perspectives

Early Childhood
Education

perspectives

Early Childhood Education

Academic Editor
Eve-Marie Arce
Shasta College

coursewise
publishing
inc.

Boulder • Bellevue • Dubuque • Madison

Our mission at **coursewise** is to help students make connections—linking theory to practice and the classroom to the outside world. Learners are motivated to synthesize ideas when course materials are placed in a context they recognize. By providing gateways to contemporary and enduring issues, **coursewise** publications will expand students' awareness of and context for the course subject.

For more information on **coursewise,** visit us at our web site: http://www.coursewise.com

To order an examination copy, contact Houghton Mifflin Sixth Floor Media: 800-565-6247(voice); 800-565-6236 (fax).

coursewise publishing editorial staff

Thomas Doran, ceo/publisher: Journalism/Marketing/Speech
Edgar Laube, publisher: Geography/Political Science/Psychology/Sociology
Linda Meehan Avenarius, publisher: **courselinks**™
Sue Pulvermacher-Alt, publisher: Education/Health/Gender Studies
Victoria Putman, publisher: Anthropology/Philosophy/Religion
Tom Romaniak, publisher: Business/Criminal Justice/Economics
Kathleen Schmitt, publishing assistant

coursewise publishing production staff

Lori A. Blosch, permissions coordinator
Mary Monner, production coordinator
Victoria Putman, production manager

from the
Publisher

Sue Pulvermacher-Alt
coursewise publishing

More or Less

"When I was a kid. . . ." Whether you are under twenty or over sixty or anywhere in between, the world is a different place and in many ways has more than it did when you were a kid—more people, more definitions of what constitutes "family," more parents working outside the home, more TVs and stereos and computers and magazines and newspapers and every other media outlet, more child-care programs and facilities, and more diversity.

As you know, more isn't necessarily better. All of the realities I just mentioned offer you challenges as a current or future educator of young children. To deal effectively with these challenges, you need to understand the issues. But you don't need more to do that. In fact, at **coursewise** we decided that less just might be better. This *Perspectives: Early Childhood Education* volume and the accompanying **courselinks**™ site have been put together to offer you less—less book bulk, less money out of your pocket, less dated material, and less wasted time surfing the Internet.

The thirty-six readings in *Perspectives: Early Childhood Education* focus on the most important topics in an introductory early childhood education course. In addition to the readings in this volume, we list web sites that will expand your understanding of the issues. The R.E.A.L. sites listed throughout this *Perspectives: Early Childhood Education* volume and at the **courselinks** site were selected because they are particularly useful sites. You, however, still need to be the one to make more or less of this information. Read our annotations and decide if the site is worth visiting. Do the activities so you can get to know the site better. Search our **courselinks** site by key topic and find the information you need to be a more informed educator.

As publisher for this volume, I had the good fortune to work with Eve-Marie Arce as the Academic Editor. Eve-Marie brought more energy and enthusiasm to this project than I had a right to expect. In making decisions about topics, readings, and web sites, she invested more time and expertise so that she could give you less. Only the most appropriate and useful content made the cut.

A top-notch Editorial Board provided feedback and expertise. At **coursewise** we're working hard to publish "connected learning" tools— connecting theory to practice and the college classroom to the outside world. Articles and web sites are selected with this goal in mind. Members of the Editorial Board then offer critical feedback and pose some interesting challenges. They know their content and are a web-savvy bunch. My thanks to Eve-Marie and the entire Editorial Board.

In conclusion, while you're striving for more, we're going after less. You're trying to get *more* out of your educational investment by taking an early childhood education course. We're trying to put together materials for your course that take *less* of your time and money. How are we doing? Did we miss any important topics or include any you don't need? What worked and what didn't work in this *Perspectives* volume and the accompanying **courselinks** site? I'd love to hear from you—more or less.

Sue Pulvermacher-Alt, Publisher
suepa@coursewise.com

Eve-Marie Arce has been on the faculty at Shasta College in Northern California since 1980, teaching early childhood education and psychology related to children and the cultural context of childhood. She has been active in statewide professional organizations that advocate for children throughout her career. Her current position as a member-at-large on the CAEYC Board is her latest involvement. Eve-Marie's varied experiences, including administration, preschool teaching, and consultancies, began in 1967 as a Head Start teacher. She has co-directed a university lab school and coordinated the implementation of the nine child development centers for the Los Angeles Community College District. A television parenting series (Channel 7, Redding, California) and conference and community presentations have given her continuing opportunities to extend community awareness of children while relating the importance of diversity and professionalism for early childhood education.

from the
Academic Editor

Eve-Marie Arce
Shasta College

Can you remember being excited about an assignment? Preparing this reader on early childhood education has been an exciting assignment for me for two reasons: First, the primary focus of this reader is on young children. Second, the reader addresses the needs of those of you who are enhancing your abilities to work with young children.

Early childhood education students are a dynamic group. Some of you are just beginning your career, while others of you are refining your abilities or expanding your knowledge. Some of you are young; some of you are middle-aged and older. Some of you are parents or grandparents. You may be highly experienced or a novice. I listen and continuously learn from you.

This reader has the most current articles and research that you will need to be successful as an early childhood educator. Child-related resources on the Internet enhance the currency of this material. The information presented here and at the reader's associated web sites will be essential as you continue your professional development.

As the Academic Editor of this reader, I blended the ideas of students and teaching faculty with my unwavering dedication to child advocacy. We need places that welcome and nurture children as they arrive from diverse families, communities, and opportunities. The articles in this reader will give you a more authentic view of children's cultures, languages, and abilities, and promote a universal appeal for acceptance and support of children and their families.

Acceptance of children should include an appreciation for variation in learning and teaching styles. My own appreciation began when I accepted a position as a Head Start teacher in 1967, and it has evolved with experiences in teaching at and directing state-funded preschools and college labs and in teaching college students for over 25 years. Perhaps, though, the realities of children's needs have been best confirmed through parenting my daughters who, born on the same day, continue after 21 years to both enhance and challenge my knowledge of human development. Today, as parents, teachers, and community members, we are all challenged by an information-driven era. Societal changes invite us to carefully apply technology while we remain sensitive to living relationships.

Research studies validate the conditions that facilitate children: feelings of belonging, strong family relations, and quality interactions between home and school. Our strength as early childhood educators lies in our commitment to provide quality programming for children and their families. If we maintain that commitment, we can achieve high standards of preparation, recognition, and compensation in our profession.

Read the articles presented in this reader, and appreciate how you, as an early care and learning professional, can contribute to a meaningful and joyful perspective of young children in the twenty-first century.

Editorial Board

We wish to thank the following instructors for their assistance. Their many suggestions not only contributed to the construction of this volume, but also to the ongoing development of our Early Childhood Education web site.

Gaye Gronlund
ECE Consulting, Inc.

Gaye Gronlund has served as president of ECE Consulting, Inc. for the past 7 years. Providing teacher and childcare provider inservice training and support, ECE Consulting has worked with clients such as the Indiana Department of Education and the YWCA/Step Ahead Program. Gronlund holds an M.A. in human development with a specialization in early childhood education from Pacific Oaks College, and she is a past president and founder of the Indianapolis Area Association for the Education of Young Children.

Judy Helm
Consultant

Judy Helm is a consultant and author of "Windows on Learning." She lives and works in Peoria, Illinois.

Peyton Nattinger
Chabot College

Peyton Nattinger holds an M.A. in human development from Pacific Oaks College. He began teaching in Head Start in 1967 and has taught adults in the California Community College system for the past 26 years. As coordinator of early childhood studies at Chabot College, he was the primary developer and co-founder of the California Early Childhood Mentor Program, of which he is now director. Professional interests include early childhood professional development and training issues, and cross-cultural studies. He lives in San Francisco with his wife, Chris, and two daughters, Lizzie and Caroline.

Beth Nason Quick
Florida State University

Beth Nason Quick, assistant professor in the College of Education at Florida State University in Tallahassee, completed her M.Ed. and Ed.D. at Peabody College of Vanderbilt University in Nashville, majoring in early childhood education. Her areas of interest include curriculum, emergent literacy, parent-teacher relations, and public policy.

Margarita Gesualdo Roig
Essex County College

Margarita Gesualdo Roig is an assistant professor of early childhood/elementary education at Essex County College in Newark. As coordinator of the Child Development Associate Program (CDA), she developed the first infant/toddler CDA training program with a bilingual component in New Jersey. Roig also serves as a consultant for both the Council for Early Childhood Professional Recognition in Washington, D.C. and the Head Start Technical Assistant Center in New York.

Kathlene Watanabe
Mount San Antonio College

Kathlene Watanabe is a professor of early childhood development at Mount San Antonio College in Walnut, California. She completed her undergraduate work in child development at California State University, Los Angeles, and postgraduate course work at Pacific Oaks College. She is a trainer for Culturally Relevant Anti-Bias (CRAB) and the chair of Taking the Lead.

Carolyn R. Wilder
West Los Angeles College

Carolyn R. Wilder is professor of child development at West Los Angeles College, one of the nine Los Angeles Community College District campuses. She is also the owner/administrator of Tender Care Child Development Center and Tender Care Elementary and Middle School. She serves as a commissioner for the Los Angeles Care Advisory Board and Commission of Human Affairs in Inglewood, California.

WiseGuide Introduction

Critical Thinking and Bumper Stickers

The bumper sticker said: Question Authority. This is a simple directive that goes straight to the heart of critical thinking. The issue is not whether the authority is right or wrong; it's the questioning process that's important. Questioning helps you develop awareness and a clearer sense of what you think. That's critical thinking.

Critical thinking is a new label for an old approach to learning—that of challenging all ideas, hypotheses, and assumptions. In the physical and life sciences, systematic questioning and testing methods (known as the scientific method) help verify information, and objectivity is the benchmark on which all knowledge is pursued. In the social sciences, however, where the goal is to study people and their behavior, things get fuzzy. It's one thing for the chemistry experiment to work out as predicted, or for the petri dish to yield a certain result. It's quite another matter, however, in the social sciences, where the subject is ourselves. Objectivity is harder to achieve.

Although you'll hear critical thinking defined in many different ways, it really boils down to analyzing the ideas and messages that you receive. What are you being asked to think or believe? Does it make sense, objectively? Using the same facts and considerations, could you reasonably come up with a different conclusion? And, why does this matter in the first place? As the bumper sticker urged, question authority. Authority can be a textbook, a politician, a boss, a big sister, or an ad on television. Whatever the message, learning to question it appropriately is a habit that will serve you well for a lifetime. And in the meantime, thinking critically will certainly help you be course wise.

Getting Connected

This reader is a tool for connected learning. This means that the readings and other learning aids explained here will help you to link classroom theory to real-world issues. They will help you to think critically and to make long-lasting learning connections. Feedback from both instructors and students has helped us to develop some suggestions on how you can wisely use this connected learning tool.

WiseGuide Pedagogy

A wise reader is better able to be a critical reader. Therefore, we want to help you get wise about the articles in this reader. Each section of *Perspectives* has three tools to help you: the WiseGuide Intro, the WiseGuide Wrap-Up, and the Putting It in *Perspectives* review form.

WiseGuide Intro

In the WiseGuide Intro, the Academic Editor introduces the section, gives you an overview of the topics covered, and explains why particular articles were selected and what's important about them.

Also in the WiseGuide Intro, you'll find several key points or learning objectives that highlight the most important things to remember from this section. These will help you to focus your study of section topics.

WiseGuide Intro

At the end of the Wiseguide Intro, you'll find questions designed to stimulate critical thinking. Wise students will keep these questions in mind as they read an article (we repeat the questions at the start of the articles as a reminder). When you finish each article, check your understanding. Can you answer the questions? If not, go back and reread the article. The Academic Editor has written sample responses for many of the questions, and you'll find these online at the **courselinks**™ site for this course. More about **courselinks** in a minute. . . .

WiseGuide Wrap-Up

Be course wise and develop a thorough understanding of the topics covered in this course. The WiseGuide Wrap-Up at the end of each section will help you do just that with concluding comments or summary points that repeat what's most important to understand from the section you just read.

In addition, we try to get you wired up by providing a list of select Internet resources—what we call R.E.A.L. web sites because they're **R**elevant, **E**xciting, **A**pproved, and **L**inked. The information at these web sites will enhance your understanding of a topic. (Remember to use your Passport and start at http://www.courselinks.com so that if any of these sites have changed, you'll have the latest link.)

Putting It in *Perspectives* Review Form

At the end of the book is the Putting It in *Perspectives* review form. Your instructor may ask you to complete this form as an assignment or for extra credit. If nothing else, consider doing it on your own to help you critically think about the reading.

Prompts at the end of each article encourage you to complete this review form. Feel free to copy the form and use it as needed.

The courselinks™ Site

The **courselinks** Passport is your ticket to a wonderful world of integrated web resources designed to help you with your course work. These resources are found at the **courselinks** site for your course area. This is where the readings in this book and the key topics of your course are linked to an exciting array of online learning tools. Here you will find carefully selected readings, web links, quizzes, worksheets, and more, tailored to your course and approved as connected learning tools. The ever-changing, always interesting **courselinks** site features a number of carefully integrated resources designed to help you be course wise. These include:

- **R.E.A.L. Sites** At the core of a **courselinks** site is the list of R.E.A.L. sites. This is a select group of web sites for studying, not surfing. Like the readings in this book, these sites have been selected, reviewed, and approved by the Academic Editor and the Editorial Board. The R.E.A.L. sites are arranged by topic and are annotated with short descriptions and key words to make them easier for you to use for reference or research. With R.E.A.L. sites, you're studying approved resources within seconds—and not wasting precious time surfing unproven sites.

- **Editor's Choice** Here you'll find updates on news related to your course, with links to the actual online sources. This is also where we'll tell you about changes to the site and about online events.

- **Course Overview** This is a general description of the typical course in this area of study. While your instructor will provide specific course objectives, this overview helps you place the course in a generic context and offers you an additional reference point.

- **www.orksheet** Focus your trip to a R.E.A.L. site with the www.orksheet. Each of the 10 to 15 questions will prompt you to take in the best that site has to offer. Use this tool for self-study, or if required, email it to your instructor.

- **Course Quiz** The questions on this self-scoring quiz are related to articles in the reader, information at R.E.A.L. sites, and other course topics, and will help you pinpoint areas you need to study. Only you will know your score—it's an easy, risk-free way to keep pace!

- **Topic Key** The Topic Key is a listing of the main topics in your course, and it correlates with the Topic Key that appears in this reader. This handy reference tool also links directly to those R.E.A.L. sites that are especially appropriate to each topic, bringing you integrated online resources within seconds!

- **Web Savvy Student Site** If you're new to the Internet or want to brush up, stop by the Web Savvy Student site. This unique supplement is a complete **courselinks** site unto itself. Here, you'll find basic information on using the Internet, creating a web page, communicating on the web, and more. Quizzes and Web Savvy Worksheets test your web knowledge, and the R.E.A.L. sites listed here will further enhance your understanding of the web.

- **Student Lounge** Drop by the Student Lounge to chat with other students taking the same course or to learn more about careers in your major. You'll find links to resources for scholarships, financial aid, internships, professional associations, and jobs. Take a look around the Student Lounge and give us your feedback. We're open to remodeling the Lounge per your suggestions.

Building Better Perspectives!

Please tell us what you think of this *Perspectives* volume so we can improve the next one. Here's how you can help:

1. Visit our **coursewise** site at: http://www.coursewise.com

2. Click on *Perspectives*. Then select the Building Better *Perspectives* Form for your book.

3. Forms and instructions for submission are available online.

Tell us what you think—did the readings and online materials help you make some learning connections? Were some materials more helpful than others? Thanks in advance for helping us build better *Perspectives*.

Student Internships

If you enjoy evaluating these articles or would like to help us evaluate the **courselinks** site for this course, check out the **coursewise** Student Internship Program. For more information, visit:

http://www.coursewise.com/intern.html

Brief Contents

Contents

section

1

Young Children in the Twenty-First Century: How Will We Meet Their Needs?

section 2

Quality Child Care and Education: What Are the Characteristics of Quality Programs?

section 3

Child-Rearing Responsibilities: How Will We Build Supportive Partnerships with Parents?

section

4

Acceptance of All Young Children: How Will We Recognize and Celebrate Each Child?

section 5

Family-Centered Communities Benefit Young Children: What Policies Enhance the Developing Child?

section 6

Societal Changes That Impact Early Childhood Education: How Will Children, Families, and Professionals Adapt?

Topic Key

This Topic Key is an important tool for learning. It will help you integrate this reader into your course studies. Listed below, in alphabetical order, are important topics covered in this volume. Below each topic you'll find the reading numbers and titles, and R.E.A.L. web site addresses, relating to that topic. Note that the Topic Key might not include every topic your instructor chooses to emphasize. If you don't find the topic you're looking for in the Topic Key, check the index or the online topic key at the **courselinks**™ site.

section

1

Key Points

- There are primary issues to be addressed before society is able to meet the needs of young children in the next century.

- Early experiences and nurturing interactions facilitate healthy brain development.

- Emotional well-being during the early years provides skills for healthy and successful lives.

- Families, communities, and schools that model sensitivity for society's many cultures prepare children for the twenty-first century.

- Effective strategies are needed to ensure quality care and educational opportunities for all children.

- Early care and learning settings that maintain play as a basic foundation prepare children for the multitude of societal challenges in the next century.

Young Children in the Twenty-First Century: How Will We Meet Their Needs?

 **WiseGuide Intro**

Rapid changes, new knowledge, and transition to another century intensify our reexamination of young children's needs. How will parents, caregivers, and teachers validate the commitment of early childhood education?

Research findings about development and learning help us to redefine agendas for programs, schools, and communities. The focus on young children brings greater visibility to the early childhood education profession that provides care and learning to the youngest children. As we shift into another era we can utilize this visibility to thoughtfully distinguish meaningful ways to best meet the needs of young children in the twenty-first century.

Section 1 of *Perspectives: Early Childhood Education* offers five readings that suggest fundamental themes related to the needs of children. If we look back and we look forward, the key features that emerge relate to the importance of early experiences and quality programming in an inclusive atmosphere where emotional health is valued. Basic ideas may be labeled and described differently, but the fundamental needs of young children direct us to create a vision upon which best policies can be built and programs designed.

The initial reading ("Starting Smart: How Early Experiences Affect Brain Development") highlights recent studies that explain the profound correlation between a baby's early experiences and brain development. In the second reading ("Up with Emotional Health"), Carolyn Pool suggests that emotionally healthy children are more likely to achieve in school and to attain career successes later in their lives.

Educators and community leaders have asked how to best prepare children for the next century. In "Educating Citizens for a Multicultural 21st Century," Lily Wong Fillmore responds firmly that it is the responsibility of the schools to facilitate awareness of multiculturalism because young children will grow up in an era that is more diverse than any other.

In "Highlights of the Quality 2000 Initiative: Not by Chance," Sharon Kagan and Michelle Neuman call for bold planning now so that the early care and education needs of all children 0–5 years are not left to chance. Similarly, the last reading in Section 1 ("Playfulness Enhancement Through Classroom Intervention for the 21st Century") suggests that we will fulfill children's needs for the twenty-first century by confirming teaching and learning strategies that maintain play experiences.

Questions

Reading 1. How can good early experiences help the brain to develop well or poorly?

Reading 2. What behaviors during early childhood promote positive lifelong social skills?

Reading 3. How will families and schools prepare children for a multicultural twenty-first century?

Reading 4. What strategies are professionals recommending for program quality in the twenty-first century?

Reading 5. How will the encouragement of playfulness prepare children for the twenty-first century?

How can good early experiences help the brain to develop well or poorly?

Starting Smart

How early experiences affect brain development

Michael Stevens is a healthy, beautiful newborn baby. As his parents admire him, they wonder, "What will Michael be like when he grows up? Will he do well in school? Will he get along with other kids and be happy?" Scientists now believe that the answers to these questions depend in large part on how young Michael's brain develops, and that this development in turn depends largely on the kinds of experiences that his parents, extended family, and community provide for him over the next few years.

Recent advances in brain research have provided great insight into how the brain, the most immature of all organs at birth, continues to grow and develop during the first years of life. Whereas this growth was once thought to be determined primarily by genetics, scientists now believe that it is also highly dependent upon the child's experiences. Research shows that, like protein, fat, and vitamins, interactions with other people and objects are vital nutrients for the growing and developing brain and different experiences can lit-

erally cause the brain to develop in different ways. It is this "plasticity" of the brain, its ability to develop and change in response to the demands of the environment, that will enable Michael to learn how to use computers as successfully as his ancestors learned how to hunt animals in the wild.

As he grows, Michael's ability to understand language, solve problems, and get along with other people will be strongly influenced by what he experiences as an infant and young child. This is not to say that individual genetic differences have no influence on how a child develops; they do. But there is mounting evidence that early experiences can dramatically alter the way genes are expressed in the developing brain. While good early experiences help the brain to develop well, poor early experiences can literally cause a genetically normal child to become mentally retarded or a temperamentally easy-going child to develop serious emotional difficulties.

Understanding How the Brain Develops

In order to understand how this happens, we need to understand a bit about how the brain works. The brain is comprised of many distinct regions, each devoted to a specific function, such as identifying what we see, processing spoken language, or assessing whether we are in danger. Within each of these brain areas are millions of neurons, or nerve cells, which are connected to each other by synapses. These trillions of synapses and the pathways they form make up the "wiring" of the brain; they allow all of the various brain areas to communicate and function together in a coordinated way. The number and organization of connections in the brain influences everything from the ability to recognize letters of the alphabet to facility at managing complex social relationships.

Neurons develop rapidly before birth, but after birth no new neurons are formed. Instead, brain development after birth

"Starting Smart: How Early Experiences Affect Brain Development" from AN OUNCE OF PREVENTION FUND PAPER, 1996, p. 5. Reprinted by permission of Theresa Hawley, Ph.D., and The Ounce of Prevention Fund.

consists of an on-going process of wiring and re-wiring the connections among neurons. New synapses between cells are constantly being formed, while others are broken or pruned away. During the first eight months after birth, connections are formed more quickly than they are broken, so that at age eight months a baby may have an astounding 1,000 trillion synapses in his brain! After the first year, pruning occurs more rapidly than synapse formation until age 10, when a child has about 500 trillion synapses, roughly the same number as the average adult.[1] Early experiences can have a dramatic impact on this brain-wiring process, causing the final number of synapses in the brain to increase or decrease by as much as 25 percent.[2]

New scientific data have taught us that the forming and breaking of neural connections depends directly on the child's experiences. The brain operates on a "use it or lose it" principle as it develops: only those connections and pathways that are frequently activated are retained.[3] The ways infants learn to understand spoken language provides a good example of this experience-dependent development of neural connections. When an infant is three months old, his brain can distinguish several hundred different spoken sounds, many more than are present in his native language. Over the next several months, however, his brain will organize itself more efficiently so that it only recognizes those sounds that are part of the language he regularly hears. For example, a one-year-old Japanese baby will not recognize that "la" is different from "ra," because the former sound is never used in his language. During early childhood, the brain retains the ability to re-learn sounds it has discarded, so young children typically learn new languages easily and without an accent. After about age ten, however, plasticity for this function is lost; therefore, most adolescents and adults find it difficult to learn to speak and understand foreign languages.

Windows of Opportunity in Brain Development

This new understanding of how the young brain develops has already altered the practices of medical professionals who work with children born with hearing and vision impairment. For example, surgeons now remove congenital cataracts as early in infancy as possible, because they know if they wait until the child is older, the neural connections between his eyes and his brain will fail to develop properly, and he will never be able to see. Similarly, scientists now know that if children born deaf do not hear people talking before they are ten, they will never learn to understand spoken language. As a result, new hearing aids called cochlear implants have been developed to provide at least some hearing for very young deaf children.

A new consensus about the importance of intervening in the first months and years is also emerging in the field of early intervention with disadvantaged children. Psychologists have long known that children of poorly educated, low-income parents are at risk for mental retardation. The recent developments in brain research have provided new insights into why this is so. Parents who are preoccupied with a daily struggle to ensure that their children have enough to eat and are safe from harm may not have the resources, information, or time they need to provide the stimulating experiences that foster brain growth. Infants and children who are rarely spoken to, who are exposed to few toys, and who have little opportunity to explore and experiment with their environment may fail to fully develop the neural connections and pathways that facilitate later learning.[4] Despite their normal genetic endowment, these children are at a permanent intellectual disadvantage and are likely to require costly special education or other remedial services when they enter school. Fortunately, intervention programs that start working with children and their families at birth or even prenatally can help prevent this tragic loss of potential.[5] *(see box below)**

An impressive example of the power of adult-child interactions to facilitate children's successful development comes from a study of early language skills.[6] Researchers found that when mothers frequently spoke to their infants, their children learned almost 300 more words by age two than did their peers whose mothers rarely spoke to them. Furthermore, the study suggested that mere exposure to language such as listening to the television or to adults talking amongst themselves provided little benefit. Rather, infants need to interact directly with other human beings, to hear people talk to them about what they are seeing and experiencing, in order for their brains to develop optimal language skills. Unfortunately, many parents are under the mistaken impression that talking to babies is not very important, since babies are too young to understand what is said.

*Not included in this publication.

Parents need to be educated about how children develop and about the importance of their early interactions with their children.

Emotional Development and the Infant Brain

One of the most fundamental tasks an infant undertakes is determining whether and how he can get his needs met in the world in which he lives. He is constantly assessing whether his cries for food and comfort are ignored or lovingly answered, whether he is powerless or can influence what adults do. If the adults in his life respond predictably to his cries and provide for his needs, the infant will feel secure. He can then focus his attention on exploring, allowing his brain to take in all the wonders of the world around him. If, however, his needs are met only sporadically and pleas for comfort are usually ignored or met with harsh words and rough handling, the infant will focus his energies on ensuring that his needs are met. He will have more and more difficulty interacting with people and objects in his environment, and his brain will shut out the stimulation it needs to develop healthy cognitive and social skills.[7]

Children who receive sensitive, responsive care from their parents and other caregivers in the first years of life enjoy an important head start toward success in their lives. The secure relationships they develop with the important adults in their lives lay the foundation for healthy emotional development and help protect them from the many stresses they may face as they grow. Researchers who examine the life histories of children who have

succeeded despite many challenges in their lives have consistently found that these children have had at least one stable, supportive relationship with an adult (usually a parent, other relative, or teacher) beginning early in life.[8]

The Effects of Trauma and Chronic Stress

Scientists have discovered that chaotic or overwhelming experiences can be as damaging to the developing brain as a lack of stimulation. Exposure to trauma or chronically stressful environments can dramatically change the way an infant or young child's brain develops, making the child both more prone to emotional disturbances and less able to learn. Unpredictable, chaotic, or traumatic experiences over-activate the neural pathways that control the fear response, causing children's brains to be organized for survival in a persistently threatening and violent world.[9] The result is that such children live life on high alert, overly quick to interpret others' actions as threatening, and quick to respond aggressively in their own defense. Although this ability of the brain to adapt to what it perceives as constant threats may help the child avoid future harm (e.g., a battered child may learn to keep out of his father's way when the father is in a bad mood) it exacts a great cost. Children exposed to severe stress frequently develop learning disabilities and emotional and behavioral problems (e.g., attention deficits, anxiety, depression) and appear to be at risk for a host of medical problems, such as asthma, immune-system dysfunction, and heart disease (*see box to the right*).*

*Not included in this publication.

It is important that we not assume that a poorly parented or traumatized child is incapable of healthy functioning later in childhood or adolescence. Research on the developing brain suggests continuing opportunity for change into adulthood and provides no evidence that there is some age beyond which intervention will fail to make a difference. In fact, this research provides exciting new clues as to what kinds of therapy might be most helpful for children who have experienced difficult lives.[10] Clearly, however, the costs (in human suffering, loss of potential, and real money) of trying to repair, remediate, or heal these children is far greater than the costs of preventing these problems by promoting healthy development of the brain during the first few years of life.

Helping Families Support Healthy Brain Development

It is now clear that what a child experiences in the first few years of life largely determines how his brain will develop and how he will interact with the world throughout his life. Parents play the most important role in providing the nurturing and stimulation that children require, but they need information and support to develop good parenting skills. In the past, extended family members were often close by, offering advice and acting as role models for inexperienced parents. Young families today often live far away from grandparents and other family and rely more on community resources for information and support in parenting. There is much that communities can do to help families promote their children's healthy brain development.

Educate parents about the importance of early experiences for their children's development.

Often parents don't know about the many little things they can do to foster their child's healthy cognitive and emotional development, like talking to the child beginning in infancy, reading to him from a very early age, and helping him play simple games. Parents, especially new or young parents, may also need help learning to recognize their child's cues that he is hungry for stimulation or has had enough.

In some cases, written materials or a few sessions of parenting education classes may be all that a parent needs to learn how to provide his or her child with appropriate stimulation. However, parenting styles and beliefs that have evolved over generations, like rarely talking to babies, can be difficult for parents to change. Many parents benefit from community-based programs in which a parent group leader or a home visitor acts as a role model and friend, supporting parents in their relationship with their children. Programs that work with parents over several years can be very successful in helping them become effective "first teachers" of their children.[11]

Prevent abuse and neglect.

Children who are abused or severely neglected are at extremely high risk of developing emotional, behavioral, social, and intellectual disabilities. By the time a child is identified as having been neglected or abused, these problems have already begun to develop. Greater attention must be given to preventing maltreatment before it starts. High-quality home visiting programs which start working with families as soon as the child is born have proven to be effective in preventing abuse and neglect.[12] The key to these programs' success is that they help parents manage the stresses of raising children before unhealthy patterns develop and things get out of control.

Provide accessible, quality mental health services for parents.

Research has shown that parents suffering from untreated depression often fail to respond sensitively to their children's cries and bids for attention, and that they are unlikely to provide the child with the kind of cognitive stimulation that promotes healthy brain development.[13] Other mental illnesses like schizophrenia can also dramatically affect a parent's ability to interact appropriately with his or her child. Proper mental health treatment for these parents can make a real difference in their ability to raise a competent, happy child.

While good early experiences help the brain to develop well, poor early experiences can literally cause a genetically normal child to become mentally retarded or a temperamentally easy-going child to develop serious emotional difficulties.

Ensure adequate nutrition prenatally and in the first years after birth.

Numerous studies have shown the devastating effects on intelligence and brain development of a lack of basic nutrients at the prenatal stage and in infancy and early childhood. Programs such as the Special Supplemental Program for Women, Infants, and Children (WIC) can be effective in ensuring that babies receive the kinds of foods they need to thrive.[14] Educational and outreach campaigns to alert women to the importance of nutrition in the first trimester of pregnancy would also be helpful in preventing problems that can arise in this critical period when brain cells begin to form.

The Importance of Quality in Infant-Toddler Child Care

Increasing numbers of American infants and toddlers spend several hours each day in various child care arrangements because their parents work or attend school. It is critical that the care these children receive promotes their healthy growth and development. Too often, however, child care providers are poorly trained and do not provide children with appropriate stimulation. Research has shown that in the majority of infant care arrangements in the U.S., children are not talked to and played with enough, and they do not have the opportunity to form the kind of comfortable, secure relationships with a caregiver that will promote their healthy emotional development.[15]

Parents should be given information about how to choose quality care for their children. In addition, special attention must be given to the development and enforcement of child care licensing standards that promote high-quality care: adequate pre-service and in-service training for caregivers, low child-to-teacher ratios, and small group sizes. Finally, child care reimbursement rates for families moving from welfare to work must be high enough to fund well-trained teachers who can deliver developmentally appropriate care and education.

Conclusion

Like most children, Michael Stevens has a family that will provide the stimulation and nurturing that he needs to grow and develop to his potential. Unfortunately, rising rates of child abuse and neglect across the country and persistently high rates of school failure in some communities indicate that far too many children do not receive what they need during their first few years for healthy brain growth and development. Our increasingly technically and socially complex society cannot afford to continue to allow large numbers of children to miss out on the positive experiences they need in infancy and early childhood; the costs, in terms of lost intellectual potential and increased rates of emotional and behavioral problems, are too high. The new developments in brain research show us what children need; our challenge is to ensure that every child receives it.

Notes

1. Huttenlocher, P. R. (1994). Synaptogenesis, synapse elimination, and neural plasticity in human cerebral cortex. In C. A. Nelson, Ed., *Threats to optimal development: Integrating biological, psychological, and social risk factors.* The Minnesota symposia in child psychology, Vol. 27, pp. 35–54.
2. Turner, A. M. and W. T. Greenough. (1985). Differential rearing effects on rat visual cortex synapses: I. Synapse and neural density and synapses per neuron. *Brain Research*, 329, 195–203.
3. Greenough, W. T. (1987). Experience and brain development. *Child Development*, 58, 539–559.
4. Ibid.
5. Campbell, F. and C. Ramey. (1994). Effects of early intervention on intellectual and academic achievement. A follow-up study of children from low-income families. *Child Development*, 65, 684–698.
6. Huttenlocher, J. et al. (1991). Early vocabulary growth: Relation to language input and gender. *Developmental Psychology*, 27, 236–248.
7. Lieberman, A. F. and C. H. Zeanah. (1995). Disorders of attachment in infancy. *Infant Psychiatry*, 4: 571–587.
8. Werner, E. E. and R. S. Amith. (1982). *Vulnerable but not invincible: A longitudinal study of resilient children and youth.* New York: Adams, Bannister, Cox.
9. Perry, B. D. *et al.* (1995). Childhood trauma, the neurobiology of adaptation, and "use-dependent" development of the brain: How "states" become "traits." *Infant Mental Health Journal*, 16: 271–291.
10. Perry, B. D. (1993). Neurodevelopment and the neurophysiology of trauma II: Clinical work along the alarm-fear-terror continuum. *The Advisor*, 6: 1, ff.
11. Olds, D. L. *et al.* (1993). Effect of prenatal and infancy nurse home visitation on government spending. *Medical Care*, 31: 155–174.
12. MacMillan, H. L. *et al.* (1994). Primary prevention of child physical abuse and neglect: A critical review. *Journal of Child Psychology and Psychiatry and Allied Disciplines*, 35, 835–856.
13. Field, T. M. (1995). Psychologically depressed parents. In M. H. Bornstein, Ed. *Handbook of parenting, Vol. 14: Applied and practical parenting.* Mahwah, NJ: Lawrence Erlbaum Associates, Inc.
14. Yip, R. *et al.* (1987). Declining prevalence of anemia among low-income children in the United States. *Journal of the American Medical Association*, 258, 1619–1623.
15. Whitebook, M; D. Phillips; and C. Howes. (1989). *Who Cares? Child care teachers and the quality of child care in America: National Child Care Staffing Study.* Oakland, CA: Child Care Employee Project.

Article Review Form at end of book.

What behaviors during early childhood promote positive lifelong social skills?

Up with Emotional Health

Emotional well-being is a predictor of success in academic achievement, employment, marriage, and physical health. Daniel Goleman, author of the bestseller *Emotional Intelligence*, spoke at ASCD's Annual Conference about the emotional intelligence of our students.

Carolyn R. Pool

Carolyn R. Pool is Senior Editor of Educational Leadership. Daniel Goleman, formerly the Senior Editor of Psychology Today, is a psychologist who has reported on the behavioral and brain sciences for The New York Times since 1984. He is the author of Emotional Intelligence (New York: Bantam Books, 1995).

Have you had an amygdala attack lately? An amygdala attack in your brain sets your heart to racing, poised for fight or flight. As the "seat of all passion," according to Dan Goleman, our two amygdalas rule our emotions, our feelings, our relationships, our learning. In fact, emotional well-being is the strongest predictor of achievement in school and on the job, according to recent research. And according to other research, today's children are *down* on all indicators of emotional health.

Goleman discussed ways to bring out the "good citizen" that is already there in our children—the person who cares, who "sees human need and acts spontaneously." Such a person may not know about the amygdala, but the good citizen—the person with a high emotional intelligence—knows what to do when it attacks.

Goleman discussed many research studies showing that a person's IQ predicts only a small part of career performance—ranging from 4 to 20 percent. But recent studies have shown that emotional intelligence predicts about 80 percent of a person's success in life.

What Is the Emotional Brain?

Goleman said that his understanding of emotional intelligence expands on Howard Gardner's "personal intelligences"—the intrapersonal (knowing yourself) and interpersonal (knowing how to get along with others). Goleman emphasized that educators need to consider "educating differently" for this intelligence, because different areas of the brain are involved.

What controls our emotions is the limbic brain, right in the middle of the three main layers of the human brain: the cortex, limbic brain, and brain stem. And in the middle of the limbic area, behind our eyes, are two amygdalas. Recent neurological research has shown that these almond-shaped organs receive and send all emotional messages. Of course, nothing in the brain occurs in isolation; the amygdala is constantly communicating with the cortex, where we do analytical and verbal tasks and where our working memory resides. Goleman said that we neglect the emotional brain at our peril—and at the peril of our students. Here is how your amygdalas work:

The emotional brain scans everything happening to us from moment to moment, to see if something that happened in the past that made us sad or angry is like what is happening now. If so, the amygdala calls an alarm—to declare an emergency and mobilize in a split second to act. And it can do so, in brain time, more rapidly than the thinking brain takes to figure out what is going on, which is why people can get into a rage and do something very inappropriate that they wished they hadn't. It's an emotional hijacking.

Our analytical thinking is always influenced by our emotions. If we have a mature, healthy connection, we can control our responses to the amygdala's messages. The cortex can tell us to forget the "fight" response. Everybody gets angry, but not everyone acts violently. Children who are chronically sad or angry or anxious experience constant interference by the amygdala; it's hard for them to concentrate, to learn.

Five Dimensions of Emotional Intelligence

Goleman said that we need to incorporate five dimensions of emotional intelligence into everything we do in school, for both adults and children.

Self-awareness. The first dimension, self-awareness, is the basis for self-confidence. We need to know our strengths and limits and how to be decisive. Kids need to learn from a young age what the words for feelings are, why they feel the way they do, and what *action options* they have. For example, a recent study found that 6th grade girls who confused feelings of anger, anxiety, loneliness, and hunger were at high risk of developing an eating disorder like bulimia or anorexia in their teens. Such children would benefit from higher self-awareness and healthier decision making.

Handling emotions generally. The second dimension, knowing how to handle upsetting feelings, or impulses, is the root of emotional intelligence. Consider the famous Marshmallow Test:

Four-year-old kids from the Stanford University preschool are the subjects. The experimenter puts a marshmallow in front of each kid and says: "You could have this marshmallow now, if you want, but if you wait until I run an errand, and don't eat it until I get back, you can have two then." The videotaped results are hilarious. Some kids go up to the marshmallow, smell it, then leap back like it's dangerous. Some go off in a corner and sing and dance to distract themselves. Some kids just grab it. And a third of the kids grab it and eat it, about a third wait just a while, and the rest wait an endless 10 minutes until the experimenter comes back, and they get two.

These kids were followed up 14 years later, when they graduated from high school. The "grabbers" were still impulsive; they were quick to anger and not very popular. The "waiters" were popular and well-balanced emotionally. But the most astonishing finding was that the "waiters" had higher scores on their SATs—210 points higher than the "grabbers," out of a possible score of 1,600.

According to the Educational Testing Service (ETS), this 210-point advantage *matches* that of economically advantaged children versus poor children and is *larger* than that of children from families with graduate degrees versus children whose parents didn't finish high school.

Here are some social consequences of being impulsive: *for boys*—three to six times more likely to be violent by the end of adolescence; *for girls*—three times more likely to get pregnant in adolescence; *for kids who are chronically sad or anxious in elementary school*—most likely to end up as a substance abuser in adolescence during periods of experimentation.

Here are some consequences of being "waiters": A U.S. Department of Personnel study of outstanding performers found that they were flexible, adaptable, and conscientious; they stayed positive under pressure and had integrity.

Motivation. Moving toward our goals is a third element of emotional intelligence. An important element of motivation is *hope*—having a goal, knowing the small manageable steps it takes to get to that goal, and having the "zeal or persistence" to follow through. Can we measure—and thus teach—hope? A psychologist, C. R. Snyder, devised such a measurement and tested freshmen as they entered college. He found that those who scored higher on hope had higher grades at the end of the year and that hope was a better predictor of good grades than were SAT scores. Goleman said, "The folks at ETS were startled to hear about this."

We can actually teach hope, and optimism, and motivation to learn. Many families do this on their own—teaching children by small steps how to set goals, how to persevere, how to work toward high achievement, how to find fulfillment in life.

Empathy. Empathy, the fourth element, means reading other people's feelings by tone of voice or facial expression, not necessarily words. Knowing how someone else feels is a fundamental human ability—seen even in infants and small children. Goleman said that 2-year-olds from loving families will often try to comfort a friend who is crying. But young children who have been seriously abused or neglected in the first years of life tend to yell at or hit crying children. He stated, "Emotional intelligence is learned, and it's learned from the earliest years straight on through."

Goleman related a disturbing story of a person who lacked empathy and compassion. A man known as the Santa Cruz Strangler was in prison for murdering seven people. When asked by an interviewer whether he felt any pity for his victims, the strangler said in a calm tone, "Oh, no. If I had felt any of their suffering, I couldn't have done it." The man had an IQ of 160.

An obvious lesson to be drawn from this story is that IQ has absolutely nothing to do with empathy. Goleman stated: "Empathy is the brake on human cruelty. It is what keeps civility alive in society."

Another example of people who seem to lack empathy is playground bullies. How do educators deal with bullies? Some researchers have found that bullies benefit from lessons in reading faces—what different emotions look like.

One psychologist decided to form a Buddies Club to help socialize some bullies he was working with (note that he did *not* call it the "Bullies Club"). In one activity, he paired all the children and had them make faces at each other, then identify what feelings the faces communicated. The bullies learned the differences between sad, angry, neutral, and hostile expressions. The psychologist also taught the children other social skills, such as how to ask other kids about themselves and how to take turns. Goleman concluded: "Guess what? They weren't bullies anymore after that."

Social skills. This is the fifth element of emotional intelligence. As Goleman noted, bullies benefit from instruction in social skills. And such skills are contagious.

Goleman's story of the "urban saint" shows such positive contagion. He described an unusually friendly bus driver who greeted passengers, pointed out interesting features on the route, and wished passengers well as they alighted—each with more energy in his or her step. Goleman said he would like to see more people like that bus driver in our classrooms.

Emotional Skills for Life

Emotional intelligence matters for school achievement, job success, marital happiness, and physical health. Goleman discussed the recent research finding that people who are chronically anxious, sad, or depressed have double the risk of getting a major disease—a higher risk than smoking.

The same risk factors apply to marriage, which is particularly prone to amygdala attacks. Many couples fall into the habit of negative emotional expressions that, if continued, leads to divorce. In this pattern, the partners make angry accusations and personal attacks in the heat of the moment—using name-calling, like "You're a slob!" Things escalate when words like "jerk" are added, and then the rolling eyes, sneers, and sarcasm that are sure signs of contempt and disgust—"very hurtful messages from someone you love."

These messages can trigger a greatly increased heart rate: an amygdala attack, an "emotional hijacking, a flooding." People in this state hate it: they strike out or they leave. Many learn to tune out completely to other people—whether a spouse, a teacher, a parent, an employer, or a friend. Goleman said that couples, as well as educators and students, need to learn how to give calm, informational feedback, and thus avoid provoking amygdala attacks.

Emotional health is also important on the job. Employers have rated "star performers" as those who are persuasive, likable, and assertive; these people can motivate and inspire others, lead teams, and work cooperatively.

We can raise the emotional intelligence of our students. We can provide supports—even one caring adult—for those children whose parents are not around. We can plan activities to get children away from TVs and video monitors. Because the amygdala doesn't mature until a child is 15 or 16, we have many chances to teach children how to handle their feelings. We can teach bullies peaceful options; we can help shy kids develop their social skills.

Goleman emphasized that social-emotional development programs should be integrated into the curriculum and the life of the school, involve parents, and include community mentors. They do best when they go for the long term and when teachers are well trained—and when we ourselves become more healthy emotionally.

 Article Review Form at end of book.

How will families and schools prepare children for a multicultural twenty-first century?

Educating Citizens for a Multicultural 21st Century

Lily Wong Fillmore

Lily Wong Fillmore is a professor of language and literacy, University of California, Berkeley. This article is adapted from her opening session address at the Third Annual Conference of the National Association for Multicultural Education, February 11, 1993.

American society is, and has always been, a diverse, multicultural society. But there is something new. Over the past two decades, with the influx of the new immigrants—people largely from Asia and Latin America, but also the Caribbean, Africa, the Middle East, and the Indian Sub-Continent—we have become visibly diverse. We have become noticeably a more colorful and variegated people than ever before.

But this same multiculturalism and diversity that some of us celebrate represents problems to others. These forces constitute, in the eyes of some people, frightening, unwanted changes in our society. The American ideal for most citizens is a monocultural society, a society with one language, one culture, one purpose, one people.

When you and I talk about the advantages of a multicultural society, when we argue about the need to accommodate the many different perspectives, histories, and experiences that are represented in our society, say in our celebrations, or in our schools, we are denounced as promoters of new heresies.

The rumblings in America these days are symptomatic of another bout of crippling xenophobia coming on. This society has never found it easy to incorporate newcomers who don't blend into the crowd easily. Despite the fact that this has always been a diverse multicultural society, Americans have never accepted that reality. We have, until recently, been able to suppress it, deny it, and even erase it—at least we have tried. We have done it by forcing people, by both subtle and not-so-subtle means, to conform to our ideal of a monocultural society. People either give up their differences or they don't get access to the society.

School is the place where this process begins and where much of it takes place. It is where children learn and come to believe that what they have been taught by their parents has no place or value in the society they live in. In what follows, I will comment on what happens, and what should be happening, in schools.

For most of us, school was the place where we—or our parents or grandparents—first came into contact with the larger society. It was where we learned English, after retiring our own languages; it was where we learned what it meant to be an American in contrast to whatever else we were when we first entered school. It was where we gained a common culture and set aside our own, the culture of our parents and our primary communities. All of that was necessary, we were told, if we wanted to be members of the larger society, if we wanted jobs, if we wanted to be Americans.

And so many of us took on American culture, the one that is about baseball, cowboys, fast cars and John Wayne, and we suppressed and set aside the other stuff—our languages, our history, our stories, ourselves—and eventually forgot about them.

This process continues. Despite our best efforts to diversify the curriculum, to accommodate the cultures and experiences of our newest Americans in the schools, it continues.

We see kids entering our schools, bringing with them a great diversity of experience, language, and cultures. Their names are novel, colorful, and delightful to the ear. In just a couple of years, these kids will be speaking English—not well, but it will be their preferred language. In dress, hair-style, and in their manner, they will become more and more American. And their names—Thuy becomes Tiffany, Guillermo is Bill, you know, like the president? and Chui-wing is no more—she's Jennifer now, please. And at home, their parents are bewildered. Their children—what has happened to their children? They have become strangers—they can hardly understand the family language anymore. When they speak to their parents at all, it is in English, a language the parents don't understand. And their tones are terse, impatient, scornful even. The parents don't understand, they just don't understand. "What has happened to our children?" they ask. "What has happened to our family?"

But as we know, culture is not easily changed. The kids adopt new ways of talking, dressing, and thinking—but they nonetheless retain a lot of their parents' early teachings in the deep structure of their thought. They retain a sense of the rightness of the patterns of behavior and beliefs that their parents have inculcated in them in the early years, even if they are no longer practice or are guided by them. And these patterns continue to exert an influence on their thinking well after children appear to

have "adjusted," as we say, to their new circumstances.

The conflict between what is and what ought to be has to be confronted by each individual who undergoes this process, and it is harder for some than for others. All of this goes into the shaping of our national psyche. Whether we like to acknowledge it or not, we are an immigrant society, and unresolved conflicts between what we are and what we might have been do affect how we look at ourselves and at others.

Here I raise issues about American society that must be confronted head-on if we are to succeed as a multicultural society. We are undeniably a multicultural society, but we are far from the kind of multicultural society we could be. There are far too many divisions among us, and there is the backlash, exemplified in the attitudes so freely expressed these days by members of the public, who view our diversity as a violation of the American ideal.

Ethnic, cultural, linguistic, religious, social, and racial differences have remained, even after most of us have bought into the idea of a common culture, a common language, and a common purpose. Our society is riddled with divisions and polarities: majority versus minority, haves versus have-nots, whites versus blacks, Asians against non-Asians, Latinos versus Anglos, native-born versus foreign-borns as in ABCs versus FOBs (in the parlance of young Chinese Americans, "ABC" refers to American-born Chinese, "FOB" to Chinese immigrants, those who are "fresh off the boat"), gays versus straights, men versus women.

Language, ethnicity, race, and cultural and social differences have never been so apparent as they are now. There is ample evi-

dence that such differences can affect every aspect of life. As citizens, we have to ask why matters like children's school performance can be predicted by skin color, parental income, ethnic group, or home language.

There is a lot of racial tension in our diverse communities these days—in fact, it is often directly proportional to the amount of diversity that is present in a community. The interracial violence in Los Angeles in the spring of 1992 following the first Rodney King trial should not have surprised anyone, and Los Angeles is not an isolated case. We have seen eruptions of violence—acts of intolerance by one group against another—by people who ought to get along a great deal better than they do in a multicultural society.

After a while, a person begins to wonder: Is a multicultural society really possible—a society in which diverse people live together harmoniously and at peace with one another? And if such a society is possible, how do you achieve it? How do we create the connections that will make a difference, as was pledged in the theme of the 1993 National Association for Multicultural Education Conference?

I will argue that connections have got to be forged on many fronts, but the most important of these must be made in the classroom. We have to help children—the next generation—acquire the means and desire to build such a society. We focus on the children, but that means that we have to include their educators—teachers and parents—the adults who must be involved in the transformation of our progeny into citizens of a diverse, multicultural world.

But how do we do it when the adults we have to begin with

are people who have been socialized in ways that have created the problems we face in the first place? The separatism, the racism that has kept most people from seeing the possibility or advantages of a truly multicultural world, has been the human legacy for much of our history on earth until now. That heritage has profoundly shaped the reality we have lived with in the twentieth century.

Until recently, it was possible for us to believe that we could live in worlds separated by borders and boundaries—crossing them only to vanquish, conquer, or subjugate others. That is how our own society was formed, after all. Almost always, each group sees itself, not as equal to all others, but superior to any other. Ethnocentrism, racial-centrism, is nothing new. It is written in our histories, imprinted on our brains. We are humans—you are less than that. Thus, we can set ourselves off as special, and it is easy to demonize all others.

When we talk about the advantages of a multicultural society, it is easy to romanticize the idea of diversity and see only the colorful, interesting, positive aspects of other groups that are different from our own, and to glorify them. But in fact, most people come from societies with long, long histories of enmity and wars with neighbors—the outsiders, the demon others in their worlds.

We humans are just only discovering that we have to live together, and it is only after living side by side, learning that we can't afford not to get along together —that it is all too easy to end up destroying one another. Those of us who work in multicultural education—who recognize that we have to build connections between the constituent groups in this society—are pretty much ahead of the game in this regard. But not everyone is. Most of all, the kids in our schools—our future citizens and leaders—their teachers, and their parents, have got to be helped to take part in this work. And that is why we have to begin with the children, and their teachers and parents.

I will argue that multicultural education must begin in kindergarten and be continuously reinforced throughout the school years. What children must learn are some fundamental attitudes and values concerning life in a multicultural, multilingual society. They must be taught, early in life, that they live in a world where people come from many different places and backgrounds, but they are more alike than they are different. They need to recognize that differences in looks, likes, beliefs, and behavior are neither good nor bad—they are just differences. They have to learn that differences are what make people interesting, and while it might be a whole lot easier to be with people who are exactly the same as we are, it can be a whole lot more interesting to be with people who are different. Most of all, they need to discover that in order to succeed socially in a multicultural world, they have to accept and respect differences in others, rather than reject and abhor them. In short, they must be educated to think and live as citizens of a multicultural world.

These might not seem like such big things, but they are core concepts, and ought to be at the heart of any curriculum for children who live in a diverse society. They are also the hardest things to teach—and that is why we have to work together to figure out how to do it right. One might think that the kids in our classrooms do not need to be taught about diversity—they, after all, are nothing if not diverse. In reality, they have no greater reason to appreciate or to know how to live with diversity than other children in the society.

How are such concepts to be taught in school? How does one incorporate them into a curriculum, and how can we impart them to children? Can children handle such notions?

In many respects, the curricular changes I have been talking about involve the inculcation of basic, fundamental ideas that make us who we are, rather than the teaching of information and skills that enable us to perform jobs or understand ideas. Some of these fundamental ideas are learned in school, ordinarily, but the really basic set is learned at home—well before children begin school, through the socialization process that takes place as family members interact with children.

It is at home that children acquire an outlook on life, a set of attitudes about themselves, about others, the environment, about their place in the world. Children acquire, along with their primary languages, a set of beliefs, expectations, and practices from family members—the significant others in their lives. By the time children come to school at age five or six, they are already well-socialized members of a particular family and cultural group.

As educators, we know how differently children can behave and respond to the experience of school, depending on the group and family they come from. The most critical results of this preschool curriculum in the home are invisible, not as obvious as the results of language socialization. The most powerful aspect of the cultural package that children receive in the socialization process is the belief in the naturalness and normality of the attitudes and practices that have been inculcated in them early in life.

What they are used to, what they have been taught is right and appropriate, what they have learned is the way to treat people, about handling conflict, or hurt, or injustice, what they regard as good or bad, beautiful or not, desirable or undesirable—all are aspects of children's culture. How do we look at these aspects of culture that children bring to school? We acknowledge the need to recognize and to respect cultural differences that children bring to school. But we are often confused about how to reconcile what we know we must achieve instructionally in school, with the beliefs, values, and understandings children have learned in the home.

Let us be clear about what educational role the family must play at home and what role the society must play at school. The family socializes its children in ways that allow the child to fit into the family and the primary group. It inculcates in the child the values and practices that will enable the child to behave and participate appropriately and effectively in the everyday activities of the family and community—whatever they happen to be. The family also prepares the child for the experience of school, teaching it ways of learning from experience and for attacking complicated problems like those they will encounter in formal instruction.

To a large degree, this process follows the traditional patterns of the cultural group of which the family is a part, but it is affected by the family's recent experiences and history, too.

Many of the families in our communities now have gone through hell before immigrating to the United States, and many of them have been deeply shaped by the problems they encountered after immigrating to the United States. Consider the experiences that have affected the lives of the South Asian and Central American refugee and immigrant families. Think about the experiences that are even now shaping the outlook of families living in inner-city ghettos where there is danger everywhere. The messages their children are being taught no doubt reflect those experiences.

And so children go to school with the teachings of the home and family, where the set of behaviors, values, and practices acquired at home are expanded to the larger world of the school and society.

Inevitably, school expands the child's world. School, especially during the early years, is advanced socialization, a process that continues throughout the school years. Ordinarily, what happens in school is a continuation of the process that begins in the home. But what happens when the socialization that takes place in school, that is, the necessary preparation for life as a member of the larger society, is in conflict with the teachings of the home?

The kinds of things I am proposing as necessary additions to the school curriculum for a multicultural society will cause many clashes with the practices, beliefs, and attitudes that are taught in many homes. In fact, that is precisely why such curricular changes are needed, and why the changes have to be for all children. There are many families, for example, who do not believe that all people are equal, or that differ-

ences in appearance, speech, belief, and practice are just differences. There are people who, by their behavior, show their children that the way to deal with things they do not understand or like is to strike out in violence.

This obviously does not make the educator's job easy. As educators, we do have to think about where our students are coming from, and what they have been taught at home. And yet, we also have a responsibility to the society we and the children we are educating live in. In order for them to live together harmoniously, peacefully, and safely, they are going to have to get along together. And no matter what their parents and families think about others, they too will have to learn to live together and be responsible for the society they live in—that is, if there is going to be society worth living in at all.

There is no choice, really. If we are going to have a future, we are going to have to inculcate in our children the rules that form a credo that will work for the multicultural Twenty-first Century. Can we do it alone? I don't think so. We have got to form partnerships with parents and people in our communities in the most real way. We need to work on a two-pronged plan—to be carried out at home and at school—that will insure that parents and teachers alike are involved in the important task of preparing our children for the future. The curricular changes I am proposing call for the teaching of a set of beliefs, practices, and attitudes that do not necessarily come naturally to the adults who have got to be involved.

All of us, teachers and parents and citizens alike, must engage in a process of learning. What ought to be happening at parent and teacher meetings is planning and learning. We ought to be learning about one another's cultures. We should be reading the poetry and history and literature of the various groups that make up this country, to get a perspective on the many groups that have contributed to the many-faceted culture that is America.

Many if not most of the parents in the schools I visit are not literate in English. This is hardly a problem. Many of the important works that have come from our multicultural society have been translated into many languages. Nor is the fact that some parents are not literate even in their own languages a problem. So what? People who can read can read to them in their language—that is the advantage of having bilingual teachers and citizens in our schools and communities. And what if the parents of the kids are not educated enough to deal with such materials? They can be educated—like everyone else.

The next step is to plan a series of activities that parents, teachers, and kids might engage in that would allow everyone to gain the kind of understanding needed to transform our ways of thinking, valuing, and behaving. The things to be learned are learned through example, and by active engagement, not by indirect means.

I think one does it by working together on projects that benefit everyone—and I do not mean activities where people who are in the dominant group do something to help the "poor, unfortunate,

down-trodden members of the society." Rather, I think about people from all segments of the society engaged in projects like cleaning up the city's streets, developing neighborhood parks, or raising funds for projects that will benefit everyone in the community, like a new fire truck, or an after-school program for the children of working parents. When people work together as a community, they become a community, and eventually they learn enough about their neighbors to regard them not only as neighbors, but as friends.

There are so many existing divisions to bridge—how do we pull together in the face of so much racism and cross-group friction as we have now? And that is the special part that multicultural educators can play. We begin by inviting our colleagues, the parents we work with, the public, to join us in considering what kind of a society we are going to have in the future and what we have to do to prepare all children to take part in that future. And we do it by example: as educators, we show our kids and their families what we want them to be by our behavior. That, after all, is how it is done in socialization.

As parents we know that it is through our behavior that we teach our kids what it means to be a person. If we treat our children with respect, they learn to be respectful. If we are tolerant and accepting of our kids and of others, they become tolerant and accepting people. If we are fair with them, they learn the meaning of

fairness. If such simple principles were followed by most of us, there would be fewer angry people in the world.

I end this discussion on how we ought to educate children for a multicultural society with a story that Vice President Albert Gore, Jr. tells in his best-selling *Earth in Balance*. The story is about a woman in Mahatma Gandhi's village who was worried about her young son's love of sweets. She thought it was not good for her child's health to eat so many sweets. She asked the revered teacher to speak to the boy about it, to suggest to him that he should give up sweets. Gandhi thought about the woman's request for a moment, and then told her to bring her son to him in two weeks time, and he would talk with him.

Two weeks later, the woman takes her son to see Gandhi, and Gandhi does as he had promised. The boy agrees to do as he has been advised, and the mother is happy. But she is puzzled. Why did Gandhi wait two weeks before talking to her son? Gandhi tells her: he could hardly ask the boy to give up sweets until he himself had done so, and he knew it would take him at least two weeks to learn to do without them.

Educating children for the kind of world we want to leave to them has to begin somewhere, and the only place where we can be certain about it is in ourselves. It is a beginning.

 Article Review Form at end of book.

What strategies are professionals recommending for program quality in the twenty-first century?

Highlights of the Quality 2000 Initiative

Not by chance

Sharon L. Kagan and Michelle J. Neuman

Sharon L. Kagan, Ed.D., senior associate at Yale University's Bush Center in Child Development and Social Policy in New Haven, Connecticut, is recognized nationally and internationally for her work related to the care and education of young children and their families and investigation of issues, including policy development, family support, early childhood pedagogy, strategies for collaboration and service integration, and evaluation of social programs.

Michelle J. Neuman was recently a research assistant at the Yale Bush Center in Child Development and Social Policy. Her research has focused on issues related to children and families, including early care and education policy, family support, children's transitions to school, school readiness, and French family policy.

The Quality Crisis in Early Care and Education

Each day 13 million children spend time in early care and education centers or family child care homes. This should be heartening given that quality early care and education contributes to the healthy cognitive, social, and emotional development of all young children (CQ&O Study Team 1995) and in particular children from low-income families (Schweinhart, Barnes, & Weikart 1993; Barnett 1995; Gomby et al. 1995; Phillips 1995; Yoshikawa 1995). Yet we know that the quality of a majority of these settings does not optimize children's healthy development; in fact, many settings seriously jeopardize it (Galinsky et al. 1994; CQ&O Study Team 1995).

We well understand many of the reasons for low quality: underfinanced services, poorly compensated teachers, precarious turnover rates, inadequate and inconsistent regulation and enforcement, fragmented training and delivery mechanisms—the litany goes on. We understand less well how to alter the situation and what it would *really* take to reverse the pattern of neglect and provide quality early care and education to all young children.

The Quality 2000 Initiative

For the past four years, hundreds of experts in early childhood education and allied fields have been examining these very questions under the auspices of an inventive initiative, Quality 2000: Advancing Early Care and Education. The primary goal of this initiative is that by the year 2010, high-quality early care and education programs will be available and accessible to all children from birth to age five whose parents choose to enroll them. Funded by the Carnegie Corporation of New York, with supportive funding from the David and Lucile Packard, W.K. Kellogg, A.L. Mailman Family, and Ewing Marion Kauffman foundations, the initiative carried out its work through a series of commissioned papers, cross-national literature reviews, task forces, and working groups. Informed by national and international research, the fruit of that work, *Not by Chance: Creating an Early Care* and *Education System for America's Children*, offers a comprehensive, long-range vision for the field.

The vision is not about adding more services or disparate programs to what exists, although additional funds and services are essential to the vision. Rather, consisting of eight recommendations, the vision sets forth new patterns of thinking and pathways for action. Some of the recommendations seem familiar; others may sound bold, if not audacious. However they are interpreted, the recommendations are not modest or quick fixes; they will take time and energy to accomplish. That is why we set them in the context of the year 2010, not the year 2000 as the project's name suggests.

Recommendations for Eight Essential Functions

The Quality 2000 recommendations are broad and represent eight essential functions or areas where action to improve quality is needed; each recommendation is accompanied by suggested strategies to be tailored to fit individual community needs. Finally, the recommendations, although individualized to reflect each of the eight essential functions, need to be read in the aggregate—as a set of linked ideas.

1. Program Quality

Imagine a time when we expect and support quality in all family child care and center-based programs (Head Start, for-profit and nonprofit child care centers, prekindergartens, nursery schools), allowing staff flexibility in using state-of-the-art strategies, technologies, and resources creatively and cost effectively.

To address the quality crisis, early care and education programs need the flexibility to explore and implement fresh ideas and strategies—strategies that consider changing demographic and technological realities as well as strategies that focus on the total program and individual classrooms or settings.

Strategies

Promote cultural sensitivity and cultural pluralism. Children, staff, and families need opportunities to better understand and express their own cultural values and beliefs and to learn about other cultures (Derman-Sparks & the A.B.C. Task Force 1989; Phillips 1994; Phillips & Crowell 1994; Chang, Pulido-Tobiassen, & Muckelroy 1996). Staff should be trained to promote cultural sensitivity and cultural pluralism, and where possible, staff should come from the communities they serve. Children should be encouraged to cherish diversity.

Encourage pedagogical inventiveness in family child care and centers. Quality may result from a variety of strategies, including working with children in mixed-age groups (Katz, Evangelou, & Hartman 1990) and working inventively with families, grouping children in new ways, and considering ways of adapting child-staff ratios to capitalize on staff abilities to meet preschoolers' needs.

Focus on improving the overall organizational climate. The organizational climate of the total early care and education program—not only classrooms—must be considered as we create positive environments for all staff, parents, and families. Such environments should focus on the program as a learning organization ready to experiment, adapt, and grow.

Increase the number of accredited programs. Research indicates that accreditation—a voluntary process of self-assessment—significantly raises program quality. Because accredited centers provide higher quality services than nonaccredited programs (Bredekamp & Glowacki 1995; Bloom 1996; Whitebook, Sakai, & Howes 1997) and because the process promotes professionalism in the field, concerted efforts must be made to significantly increase the numbers of accredited programs.

Link programs to networks, supportive services, or other community resources. Linking early care and education programs with other services, especially resource-and-referral agencies, can help address unmet needs, expedite service delivery, minimize duplication of services, ensure smooth transitions for children, and help parents navigate through the social services maze (NACCRRA 1996). In addition, by creating family child care systems or networks, family child care providers can reduce their isolation and be more effectively linked to each other and community services.

2. Results for Children

Imagine a time when clear results and expectations are specified and used to guide individual planning for all three- and four-year-old children, based on all domains of development (social/emotional, physical/motor, cognitive, language) and approaches to learning.

Traditionally, researchers have focused on inputs (e.g., child-staff ratios, group size, staff training and education) and on the manner in which services are delivered (e.g., the nature of adult-child interactions) (Hofferth

& Chaplin 1994). Recently, however, there has been mounting interest in gauging quality in terms of the results that programs or interventions produce for preschool-age children and their families (Schorr 1994; CCSSO 1995). A focus on results for three- and four-year-olds can assist teachers with pedagogical planning and improvement as well as for purposes of evaluation and accountability. By defining desired goals and results, practitioners who work with young children can plan and tailor their activities to foster individual children's development. In addition, specified goals and results can provide programs with the feedback they need to evaluate their effectiveness and identify areas for improvement. Results also can be used to help assess the overall status of young children in communities, states, and the nation (Schorr 1994). With this information in hand, parents, practitioners, and the public can hold decisionmakers at all levels accountable for investing in early care and education (Kagan, Rosenkoetter, & Cohen 1997).

Strategies

Identify appropriate results. To move toward a results-focused approach and to safeguard children from the misuses of results, parents, practitioners, policymakers, and the public need to come together to define results and expectations for three- and four-year-old children, taking into consideration the child, family, and community conditions that promote healthy development. In particular, results should be considered from the perspective of children—across programs and over time. Results should be specified at the local, state, and national levels, increasing the customization and specificity at each level.

Develop appropriate strategies and instruments. Developmentally appropriate and culturally sensitive instruments should be developed to evaluate progress toward the achievement of specified results in all domains of development. These strategies should include capturing children's development via portfolios and other documentation of children's work.

Share results effectively, ensuring safeguards for children. Demonstration projects, evaluation, and basic research will expand the knowledge base of what helps children achieve positive results. This information needs to be shared in ways that increase public understanding of the connection among child results, effective services, and the expenditure of public funds, not in ways that may label or stigmatize children. Guidelines for the effective use of results should be developed.

3. Parent and Family Engagement

Imagine a time when parents of young children are actively involved in their children's programs and when programs provide diverse opportunities for such involvement. Imagine a time when parents have the user-friendly information and support they need to be effective consumers in choosing programs for their children. Imagine a time when employers provide policies that enable parents to become involved in their children's early learning and education.

Research shows that parent and family engagement in early care and education programs improves results for children, increasing the likelihood of children's success and achievement and decreasing the likelihood of negative outcomes, both in school and later in life. (Bronfenbrenner 1974; Bronson, Pierson, & Tivnan 1984; Powell 1989).

Strategies

Support parents as partners in early care and education programs. By focusing on developing regular communication among practitioners and parents (Weissbourd 1987), parents can be more effectively engaged as equals, with valuable information and resources. To that end, programs can offer multiple activities to involve parents (Henderson, Marburger, & Ooms 1986; Epstein 1995), taking into consideration how parent's interests, needs, and work and family responsibilities may influence their participation. Parents also should be engaged in governance opportunities (Kagan 1994).

Support parents as effective consumers. Parents can benefit from objective information about programs so they can make educated decisions that will promote their children's early development and learning. Well-funded resource-and-referral agencies, along with other parenting education efforts, can assist parents in learning about and evaluating their early care and education options. Such efforts must acknowledge and respect parents' diverse backgrounds, cultures, and needs.

Increase the family-friendliness of workplaces. Parents need support from their employers so they can fulfill their roles as partners in their children's programs, as effective consumers of early care and education services, and as productive employees (Staines &

Galinsky 1991; Galinsky, Bond, & Friedman 1993). Employers should consider offering significantly greater employee benefits, at a minimum providing time for parents to find a program and monitor and participate in their children's early care and education. Corporations should offer parents the choice of working part-time, paid sick days to care for sick children, and job-protected paid maternity and parental leave.

4. Staff Credentialing

Imagine a time when all individuals working with children in early care and education programs have—or are actively in the process of obtaining—credentials related to the position they hold or seek. Imagine a time when all staff are encouraged to pursue ongoing training and education—a course of lifelong learning.

Because individuals who work with children in early care and education programs have a major impact on children's early development and learning experiences, their credentialing/licensing is critical. Licensing individual early childhood educators has many benefits. Licensing

- holds promise for increasing the compensation of staff
- increases professionalization in the field,
- promotes the creation and coordination of quality training and education as well as career mobility, and
- helps prevent harm to children and ensure the quality of programs (APHA & AAP 1992).

The model for individual licensing can be found in Western European nations and Japan, which require significantly more training and education of

An Approach to Licensing Individuals: Requirements for Early Care and Education Staff

Administrator License

For center directors and directors of family child care support services,

- at least a bachelor's or master's degree in early childhood education or child development from an accredited institution, including at least 15 credits in early childhood administration
- certification in pediatric first aid
- demonstration of competency in management and in working with children and families

Educator License

For center teachers and public school teachers of children ages three and four,

- at least an associate's or bachelor's degree in early childhood education or child development from an accredited institution
- practicum with the age of children with whom individuals would work
- certification in pediatric first aid
- demonstration of competency in working with children and families

Associate Educator License

For lead providers in large family child care homes and assistant teachers in centers

- at least a Child Development Associate (CDA) credential, the revised National Association for Family Child Care (NAFCC) accreditation or equivalent—meaning at least 120 clock hours of formal education in child development/early childhood education and the demonstration of competency in working with children and families
- practicum with the age group with which individuals would work
- certification in pediatric first aid

Entry-Level Position Requirement

For aides in centers and in large family child care homes and for family child care providers in small family child care homes,

- interest in and aptitude for working with children and families
- commitment to participating in ongoing training leading to licensure

practitioners and a more coordinated and sequenced training delivery system (Pritchard 1996). Structures to support licensing individuals are well established in many other occupations in the United States, including helping professionals (e.g., social workers, registered and licensed practical nurses, teachers), technical professionals (e.g., architects, engineers), tradespeople (e.g., electricians), and even service workers (e.g., cosmetologists) (Mitchell 1996).

Individual licenses should be distinct from, but complementary to, facility licenses. They should specify the preparatory and ongoing training that staff need to work with children in a variety of roles. While there are many ap-

proaches to individual licensing, Quality 2000 offers one that calls for a series of three licenses for early care and education workers (see "An Approach to Licensing Individuals" chart).

Strategies

Create early childhood administrator licenses. All center directors and directors of family child care support services would be required to have early childhood administrator licenses. To obtain this license, an individual would need at least a bachelor's or master's degree in early childhood education or child development from an accredited institution, including at least 15 credits in early childhood administration, certification in first aid, and demonstrated competency in management and in working with children and families.

Create early childhood educator licenses. All teachers in centers would be required to have early childhood educator licenses. Teachers of three- and four-year-old children in public schools would have the option of obtaining public school teacher certification/licenses or the early childhood educator license. To obtain the early childhood educator license, individuals would need to have at least an associate's or bachelor's degree in early childhood education or child development from an accredited institution; have practicum experience with the age group with which they would work; be certified in pediatric first aid; and pass a competency-based assessment in working with children and families.

Create early childhood associate educator licenses. All assistant teachers in centers, as well as lead providers in large family child care homes, would be required to have early childhood associate educator licenses. To obtain the license, an individual working in a center would need to have a Child Development Associate (CDA) credential or the equivalent; an individual working in a family child care home would need to have a CDA, the revised National Association for Family Child Care (NAFCC) accreditation, or equivalent certification. Each of these certifications requires at least 120 clock hours of formal education in early childhood development and education and the demonstration of the competencies needed to work with young children and

their families. Assistant teachers and lead providers also would need to have practicum experience with the age group with which they would work and certification in pediatric first aid.

Maintain access to entry-level positions. Individuals who do not have training or education in child development or early childhood education, but who have an interest in and aptitude for working with young children and families and a commitment to seeking training in the field, would have access to entry-level jobs as aides in child care centers and in large-group family child care homes or as providers in small family child care homes. These individuals would be considered an integral part of the profession as long as they are actively pursuing training to achieve licensure as early childhood associate educator or educator.

5. Staff Training and Preparation

Imagine a time when all training for early childhood positions is child and family focused, reflecting and respecting cultural and linguistic diversity. Imagine a time when all approved training bears credit, leads to increased credentials and compensation, and equips individuals for diverse and advanced roles.

The quality of the credentials just discussed is contingent upon the quality of the training individuals receive. All training and education sequences should, at a minimum, address the CDA competency areas (establishing and maintaining a safe, healthy learning environment; advancing physical and intellectual competence; supporting social and emotional development and providing positive guidance; establishing

positive and productive relationships with families; ensuring a well-run, purposeful program that is responsive to participant needs; and maintaining a commitment to professionalism [Council for Early Childhood Professional Recognition 1992]). More preservice and inservice training, particularly at intermediate and advanced levels, needs to be developed and made available to practitioners in the following areas (Morgan et al. 1993): engaging and supporting families; developing cultural competency; observing and assessing children; working with mixed-age groups and larger groups, and team teaching; working with infants and toddlers; working with children with special needs; promoting ethics; working across human service disciplines; and developing management and leadership skills.

Strategies

Revise and develop staff training/preparation curricula and sequences. Revamping the content of and opportunities for practitioner training/preparation will necessitate the participation of many stakeholders. State licensing boards for early care and education should require staff to have appropriate ranges of skills to earn and maintain licenses, including appropriate preparatory and ongoing course work. Colleges and community organizations that educate and train early care and education staff should revise and develop curricula and sequences to address the broad-based knowledge (early childhood pedagogy and content from allied disciplines) and skills that practitioners need to be competent in today's early care and education programs.

Promote the development of leaders and managers. To promote the development of leaders and managers at the local, state, and national levels, program administrators with strong leadership potential should be supported through fellowships and training and mentoring opportunities. Such mentoring programs are an effective strategy to support staff as they acquire knowledge and skills and to enhance the professional development of more skilled and experienced mentor-teachers (Whitebook, Hnatiuk, & Bellm 1994; Breunig & Bellm 1996).

6. Program Licensing

Imagine a time when all early care and education programs are licensed, without any legal exemptions. Imagine a time when facility licensing procedures are streamlined and enforced to ensure that all programs promote children's safety, health, and development. Imagine a time when incentives exist for programs to continually enhance their facilities.

Research demonstrates that about 40% of center-based programs—including many part-day, school-based, and church-based programs (Adams 1990)—and as many as 80 to 90% of family child care providers (Willer et al. 1991) are legally exempt from regulation despite the fact that states with more stringent regulation yield higher quality programs (CQ&O Study Team 1995).

Strategies

Eliminate exemptions. All programs available to the general public should be required to meet basic safeguards that protect children's well-being and foster equity in the early care and education field; there should be no legal exemptions. For example,

programs should not be legally exempt from facility regulations because of their size, hours of operation, location, or auspices.

Streamline facility licensing. State facility licensing should be streamlined to focus on essential safeguards of safety, health, and development and to complement the system of individual licensing described earlier (U.S. ACIR 1994; Gormley 1995; Gwen Morgan, personal communication, 22 March 1996). Standards for staffing levels should allow programs the flexibility to group children and organize staff in ways that maximize quality.

Enforce requirements. To fully promote children's safety, health, and development, states must not only eliminate exemptions and streamline regulations but also enforce requirements. Licensing agencies must have the appropriate resources to carry out enforcement functions. State monitoring and enforcement systems should employ positive, incentive-based strategies to enable programs to meet licensing requirements. State licensing systems also should provide incentives for programs to invest in facility enhancement to increase capacity for meeting the increasing demand for early care and education services.

Develop national licensing guidelines. Although the main responsibility for the development and issue of facility licensing requirements should remain at the state level, national licensing guidelines should be developed to promote regulatory consistency across the country.

7. Funding and Financing

Imagine a time when young children's early care and education is funded by the public and private sectors at per-child

levels commensurate with funding for elementary-age children and when 10% of the funds are set aside for professional and staff development, enhanced compensation, parent information and engagement, program accreditation, resource-and-referral services, evaluation, research, planning, and licensing and facility enhancement.

Adequate funding is essential to ensuring that all children have access to quality early care and education services and that their parents have choice in selecting services. The costs must be shared by the public at large, parents (according to income), employers, government, and community organizations. While parents need access to and choice of quality early care and education services, they also need the option of caring for their own very young children; therefore, paid parental leave for parents of very young children should be provided. These efforts to increase investment necessitate additional research and planning.

Strategies

Estimate the actual cost of a quality early care and education system. The field needs to estimate the actual cost of mounting and sustaining a comprehensive quality early care and education system. In making such estimates, early care and education professionals need to work closely with funding and financing experts, using cost-calculation approaches that other fields have found useful. Such an analysis also should estimate the revenues that the early care and education system would generate in both the short and long term. Longer-term cost-benefit accounting should be used to determine the extended benefits of a quality early care and education system, benefits that include savings in special education, corrections, public assistance, and other social services.

Identify several revenue-generation mechanisms. Several revenue-generation options for funding for a comprehensive early care and education system—including increased staff compensation—need to be considered and implemented. Some possible mechanisms include establishing individual and corporate income taxes, federal payroll taxes, and new sales or excise taxes; expanding the populations eligible to receive the school aid formula; cutting other government expenditures to raise some of the needed funds; and procuring funds as part of a larger revenue-generation package designed to support a range of social services that families need. None of these approaches are easy to sell to the public or policymakers, but each would help improve the amount of funding available to support early care and education.

Develop model approaches for distributing funds to parents. State-level agencies may be best suited for administering funds to parents. Mechanisms to distribute funds to parents should promote parent choice, such as vouchers, direct payments to programs of parents' choice, and/or tax credits. Parents should receive assistance in paying for early care and education programs based on a sliding scale linked to parents' income. (As family income increases over time, public assistance for early care and education would decrease proportionately but not be completely cut off [Stangler 1995]).

Create a targeted, coordinated funding initiative. Scholarship and knowledge of how to generate increased revenues for the development of a comprehensive early care and education system is emerging but remains piecemeal and embryonic. Focused research is needed to carry out the analyses mentioned above. Therefore, it will be necessary to create a targeted, coordinated initiative focused on funding a quality early care and education system.

8. Governance Structures

Imagine a time when early care and education is governed rationally. Imagine a time when mechanisms (councils, boards) are established or built upon in every community and state to carry out planning, governance, and accountability roles in early care and education.

To increase coordination, efficiency, and continuity of services for young children and their families, it is critical to establish a rational governance system. Quality 2000 recommends establishing governance entities in every state and locality—to be called State Early Care and Education Board and Local Early Care and Education Board, respectively. Where these governing boards or coordinating councils already exist, the State or Local Early Care and Education Board could be built from the existing body or created in collaboration with it.

Strategies

Establish state boards. State boards should be responsible for ensuring quality and achieving agreed-upon results for children. They should engage in planning, collecting, and analyzing data; defining eligibility and subsidy levels and parental-leave conditions; and determining how to allocate funds to parents. They would also develop state standards for results to align with national goals. As with other governance entities, state boards would facilitate collaboration, service integration, and comprehensive services delivery. State boards would be composed of appointed or elected board members, including equal numbers of parents/consumers; practitioners; community and state leaders, including clergy; and municipal or government agency representatives.

Establish local boards. Local boards would have responsibility for both the governance and the coordination of early care and education for children birth to age five. They could be geographically aligned with school districts, but would be distinct entities. Like their state counterparts, they should be composed of a broad-based group of appointed or elected board members who would be responsible for developing performance benchmarks for child results, taking into consideration local strengths, needs, priorities, and resources. Local boards would involve consumers and citizens in comprehensive needs assessment and planning.

Support effective federal governance. To support these efforts, the federal government will need to provide mandates and incentives to these boards. In addition, the federal government will guide states as they develop standards and communities as they develop benchmarks to meet state standards and national goals. The federal government also will collect national data, provide funding for evaluating demonstration efforts, and offer technical assistance to states and localities. Their well-being, and the nation's, simply cannot be left to chance.

The quality of daily life for millions of American children and families depends on how the United States solves—or fails to solve—the quality crisis in early care and education. Quality 2000 and the *Not by Chance* report address this crisis by recommending that the nation make a planned, significant, and immediate advance to improve quality and to create a system of services. It is the hope of those involved in the Quality 2000 initiative that the ideas put forth in these recommendations will provoke discussion, advance our collective thinking, and spark bold, new action on behalf of our nation's children. Their well-being, and the nation's, simply cannot be left to chance.

References

Adams, G. 1990. *Who knows how safe? The status of state efforts to ensure quality child care.* Washington, DC: Children's Defense Fund.

APHA (American Public Health Association), & AAP (American Academy of Pediatrics). 1992. *Caring for our children: National health and safety performance standards—Guidelines for out-of-home child care programs.* Washington, DC: APHA.

Barnett, W.S. 1995. Long-term effects of early childhood programs on cognitive and school outcomes. *The Future of Children* 5 (3): 25–50.

Bloom, P.J. 1996. The quality of work life in early childhood programs: Does accreditation make a difference? In *NAEYC accreditation: A decade of learning and the years ahead,* eds. S. Bredekamp & B.A. Willer, 13–24. Washington, DC: NAEYC.

Bredekamp, S., & S. Glowacki. 1995. The first decade of NAEYC accreditation: Growth and impact on the field. Paper prepared for an invitational conference sponsored by the Robert McCormick Tribune Foundation and NAEYC, 18–20 September, Wheaton, Illinois.

Breunig, G.S., & D. Bellm. 1996. *Early childhood mentoring programs: A survey of community initiatives.* Washington, DC: National Center for the Early Childhood Work Force.

Brofenbrenner, U. 1974. *A report on longitudinal evaluations of preschool programs, Vol. 2: Is early intervention effective?* Washington, DC: Office of Child Development, U.S. Department of Health, Education, and Welfare.

Bronson, M.B., D.E. Pierson, & T. Tivnan. 1984. The effects of early education on children's competence in elementary school. *Evaluation Review* 8: 615–29.

Chang, H.N., D. Pulido-Tobiassen, & A. Muckelroy. 1996. *Looking in, looking out: Redefining care and early education in a diverse society.* San Francisco: California Tomorrow.

CCSSO (Council of Chief State School Officers). 1995. *Moving toward accountability for results: A look at ten states' efforts.* Washington, DC: Author.

Council for Early Childhood Professional Recognition. 1992. *Child Development Associate assessment system and competency standards.* Washington, DC: Author.

CQ&O (Cost, Quality, & Outcomes) Study Team. 1995. *Cost, quality, and child outcomes in child care centers.* Denver: Department of Economics, University of Colorado at Denver.

Derman-Sparks, L., & the A.B.C. Task Force. 1989. *Anti-bias curriculum: Tools for empowering young children.* Washington, DC: NAEYC.

Epstein, J.L. 1995. School/family/community partnerships: Caring for the children we share. *Phi Delta Kappan* (May): 701–12.

Galinsky, E., J.T. Bond, & D.E. Friedman. 1993. *The changing workforce: Highlights of the National Study.* New York: Families and Work Institute.

Galinsky, E., C. Howes, S. Kontos, & M. Shinn. 1994. *The study of children in family child care and relative care.* New York: Families and Work Institute.

Gomby, D.S., M.B. Larner, C.S. Stevenson, E.M. Lewit, & R.E. Behrman. 1995. Long-term outcomes of early childhood programs: Analysis and recommendations. *The Future of Children* 5 (3): 6–24.

Gormley, W.T. 1995. *Everybody's children: Child care as a public problem.* Washington, DC: Brookings Institution.

Henderson, A.T., C.L. Marburger, & T. Ooms. 1986. *Beyond the bake sale: An educator's guide to working with parents.* Columbia, MD: National Committee for Citizens in Education.

Hofferth, S.L., & D. Chaplin. 1994. *Child care quality versus availability: Do we have to trade one for the other?* Washington, DC: Urban Institute Press.

Kagan, S.L. 1994. *Defining America's commitments to parents and families: An historical-conceptual perspective.* Kansas City, MO: Ewing Marion Kauffman Foundation.

Kagan, S.L., S. Rosenkoetter, & N.E. Cohen, eds. 1997. *Considering child-based outcomes for young children: Definitions, desirability, feasibility, and next steps.* New Haven, CT: Bush Center in Child Development and Social Policy, Yale University.

Katz, L.G., D. Evangelou, & J.A. Hartman. 1990. *The case for mixed-age grouping in early education.* Washington, DC: NAEYC.

Mitchell, A. 1996. Licensing: Lessons from other occupations. In *Reinventing early care and education: A vision for a quality system,* eds. S.L. Kagan & N.E. Cohen, 101–123. San Francisco: Jossey-Bass.

Morgan, G., S.L. Azer, J.B. Costley, A. Genser, I.F. Goodman, J. Lombardi, & B. McGimsey. 1993. *Making a career of it: The state of the states report on career development in early care and education.* Boston: Center for Career Development in Early Care and Education, Wheelock College.

NACCRRA (National Association of Child Care Resource and Referral Agencies). 1996. *Creating and facilitating health linkages: The role of child care resource and referral.* Washington, DC: Author.

Phillips, C.B. 1994. The movement of African-American children through sociocultural contexts: A case of conflict resolution. In *Diversity and developmentally appropriate practices: Challenges for early childhood education,* eds. B.L. Mallory & R.S. New, 137–54. New York: Teachers College Press.

Phillips, D.A., ed. 1995. *Child care for low-income families: Summary of two workshops.* Washington, DC: National Academy Press.

Phillips, D.A., & N.A. Crowell, eds. 1994. *Cultural diversity in early education: Results of a workshop*. Washington, DC: National Academy Press.

Powell, D.R. 1989. *Families and early childhood programs*. Washington, DC: NAEYC.

Pritchard, E. 1996. Training and professional development: International approaches. In *Reinventing early care and education: A vision for a quality system*, eds. S.L. Kagan & N.E. Cohen, 124–41. San Francisco: Jossey-Bass.

Schorr, L.B. 1994. The case for shifting to results-based accountability. In *Making a difference: Moving to outcome-based accountability for comprehensive service reforms*, eds. N. Young, S. Gardner, S. Coley, L. Schorr, & C. Bruner, 13–28. Falls Church, VA: National Center for Service Integration.

Schweinhart, L.J., H.V. Barnes, & D.P. Weikart, with W.S. Barnett, & A.S. Epstein. 1993. *Significant benefits: The High/Scope Perry Preschool Study through age 27*. Ypsilanti, MI: High/Scope Press.

Staines, G.L., & E. Galinsky. 1991. *Parental leave and productivity: The supervisor's view*. New York: Families and Work Institute.

Stangler, G. 1995. Lifeboats vs. safety nets: Who rides . . . who swims? In *Dollars and sense: Diverse perspectives on block grants and the Personal Responsibility Act*, 67–72. Washington, DC: The Finance Project and Institute for Educational Leadership.

U.S. ACIR (Advisory Commission on Intergovernmental Relations). 1994. *Child care: The need for federal-state-local coordination*. Washington, DC: Author.

Weissbourd, B. 1987. A brief history of family support programs. In *America's family support programs*, eds. S.L. Kagan, D.R. Powell, B. Weissbourd, & E.F. Zigler, 38–56. New Haven, CT: Yale University Press.

Whitebook, M., P. Hnatiuk, & D. Bellm. 1994. *Mentoring in early care and education: Refining an emerging career path*. Washington, DC.. National Center for the Early Childhood Work Force.

Whitebook, M., L. Sakai, & C. Howes. 1997. *NAEYC accreditation as a strategy for improving child care quality, executive summary*. Washington, DC: National Center for the Early Childhood Work Force.

Willer, B., ed. 1990. *Reaching the full cost of quality in early childhood programs*. Washington, DC: NAEYC.

Willer, B., S. Hofferth, E. Kisker, P. Divine-Hawkins, E. Farquhar, & F. Glantz. 1991. *The demand and supply of child care in 1990: Joint findings from the National Child Care Survey 1990 and a profile of child care settings*. Washington, DC: NAEYC.

Yoshikawa, H. 1995. Long-term effects of early childhood programs on social outcomes and delinquency. *The Future of Children* 5 (3): 51–75.

 Article Review Form at end of book.

How will the encouragement of playfulness prepare children for the twenty-first century?

Playfulness Enhancement through Classroom Intervention for the 21st Century

W.A.R. Boyer

W.A.R. Boyer is Assistant Professor, Department of Psychological Foundations, Faculty of Education, University of Victoria, Victoria, British Columbia, Canada.

What attributes do we believe our children will need in order to maintain physical and mental health, and to foster a more balanced, yet vigorous, life for the challenges of the 21st century?

If asked to consider this question, we might include one or more of the following characteristics: imagination, humor, emotional expressiveness, a penchant for novelty seeking, curiosity, openness, communicativeness, flexibility and persistence. Remarkably, all of these attributes have been related to play and playfulness (Athey, 1984; Barnett, 1990; Cattell, 1950; Singer & Rummo, 1973).

Lieberman (1977) supported the relationship among play, imagination and creativity, and dubbed them "first order" elements in human functioning. These first order elements lead to a *style of play* that attracts, preoccupies and enhances children's intrinsic motivation to learn. This style of play, which can be applied to areas of work and academic functioning, is called "playfulness." Playfulness, or a playful attitude in learning, therefore can be defined as an "indifference to extrinsic payoffs [that] allows a new response for the person or a new transformation of information. Novel engagements with elements in the environment are self-reinforcing and sustain the behaviour leading to new knowledge" (Ellis, 1973, p. 121).

Thus, playfulness provides children with the opportunity to freely discuss and explore personality dimensions and personas, discover alternative strategies for handling daily concerns, and use their senses to sample the world in a healthy, structured manner (Fineman, 1962; Freyberg, 1973; Glickman, 1984; Singer, 1973; Singer & Singer, 1977).

Keeping a playful attitude toward learning is an integral part of acquiring the adaptive skills necessary to thrive and meet the upcoming challenges of the 21st century. According to Sinetar (1991), members of the global society in the 21st century will require:

- a synergistic frame of reference, which is the ability to wholeheartedly work with others to regenerate, renew and revive learning and thinking to an extent that could not be achieved alone

- an ability to see the whole project or process

- an ability to look beyond form and content to context

- an ability to integrate, unify and feel connected to life and work

- the motivation to work with one's heart or for the love of the task.

Playfulness can help individuals achieve each of these components of Sinetar's conceptual framework. Playfulness, in a learning context, deemphasizes the need to be perfect and, thus, increases children's self-esteem; therefore, it also increases children's willingness to develop interpersonal relationships through synergistic endeavors. For example, "Latonya, that's an even better idea. Let's try it first. It might make our project even better." Playful learning behaviors also can allow a child to see the whole project or process, and understand why the project is important, and how it fits within a larger thematic *context*. Experimenting with answers, using free associative imagination and tinkering with reality's boundaries are highly motivating strategies that can promote self-regulated and metacognitive thinking processes. For example, "I wonder what would happen if I just changed this one piece of my project? Would it help or hurt? I think this is how Daddy always finds bugs in computer programs." By learning to use a playful approach to real-life decisions, children will learn to accept making mistakes and be more likely to learn from them. Successfully handling the responsibility of these decisions allows a child to feel connected to life and work. Furthermore, a child who employs a playful approach is likely to see academic and personal problems as puzzles or challenges that fuel motivation

and capture the desire to pursue solutions.

On the other hand, Schafer (1969) has traced insufficient make-believe or playful learning experiences in early childhood to differences in high school students' creative problem-solving skills. Furthermore, authors such as Meichenbaum (1971) and Spivak and Levine (1964) believe that children who do not have sufficient fantasy play and playful experiences with the environment in early childhood could later develop problems with impulsiveness, antisocial behavior and a susceptibility to delinquency.

Playfulness is an important part of learning to work with others, as well as for attaining such traits as flexible thinking, persistence, commitment, and a love of and fascination with learning. The author will present a unified review of playfulness development, focus on children ages 3 to 5, and describe playfulness enhancement through classroom intervention for the 21st century.

Developmental Progression of Playfulness and Imagination

How do children develop the creativity and imagination skills that support playfulness? In order to respond to this question, the author examined Valett's (1983) theory of the developmental progression of playfulness and imagination. Valett proposes that creativity and imagination are factors within an integrated process composed of sensory impressions acquired by time, experience and education. Dynamic entities such as images and novel ideas are activated within the mind by personal receptiveness, volition

and action. The development of creative and imaginative play is influenced by training and experience and can be best described by five phases: sensory exploration, egocentric speculation, personal experimentation, symbolic representation and functional verification (see Table 1). The author will focus on sensory exploration, which Valett's conceptual paradigm portrays as age-appropriate for 3- to 5-year-olds.

At first, the reader may not find anything new here; after all, most early childhood teachers present a unit on the senses to the children. The unit, however, usually focuses on identifying specific sensations (e.g., this is the pickle smell and this is the flower smell), on using a physical sense as an end rather than as a means to an end (e.g., today we are going to cook and use our sense of taste on the food), or on naming the appropriate body part responsible for a sense (e.g., what would you use to see the color of a pickle?).

Less often do educators consistently direct and guide students to use their senses in a metacognitive and self-regulatory manner that encourages "individuals to monitor their own learning by strategically adopting and effectively using learning and problem-solving strategies that meet their individual needs. . . . Self-regulatory practices encourage children to recognize what they have learned and what they need to learn" (Boyer & Sweeting, 1996, p. 20). Metacognition "is any knowledge or cognitive activity that takes as its object, or regulates, any aspect of any cognitive enterprise" (Flavell, Miller & Miller, 1993, p. 150). Within the context of this definition, the goal is not only to get children to use their senses, but also to teach them to think for themselves about when and why

Table 1 — Developmental Progression of Playfulness and Imagination

Sensory exploration is a playful phase in which a child flexibly and enthusiastically encounters the environment. This phase begins shortly after birth and continues through the preschool years. (approximate ages, birth to 5)

Egocentric speculation is dominated by fantasy and the exaggeration of intuitive impressions. Children in preschool to early school years are enthralled by the possibility of having "magical" powers. Dolls, toy animals and imaginary friends are imbued with life and special qualities. (approximate ages, 2–7)

Personal experimentation during the early school years results in a systematic trial-and-error approach to the world. Visual and auditory images are "put to the test" experientially. (approximate ages, 6–10)

Symbolic representation is the phase reached by early adolescence. It is characterized by the representation of imaginative experiences in symbolic forms such as drawings, formulas, words, dance, paintings, sculpture and other forms. (approximate ages, 11–15)

Functional verification is marked by the emergence of inventive, productive and applied behaviors, resulting from the accumulated experience and the wisdom of adulthood, that create new changes in the self and the environment. (approximate ages, 23 and older)

---

to use their senses. To help a child cope with the demands that a new sibling places on the family, for example, we might start by pretending that a cotton ball is a new baby. The playfulness aspect emerges from comparing a soggy cotton ball to a soggy baby:

Teacher: What does it feel like when the baby wets? (Soaks cotton ball in muddy pond water.)

Child: Soggy and droopy, like a garbage bag filled with water. Oh, yuck.

Teacher: What does it smell like?

Child: Stinky. It's like the dog, only he does it outside.

Teacher: What does it sound like when the baby has been wet for a little while?

Child: WAHHHHHHHH! She really cries loud.

Teacher: Do you like that sound?

Child: No, I wish she would stop it.

Teacher: When she cries so loud, do you think she's comfortable?

Child: No, I guess not. I guess she feels bad.

Teacher: What does your dog sound like when it has to go?

Child: Hey, the dog barks to go out but my sister can't go out on her own. She needs us to help her.

Teacher: What does the baby look like/smell like/feel like when it has just had a bath? (Washes out the cotton ball.)

Child: It looks white and clean, it feels soft and a little wet, and it smells a lot better.

Teacher: Isn't this the good part about your new sister?

Child: Yes. I like that part. Maybe I shouldn't get upset with my baby sister because she needs me sometimes.

Child: I want to know if all babies are alike, or is it just my sister?

Teacher: I think we can find out together. Perhaps we can share this with the class and see if they feel the way you did. Maybe we can help them, too.

By using their senses, children can learn that life is full of experiences, both pleasant and unpleasant. They can learn how to offset what may be bothersome by focusing, through the senses, on something that is good.

In summary, we now find that there is a hierarchical goal structure, in which enhancing playfulness seems to be the central theme. We can use a goal-driven search method to analyze this structure. Since the goal is to enhance playfulness, and consequently derive all the benefits that researchers have associated with it, we must ask how we can enhance playfulness. First, we enhance playfulness in this age group by using sensory exploration (Valett, 1983). Therefore, we must increase children's opportunities for sensory exploration. How do we maximize the benefits of such opportunities? By teaching children how, when and why to use their senses. Thus, metacognition regarding the use of senses becomes a goal. Ultimately, self-regulated metacognition, both in sensory exploration and in later phases, is a tool for enhancing playfulness, which in turn is a tool for deriving long-term, positive benefits throughout life.

Strategies for Sensorial Stimulation

The author (Boyer, 1994) found, in a study of 105 children, ages 3 to 5, that deliberate strategies for sensorial stimulation could enhance playfulness. The experimental group received a sensory stimulation intervention, and consequently demonstrated heightened manifest levels of joy, humor and social spontaneity in their everyday interactions, compared to the control group. Boyer (1994) found that enthusiastic, playful, joyful and fun exploration of the environment through the senses involved 12 general teaching/

learning strategies that encourage children to think, by:

- *Encouraging and modeling different ways in which children can use a variety of familiar and unfamiliar objects.* In the above text about a new-born baby, for example, a familiar object (a cotton ball) was used in an unusual way. The senses were not simply used; they were used in playful exploration of feelings regarding a stressful situation. Confronted with an unfamiliar object, such as a tire iron for fixing a flat tire, a child might respond, "I don't know what this is, but to me it is a paddle for a boat." Further exploration could be encouraged by asking follow-up questions: "What does it sound like as you dip the 'paddle' into the water to row?" "Does it make a different sound from a wooden paddle?" "Do you think it would be easier or harder to row with this new paddle?" "What would the air smell like right now if you were paddling on a lake?" "Would you rather be paddling on a sunny lake or along a shady stream?"

- *Examining and discussing how certain sensory perceptions make us feel.* Statements that reflect this strategy include: "I feel happy when I *see* the beautiful colors of the sunrise because it means a new day of fun." "I feel shy when I *smell* this sweet perfume my aunt wears. She always rushes over to me in a crowd and grabs me and kisses me in front of everyone." "I get excited when I *feel* the cold air on my cheeks and *see* the big puffy clouds in the sky

because I know it is going to snow." "I feel surprised when I *taste* the bitter flavor of dark unsweetened chocolate—yuck!!!" "I feel angry when I *hear* an ambulance siren because I think someone was hurt in an accident that didn't have to happen." "I am ready to laugh when I *see* my teacher make a funny face at me." These discussions of feelings help children feel connected to and appreciative of events that occur in their lives.

- *Thinking of ways to use our senses in indoor and outdoor play in order to support and generate more fun-filled and exciting experiences.* Knowing what one likes and dislikes and how to generate or avoid these activities makes us more motivated to learn. "When I am on the swing, I can hold on tight and close my eyes and feel the world spin just for me. I really like these quiet moments. They give me time to think for myself." Or, "Swings make me dizzy, but the world spins for me when I lie on the ground and look at the moving clouds. I like that better."

- *Isolating the senses to discover their importance, their uses and their limitations (without the other senses).* Through directed reflection and self-regulation, children can see the senses' importance to human functioning. "Smelling, seeing, touching and tasting help me to avoid vinegar. If I only used my sense of taste I

might accidentally drink vinegar like I would water—yuck! If I just saw it or touched the vinegar it would seem like water and I might drink it. What a mistake! If I smelled the vinegar it wouldn't give away the bad taste so I need all of my senses for some things."

- *Encouraging children to use words to describe how they use their senses when working with objects in their environment.* Knowing that our hands are our servants motivates us to find ways of constructively working with them to perform beautiful, pleasing tasks. "When I work with clay, my hands feel like they are a part of the clay. They are soft, bendable, squeezable, stretchable. I can make my hands take any form and do anything beautiful for me."

- *Using humorous poetry, riddles, songs and jokes to inspire and evoke curiosity, interest and motivation in a lesson.* Teacher: "What equipment does a taste tester need?" Children: "A tongue." Teacher: "Today we have used our sense of touch; we need this sense so very much. To touch a zipper that is as hard as steel, makes this object very real. Things that hide in a magic sock, have texture, shape and may weigh a lot."

- *Using guided recall of sensory episodes or experiences.* "I remember when I first smelled spring. I was with my best friend. The sun was shining and there was a wet smell of gritty earth and mud, along with a faint smell of spinach and green beans in the air."

If we do not practice the act of remembering the things that happen to us, then we will not be as good at enjoying the present and the future.

Discussions of feelings help children feel connected to and appreciative of events that occur in their lives.

Any episode can be used as a memory trigger to connect us with our past and help us to think about what we might do in the future. This is not only applicable to choosing leisure experiences, like going back to a place for which we have fond memories, but also lets us revisit a mistake, so we can figure out how to avoid repeating it. If we do not practice the act of remembering the things that happen to us, then we will not be as good at enjoying the present and the future.

- *Evoking speculation from stimulating objects in the child's environment through directed fantasy activities.* Children could be asked to imagine that they could communicate with life on other planets by means of radio or television. They could be encouraged to consider questions they would ask the life forms. These fantasies might result in ingenious ideas, designs or inventions.

- *Providing fun opportunities to compare real events with hypothetical events, and providing children with practice in productive thinking through imaginative games.* Consider, for example, the game called HOME (de Mille, 1973). In this game, children are asked to reflect on what home looks like and what it would look like if things were changed around (e.g., "Let us take the stove out of the kitchen and put it in some other room. What room would you like to put it in and why?"). The game is fun because it uses a well-known milieu that offers the child many objects from which to choose and use in unconventional ways.

- *Having children imagine a situation in as much detail as possible, and exploring it verbally and pictorially through imaginative situations.* Wherever possible, provide physical enactment through dramatic arts, drawings, constructions or other means. In order to travel to the sun, for example, the children could pack their "sensory" travel bag, which might include liquid imagination for their heads, a nose key to control their sense of smell, spectrum goggles to shield their eyes from the sun and to see its different kinds of light, and, of course, oven mitts to protect their hands from the intense heat.

- *Presenting realistic problems for thought and consideration through creative problem-solving activities.* "Mommy said she wanted you to have one apple with your lunch on each school day. If she buys 6 apples, will you be able to have an apple for every day of the school week?"

- *Using linguistic strategies that involve activities such as finding:*

(a) *commonalities* (attributes: I spy with my little eye something that is [attribute]; similarities: a child is like a little tree growing every day; analogy: my aunt is to my cousin as my mommy is to me)

(b) *opposites* (attributes; incongruities: "You are looking so somber on such a cheerful occasion"; analogies: hot is to cold as day is to night)

(c) *absurdities* (the foolish or insensible: "What if gravity stopped working?" "We would fly off the surface of the earth out into space, and furthermore, the earth would fly apart.")

(d) *innovative forms* (popular phrases from song, slang, etc.: "This is a hot book. I really think the little boy and girl in the story are cool. This is a major cool story." The words "hot," "cool" and "major" are used here to indicate a preference for something)

(e) *metaphors* (how words represent many different ideas: e.g., *This Little Light of Mine*).

As these strategies fill the child's playfulness toolbox, the child will begin to approach new scenarios by pulling out various "tools" for coping with, enjoying and learning from the environment. If we invert the metaphor, however, it is easy to see that a child cannot employ tools that he does not possess. Moreover, the child is unlikely to acquire most of these tools without consistent direction from teachers.

Learning activities that accentuate the senses must form the basis for children's comprehension and manipulation of abstract verbal and written symbols (Piaget & Inhelder, 1971). Furthermore, O'Neill, Astington & Flavell (1992) suggest that children between 3 and 5 can develop an appreciation of the different types of knowledge that the senses can provide. Singer and Singer (1980) assert that "it seems important that we find such a dimension emerging so early with preschoolers"

Playfulness is appropriate in the regular curriculum when children are just starting to be involved in a field of study . . .

(p. 153). Recognizing the need for sensorial experiences and the development of modality specific sensorial knowledge requires that we provide "opportunities for impression and expression" (Stern, 1924, p. 313).

Conclusion

By integrating playfulness with school or center activities, we give children the opportunity to explore the possibilities of a given situation. Playfulness allows children to be happier, and have a sense of how to please themselves and personally engage themselves in the active, positive and fruitful pursuit of learning. Playfulness is appropriate in the regular curriculum when children are just starting to be involved in a field of study, when they need to become more committed to a learning endeavor, or when they are nearly finished with a project and need the added enthusiasm and energy to satisfactorily complete the task.

Furthermore, playfulness is well suited to scientific investigation, mathematical inquiry and language investigation in the classroom, because it allows children to develop self-awareness as well as control over environmental objects, their movements and their bodies. Playfulness allows a child to pretend that a fluffy piece of cotton is a baby who moves, talks, wets or smells. Playfulness allows children to practice verbal skills by allowing them to hear their own words or those of their playmates. Through playfulness, children can develop emotional awareness and sensitivity by taking the part of one character, or several characters, or assuming the role of a parent, a doctor or a teacher. Children may not only

mimic adults' speech, but also imitate adults' sense of concern for children, which is the cornerstone of empathy and sympathy. Playfulness allows children to learn roles for new social situations, allowing a child to shift from "I'm Daddy" to "I'm the baby" or "I'm the giant." In this way, children develop an awareness of different figures and their functions. This will help them work through their feelings of rivalry, jealousy and self-doubt.

In order for teachers and parents to stimulate and support children's playfulness and the development of imaginative play, an appropriate fit must exist between the child's playfulness and the objects and experiences found in the interactive setting. The National Association for the Education of Young Children (1986) emphasizes that children must be provided developmentally appropriate, environmental experiences. Early childhood is an appropriate age for acquiring sensorial awareness, which is critical for the improvement of imagery in memory development and the reproduction of sensations (Fineman, 1962; Freyberg, 1973). With practice, individuals have the capacity to express or reproduce sights, sounds, smells, tastes and touches (Singer & Singer, 1977). "Inside each person there is a wonderful capacity to reflect on information and the various sense organs register, direct and control these experiences" (Csikszentmihalyi, 1993, p. 22).

The 12 teaching/learning strategies presented in this article can be used to develop playfulness and allow children to direct and control their personal learning experience. As Pritchett (1995) indicates, "Considering the scope and speed of change these days, there will be precious gifts—many

priceless opportunities—for those of us who play by the new rules, position ourselves right, and take personal responsibility for our future" (p. iv). Playfulness is a precious gift that will provide priceless opportunities for children to think, plan and enjoy life with all of the incipient changes and challenges offered by the 21st century.

References

Athey, I. (1984). Contributions of play to development. In T. D. Yawkey & A. D. Pellegrini (Eds.), *Child's play: Developmental and applied* (pp. 9–28). Hillsdale, NJ: Erlbaum.

Barnett, L. A. (1990). Playfulness: Definition, design, and measurement. *Play & Culture, 3,* 319–336.

Boyer, W. A. R. (1994, October). *Enhancing playfulness and creativity with sensory stimulation.* Paper presented at the International Conference on Innovations in Education, Penang, Malaysia.

Boyer, W. A. R., & Sweeting, T. (1996). Portfolio assessment in primary physical education programs. *Canadian Children, 21*(l), 19–25.

Cattell, R. B. (1950). *Personality. A systematic theoretical and factual study.* New York: McGraw-Hill.

Csikszentmihalyi, M. (1993). *The evolving self. A psychology for the third millennium.* New York: HarperCollins.

de Mille, R. (1973). *Put your mother on the ceiling. Children's imagination games.* Middlesex, England: Penguin Books.

Ellis, M. J. (1973). *Why people play.* Englewood Cliffs, NJ: Prentice-Hall.

Fineman, J. (1962). Observations on the development of imaginative play in early childhood. *Journal of the American Academy of Child Psychiatry, 1,* 167–181.

Flavell, J. H., Miller, P. H., & Miller, S. A. (1993). *Cognitive development* (3rd ed.). Englewood Cliffs, NJ: Prentice Hall.

Freyberg, J. (1973). Increasing the imaginative play of urban disadvantaged kindergarten children through systematic training. In J. L. Singer (Ed.), *The child's world of make-believe* (pp. 129–154). New York: Academic Press.

Glickman, C. D. (1984). Play in public school settings: A philosophical question. In T. D. Yawkey & A. D. Pellegrini (Eds.), *Child's play: Developmental and applied* (pp. 255–271). Hillsdale, NJ: Lawrence Erlbaum Associates.

Lieberman, J. N. (1977). *Playfulness. Its relationship to imagination and creativity.* New York: Harcourt Brace Jovanovich.

Meichenbaum, D. H. (1971). *The nature and modification of impulsive children: Training impulsive children to talk to themselves* (Internal Report No. 23). Waterloo, ON: University of Waterloo.

National Association for the Education of Young Children. (1986). Position statement on developmentally appropriate practice in early childhood programs serving children from birth through age 8. *Young Children, 41*(6), 4–19.

O'Neill, D. K., Astington, J. W., & Flavell, J. H. (1992). Young children's understanding of the role that sensory experiences play in knowledge acquisition. *Child Development, 63,* 474–490.

Piaget, J., & Inhelder, B. (1971). *Mental imagery in the child. A study of the development of imaginal representation.* London: Routledge & Kegan Paul.

Pritchett, P. (1995). *New work habits for a radically changing world. 13 ground rules for job success in the information age.* Dallas, TX: Pritchett & Associates, Inc.

Schafer, C. E. (1969). Imaginary companions and creative adolescents. *Developmental Psychology, 1,* 747–749.

Sinetar, M. (1991). *Developing a 21st century mind.* New York: Ballantine Books.

Singer, J. L. (1973). *The child's world of make-believe.* New York: Academic Press.

Singer, D. G., & Rummo, J. (1973). Ideational creativity and behavioral style in kindergarten aged children. *Developmental Psychology, 8,* 154–161.

Singer, D. G., & Singer, J. L. (1977). *Partners in play. A step-by-step guide to imaginative play in children.* New York: Harper & Row.

Singer, J. L., & Singer, D. G. (1980). A factor analytic study of preschoolers' play behavior. *Academic Psychology Bulletin, 2,* 143–155.

Spivak, G., & Levine, M. (1964). *Self-regulation and acting-out in normal adolescents.* (Progress Report for National Institute of Mental Health Grant M-4531). Devon, PA: Devereaux Foundation.

Stern, W. (1924). *Psychology of early childhood up to the sixth year of age.* New York: Henry Holt.

Valett, R. E. (1983). *Strategies for developing creative imagination and thinking skills.* (Report No. EC 160 059). (ERIC Document Reproduction Service No. ED 233 533)

This study was supported in part by research grants from the University of Victoria and the Social Sciences and Humanities Research Council of Canada (SSHRC).

 Article Review Form at end of book.

WiseGuide Wrap-Up

- Quality early experiences for young children will remain a primary goal for early childhood educators throughout the next century.

- A society that nurtures mental health, cultural sensitivity, and play-enhanced learning opportunities will meet the needs of young children.

R.E.A.L. Sites

This list provides a print preview of typical **coursewise** R.E.A.L. sites. (There are over 100 such sites at the **courselinks**™ site.) The danger in printing URLs is that web sites can change overnight. As we went to press, these sites were functional using the URLs provided. If you come across one that isn't, please let us know via email to: webmaster@coursewise.com. Use your Passport to access the most current list of R.E.A.L. sites at the **courselinks**™ site.

Site name: National Institute on Early Childhood Development and Education
URL: http://www.ed.gov/offices/OERI/ECI/
Why is it R.E.A.L.? Review of comprehensive research, conducted by the U.S. Department of Education, is available at this site. The Office of Educational Research and Improvement sponsors projects to promote quality of life for children and families. A biannual newsletter, *ECI News and Views*, is available online. Students can link to other sites such as the National Institute for Family Literacy.
Key topics: early care and learning, early experiences, program quality
Activity: Locate *ECI News and Views* and summarize one article from the most recent newsletter.

Site name: Education Resources Information Center (ERIC)
URL: http://ericir.syr.edu/
Why is it R.E.A.L.? Resources and information related to the development of children, ages zero through early adolescence, are available in an extensive data base. Students will find a research tool called AskEric.
Key topics: curriculum, early care and learning professionals, program quality
Activity: Describe and record the procedure for ordering an AskEric poster.

Site name: National Association for the Education of Young Children (NAEYC)
URL: http://www.naeyc.org/
Why is it R.E.A.L.? NAEYC is the largest national organization of early childhood professionals. This site provides information about the association's accreditation criteria, Week of the Young Child, public policy, catalog for resources, and a searchable index to journal articles in *Young Children*.
Key topics: early care and learning, curriculum, developmentally appropriate practices, guidance
Activity: List the stated motto for the National Association for the Education of Young Children.

Site name: Children's Defense Fund (CDF)
URL: http://www.childrensdefense.org
Why is it R.E.A.L.? The Children's Defense Fund is a nonprofit advocacy organization that seeks to educate the nation about the needs of children "who cannot vote, lobby or speak out."
Key topics: cultural sensitivity/diversity, identity, intervention
Activity: Describe the Children's Defense Fund, as it is presented on the web site, and provide the mailing and email address.

section

2

Key Points

- Meaningful programs for young children that nurture quality care and educational experiences evolve from children's needs and interests.

- Inclusive early childhood settings feature both developmentally appropriate practices and early childhood education practices.

- Early childhood care and learning must balance costs to parents with budgets that maintain quality child care and appropriate compensation.

- The definition of quality child care is related to the interpretation of research and the focus of services provided.

- Quality begins with an appreciation of children's natural way of knowing.

- A trust in children's views and interests motivates emergent curriculum.

Quality Child Care and Education: What Are the Characteristics of Quality Programs?

 **WiseGuide Intro**

The spotlight on young children is also reflecting on the practitioners who provide for their care and learning. Excitement about children's issues has not been this apparent since the mid 1960s when national legislative priorities led to the initiation of programs such as Head Start. The attention to children's needs has been driven by the entry of more women into the work force and the trend toward more single-parent families; these social forces have changed our view of the needs of children under age 5 forever, but the level of commitment to address the needs of young children has only recently gained renewed attention.

A large number of young children, by necessity or the choice of the parent, now are cared for outside their home for part of the day. The question is no longer whether children benefit from early experiences with other than the primary family unit, but instead, how can we ensure quality child care and education?

The field does not have a universal definition of "quality." The characteristics that mark quality programming seem to relate to specific goals, identification of children's needs, and interpretation of research findings. There is greater variation in the definition when we look at the views of early care and learning providers, parents, legislators, geographical areas, academic disciplines, and special interest groups. However, research has shown that for very young children the quality of child care affects the mother-child relationship. The National Institute of Child Health and Human Development (NICHD) study also revealed a correlation between the quality of child care and the development of children's language and cognitive abilities.

Although a consensus of what constitutes quality may not exist, there are quality characteristics that reappear. Programs that place children's needs first gain professional respect. Meeting these needs requires that staff have suitable levels of educational preparation and compensation. Quality occurs when programs and professionals engage children in experiences that facilitate their optimal growth and development. The advocacy of parents and professionals has required care programs to balance the increasing need for child care with the development and implementation of quality standards.

The selected readings in Section 2 discuss the quality of children's programming. In the first reading, "Quality Programs That Care and Educate," Anne B. Smith advocates the educare concept that combines both quality care and education. The second selection ("From Philosophy to Practice in Inclusive Early Childhood Programs") similarly calls for combining concepts, developmentally appropriate practices, and early childhood special education practices in inclusive programs for young children.

The next two readings ("The Great Day-Care Paradox" and "New Research on Day Care Should Spur Scholars to Reconsider Old Ideas") raise two dilemmas: fees for child care that do not burden parents, and compensation for experienced and skilled professionals. A challenge to the definition of quality care for young children is presented in the second of these two readings, with commentary about changing family patterns.

The last three selections offer insight into curricula that encourage children's acquisition of skills and knowledge. The value of natural settings is featured in "The Wonders of Nature: Honoring Children's Way of Knowing." In "Reggio Emilia: What Is the Message for Early Childhood Education?" Jan McCarthy provides a concise review of the characteristics of Reggio Emilia schools that are applicable for early childhood educators. The last reading, "The Fiber Project: One Teacher's Adventure Toward Emergent Curriculum," describes a teacher's adventure in using the Project Approach.

Questions

Reading 6. How do adults help children acquire cognitive skills through social interaction?

Reading 7. How can educators blend developmentally appropriate practices with early childhood special education recommended practices?

Reading 8. How can directors of children's programs effectively budget income received from child-care fees?

Reading 9. Why would Sandra Scarr's interpretation of research on quality care differ from a developmental viewpoint?

Reading 10. How can early childhood professionals foster early awareness of nature?

Reading 11. What benefits might an early childhood teacher gain by collaborating with an atelierista in a Reggio Emilia School?

Reading 12. What did Cleta Booth learn about facilitating a project, and what additional methods did she suggest?

Principles of Early Childhood Special Education

- Intervention focused on functional goals
- Family-centered services
- Regular monitoring and adjustment of intervention
- Transition planning
- Multidisciplinary services

time. Each child is given the support he or she needs to be successful in the setting. For children age 3 to school age, these settings are most often public and private community preschool and child care programs.

The most comprehensive and widely disseminated guidelines defining quality services in these settings are *developmentally appropriate practices,* as defined by the National Association for the Education of Young Children (NAEYC).

Research in early childhood special education indicates that those using these developmental guidelines as the *sole* principles for providing services to young children with disabilities would fall short of providing the full range of services these children need. Carta, Schwartz, Atwater, and McConnell (1991) warned against the adoption of these guidelines to the potential exclusion of principles and practices that we know are effective for children with disabilities, but also suggest that educators not overlook developmentally appropriate practices in providing inclusive services for these children. Indeed, Bredekamp and Rosegrant stated in a 1992 NAEYC publication:

Experiences with mainstreaming over the past two decades suggest a conclusion that probably will be made concerning the guidelines . . .

and children with special needs 20 years from now: The guidelines are the context in which appropriate early education of children with special needs should occur; however, a program based on the guidelines alone is not likely to be sufficient for many children with special needs. (p. 106)

Let's look at both recommended practices—developmentally appropriate practices and early childhood special education practices—and find points where educators, children, families, and communities can work together to make inclusive programs successful.

Developmentally Appropriate Practice

NAEYC published a widely used position statement about developmentally appropriate practices for serving young children from birth to age 8 in early childhood programs (Bredekamp, 1987). The association compiled and published this statement in reaction to the concern of early childhood educators with the increasing academic demands made of young children in early childhood programs and general misconceptions about how teachers should provide instruction to young children.

This position statement became the most widely recognized guideline in the field of early childhood education. In 1997 NAEYC published the revised *Developmentally Appropriate Practice in Early Childhood Programs* (Bredekamp & Copple, 1997), clarifying the misunderstandings and misinterpretations that arose from a decade of extensive dissemination of the original position statement.

Based on the developmental theories of Piaget and Vygotsky,

the NAEYC guidelines convey the primary message that *learning occurs through exploratory play activities* and that formal instruction beyond the child's current developmental level will result in nonfunctional, rote learning at best. Developmentally appropriate practice suggests that teachers should not attempt to direct or tightly structure learning experiences and that formal academic instruction at the preschool level should not occur.

These guidelines have three dimensions, as follows:

1. *Age appropriateness.* According to child development knowledge and research, all children grow and change in a universal, predictable sequence during the first 9 years of life. This knowledge about typical child development allows teachers to plan appropriate environments and experiences.

2. *Individual appropriateness.* Each child has his or her own unique pattern of growths, strengths, interests, experiences, and backgrounds. Both the curriculum and adults' interactions with children should be responsive to these individual differences.

3. *Cultural appropriateness.* To truly understand each child, teachers and child care providers must recognize and respect the social and cultural context in which the child lives. When teachers understand the cultural context in which children live, they can better plan meaningful experiences that are relevant for each child (Bredekamp & Copple, 1997).

Teachers should use knowledge of child development to identify the range of appropriate behaviors, activities, and materials for a specific age group. As well, they should use this knowledge in conjunction with an understanding of each child in the classroom and his or her unique personalities, backgrounds, and abilities to design the most appropriate learning environment.

NAEYC recommends that instructional practices emphasize child-initiated, child-directed play activities, based on the assumption that young children are intrinsically motivated to learn by their desire to understand their environment. Teaching strategies include hands-on exploratory activities with emphases on the use of concrete, real, and relevant activities.

> **Effective early childhood instructional practices emphasize child-initiated, child-directed play activities, based on the assumption that young children are intrinsically motivated to learn by their desire to understand their environment.**

Rationale of Early Childhood Special Education

Early childhood special education is based on the premise that early and comprehensive intervention maximizes the developmental potential of infants and children with disabilities. Such intervention produces child outcomes that would likely not occur in the absence of such intervention (McDonnell & Hardman, 1988).

Since the initiation of publicly supported services for preschool children with disabilities in the mid-1970s, professionals in early childhood special education have developed a body of practices. This body of practice has evolved from research, model demonstration, and evaluation efforts and is currently referred to as *early childhood special education recommended practices*. Researchers have documented syntheses of

desired characteristics, or recommended practices, of exemplary, early childhood special education models (DEC, 1993; McDonnell & Hardman, 1988; Wolery, Strain & Bailey, 1992; Wolery & Wilbers, 1994). We have selected components of these models and practices that researchers have shown to be essential, effective, and compatible with the NAEYC guidelines (see Carta et al., 1991, for evaluation criteria). These components include setting functional goals and monitoring children's progress toward these goals, planning for transitions, and working closely with families.

Intervention Focused on Functional Goals

Intervention for children with disabilities should focus on producing specific and measurable child goals. To make meaningful changes in children's behavior, these goals need to be functional for each child and for the environments in which the child participates. A *functional* skill is one that is essential to participation within a variety of integrated environments. In early childhood settings, functional skills are those that assist children to interact more independently and positively with their physical and social environments.

For example, it is probably more functional for a child to be able to carry out his or her own toileting functions independently than to be able to name 10 farm animals. Shouldn't we give preference to skills that will enable the child to participate more fully

in an integrated setting, as opposed to those skills that would be indicated in the developmental hierarchy or sequence? If our answer is yes, these goals then become the focus for providing individualized intervention. Teachers or care providers design services and instruction to produce a specific outcome—like independent toileting—and this outcome becomes the standard against which the success of an intervention is measured.

Family-Centered Services

The family is the heart of all early childhood programs. Families participate in planning and decision making in all aspects of their children's program.

A good school-family partnership includes a system for a child's family to have regular communication with the classroom staff and have frequent opportunities to participate in their child's program. Quality programs also include procedures for helping families link into existing community resources.

Regular Monitoring and Adjustment of Intervention

Educators and care providers should systematically monitor the effects of specific interventions. Researchers have shown the effectiveness of using *formative* assessment data to monitor children's

Key Aspects of Developmentally Appropriate Practices

- Developmental evaluation of children for program planning and implementation
- High staff qualifications
- High ratio of adults to children
- Strong relationship between home and program

progress toward their individual goals and objectives (McDonnell & Hardman, 1988).

We know that such data must be gathered frequently enough to monitor the subtleties of progress or failure. Data-collection systems must measure child progress toward the acquisition of predetermined goals, including the application of skills in a variety of settings.

Transition Planning

Educators and care providers of all children—and particularly children with disabilities—must plan for transition from one school or child care setting to the next one. Early childhood special educators are particularly concerned with transition from preschool to kindergarten because this move signals a major change for the child and the family from familiar and secure surroundings to a new, unknown setting.

This is a time of considerable stress, and teachers and child care providers must engage in careful, timely planning to smooth the process. Many people are involved in the transition planning process: the child's family, the sending teacher, the early intervention specialist, support personnel, and the future receiving teacher. An effective transition plan often begins 1–2 years before the actual move. This preliminary planning enables the sending teachers to identify skills needed in the future environment. These skills are included in the child's curriculum during the last preschool years.

Multidisciplinary Services

Professionals from many disciplines need to participate in the planning of comprehensive services for children with disabilities and their families. Because many

of these children and their families have complex needs, no single professional and not one discipline can provide a full range of services.

The specific needs of each child and family determine what disciplines should be involved in assessing, planning, implementing, and monitoring services. The following disciplines are commonly involved in early childhood special education:

- Speech and language therapy.
- Occupational and physical therapy.
- Audiology.
- Disability-specific specialists, such as a vision specialist or autism specialist.

Professionals in these disciplines provide services in an integrated manner: They share knowledge and methods across disciplines, and the entire team develops and implements one comprehensive plan. Following this plan, team members provide consultation services within the early childhood environment.

Merging Programs Through Developmentally Appropriate Practices

The first step to merging these approaches is to recognize the advantages a program adhering to developmentally appropriate practices offers for the successful inclusion of children with disabilities. Such a program will have high-quality components, many of which facilitate the inclusion process.

Facilitating Inclusion

The nature of developmentally appropriate practices allows for

the inclusion of children with great variation in development within the same setting. Even in a group of young children without disabilities, of the same age, children can be as much as 2 years apart developmentally.

Thus, planning developmentally appropriate activities and providing equipment and materials for the preschool setting already accommodates children in a wide development range. This allowance in planning and material selection makes it possible to include children with mild and moderate disabilities without additional adaptation.

This developmental approach to planning creates an ideal environment for embedding instruction on individually targeted skills. The developmental emphasis on learning as a process rather than a product also facilitates targeting a variety of individualized objectives. To illustrate the process-versus-product approach, let's look at ways teachers might provide art experiences—and individualized instruction—for children.

The *process* approach to art allows children to explore available materials, experiment, and create individual designs with little regard for the end product. This approach also allows for intervention on a variety of instructional objectives for children with disabilities while all children are involved in the same activity. For example, all children are involved in a finger-painting activity; one child may be working on requesting objects, another on identifying colors, and yet another on staying with the group.

Providing Quality Indicators

Developmentally appropriate practices are not a curriculum, nor do they dictate a rigid set of standards.

Developmental programs will not all look the same, but they will have a similar framework that pays careful attention to child development knowledge and will assist educators in providing quality services for children. The use of developmentally appropriate practices ensures quality in programs in many ways, such as developmental evaluation of children for program planning and implementation, high staff qualifications, a high ratio of adults to children, and strong relationship between home and program.

- *Developmental evaluation.* Decisions about enrollment and placement have a major effect on children. Educators and care providers base these decisions on multiple assessment data emphasizing observations by teachers and parents. Teachers use developmental assessment of child progress and achievement to adapt curriculum, communicate with families, and evaluate program effectiveness. Developmental evaluations of children use valid instruments developed for use with young children; these assessment tools are gender, culture, and socioeconomically appropriate (Bredekamp, 1987).

- *Staff qualifications.* The NAEYC guidelines for developmentally appropriate practice emphasize the need for staff with preparation and supervised experiences specific to working with young children. Early childhood teachers should have college-level preparation in early childhood education and child development.

- *High adult/student ratios.* A key to implementing developmentally appropriate practices is to have a small number of children per classroom and a high ratio of adults to children. Ratios suggested in the NAEYC position statement are higher than those required for licensing in most states. NAEYC recommended standards describe a ratio of 2 adults to 20 children ages 4–5, with younger children requiring smaller groups with higher adult-to-child ratios.

- *Home-to-program relationship.* NAEYC guidelines recommend parent involvement in all decision making, regular communication between parents and teacher, and encouragement of parent involvement in the day-to-day happenings of the program. These practices help in building a strong relationship between home and the child's community program.

Developing a Conceptual Base

We have developed a conceptual base, recognizing the two sets of practice, that will allow both developmentally appropriate practices and special education principles to exist within the same setting. The Teaching Research Early Childhood Program has developed a philosophy that views developmentally appropriate practices as the foundation on which individualized programs are built, adding special education instruction when needed for individual children. We believe that the two approaches to early childhood are not mutually exclusive.

Figure 1 illustrates this dilemma. The builder has two sets of clearly different materials and cannot decide which to use. The key to moving beyond this dilemma is to recognize that these practices serve distinctly different purposes—and we can view them as different types of resources.

- *Developmentally appropriate practices* are used to design an age-appropriate, stimulating environment supportive of all children's needs. These practices, however, were not developed to reflect or address specific individual needs of children with disabilities and offer little information about specific intervention strategies needed to serve these children.

- *Early childhood special education* practices are used to complement the basic program

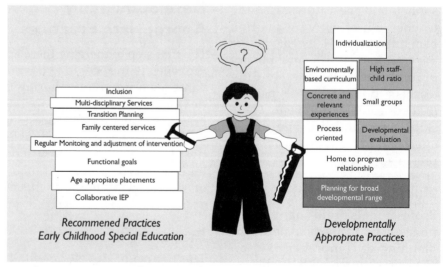

Figure 1. Combining ECSE and DAP.

for children with exceptional developmental needs and to emphasize individualized strategies to maximize children's learning opportunities. These practices, however, do not provide guidelines for designing a quality early childhood learning environment.

When educators recognize these practices as being different, but compatible, they can then plan a single comprehensive program, as shown in Figure 2. The completed school uses developmentally appropriate practices as the material from which the foundation is built and special education practices as the material that completes the structure.

Implementing Both Practices within the Same Setting

Let's look more closely at how this merger might work. A well-designed early childhood education program, following developmentally appropriate practices, uses a planned, well-organized environment where children interact with materials, other children, and adults. Here the NAEYC guidelines are apparent: Young children are intrinsically motivated to learn by their desire to understand their environment; the program is set up to allow children to self-select activities from a variety of interest centers.

When children show they need further support, educators use special education strategies that are made available in the program. These strategies include the following:

- *Directly prompting practice* on individually targeted skills, based on functional behavioral outcomes.

- *Reinforcing* children's responses.

- *Collecting data* to monitor children's progress and make intervention changes.

Some educators view these strategies as conflicting with developmentally appropriate practices. Some people liken this to direct prompting to the formal instruction that NAEYC deplored for use with young children. We believe that this view is a misinterpretation of NAEYC's position statement and the guidelines for developmentally appropriate practices.

As we mentioned earlier, however, NAEYC guidelines do not exclude intervention strategies for children with identified special needs (Bredekamp & Rosegrant, 1992). We hope that by clarifying this misinterpretation, we might encourage teachers to view these intervention strategies as individually appropriate for some children.

As educators begin to merge these two approaches to early childhood education, we will find all children participating in the same well-organized, systematically planned environment—with direct instruction being provided to children who need this type of intervention. This direct instruction is blended into naturally occurring opportunities throughout the on-going daily routine, such as play at the water table or learning independent toileting. An early childhood program adhering to developmentally appropriate practices provides a strong foundation for the provision of consultation services from professionals across different disciplines.

Consider transition services—an area of special education services that some educators believe conflicts with a child-centered developmental program. The transition planning process has an apparent conflict with developmentally appropriate practice because it presumes that the needs of some future environment should drive the child's curriculum at present. Guidelines for developmentally appropriate practices reject the idea of current curriculums being driven by the needs of a future environment.

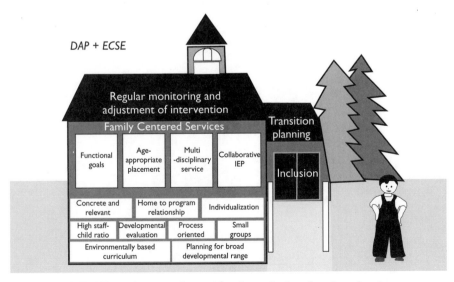

Figure 2. A DAP setting produces the foundation for developing comprehensive programs for children with disabilities.

To resolve this conflict we can look to the *foundation* concept. In developmentally appropriate practice, we find children participating in an environment planned to fit their current developmental demands and individual backgrounds and interests. Within this environment, children with special needs receive instruction on specific skills that will assist them to be successful in their next setting. Teachers have selected these specific skills or objectives with direct regard to the child's current needs and level of functioning, with some, but not predominant, focus on transition skills needs as dictated by future environments. Skills selected because of the demands of a future environment are ones that can be facilitated without disruption in the current environment. These skills are also within the boundaries of being developmentally appropriate in the future environment.

Mutually Beneficial, Not Mutually Exclusive

In inclusive early childhood education programs, we must caution against adopting developmentally appropriate practices to the exclusion of research-supported special education practices. Similarly, we must not fail to recognize the benefits offered by placing children with disabilities in developmentally appropriate programs. We need to develop an understanding of both sets of practices and to develop a program, from philosophy to practice, that merges practices.

References

Bredekamp, S. (Ed.). (1987). *Developmentally Appropriate Practices in Early Childhood Programs Serving Children from Birth Through Age 8* (Exp. ed.). Washington, DC: National Association for the Education of Young Children.

Bredekamp, S., & Copple, C. (Eds.). (1997). *Developmentally Appropriate Practices in Early Childhood Programs* (Rev. ed.). Washington, DC: National Association for the Education of Young Children.

Bredekamp, S., & Rosegrant, T. (Eds.). (1992). *Reaching potentials: Appropriate curriculum and assessment for young children* (Vol. 1, pp. 92–112). Washington, DC: National Association for the Education of Young Children.

Carta, J. J., Schwartz, I. S., Atwater, J. B., & McConnell, S. R. (1991). Developmentally appropriate practice: Appraising its usefulness for young children with disabilities. *Topics in Early Childhood Special Education 11*(1), 1–20.

DEC Task Force on Recommended Practices. (1993). *DEC recommended practices: Indicators of quality in programs for infants and young children with special needs and their families.* Reston, VA: The Council for Exceptional Children, Division of Early Childhood Education. (ERIC Document Reproduction Service No. ED 370 253).

McDonnell, A., & Hardman, M. (1988). A synthesis of "best practice" guidelines for early childhood services. *Journal of the Division of Early Childhood, 12,* 328–337.

Wolery, M., Strain, P. S., & Bailey, D. B. (1992). Reaching potentials of children with special needs. In S. Bredekamp & T. Rosegrant (Eds.), *Reaching potentials: Appropriate curriculum and assessment for young children* (Vol. 1, pp. 92–112). Washington, DC: National Association for the Education of Young Children.

Wolery, M., & Wilbers, J. S. (Eds.). (1994). *Including children with special needs in early childhood programs.* Washington, DC: National Association for the Education of Young Children.

We would like to thank Kathy Haydon for her illustrations.

Article Review Form at end of book.

How can directors of children's programs effectively budget income received from child-care fees?

The Great Day-Care Paradox

How can this vital service cost too much and too little at the same time?

Jane Bennett Clark

To get in the door at Smoky Row Children's Center, it helps to be short. One of the double entry doors to each of the center's two wings is only four feet high, just right for the 200-plus toddlers and preschoolers who march through Smoky Row's bright blue portals every working day.

It also helps to be lucky. Families at Smoky Row have inched their way up a permanent waiting list to attend this center in suburban Columbus, Ohio, even though it charges more than many in the community. For infant care (the most costly to provide), Smoky Row parents pay $143 a week, or $7,436 a year. Full-time tuition for two children—an infant and a toddler—runs a gut-sucking $14,000 annually. That's about what it costs to send *three* kids across town to Ohio State University—and have $4,000 left over for books and pizza.

One reason parents pay a premium to walk—or duck—through the doors at Smoky Row is that the center is accredited by the National Association for the Education of Young Children,

How Smoky Row Spends Its Allowance

Here's how Smoky Row allocates the $270 a week a family pays for two children.	
Teacher salaries and benefits	$194
Housing and maintenance	50
Food and paper supplies	12
Toys and supplies	7
Administration, insurance and training	7

which dictates teacher qualifications and staff-child ratios (about 10% of all centers nationwide are accredited by the NAEYC). In fact, Smoky Row is a bargain compared with other accredited centers in the area, which charge up to $160 a week for infant care—a $17-a-week difference that saves Smoky Row parents $884 a year. Still, it costs about $30 a week more than the average facility in Columbus and elsewhere.

As an independent, for-profit operation, Smoky Row has one economic disadvantage: It competes with nonprofit centers whose operating expenses are subsidized by a church or other institution (see the box on page 00) as well as with for-profit chains that enjoy economies of

scale. But for any child-care center, delivering good care on a budget is like trying to create tuna sandwiches for 200 from a few loaves and fishes. Says Judy Chosy, director and owner of Smoky Row: "To be honest, I run this school the way you run your household—if we've got it, we spend it."

Talking Turkey

On a bright winter's morning in Smoky Row's East Building, teacher Michelle Salomone is leading a group of 3- and 4-year-olds in a rousing version of the song "Albuquerque Turkey," part of a daylong theme focusing on early-American life. Behind them a parent volunteer sets up the morning's art project: turkeys to be crafted using paper plates, construction paper, paint, scissors, pens and a glue stick. Another teacher, Janet Mitchell, arrives in the classroom bearing hot muffins for the morning snack. Meanwhile, across the yard in the West Building, teacher Diana Castrillon engages in a constant activity: changing one of the 50 diapers that will be used and discarded in the infant room in a single day.

Paying teachers and assistants to perform the myriad tasks undertaken between 7 A.M. and 6

P.M. each day is Smoky Row's biggest expense—the center devotes more then 70% of its budget to salaries and benefits. That's high, almost approaching the outlay of nonprofit centers, which are able to pony up as much as 80% because their other expenses are subsidized. Many for-profit centers, including large chains such as KinderCare, devote as little as half of every day-care dollar to wages and benefits.

Smoky Row's teacher expenses are high in part because most of the staff have degrees in early-childhood education, exceeding Ohio licensing standards, which demand only a high school diploma or equivalency. (State licensing standards vary widely; Ohio's are considered average.) Chosy pays top salaries by day-care standards, but still they're about one-third less than the going rate for public-school teachers. Full-time teachers at the center earn more than $9 an hour, plus such benefits as vacations and health insurance, compared with $5 or $6 an hour with no benefits at other Franklin County centers.

Because their salaries are relatively generous, Smoky Row's teachers have one of the lowest turnover rates in the area, while other local centers are struggling to keep their staff. Unemployment is low in Columbus, and even a nearby McDonald's can match the average hourly rate for most child-care workers—plus McDonald's offers benefits, a rarity in the day-care world.

Parent Dana Ullom-Vucelich says that low turnover is one reason she sought out Smoky Row, though it costs almost $12,000 a year for her two children. As a vice-president of human resources at a local hospital, Ullom-Vucelich says, "I know how important low turnover can be."

Good qualifications and salaries aren't the only reason Chosy's budget tilts toward teachers: She also employs more of them than other day-care centers do. Smoky Row follows staff-child ratios recommended by the NAEYC—that is, one adult for every four infants, for every five toddlers, and for every ten 4-year-olds. Those standards, tougher than those of many states, including Ohio, are "critical" in providing quality care, says Anne Goldstein of the National Child Care Information Center, in Vienna, Va. But they soak up budget dollars faster than Pampers absorb—well, what they absorb.

In fact, infant and toddler care, which has the highest proportion of teachers to children, usually loses money. Last year the infant room at Smoky Row, with 12 children, posted a $23,400 deficit, and the toddler room lost $17,600. Making up the difference are classes for older kids, whose higher ratios also provide a higher return. Says Chosy: "The money is in the preschool"—a truism for most centers.

A Roof Over Their Heads

The weather today is unseasonably cold, so instead of playing outside, a group of toddlers are careering around the indoor playcourt, a recessed area outfitted with climbing equipment, a seesaw, plastic toys and the other implements of childhood. Grant, 2 1/2, hurls himself across the room to greet a visitor, while Samuel steers his riding toy through a floor mined with brightly colored balloons. Across the yard, it's sharing time in the kindergarten class, where MacKenzie

proudly displays this morning's contribution: her shoe.

Keeping the kids at Smoky Row housed and heated is the next biggest item in Chosy's budget: 18.6% goes toward payments on two 20-year mortgages and for taxes, maintenance and utility bills. With 261 children hitting the halls each week, maintenance is a challenge. "We're very, very hard on things," she says. Last spring Chosy spent $6,000 to have the outside of the six-year-old building painted; she anticipates paying about $3,000 to have the inside painted this year and recently spent $12,000 for new carpeting.

Chosy economizes by forgoing a few big-ticket items offered by other centers—Smoky Row doesn't provide transportation and asks parents to pack lunch—and by hunting down bargains such as locally built playground equipment instead of purchasing from a catalog. She also saves on costs by bypassing high-priced service contractors in favor of a college student who cleans the center and a high school student who cuts the grass. Chosy's husband, Bob, comes over once a week to perform minor repairs; a retired obstetrician, he's one of the more overqualified (and underpaid) handymen in the Columbus area. Jim Emanuelson, father of a Smoky Row teacher, charges bargain rates to work on accounts receivable. Chosy's son-in-law, a mutual fund accountant, pays the center's bills for free.

As for the piles of puzzles, the bins of blocks and the buckets of Barbies, despite their bulk they constitute a relatively small part of the budget, less than 3% of the total. Chosy considers the allotment generous, but teachers occasionally kick in for other supplies, including food for Bunny Foo-Foo

Nonprofit Centers: Help from Their Friends

Not all child-care centers can expect parents to cover the entire cost of tuition. Nonprofits, such as Fruit and Flower Child Care Center, in Portland, Ore., get a lot of help from other friends.

Fruit and Flower has been in business for almost a century. In the late 1920s it received an endowment whose earnings continue to help finance operations. The center, which raked in more than $90,000 last year from donations and fund-raisers, boasts clear title to its current building, which was financed by community funds in 1970.

With no mortgage payments, Fruit and Flower devotes only 6% of its budget to its physical plant, mainly in maintenance costs and utility bills—a third of the proportion that the Smoky Row Children's Care Center, near Columbus, Ohio, earmarks (see the accompanying story). The freed-up funds allow Fruit and Flower to allocate up to 85% of its budget to teacher salaries and benefits, a high proportion for any day-care center. Teachers here start at $8 or

$8.50 an hour and receive two raises a year for the first ten years of employment.

Parents get a break at Fruit and Flower, too. Although tuition is stiff, at $187 a week for infants and toddlers, low-income families receive subsidies from the state, and United Way funds let the center charge some families on a sliding scale. Even affluent and middle-income parents don't pay full freight, according to director Roberta Recken, who says the center spends $943 a month for every toddler, about $200 more than what parents are charged. "I don't think anyone will pay $943," says Reckon. "It's more than the market will bear."

While few nonprofit centers boast an endowment like Fruit and Flower's or heavy-hitter fund-raising to help them offset costs, most depend on community resources such as churches and universities to provide space or materials, discounts on maintenance and utilities, cash contributions and some volunteer labor.

(a rabbit) and Rosie the red-eared slider (a turtle). Two fund-raisers a year finance new outdoor toys and computer software. In recent years AT&T, which employs the parents of several Smoky Row kids, has awarded grants of up to $10,000 to the center to help pay for materials and field trips. The full-day kindergarten also picks up about $800 a year from the Ohio Department of Education, which goes for library books and other teacher resources.

The Parents' Part

That help aside, parents basically finance Smoky Row's costs, a major distinction from nonprofit centers, where public and private subsidies can make up almost half of a center's revenues. And other for-profit centers get some help from government and private-sector programs, which each kick in about 12% of the typical center's budget. Because families are lining up to pay full tuition at Smoky Row, Chosy doesn't take families receiving government assistance. The combination of government payments and a limited contribution required from families falls short of the full fee at Smoky Row. Many families on assistance cannot afford to pay their share, says Susan Jakob of Action for Children, a child-care referral agency in Columbus, so other centers in demand allocate only a small number of spaces to subsidized families. "They can't afford it. It's a drain on their program," she says. On the other side, poor working families are being squeezed out of state assistance programs to make room for those

getting off welfare rolls, creating a shortfall in care for parents who are barely managing as it is.

Of course, every family whose kids are in day care so that parents can work qualifies for the federal child-care tax credit (some states offer additional tax credits), which can be worth $480 to $1,440 a year. Most day-care centers also give tuition breaks to siblings—at Smoky Row, older sibs get a 10% discount—and offer a sliding sale to a small number of parents who earn too much for state programs but not enough to afford full fees. A growing number of employers have also joined forces with day-care providers to help parents pay for care, says Goldstein. KinderCare, for instance, operates 42 on-site or nearby centers for corporations, including Ford Motor Co., and provides a 10% discount to employees of more than 400 companies nationwide, with many companies kicking in another 10%.

Too Much, Too Little

In the early days Chosy worked 11-hour days and skipped a salary altogether, but 1996 was a good year. Smoky Row showed a profit of about 4% after taxes (although Chosy took home less during the year than the $25,000 to $30,000 other directors make). That margin compares favorably with the average for-profit center, which earns 3% to 4%. Last year, KinderCare, the country's biggest chain, reaped a 4% profit after rebounding from bankruptcy in 1993; another chain, Children's Discovery Centers, lost money in the early 1990s, but earned 3.4% in 1995.

The real bottom line, experts agree, is that day care costs both too much and too little, taking up to one-fourth of income from young families at the beginning of their earning power, yet not always generating enough revenue for centers to offer the kind of care that families want. High tuition doesn't guarantee good quality, but even a slightly higher-than-average fee helps maintain standards in an industry whose members are often undertrained and underpaid, says Jakob.

The too-much, too-little paradox is one that parent Dana Ullom-Vucelich has seen from both sides. She earned a degree in early-childhood education but changed careers when she realized she would be making only minimum wage as a day-care teacher. Now she and her husband, Sam, are contemplating paying five-figure day-care bills for at least another year. Says

Ullom-Vucelich: "This is the most significant long-term investment decision I have ever made. It touches the root of everything we hope and dream for." And the price? "No matter what it is, in your heart, you know it's never enough."

 Article Review Form at end of book.

Why would Sandra Scarr's interpretation of research on quality care differ from a developmental viewpoint?

New Research on Day Care Should Spur Scholars to Reconsider Old Ideas

Sandra Scarr

Sandra Scarr is a professor emerita of psychology at the University of Virginia and former chairman and chief executive officer of Kindercare, a national chain of day-care centers. She was president of the American Psychological Society in 1996–97.

American child-rearing practices are undergoing a sea change. As increasing numbers of mothers rejoin the labor force earlier in their children's lives, day care has become a standard experience for infants and young children. Many experts worry that children are not getting sufficient attention from their parents to develop solid foundations of intelligence and mental health. Indeed, we should worry about the small minority of children whose caregivers are truly abusing or neglecting them. But much of the experts' concern—which unnecessarily alarms working parents—is caused by their reliance on past assumptions about children's development that no longer match reality. Experts should re-examine their theories in light of research showing that children in day care develop as normally and as quickly as children who stay home with their mothers.

Renewed interest by researcher in how infants' brains develop is one symptom of experts' unwarranted fear about changes in parenting. Are parents giving infants and toddlers enough of the right kinds of stimulation to develop proper neuronal connections? The recent White House Conference on Early Childhood Development and Learning and articles in *Newsweek* and *Time* all have promoted the idea that early experiences mold infants' brains, determining future brainpower. Experts claim that it is critical to babies' later cognitive and linguistic development that parents read, talk, and provide visual stimulation to babies.

Can it be true that babies must have specific early experiences to become normal adults? Hardly. If our species had evolved to require scarce or unusual experiences for normal development to occur, humans would be extinct. Cultural variations in child-rearing practices around the world demonstrate that normal human development occurs in many different environments. Reading is one way to interact with babies, but it's not the only right way.

Language acquisition depends on hearing adult speech, but what infant is not exposed to any human speech? Even the hearing children of deaf parents develop into normal speakers of their native languages, if they hear other people speak for only a few hours each week. This is not to say that we shouldn't talk and read to babies; I did, and so do many other parents. But it is wrong to say that this is the only

"New Research on Day Care Should Spur School Scholars to Reconsider Old Ideas" by Sandra Scarr as appeared in THE CHRONICLE OF HIGHER EDUCATION, August 8, 1997, Vol. XLIII, #48. Reprinted by permission of the author.

way to produce cognitively and linguistically normal human beings. Equally, a mobile over the crib may be entertaining, but everyday life gives babies all of the visual stimulation that they really need.

Critics will be quick to point out that getting parents to focus positive attention on their babies for any reason can't hurt. But why evoke worry and guilt in working parents about their children's development, when we know that caring parents who engage in culturally ordinary interactions with their children will do just fine?

Another symptom of experts' misplaced concern about recent child-rearing practices is the repetition of studies about the potentially harmful effects of low-quality child care. In April, the National Institute of Child Health and Human Development released a report concluding that young children cared for by adults other than their parents have normal cognitive, linguistic, social and emotional development. The report, based on an $88-million longitudinal study, is hardly the first to reach this conclusion. And the researchers reported another reassuring, but not novel, finding: The quality of infant care, which ranged from poor to excellent for the 1,200 children in this study, had no impact on young children's development, although good-quality day care can to some extent make up for poor parenting.

Several other large studies also have shown that vast differences in the quality of care that children received had only small effects on their preschool cognitive, social, and emotional development. Further, by the time the children reached school age, the studies found that the small early differences had vanished. By implication, ordinary homes and day-care centers provide adequate environments for children's healthy development.

These results, which could be so reassuring to hard-pressed working parents, have not stopped the fretting by some experts, however. Quality of care must matter, they argue, or most developmental theories, which stress the lasting importance of children's early environments, must be wrong. The fact that child care judged by early-childhood researchers to be of poor to medium quality could have little negative effect on children is unpredicted and disturbing. That day care is just as beneficial to children as full-time parental care is a theoretical and emotional blow to some experts.

No one wants to see children in dangerous or debilitating environments, at home or in day-care settings. Unfortunately, some environments *are* so poor that they endanger children's lives and development, and those should not be tolerated. But the need to improve some very poor care does not justify frightening American parents in general, when the results of several major studies could be used to calm their worst fears about their children's development.

Scholars need to take a good look at their old theories and assumptions in light of this research. We can no longer say that children need full-time maternal care, when studies show that other arrangements work just as well to promote healthy development. We should not claim that children need a carefully tailored environment of sensory and intel-

"Can it be true that babies must have specific early experiences to become normal adults? Hardly."

lectual stimulation and emotional support from two parents (preferably one male and one female). We need to re-examine the ideal that children should be so securely attached to their mothers that they suffer when their mothers are absent. And we need to look beyond the quality of day care to its costs and benefits for working parents, now that a good deal of competent research has shown how little impact variations in quality have on children's development.

The vast majority of middle-class mothers already work, and welfare reforms are pushing poor mothers into the labor force as well. Further, in the 21st century, experts predict that adults will change jobs frequently and move often from one community to another. The children who will succeed in the future need to be more sociable and more secure with large numbers of new people than children of the past were.

What should experts in the next century focus on concerning child development? It seems to me they should stress that children benefit from multiple attachments, rather than an exclusive attachment to their mothers. The experts might even argue that being isolated at home with one adult and no peers could retard toddlers' social and emotional development.

The revolution in information and communication that is well under way will accelerate in the next century, requiring children to have better cognitive and linguistic skills. Experts may well decide that only a demanding, knowledge-based curriculum can prepare the young for this world. Therefore, all children may enter educational settings at earlier ages. (France has already moved in this direction.) Nations may well set standards for the content of preschool education.

The noted anthropologist Robert LeVine of Harvard University once observed that every culture gets the children it deserves. The worries of today's experts largely reflect their own discomfort with cultural shifts in ideals for children and child rearing. Fortunately, the human species will endure in spite of these shifts, because children can thrive in many different kinds of environments. But experts can make such shifts less stressful for themselves and for parents by accepting what research has shown us and using it to fashion theories and research questions more relevant to children's needs in the next century.

 Article Review Form at end of book.

How can early childhood professionals foster early awareness of nature?

The Wonders of Nature

Honoring children's ways of knowing

Ruth A. Wilson, Ph.D.

Ruth Wilson, Ph.D., is an associate professor at Bowling Green State University in Bowling Green, Ohio. Dr. Wilson has been actively involved in curriculum and program development in the area of early childhood environmental education over the past six years and has published numerous articles in this field. She is also a frequent presenter at professional conferences and has developed a teacher inservice guide focusing on how to infuse environmental education into all aspects of an early childhood curriculum. Dr. Wilson has also been involved in research relating to the development of the ecological self and the use of ecological narratives as a tool for enhancing environmental sensitivity.

"There was a time when the world was a song and the song was exciting." These words, from the musical *Les Miserables,* haunt me. I find that they bring back rich memories from childhood, when the world to me was a marvelous place for adventure and exploration, for discovering beauty and mystery, and for stirring the imagination. Almost all of my favorite memories from childhood relate to experiences with the natural world—watching and catching minnows and tadpoles, making corn husk dolls with shiny corn silk hair, picking cherries and plums from the trees in our yard, watching daffodils unfold in early spring, and rejoicing in the sweet scent of the lilacs that grew near our house. Such experiences filled my world with song, and I remember being swept away in a joyful childhood dance.

Today, I miss the music, the dance, and the enchantment of childhood. "Earth song" has been replaced by the noise of traffic, and daily life feels more like a race than a dance. The enchantment of knowing the world as a song is a treasured memory—a memory that still adds joy to my life. This memory, however, also brings a touch of sadness, because I feel that over the years to adulthood, I've truly lost something special along the way. This "something special" is a way of knowing the natural world as a place of beauty and mystery. While I still maintain the belief that the world is full of mystery and wonder, my way of knowing it as such is not as direct and experiential.

The Child's Ways of Knowing

Researchers who have studied how children know and perceive the world suggest that my experience is shared by children across different cultures. Rachel Sebba (1991), a researcher from Israel, investigated children's relation to the environment from actual and retrospective points of view. In conducting her research, Sebba looked at the environmental preferences and the nature of the experiences of being outdoors as reflected in adults' recollections and in children's actual approaches to investigating the world. Her findings suggest that children experience the natural environment "in a deep and direct manner, not as a background for events, but, rather, as a factor and stimulator" (p. 395).

Sebba's findings are consistent with the work of Edith Cobb (1977), who concluded from her research that "experience in childhood is never formal or abstract." "Even the world of nature," she says, "is not a 'scene,' or even a landscape.

Nature for the child is sheer sensory experience" (pp. 28-29).

Sebba's findings are also consistent with other researchers. Joseph Clinton Pearce (1971), for example, in discussing the primary perceptions of a child, used the term *magical thinking* to describe the child's way of knowing the world. These primary perceptions, Pearce notes, "are developmental in that they tend to disappear" (p.131). Pearce describes these primary perceptions as "bondings to the earth" (p. 136) and suggests that interaction with the physical substance of the living earth (e.g., rocks, trees, wind) is critical to the child's developing brain and intelligence.

It is clear that children have a special affinity for the natural environment—an affinity that is connected to the child's development and his or her ways of knowing. Sebba (1991) refers to this way of knowing as a "unique and unrepeatable ability . . . to grasp surroundings"—an ability, she says, that for most people "recedes over time" (p. 398). Sebba (1991) describes the interaction between the child and the natural environment as "an authentic childhood experience that carries with it the original stamp of childhood and that will disappear with its passing" (p. 410).

These findings and conclusions are in line with our current understanding of how young children learn. According to Piaget and other developmental theorists, learning early in life is dependent on concrete perceptual information. For the young child, learning is experienced as *sensory absorption* or *sensorimotor stimulation*. During the early stages of cognitive development, perception *conducts* thought. This is in contrast to the adult's ways of

knowing and experiencing the world, where perception *obeys* thought (Sebba, 1991). Shifting from the child's to the adult's way of knowing the world involves a deflection from sensory absorption to cognitive reasoning. According to Sebba (1991), "this deflection is accompanied by a weakening of the direct link with the physical environment, by a lessening of the importance placed on information from the senses, and by an essential change in the child's conception of the world" (p. 413).

Imagination and Knowledge

Early experiences with the natural world have been positively linked with development of imagination. The work of Edith Cobb (1977) is perhaps the most noteworthy in this regard. Her work, based in large part on a search for the creative principle in the human personality, involved a careful analysis of a wide variety of autobiographical recollections of highly creative adults. Many of these recollections reflected an "early awareness of some primary relatedness to earth and universe" (Cobb, 1977, p. 17–18). Based on these and similar findings over her 20 years of research, Cobb concluded that childhood represents a special phase in life "during which the most actively creative learning takes place" (Cobb, 1977, p. 17).

Early experiences with the natural world have also been positively linked with the sense of wonder. *Wonder*, as described by Cobb (1977), is not an abstract term or a lofty ideal. It is, instead, a phenomenon concretely rooted in the child's developing perceptual capabilities and his or her

ways of knowing. This way of knowing, if recognized and honored, can serve as a life-long source of joy and enrichment, as well as an impetus, or motivation, for further learning (Carson, 1956).

Separation from Nature

Sadly, the ability to experience the world as a "song," or as a source of wonder, tends to diminish over time. This seems to be especially true in Western cultures, where for the sake of objective understandings, children are encouraged to focus their learning on *cognitive models* rather than on a first-hand investigations of the natural environment. Cognitive models encourage children to make a transition from reliance on sensory criteria as a way of knowing the world to cognitive criteria, and in the process, construct a more objective or scientific understanding of the natural environment.

Such a transition carries with it a heavy price, including both a physical and psychological separation from the environment. "As a result, the child goes from an adaptive and sympathetic attitude to a critical and analytical one. . . . The child no longer creates a concept of the world from experience but rather receives it from others. The child's individual, multidimensional world becomes a scientific one—identical to that of his/her friends" (Sebba, 1991 pp. 414-415).

The physical and psychological separation from the environment that accompanies the transition from the child's ways of knowing the world deserves careful reflection and discussion by early childhood educators and child development specialists. The lens of cognition through which most adults view the world has serious limitations. Through this lens, we see no more than "a defective second edition" (Bailik, 1938) far removed from the child's way of seeing the world. As we move from childhood into adulthood, our receptivity diminishes. A child's way of knowing allows him or her to "linger in self-forgetfulness: she is all eyes and ears. Nor is she projecting anything, nor generalizing or classifying" (Hinchman, 1991, p. 10), as adults are inclined to do.

The richness of young children's way of perceiving the world is based, in part, on their gift of *primal seeing*. Rather than being incorrect or inferior, primal seeing allows children to experience the "embodiment of things, their very quintessence" (Bailik, 1938/1939, p. 43). Because, for most people, primal seeing is experienced only during childhood, it would be good and right and beautiful for parents and early childhood educators to honor and celebrate this way of knowing and experiencing the natural world.

Failing to recognize and support children's ways of knowing can have serious implications on how they will relate to the natural world over the span of their lifetime. "The way we think, the mental maps that we construct to make meaning of the world . . . affect the way we feel about it, and the way we behave toward it" (Shaw-Jones, 1992, p. 16). By validating and reinforcing the child's ways of knowing, we will be fostering a life-long love of the natural world. By failing to do so, we could be contributing to the increasingly more complex environmental crisis, which is considered to be due, in large part, to a growing psychological detachment from and prejudice against nature (Cohen, 1984; Devall, 1984/85; Raglan, 1993). By forcing the child

to work prematurely with abstract thought, we "break up the vital unity of self and world" (Pearce, 1971, p. 188).

Biophilia and Biophobia

Ecologists, environmental psychologists, and others suggest that we all have a natural attraction, or affinity, for life (Kaplan & Kaplan, 1989, Orr, 1994). This affinity for life has been referred to by E. O. Wilson (1984, 1992) as *biophilia* (i.e., a love of nature). If this natural attraction is not encouraged or given opportunities to flourish during the early years of life, the opposite, *biophobia* (i.e., an aversion to nature), may occur (Orr, 1994). "Biophobia ranges from discomfort in 'natural' places to active scorn for whatever is not man-made, managed, or air-conditioned" (Orr, 1994, p. 131). Biophobia is also manifested in the tendency to "regard nature 'objectively' as nothing more than 'resources' to be used" (Orr, 1994, p. 131). Disregarding young children's ways of knowing and pushing them to early abstractions about the natural world (i.e., cognitive models) may lead to biophobia at the expense of biophilia.

Biophobia tends to create havoc with both the natural environment and the spirit and soul of humankind. Physical manifestations of biophobia include strip mines, clear-cuts, blighted cities, polluted rivers, and toxic air (Orr, 1994). Psychological and spiritual results of biophobia include a shrinking of "the range of experiences and joys in life in the same way that the ability to achieve close and loving relationships limits a human life" (Orr, 1994 p. 135).

Experiences during the early childhood years give form to the values, attitudes, and basic orientation toward the world that

Take a Belly Hike

By Bill Weightman

Mark off a circle, about one foot in diameter, on a patch of grass. Give each child a small magnifying glass and have each stand a few feet from the circle. Instruct the children to crawl to their circle while looking for signs of wildlife along the way. This is their *belly hike*. Most often the young children will claim that they saw no wildlife en route to their circle.

Explain that wildlife isn't just dogs and birds and lions. It also includes small life forms like blades of grass, ants, and spiders. Even small life forms need air, water, and light.

Finally, ask the children to use their magnifying glasses to identify wildlife in their circles. Suddenly a whole new world will open up to them! They will begin to develop a respect for these important, though small, life forms.

Bill Weightman is an education specialist at the Steel Recycling Institute.

individuals carry with them throughout their life (Wilson, 1994a). Thus, it is not surprising that early positive experiences with the natural environment have been identified repeatedly as one of the "significant life experiences" associated with responsible environmental behavior (Chawla & Hart, 1988; Peterson, 1982, Tanner, 1980) and the development of biophilia (Orr, 1994). "If by some fairly young age . . . nature has not been experienced as a friendly place of adventure and excitement, biophilia will not take hold as it might have" (Orr, 1994, p. 143).

One manifestation of biophilia is *bonding* with the earth. Because we tend to bond with what we know well, it is critical that young children be given many opportunities to learn about and become familiar with the natural world. It is also critical that their ways of knowing the world are recognized and validated.

Children's ways of knowing reflect a "plasticity of perception and thought [and] are the gift of childhood to human personality" (Cobb, 1977, p. 35). Unfortunately, this truth is "sorely abused, in our attitudes . . . toward the children in society" (Cobb, 1977, p. 35) and can lead to early psychic injury and a great loneliness of spirit (Slade, 1991; Wilson, 1996).

Fostering a Love of Nature

Recognizing and honoring young children's ways of knowing can make an important contribution to the enhancement of the human experience and a healthier relationship with the natural environment. To honor young children's ways of knowing, early childhood professionals should:

- provide frequent access to natural places,
- foster "natural play" activities, and
- encourage aesthetic representations of children's ways of knowing.

Provide Frequent Access to Natural Places

Natural places might be defined as outdoor areas featuring primarily materials that are produced by nature versus being manufactured by humans. Natural places feature native plants and often provide habitat for a variety of native animals. Nabhan and Trimble (1994), in *The Geography of Childhood*, present a compelling discussion as to why children need access to natural places and what we might do to assure children frequent opportunities for interacting with the

world of nature. They suggest that a logical place to start is rethinking the concept of playgrounds. As Nabhan (1994) says: "To counter the historic trend toward the loss of wildness where children play, it is clear that we need to find ways to let children roam beyond the pavement, to gain access to vegetation and earth that allows them to tunnel, climb, or even fall. And because formal playgrounds are the only outdoors that many children experience anymore, should we be paying more attention to planting, and less to building on them?" (p. 9).

Natural places match children's ways of knowing in that they offer varied opportunities for adventure, construction, and re-invention. The "rough ground" aspects of natural places offer the "qualities of openness, diversity, manipulation, explorability, anonymity, and wildness . . . The indeterminacy of rough ground allows it to become a play-partner, like other forms of creative partnership: actress-audience, potter-clay, photographer-subject, painter-canvas. The exploring/ creating child is not making 'art' so much as using the landscape as a medium for understanding the world" (Moore, quoted in Trimble, 1994, p. 27).

While most playgrounds for young children in the United States still focus predominantly on equipment versus "a sense of place," ideas on how to transform a traditional playground into an environmental yard have been presented in the literature (Wilson, 1994b; Wilson, Kilmer, & Knauerhase, 1996). Such ideas include:

- developing a variety of gardens (e.g., herb gardens, flower gardens, rock gardens, alphabet gardens);

- providing places and materials that invite wildlife (e.g., rock piles, bird baths, bird feeders);
- providing materials that draw attention to environmental features (e.g., wind sock, thermometers, rain gauge, sun dial); and
- providing materials that encourage direct interaction with the natural environment (e.g., child-size shovels and rakes; water source accessible to the children; natural materials that the children can manipulate such as rocks, shells, pine cones, and other plant materials).

Foster "Natural Play" Activities

While the value of play to child development has long been recognized (Johnson, Christie, & Yawkey, 1987), the activity we call *play* has changed considerably over the years. Fifty years ago, play was much more "natural: than it is today. Children at play tended to be engaged with natural materials—stones, sticks, sand, dirt, shells, clay—and the play itself was much more open-ended and child-directed. Children used the natural materials to construct their own toys and games. Sticks and pieces of bark became boats to float down the stream; leaves stirred in a bucket of water became the "soup of the day"; and burrs from burr-reed plants were shaped into stick people or animal figures.

Cross-culturally, young children—if given the opportunity—tend to create nestlike structures during their play activity. (Kirkby, 1989, Sobel, 1994). This phenomenon tends to occur without any prompting from adults. An important condition for this type of play to occur, however, is that children be provided with the necessary materials, space, and time. Unfortunately, play for many young children today revolves around commercially made toys and/or computer programs, and is often relegated to indoor activities. Play is thus no longer natural, in the sense of connecting children with the natural environment.

Because natural play is much more consistent with the child's ways of knowing and is more likely to foster the imagination of the child, it should be encouraged by both parents and teachers. Natural play can be encouraged, not only by providing a variety of natural materials for children to explore and manipulate, but also by suggesting that children take on the role of other creatures. With a little encouragement and a few simple props, young children delight in pretending to be something else. While many young children take on the roles of people they know or are familiar with (e.g., parent, teacher, fire fighter, police officer), they also enjoy "becoming" animals they know or have heard about (e.g., bears, rabbits, birds). While such dramatic play should usually be left child-initiated and open-ended, adults can add richness and excitement by providing appropriate costumes and related props (e.g., "dens" and/or nesting materials for the animals' homes). At times, adults may also suggest that children act out the experience of such natural phenomena as metamorphosis, migration, or hibernation. Such natural play experiences can help children gain a deep appreciation for the wonders of the world around them.

Encourage Aesthetic Representations of Children's Ways of Knowing

Aesthetics has been defined as being sensitive to beauty in nature and art (Wilson, 1995) and as "pertaining to the senses" (Adams, 1991). Children tend to find beauty without direct instruction, in that they are naturally inclined to hear the song of the earth and see the wonder of its workings. Encouraging children to express their ways of knowing the world through aesthetic, or artistic, representations is an excellent way of validating and enriching these experiences. Art-based experiences "encourage contemplative, reflective thought, which can extend environmental awareness, and essential basis for environmental understanding" (Adams, 1991, p. 21).

Suggestions on how to foster aesthetic learning include the following:

- involving children in classroom and school beautification and ecological projects.
- increasing the amount of time children spend outdoors interacting with natural materials.
- focusing children's attention on the beauty of the natural world versus "teaching" them facts about nature.
- encouraging children to sing, dance, draw, and paint their feelings about the world around them. Dighe (1993) suggests setting easels up outside to encourage children to paint trees or their feelings about trees. She also suggests that children be encouraged, through movement and dance, to capture the wiggle of a

caterpillar or the story of birds. Nature sounds, such as the chirp of crickets or the hum of bees, can be imitated through voice or musical instruments. Nature-theme picture books and poetry can also be used to foster aesthetic learning and reinforce enchantment with the earth.

Conclusion

Young children's ways of knowing the world are characterized by a sense of wonder and joy. By providing opportunities and encouragement for children to enter fully into these ways of knowing, we can make important contributions to both their quality of life and long-term commitment to care for the earth.

References

Adams, E. (1991). Back to basics: Aesthetic experience. *Children's Environments Quarterly, 8 (2), 19-29.*

Bailik, H.N. (1938). Aftergrowth (I.M., Trans.) Philadelphia: The Jewish Publication Society of America. (Original work published 1938).

Carson, R. (1956). *The sense of wonder.* New York: Harper & Row.

Chawla, L. & Hart, R. (1988). *The roots of environmental concern. Proceedings of the 19th Annual Conference of EDRA,* Pomona, CA. Reprinted in *The NAMTA Journal,* 1995, 20 (1), 148-157.

Cobb, E. (1977). *The ecology of imagination in childhood.* New York: Columbia University Press.

Cohen, M. J. (1984). *Prejudice against nature.* Freeport, ME: Cobblesmith.

Devall, W. (1984/85). A sense of earth wisdom. *Journal of Environmental Education,* 16(2), 1–3.

Dighe, J. (1993). Children and the earth. *Young Children,* 48 (3), 58–63.

Hinchman, H. (1991). *A life in hand: Creating the illuminated journal.* Layton, UT: Gibbs Smith Publishing.

Johnson, J. E., Christie, J. F., and Yawkey, T. D. (Eds.) (1987). *Play and early childhood development.* New York: Harper Collins Publishers.

Kaplan, R., & Kaplan, S. (1989). *The experience of nature.* New York: Cambridge University Press.

Kirkby, M. A. (1989). Nature as refuge. *Children's Environments Quarterly,* 6 (1), 7–12.

Moore, R. *Childhood's Domain.* Quoted in Trimble (1994), The scripture of maps, the names of trees: A child's landscape. In G. P. Nabhan and S. Trimble (1994). *The geography of childhood.* Boston: Beacon Press, pp. 15–32.

Nabhan, G. P. (1994). A child's sense of wildness. In G. P. Nabhan and S. Trimble (1994). *The geography of childhood.* Boston: Beacon Press pp. 1–14.

Nabhan, G. P., and Trimble, S. (1994). *The geography of childhood.* Boston: Beacon Press.

Orr, D. W. (1994). *Earth in mind.* Washington, DC: Island Press.

Pearce, J.C. (1971). *Magical child–Rediscovering Nature's plan for our children.* New York: E. P. Dutton.

Peterson, N. J. (1982). *Developmental variables affecting environmental sensitivity in professional environmental educators.* Unpublished masters thesis, Southern Illinois University at Carbondale.

Raglan, R. (1993). Reading the world: Overt and covert learning in environmental writing for children. *Journal of Environmental Education,* 24 (4), 4–7.

Sebba, R. (1991). The landscapes of childhood—The reflection of childhood's environment in adult memories and in children's attitudes. *Environment and Behavior,* 23 (4), 395–422.

Shaw-Jones, M. A. (1992). *Ecological world-views: An exploratory study of the narratives of environmental studies students.* Unpublished masters thesis. Keene, NH: Antioch University.

Slade, A. (1991). *A developmental sequence for the ecological self.* Unpublished masters thesis. University of Montana.

Sobel, D. (1994). *Children's special places.* Tucson, AZ: Zephyr Press.

Tanner, T. (1980). Significant life experience: A new research area in environmental education. *Journal of Environmental Education,* 11 (4), 20–24.

Wilson, E. O. (1984), *Biophilia.* Cambridge: Harvard University Press.

Wilson, E. O. (1992). *The diversity of life.* Cambridge, MA: Harvard University Press.

Wilson, R. A. (1994a). *Environamental education at the early childhood level.* Washington, DC: North American Association for Environmental Education.

Wilson, R. A. (1994b). Enhancing the outdoor learning environments of preschool programs. *Environmental Education,* 47, 11–12.

Wilson, R. A. (1995). Nature and young children: A natural connection. *Young Children,* 50, (6), 4–11.

Wilson, R. A. (1996). Earth—A "Vale of Soul-Making." *Early Childhood Education Journal,* 23, (3), 169–171.

Wilson, R. A., Kilmer, S., & Knauerhase, V. (1996). Developing an environmental outdoor play space for young children. *Young Children,* 51, (6), 56–61.

Article Review Form at end of book.

What benefits might an early childhood teacher gain by collaborating with an atelierista in a Reggio Emilia School?

Reggio Emilia

What is the message for early childhood education?

Jan McCarthy

Jan McCarthy, director of Center for Child and Family Studies, University of South Florida, and professor emeritus, Indiana State University, is past president of the National Association for Education of Young Children, has served as chair of the National Council for Accreditation of Teacher Education, and is president of the Council for Professional Development.

One of the most exhilarating and sustaining features of education is the continuous search for a better way to facilitate learning. The quest for knowing and responding to the complex art and science of teaching is an endeavor that distinguishes leaders in the field. In Reggio Emilia, Italy, the teachers, under the guidance of the late Loris Malaguzzi have spent slightly more than three decades honing ways of knowing that have produced remarkable results and captured the attention of early childhood educators throughout the world.

The philosophical orientation which holds that each child constructs knowledge through interactions with materials/equipment and people in an integrated process parallels the dominant view among early childhood educators in the United States. However, the Reggio schools must be examined within the context of conditions that have supported their development in a comprehensive manner that is truly exemplary. Educators must ponder how all of the schools for young children in a town of approximately 100,000 people are able to bring together hundreds of children, parents, teachers, and education specialists in a working relationship that retains the commitment to both the philosophy and the practices that distinguish their work.

One can find classrooms in the United States that exemplify the commitment to "learning by doing" through an integrated process and even more teachers who espouse this point of view but lack the support and/or the capabilities to demonstrate their beliefs in practice or to sustain them over time. Therefore, the thoughts about Reggio Emilia schools contained herein, based on on-site visitations, seminars with Reggio leaders, and dialogues with Reggio teachers, will emphasize the salient features that are vital to the development and continuation of successful schools. The commitment to the well-being of young children, the sensitivity to the unique needs of young children, the patience to listen to children's thoughts, and the critical analysis of conditions in the municipality-run schools are significant factors in the evolutionary history of Reggio schools for young children from infants through age 6.

Historical Perspectives

At the end of World War II, Loris Malaguzzi discovered a group of people in a small village near Reggio Emilia who were determined to overcome their devastation from the war by building and running a school for young children. They salvaged pieces of brick and beams from bombed houses, and they sold trucks, a tank, and some horses abandoned by the Germans to raise money to acquire the necessary resources.

The teachers were eager and energetic and exhibited tremendous dedication to what they were doing. As Malaguzzi and the teachers worked together, they

"Reggio Emilia: What is the Message for Early Childhood Education?" by Jan McCarthy from CONTEMPORARY EDUCATION, Spring 1995, Vol. 66, No. 3, pp. 139–142. Reprinted by permission.

became aware of the children's many needs. Some were undernourished and in poor health, and many spoke only in a local dialect, not standard Italian. Through observation and extended dialogue, Malaguzzi and the teachers concluded that they needed to develop ways of learning that departed from the traditional education program that lacked sensitivity to individuals. To make changes, they knew they needed to elicit help from the parents in a cooperative endeavor.

Implementing a new program that is well-conceptualized is usually very challenging; however, the trust and support from parents, the enthusiasm of the teachers, and the liberating thought that they could learn from children, gave them strength and a collective wisdom to move forward.

Learning from Children

Malaguzzi had studied in Piaget's School for Young Children in Geneva as well as at the Rousseau Institute. He was inspired by Piaget and the writings of Vygotsky and was convinced that explorations belong spontaneously to children's everyday experiences of living, playing, negotiating, thinking, and speaking by children (Malaguzzi, 1994). He felt that explorations provide a natural opportunity to work with numbers, quantity, classification, measurement, change, and space. This perspective formed the basis for his vision of a school that was more child-centered, where children are interactive constructivists.

The transition to a different way of learning required continuity as beliefs about schools and learning broke from the past. It was necessary for teachers to maintain human warmth, sustain each child's spontaneous curios-

ity, and preserve their decision to learn from children. The latter was accomplished through maintaining a constant readiness to change points of view or directions as they observed the children's work, engaged in dialogues with the children, and gained deeper insights about the children's thinking. Through this process, they acquired understandings that were incorporated into their pedagogy.

The teachers and Malaguzzi realized that putting together a new set of experiences for learning requires the recognition of the right of each child to be a protagonist—a child should be encouraged to have ideas. Additionally, they learned that families and teachers were central to this process and that focusing only on children would not produce harmony and higher levels of results. They found that building interrelationships was integral to the success of interactive learning experiences.

Relationships, Learning, and Communication

In Reggio Emilia, the goal is to build amiable schools where families, children, and teachers feel comfortable and all are valued as partners in the system. To maintain this shared responsibility for learning, there must be planning that encourages all three groups to be protagonists. Communication through meetings with families to discuss curriculum/projects, seek assistance in organizing activities, set up the space, build furnishings and toys, and organize dinners and celebrations is continuously maintained.

The interactive nature of the relationship among teachers, families, and children creates a spirit of cooperation, an individual and collective effort in support of the

schools, and political support. Furthermore, this approach fosters new dispositions on the part of teachers. They tend to question their beliefs and become more aware of the perspectives of others, more astute in providing a steady flow of documentation of their understanding of the children, and more available to children and parents. Additionally, as a result of the documentation, parents begin to re-think their parental roles and their views about how children learn. They tend to become more actively engaged in their children's experiences. These two scenarios lead to an equally pleasant outcome for children. The children demonstrate enhanced curiosity, persistence in trying new ideas, a sustained effort in solving new challenges, increased confidence in the ability to achieve self-determined goals, and a level of performance that often exceeds the expectations associated with their particular age.

Providing the Conditions for Learning

Malaguzzi saw the need for a new type of school with areas where children's minds and hands would find the means for active exploration—a place rich with materials, tools, and resourceful people; a place where children invented with their hands, tested hypotheses, played, had fun, and demonstrated how they were thinking. To some degree, this was achieved through the physical space. Each classroom is designed with wall-sized windows that connect visually with the rest of the school. The piazza (an open shared space for group gatherings and large projects), the atelier (a studio/workshop housing an abundance of materials) and courtyards (connecting the indoor learning environment with the outdoor environment) are all designed to inspire children and encourage exploration in a peaceful atmosphere.

The environment informs and engages the children. They experiment with many modalities, techniques, instruments, materials, and themes in what Malaguzzi called the many languages of children. Teachers learned that work initiated in the atelier soon permeated the entire school and often extended to the environment surrounding the school and into the entire community. Through observing children at work, listening to their verbalizations, and studying their creations, teachers had a natural laboratory for learning more about children and how to record what they were learning. The recordings provided documentation for facilitating effective communication with parents while keeping them informed about their children's activities at school.

This process supports teachers and helps them validate their ideas.

Another condition for learning centered around reconciling the dilemma between teaching and learning. If teachers believed that they could learn from children and that children should be protagonists, then those who work with children must allow children to assume a role in the construction of self and knowledge. Learning is the focal point of this perspective, and teaching becomes a complementary set of resources that offers multiple options, numerous alternatives, and a major source of support. The process becomes a reciprocal exchange, and teachers no longer view the children as "empty containers to be filled." This form of learning is exemplified in many

ways in the schools. Some of the activities are similar to those found in U.S. schools that engage children in brief individual or small-group problem-solving actions such as science explorations, dramatic play, and block building. Other learning experiences are long-term projects, in some ways similar to thematic experiences, although very different in the ways they are carried out. The extensive dialogue with children, the encouragement for children to express their ideas through some form of representation, the challenges from their peers or teachers that create a desire for children to revise their thinking and create new representations, and the teachers' support for the evolving process promote project learning to a much deeper level of thinking and problem solving than typically associated with thematic experiences in U.S. programs.

Collegial Support

Through co-teaching, working with the atelierista, the teacher trained in art education in charge of the atelier, and the pedogogista, the resource consultant, a collegial work environment is created for the faculty. This collaborative arrangement removes the feelings of isolation and uncertainty that teachers often experience. Through weekly discussions of the children's work, shared perspectives and observations are brought to the planning table. The wide variety of documentation techniques—tape recordings and transcriptions of dialogues, photographs, videos, observation notes, and the children's work—add to their insights. Consequently, as themes for projects emerge, the team of people

considers the possible directions that children might pursue. This anticipatory process includes identifying the skills and cognitive schemes that might be worth bolstering, the method for advancing words, and what resources will be needed for the children's pursuits. They discuss the range of graphic representations and thoughts that might occur, as well as ways that body language, symbolic language, fantasy, and play might be enhanced.

This process supports teachers and helps them validate their ideas. New teachers find the process especially beneficial. Consequently, the new teachers construct beliefs about how children learn that are compatible with the guiding principles of the schools and are provided authentic opportunities to develop their skills in creating a learning environment based on the observed interests and needs of children.

Engaging Parents and the Community

Parents often participate in the weekly planning meetings. They become aware of the sincere commitment to each individual child, the teachers' desires to develop thinking individuals, and the hard work that teachers do. In addition to learning new ways of parenting, they share insights about their child, secure resources for the schools, and volunteer to assist in numerous ways. Since the parents came from various professional or work roles in the community, they became a strong link to all parts of the community as well as advocates for the schools. They are a part of the process; therefore, they are well-informed and speak with insight and authority.

Constant Scrutiny

Another distinguishing feature of the Reggio schools is the constant evaluation of what they are doing. No task is looked upon as complete. Each year is viewed as a chance to improve on past experiences. Because the curriculum is not a preplanned set of experiences, the teachers engage in dialogues to determine the interests of the returning children, and they seek to know the minds of the children who are new to the school. They incorporate information from previous experiences, and ponder ways of enriching the opportunities for learning. They undertake challenges such as examining the differences that boys and girls demonstrate in how they approach an idea, how children approach computers, or how children respond when the teachers introduce materials or raise questions that provoke the children's thinking when they are exploring a topic or engaged in a project.

An evolving curriculum, new children, new parents, and, in some cases, new teachers create a set of conditions that are totally different each year. For success to prevail a continuous assessment of the process and the willingness to modify or change directions become a way of living, thinking, and acting in the Reggio schools. The exhilaration inherent in fresh thoughts and ideas permeates the beginning of each new year, captures the children's desire to explore their world, and the curriculum evolves anew.

Conclusion

Reggio schools reflect a theoretical base that is closely akin to a constructivist perspective, which is the base for developmentally appropriate practices supported by the early childhood profession in the United States. The major differences are associated with the processes that are used to enhance learning. Projects, often long-termed, are initiated with no clear focus on the outcome. Directions are determined by interests of children and challenges to their thinking by their peers or their teachers. Even if it is flawed, children are encouraged to pursue an idea in order to determine how to revise their thinking. Peer group discussions, negotiations, and conflict resolutions are encouraged, and multiple points of view are valued. In Reggio Emilia, there is a trust that children will engage in worthwhile pursuits that nurture learning and that parents are valued partners in this exciting and productive venture.

Reference

Malaguzzi, L. (1993). History, ideas, and basic philosophy. In C. Edwards, L. Gandini, and G. Forman (Eds.), *The Hundred Languages of Children.* (pp. 41-89). Norwood, NJ: Ablex Publishing Corp.

 Article Review Form at end of book.

What did Cleta Booth learn about facilitating a project, and what additional methods did she suggest?

The Fiber Project

One teacher's adventure toward emergent curriculum

Cleta Booth

Cleta Booth, M.Ed., is the prekindergarten teacher at the Wyoming Center for Teaching and Learning at Laramie, the laboratory school for the University of Wyoming College of Education, where she enjoys both teaching young children and mentoring college students.

It all started one Christmas break as I was driving through west-central Texas for the first time in years. I was luxuriating in the warmth, having left Wyoming's expanse of snow and ice far behind. Then, suddenly up ahead, there were snow-covered fields. It took a moment to reset my expectations. Cotton!

The harvest was nearing completion, and both the stubble in the fields and the weeds along the roadway wore tufts of white fibers missed by the mechanical harvesters or spilled from trucks. Just ahead, right beside the road, was an unharvested field.

My preschoolers would have been amazed by the scene. They are very familiar with a snow-blanketed landscape, but few have had the opportunity to see a cotton field ready for harvest. In fact, these three- to five-year-olds see little in the way of farming—

an occasional hay field, perhaps, but mostly where we live it's cattle or antelope grazing on a stubble of grass or sagebrush.

I stopped. The field was muddy from recent rain. If anyone had been around, I would have asked permission. But it was a Sunday, and there was no one in sight. My impulse seemed justifiable on educational grounds, so I waded into the field and pulled up one fluff-covered plant, roots and all. What a surprise for my children! A stick with dry leaves and roots but decorated as if for Christmas by balls of soft white cotton.

I also picked a handful of bolls that hadn't fully developed, ranging from small, hard nutlike balls to almost mature bolls, split open in quarters at the top, revealing tightly packed white fibers damp and matted. I had never looked at cotton bolls so carefully before. Finally I picked two fully opened bolls for each of the children in my class, my two apprentice teachers, and myself, plus a few extras in case of loss or accident. I silently promised to repay the unknown owner by talking with my children about how cotton is grown and the important work farmers do.

A Project Is Born

After Christmas break, with some trepidation, I gave the children my present. Would they really accept this as a gift? Or would they be too jaded by holiday troves of Ninja Turtles and Little Mermaids to find something from a plant even mildly interesting? Each child was handed a plastic bag with two cotton bolls inside, one to be saved whole to take home, the other to be immediately explored.

The children spent a while guessing what the strange looking ball could be and looking, feeling, and smelling it. Then I encouraged them to take it apart. Perhaps my enthusiasm was catching. There was genuine excitement when they discovered the seeds inside. "If we plant them, will they grow?" one child asked. I didn't know but promised to bring dirt the next day. As we pulled the fibers away from the seeds, I showed the children how to twist them between their fingers to make a thread. So that's what thread is, the children seemed to be thinking.

My two apprentices, both undergraduates studying to become teachers, seemed as intrigued as the children. One of them put a name to the process that had begun: "The Fiber Project."

It didn't start out to be so grand. It just grew. In fact, when I had entered the cotton field, I didn't realize I was setting a project in motion. And I didn't consult with the children (as I usually do now when we begin a project). But according to Katz and Chard (1989), good projects can begin either with the children's ideas or with a proposal by the teacher.

I teach at a university lab school, and I find myself continually challenged to grow as a teacher by both my preschool children and my college students. Many years earlier I had read about projects as an approach to teaching, but I had limited practical experience with them. I'd recently reread some of John Dewey's work for a college class I taught, and I was reminded again how important it is for children to come to understand the interconnectedness of the natural world and society through firsthand experience with real processes. At the time of this project, I had only recently become familiar with the work of Katz and Chard and was just beginning to read contemporary work on "emergent curriculum." What followed was "emergent" in the sense of "evolving." I was, and am, still learning how to listen to the children and to construct a negotiated curriculum, guided by my awareness of important developmental, cognitive, and skills goals, following children's interests and challenging their understanding.

The Possibilities Grow

My college students and I brainstormed ideas about where this exploration of cotton bolls might take us. We made a web of possibilities (see accompanying web, p. 68). We knew we'd never have time for all the possibilities, and we knew the children, and perhaps even their families, would suggest more. The web was to help us be open to possibilities and to begin to prepare materials and plan for activities that might make this a better opportunity for learning (Katz & Chard 1989). I wrote a note to parents explaining the cotton bolls and asking for their ideas. (If I were doing this now, I would include the children in making the original planning web, but I had not yet learned from experience how helpful that can be for engaging children's interest and assessing their current knowledge.)

The next day I brought potting soil and paper cups. Most children chose to plant seeds in two cups, one to take home and one to care for at school. I planted the extras in a big pot. We watched and watered. Many seeds failed to sprout, but a few grew. Over the next several weeks we watched one especially sturdy plant develop green leaves, and we measured it weekly as it grew taller, with different children choosing to trace the growth on paper posted behind it. One child wondered if the plant would make cotton too. Would it take a whole year? I wondered if it could do it without other cotton plants around.

I found magazine pictures of cotton fields and of cotton being harvested by hand and by machine. I kept my promise to the unknown Texas farmer and talked about the important work of farmers. We read about cotton—how it grows and how it is changed into thread and cloth. Children began to bring in pictures and books related to the subject, which we added to a growing classroom library. One child brought in a book about wool, and I searched in my personal library for *Pelle's New Suit*.

From Cotton on to Wool

Evan told the class about his two sheep, Lucky and Lucy, and asked if he could bring them to school. His parents agreed to meet us in the school parking lot. On a cold January day we all took turns burying our hands in the warm but dirty, oily, smelly wool. It went so deep! The braver children looked Lucky and Lucy in the eye and petted their noses. Evan's dad took sheers and cut us a large handful of raw wool. "Does it hurt?" Melissa asked. "Does it hurt when you get a haircut?" Mr. S. asked in reply. A few days later, Evan brought us a picture of Lucky being sheared. On her back, with her front feet in the air, Lucky looked uncomfortable and annoyed but not in pain, the class decided.

Some of the children remembered how I had first twisted some cotton fibers together, and they connected the idea with yarn being made from wool. When I told them I knew a local craftsperson who spins and weaves yarn to make cloth, they asked me to invite her to come to class to show us how. I quickly telephoned to make an appointment, afraid that the children's interest would start to fade. (How that interest might have grown if the children had been involved in writing a letter telling of their questions and inviting her to come, then enjoying the suspense of waiting for her reply. What a learning opportunity I missed! I hadn't yet learned how to slow down and involve children in all the steps of a project.)

My friend gave me instructions for preparing the wool in

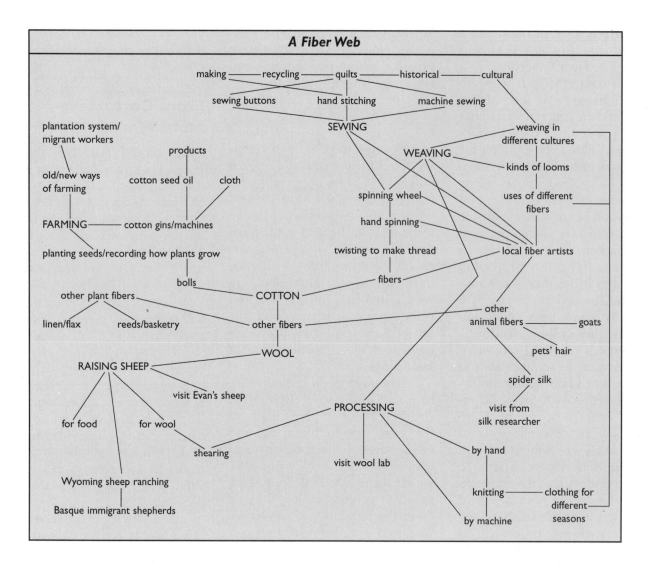

A Fiber Web

advance. I followed them at school, with children joining in as they became interested. We washed the wool with soap to get out the lanolin oil. My friend also had suggested we might want to try dying some of the wool. We boiled onion skins for a natural golden brown dye and used Kool-Aid for brighter pinks and purples. At one child's suggestions, we dyed some of the cotton too. The children wee fascinated with the change in color. They also noticed that the colors of the wool and cotton were different, and we decided to ask our visitor about the mystery.

When our expert came to class, she brought along a spinning wheel, a simple loom, and other tools. She let us, children and teachers exploring together, use carding combs to straighten out the wool fibers. She demonstrated a hand spindle and let everyone have turns holding the wool as the spindle dangled below, winding the fiber into yarn. She demonstrated how much faster the work went on her spinning wheel, and she let each child press the treadle. While some children spun, others took turns using the simple loom to weave the yarn into cloth. Our guest also let us feel other kinds of fibers—special goat's wool called mohair and even silk make by silkworms.

The children showed their discovery about the colors to our visitor, and she explained that plant fibers and animal fibers take dye differently and need different chemicals to make them set. We settled for an explanation and went on. (Now I see that the children's observation and curiosity could have opened up a whole new area of investigation.)

The following day the children recalled the visit, and they used their language, writing, and drawing skills to write thank-you notes, each telling what he or she had enjoyed most. One child drew the loom, and another surprised me by drawing details of the spinning wheel. I mailed the thank-you notes, pleased that they had occasioned meaningful work in language and fine-motor skills and that the great detail in verbal description and drawing revealed how much the children had learned.

I make a "Wool Book" that documented, with photographs, drawings, and samples, the processes from start to finish. This became part of the class library. (I had not yet begun reading abut the importance of "documentation" as used in the preschools of Reggio Emilia, Italy [Edwards, Gandini, & Forman 1993]. Today, instead of doing it myself, I would have merely assisted the children in making the "Wool Book." I also would have photographed or photocopied the drawings and notes we mailed away so that they—along with the photographs of and the children's comments on Lucky and Lucy's visit, the experience of spinning and weaving, and our exploration of the original cotton plants—could have become part of a display of the entire process. Children, teachers, and families could view the display to confirm memories and discover new questions to pursue.)

A Visit to a Wool Lab

The year before, seeking a convenient firsthand experience that would help illustrate some of John Dewey's educational ideas to college students, I had learned that the small old building behind the nearby Agriculture Building was a wool lab. Recalling that resource, I contacted the professor in charge of the lab. He invited my preschool class to visit his lab as my college class had done.

(I wish now that I had arranged, before we visited the wool lab, to keep a hand spinning wheel and loom in the classroom for an extended time, so the children could have satisfied themselves about how these particular machines worked, perhaps actually making something from cloth they had created themselves. In my "teacherly" eagerness to expose the children to many ideas and experiences, I didn't follow through in depth.)

The children thoroughly enjoyed the field trip next door. Dewey was right, that experiencing where things come from is important to children. The children were amazed by the size and complexity of the machines and the volumes of wool they processed. Each child got to take home a swatch of very finely combed "top wool." The machines themselves stimulated more general interest in how machines work, a subject we decided to pursue soon.

Weekly newsletters kept the parents informed of our activities. One parent volunteered to come in and teach any interested children to knit. One of the apprentices taught finger-knitting. The other apprentice shared her embroidery skill. We had set up a variety of sewing and weaving activities among which interested children could choose. Some children sewed and stuffed small pillows, and everyone chose to sew a button on a piece of cloth held by embroidery hoops. One college student taught a few of the older children to make a mat by weaving strips of paper, and the activity caught on. Seeing the interest, I provided a simple frame and a variety of yarns and fabric strips to make a larger class weaving.

Children Choose Activities

We worked on the fiber project for three weeks. However, it wasn't the only thing we did. Being relatively new to project work, I was more comfortable adding it gradually to my program, furthering the project at circle time and during free-choice time, with different children choosing to participate to different degrees. We maintained our regular weekly schedule of music, art, and physical education, sometimes including fiber-related activities, sometimes not.

The art teacher worked with us to incorporate weaving and fabric texture-based activities in her plans. (If I were doing this now, I would have worked with her to develop art and aesthetic goals that were integral to the children's explorations, but, like her, I still tended to plan mostly in terms of teaching certain predetermined concepts or skills by providing certain activities. I am gradually learning how to think in terms of observing more deeply what children are trying to understand or accomplish and planning in terms of challenges I can provide to further their efforts.)

The music teacher introduced theme-related songs such as "Jump Down, Turn Around, Pick a Bale of Cotton." That provided an opportunity for gross-motor activity, though not so much as if we had really been doing the labor we mimed. (If we had lived near the fields, we might have spent a while hoeing or picking to learn the difficult and hot work firsthand. This, as well as the dialect of the song, might have led to new questions and explorations about the history of cotton growing and the experience of slavery. More attention to context might have led to exploration of deeper issues.)

Our usual centers were available during an hour or more of free-choice time each day. While some children worked on an aspect of the fiber project, others used the centers to explore any ideas they wished. I enhanced the centers with activities and materials related to cotton, wool, and the processing of fibers just as I would with any thematic unit, hoping to spark new questions in some of the less-involved children. To our changing assortment of books in the book corner, both the children and I continued to add a variety of stories and non-fiction related to our fiber study (see "Selected children's books for a fiber project).*

I added a variety of sewing, weaving, and braiding activities to the sensory-perceptual area and enhanced the art supplies with both processed and raw cotton and wool and fabric scraps to encourage three-dimensional representation of ideas related to our work. In our family-play area, I chose dress-up clothes with interesting textures and designs. (But I could have done so much more! For example, the beautiful children's book *Abuela's Weave,* set in Guatemala, might have inspired another household environment, furnished with baskets [another woven fiber product!], balls of colored yarn, a backstrap loom, and colorful Guatemalan fabrics. Through fantasy play, stories, and discussion with adults, a context for understanding the place of weaving in another culture might be built up. Other children's books, such as *The Goat in the Rug,* about weaving in Navajo culture, might have provided inspiration for a different presentation of the dramatic-play area and an exploration of yet another culture.)

To the math/science center, I added our cotton plant, placing a paper behind it for tracing new growth, a ruler nearby for measuring, and a tray with cotton bolls for estimating and counting the seeds. (Balance scales, scissors, magnifying glasses, and even a

microscope might have further encouraged different explorations of the property of fibers.)

We assembled a display of planted seed in various stages of sprouting and growing, cotton bolls of differing maturity, and swatches of dyed and undyed fibers at various stages of processing—and supplied a magnifying glass. The children brought fabric items from home that were made from different types of fibers. (At the time I was thinking of this collection as part of the science center to encourage closer observation. Now I think of it as one aspect of documenting the project so that children, teachers, and visitors could refer to specific discoveries and observations as we reflected on our work and challenged each other to continue making new discoveries. For this documentation function, more photographs, labels, and transcripts of conversations were needed.)

Time to Move On

As a result of the fiber project, interest in machines was growing. We were invited to one child's house to see a knitting machine, but the mother knew we also would be interested in the machines in her professional kitchen, where she bakes for local restaurants. After we had turns using the knitting machines, she invited us to watch her mix dough in a giant commercial mixer, then allowed each child to process some dough in a pasta maker. We cooked and ate our own fresh pasta.

It was a terrific event, far eclipsing the interest in knitting. Clearly, it was time to bring some kind of closure to our fiber activities and turn our attention to the new possibilities opened up by machines as a subject of study.

Children and teachers talked about the transition and decided to conclude the fiber project by making a class quilt. I suggested the ideas, but the children were enthusiastic and had many suggestions about how the quilt should be made. Each child would contribute a square that reflected his or her own individuality and make use of one or more of the fiber-related processes or skills learned. The squares would be combined to make a group product and record of the project, enhancing everyone's sense of belonging and making a permanent contribution to the class culture.

Each child was given a choice of a variety of materials, including cotton embroidery thread, wool yarn, buttons, and puffy fabric paint, and was encouraged to make a design on a white cotton square. Some children stitched randomly. Some carefully drew designs, people, and scenes, then stitched over them. Some strung buttons loosely on thread; others carefully and tightly sewed them on. Some children were far more interested in the puffy fabric paint than in the sewing (I realized that the paint was an unnecessary and irrelevant distraction). Others combined the two mediums effectively, however. One of the youngest girls, a purist with very advanced fine-motor skills and a long attention span, refused the buttons and paints and spent three days meticulously stitching a multicolored rainbow on her square.

After each child had hand sewn a square and we had reviewed the stages of the project, I brought in my sewing machine. Each child had a turn to explore the levers and buttons on the machine, operate the switch pedal, and then, with my help, guide her or his square safely

*Not included in this publication.

through the machine, sewing it onto a matrix of calico strips that outlined the squares and made a coherent whole.

Two days later, when the top was complete, I padded it with part of an old thermal blanket and backed it with the calico material. The class quilt now covers the small mattress that defines our reading corner. Everyone felt pride in the way they, as a group, had made something beautiful to enhance our classroom. Sometimes, when children are tired or irritable, they find comfort crawling under the quilt and cuddling it up to their chins.

Meanwhile, we gradually worked deeply into our next topic of study. With some solid experience with spinning wheels and looms, wool processing and knitting machines, cooking machines, and sewing machines, as well as experiences doing similar jobs by hand, the children were able to appreciate the differences machines make in our lives. We took other field trips and began to learn more about other kinds of machines.

Seizing the Possibilities

That we began with exploring a cotton boll and ended with a new exploration is typical of emergent curricula. The underlying premise is that learning is organic and whole. One project leads to another, following the interests of the class members, child and adult. A good project starts from something that someone is *excited* about. It also has clear educational relevance, as *where things come from* always does.

A good project provides opportunities for work in many curriculum areas (as this one did in science, math, communication, so-

cial studies, and arts) and invites the exercise of many different kinds of skills. It also offers opportunities for the ongoing social-emotional curriculum of early childhood: opportunities to take turns, share, help each other, listen appropriately, challenge and question ideas, exhibit skill, create and foster pride, and contribute to a group effort.

In short, the fiber project offered a very rich developmentally appropriate curriculum for a wide age range. Working collaboratively, the apprentice teachers and I, with input from parents and the children themselves, selected what was most appropriate for our group of three- through five-year-olds. We based many of our choices on the skills and interests of individual children (although I missed many other such opportunities), on the teachers' knowledge of appropriate and worthwhile curriculum goals, and on the physical and human resources available.

As I've learned more about project work and emergent, or negotiated, curriculum by undertaking and reflecting on a variety of further projects, by rereading the early works that influenced me to begin this approach, and by exploring newer works such as *Emergent Curriculum* (Jones & Nimmo 1994), I have continued to experiment and change how I think about children's learning and what I do in class. A variety of articles in *Young Children*, presentations I've heard at NAEYC state meetings and national conferences, and conferences on project work, emergent curriculum, and Reggio Emilia keep pushing me to rethink theory and practice.

Most recently a series of exchanges on the computer bulletin boards ECEOL-L (Early Childhood Education On Line List), PROJECT -L

(Project Approach List), and REGGIO-L (Reggio Emilia List) have challenged me to think more deeply about the possibilities of this kind of emergent project work. The newest resources I've discovered are the ECEOL and Projects home pages on the World Wide Web, where, among other things, teachers can share examples of successful projects. The kind of collaboration that is so helpful, even necessary, for this work is now available through a growing worldwide network of teachers with similar interests.

To me, the two most important lessons of the fiber project were practical experience with the children as collaborators and guides in determining the direction of curriculum and firsthand evidence that children can become deeply engaged with a project over an extended period of time. For years I had planned a thematically integrated curriculum. But with the fiber project, I gradually moved toward increased coherence and meaningfulness of activities. I found that many developmental domains and curriculum goals can be effectively integrated through one project. And as new questions arise, one subject of study can lead naturally into a variety of other valuable subjects.

References

Edwards, C., L. Gandini, & G. Forman, eds. 1993. *The hundred languages of children: The Reggio Emilia approach to early childhood education.* Norwood, NJ: Ablex.

Jones, E., & J. Nimmo. 1994. *Emergent curriculum.* Washington, DC: NAEYC.

Katz, L., , & S. Chard. 1989. *Engaging children's minds: The project approach.* Norwood, NJ: Ablex.

 Article Review Form at end of book.

- The characteristics of quality care and education for young children relate to practices that nurture children's needs developmentally within settings that encourage emergent and guided experiences.

- Early care and learning professionals must find ways to balance issues of quality care, affordability, and compensation to realistically meet the needs of children and their families in the next century.

R.E.A.L. Sites

This list provides a print preview of typical **coursewise** R.E.A.L. sites. There are over 100 such sites at the **courselinks**™ site. The danger in printing URLs is that web sites can change overnight. As we went to press, these sites were functional using the URLs provided. If you come across one that isn't, please let us know via email to: webmaster@coursewise.com. Use your Passport to access the most current list of R.E.A.L. sites at the **courselinks**™ site.

Site name: National Child Care Information Center (NCCIC)
URL: http://nccic.org/
Why is it R.E.A.L.? The National Child Care Information Center is an adjunct of ERIC Clearinghouse for Child Care. Access to the *Child Care Bulletin,* publications, a conference calendar, and links to other child care resources are provided.
Key topics: child care, families, licensing
Activity: List the most current White House Initiatives.

Site name: The Association for Childhood Education International (ACEI)
URL: http://www.udel.edu/bateman/acei/
Why is it R.E.A.L.? The Association for Childhood Education International (ACEI) was founded in 1892 as the International Kindergarten Union and is known as the oldest early childhood organization of its kind. *Childhood Education* is the featured professional publication.
Key topics: curriculum, early care and learning professionals, program quality
Activity: Locate the Association for Childhood Education International (ACEI) branch affiliation nearest your institution or program. Record the local president's name and address.

Site name: Child Care Bureau
URL: http://www.acf.dhhs.gov/programs/ccb/
Why is it R.E.A.L.? The Child Care Bureau is administered by the Administration for Children and Families, U.S. Department of Health and Human Services. This agency sets out to improve the quality, affordability, and supply of child care available for all families. Research, policy, funding, and special event information are all listed.
Key topics: caregiving, child care, working families
Activity: Click on *Research, Data and Systems.* Describe the Profile of the Child Care Work Force.

Site name: The Project Approach
URL: http://www.ualberta.ca/~schard/projects.htm
Why is it R.E.A.L.? The Home Page for the Project Approach provides descriptions of projects, activities, and examples. Dr. Sylvia Chard maintains the site for the Clearinghouse on Elementary and Early Childhood Education. Chinese language and Spanish language translations are available.
Key topics: child-centered curriculum, emergent curriculum
Activity: When and where are the *Engaging Children's Minds: The Project Approach* Summer Institutes held?

section

3

Key Points

- Supportive partnerships with parents will begin when early care and learning professionals acknowledge familial factors that influence parents' choices for child care.

- Busy families create quality time with priority planning centered on their children.

- Understanding and promoting the true meaning in discipline merges ideas of early childhood professionals with parental responsibilities.

- Creative and spontaneous teaching approaches guide children's abilities to transition from one activity to another and to control their own behaviors.

- Parents and teachers will reduce bullying in schools when zero tolerance becomes policy and is complimented with expanded counseling.

- Family-friendly policies increase workplace efficiency and help parents balance demands of family and work.

- Culturally consistent caregiving begins when professionals challenge previously accepted child development principles and practices.

Child-Rearing Responsibilities: How Will We Build Supportive Partnerships with Parents?

 **WiseGuide Intro**

Greater acceptance of the enduring influence that parents have on their young children's development is obvious in both professional journals and books about children. Children and families are central in local and national initiatives concerning parent-child relationships, guidance of children, and balance of family and work. Respecting the significance of familial and cultural values greatly enhances opportunities to build supportive partnerships with parents.

Early care and learning professionals will find that their ideas about the selection of child care are not necessarily congruent with those of parents. Attempts to define and promote the selection of quality child care have not significantly influenced parental child-care choices. The first reading, "How Do Parents Really Choose Early Childhood Programs?" sends a firm message. We must identify strategies that consider parents' values and beliefs and incorporate more "parent culture" into the definition of quality child care.

The media have responded to the "parent culture," highlighting reports about parental roles and expectations. It is apparent from surveys that parents want to be "good parents"; nevertheless, parents today face enormous challenges to balance their time commitments. The second reading, "Making Time for Family," suggests practical time scheduling ideas that place children at the top of all family agendas.

Inquiries from parents about discipline rank high whenever discussions about child-rearing responsibilities occur. In the third reading, "Say What You Mean . . .," former editor-in-chief of *Parenting*, David Markus responds with recommendations about discipline that validate many of the premises that early childhood professionals promote.

Sharing the guidance strategies that skilled and innovative teachers practice provides useful insight for parents. In "Creative Strategies in Ernie's Early Childhood Classroom," Ernie engages and redirects children with flexibility and creativity that allow children to successfully make transitions from one activity to another and to learn to control their own behaviors.

There is a dual responsibility to create both safe places and places for children to learn. Achieving this goal requires that teachers and parents first recognize that bullying behavior in schools is a problem, as detailed in the reading "Bullying in School: It Doesn't Have to Happen."

Counseling is suggested as a first-order remedy, with parent, teacher, and student input to formulate an anti-bullying policy.

The supportive network for parents is expanding to include employers. Companies are beginning to endorse positive outcomes, such as increased efficiency, that relate to employee satisfaction. The reading "Companies in a Family Way" offers a brief look at companies that adopt family-friendly policies to help their workers, who are parents, achieve balance between family and work.

The final reading in Section 3, "The Cultural Context of Infant Caregiving," proposes acknowledgment of cultural and socioeconomic variation of families to ensure more consistent caregiving. Acknowledgment and acceptance create core intentions for early childhood professionals, establishing strong, supportive partnerships with parents.

Questions

Reading 13. How will early care and learning professionals influence parents' child-care choices?

Reading 14. How can parents plan and organize for effective family communication?

Reading 15. What parental behaviors contribute to appropriate discipline of children?

Reading 16. How can a teacher help young children successfully change from one activity to another?

Reading 17. What key features did Daniel Olweus's program include to reduce bullying in schools?

Reading 18. Why would companies redesign workplaces?

Reading 19. How can early childhood educators avoid judging the infant sleeping routines of children from cultures different than their own?

How will early care and learning professionals influence parents' child-care choices?

How Do Parents Really Choose Early Childhood Programs?

Ellen Zinzeleta and Nancy King Little

Ellen Zinzeleta, Sc.D., is director of Nova Southeastern University's Family Center of Tampa Bay in Tampa, Florida. She directs accreditation facilitation, staff training, and family support initiatives.

Nancy King Little, B.S., is the founding director of the Palma Ceia Presbyterian Preschool, an NAEYC-accredited, inclusive early childhood program in Tampa.

The authors cochaired a Tampa-based, child care public awareness task force and have actively advocated for quality early childhood experiences.

How could a devoted parent choose less than the best early childhood setting for a beloved child? The majority of American early childhood centers provide poor or mediocre care to the children they serve, according to early childhood professionals. Yet much of the time, parents rate these substandard care settings as providing high-quality care (Helburn & Culkin 1995). What accounts for these divergent perceptions? Are parents' views merely attempts to

justify the only choices available to them, or is there more to the story?

For decades, professionals have tired to influence parents' choices of early education and care options by describing the elements of quality in readily available checklists, articles in the popular press, and brochures (Bogat & Gensheimer 1986; Mitchell, Cooperstein, & Larner 1992). Because the majority of American children are in substandard care, one or more of the following appears to be operating.

1. parents are not using the available program evaluation materials;

2. parents are using these tools and arriving at choices that do not reflect the elements of quality as defined by the tools and the field of early childhood education; or

3. cost, location, availability, and other factors preclude parents' access to high-quality early childhood programs.

As part of our work with a Tampa-based child care public-

awareness task force, we encountered many parents who used resources describing the elements of quality and then chose an early childhood program that did not match the characteristics outlined in these materials. In some cases this occurred in spite of having access to NAEYC-accredited centers.

Could it be that these materials are not congruent with parents' basic beliefs and values?

We suggest that many currently used program evaluation materials may not dovetail with a parents' beliefs about quality early childhood care, so parents override them. The development of parents' and educators' constructs of quality may be based on different, sometimes even competing, beliefs.

For example, during a discussion group some parents with whom we spoke expressed a belief that elementary schools were too overburdened to teach basic reading skills. Therefore, these parents reasoned, early childhood programs with a heavy emphasis on academics would be the best choice for their children. Consistent with their beliefs, these parents chose a preschool that professionals would not call developmentally appropriate.

In another discussion group we learned that participants who could describe some elements of quality chose a religious program that did not demonstrate those characteristics. It may be that the religious/cultural component is the most significant quality indicator for some parents.

The research literature identifies a myriad of other cultural or familial factors that influence parents' choices of child care options. Bogat and Gensheimer found "vague yet positive qualities of the caregiver" to be important to a sample of white middle-class mothers in their late twenties (1986, 167). Zinsser's sample of middle-class and working-class mothers echoed this sentiment when describing "instant reactions of 'gut feelings' and 'stomach turnings'" (1987, 22) that influenced their child care choices.

Mitchell, Cooperstein, and Larner concluded that, for some working-class and lower-income families, "formal institutions such as nursery schools and child care centers embody a set of distinct cultural values from which parents want to protect their children" (1992, 28). This belief was described candidly by a parent who chose relative care in Rubin's classic description of working-class life: "We don't have to worry about what kind of stuff some stranger is teaching them. We know they're learning right from wrong" (1976, 87).

Our field is beginning to address the importance of considering the family's cultural beliefs in the caregiving relationship (Far West Laboratory 1993; Lally et al. 1995; Bredekamp & Copple 1997). But have we considered them in relation to how families define quality and choose child care? With this question in mind, we examined brochures and other instruments in an effort to identify ways in which parents' beliefs, values, and culture may be incongruent with the behaviors we are asking them to adopt.

Figures 1 and 2 are diagrams demonstrating parents' decision-making processes when choosing child care and how parents' use of available resources might influence their decisions. Many brochures, checklists, and other resources seem to attempt to influence choice in the way shown in Figure 1.

A notable feature of the Figure 1 model is the assumption that parents will set aside their beliefs and make choices based on the suggestions of others

While we are striving to understand the contribution of cultural beliefs to other aspects of early care and education, have we given as much attention to their role in parents' selection process? Can we find ways to consider parents' beliefs and values when attempting to influence their choices of programs?

We hypothesize that decisionmaking may actually work as diagrammed in Figure 2

This model suggests that commonly used techniques to influence parents' behavior are not always successful.

Another possible reason that checklists and other educational resources are not producing the desired outcome is that some parents may not be using them at all. There is some support for this theory. A sample of 136 parents calling a child care resource-and-referral line were sent checklists

---

Figure 1 How Educators Expect Available Resources to Influence Parents' Child Care Choices

Some Commonly Used Tools Attempt to Influence Choice at This Point.

| Parents read a description of characteristics associated with high quality as defined by the field of early childhood education (educators' construct) | → | Parents replace their own construct of high-quality care with educators' construct | → | Parents observe early childhood programs | → | Parents compare programs to educators' construct | → | Parents choose the program that most closely matches educators' construct |

Figure 2	How Parents May Actually Choose Child Care

Some Commonly Used Tools Intervene Here

Parents possess beliefs and values based on a lifetime of experiences within a culture → Parents develop and maintain a construct of quality early childhood education → Parents read a description of characteristics associated with high quality as defined by the field of early childhood education (educators' construct) → Parents adopt elements of educators' construct consistent with their own beliefs and values; **OR**

Parents maintain their own construct if educators' construct is inconsistent with parent's own beliefs and values

→ Parents observe early childhood programs → Parents compare programs to their own construct → Parents choose the program that most closely matches their own construct

---

and verbally encouraged to use them. Forty-three percent of the parents reported that they did not use the checklist. Reasons included believing that the checklist was irrelevant, having their own system, misplacing the checklist, not having the time (Bogat & Gensheimer 1986, 167).

Since traditional attempts to educate parents have not produced the outcomes we have desired for all parents, what strategies might effect this change? Social-marketing techniques may be uniquely suited to this challenge. Social marketing uses commercial marketing technologies to influence behavioral change in a social context (Andreasen 1995).

In other fields, social-marketing methods have successfully influenced behavioral choices where traditional educational techniques did not. For example, conventional educational techniques failed to increase the rate of breastfeeding among low-socioeconomic teen mothers. Social marketers studied the beliefs related to teens' reluctance to breastfeed and learned that the teens believed that breastfeeding was only for wealthy mothers with good diets. The social marketers developed strategies to counter these beliefs including the use of peers in videotapes, the use

of teen mothers as spokespersons, and pictures of peers in magazines. These techniques, combined with a comprehensive social-marketing campaign, increased the rate of breast-feeding among the low-socioeconomic teen mothers (Bryant et al. 1992).

It may be that our focus on "education" has been too narrow to create the kinds of change in parents' choosing behavior that we desire.

What changes would shifting to a broader social-marketing framework entail?

First, "all strategies begin with the customer" (Andreasen 1995, 14). When faced with educational techniques that are not producing the desired behavioral change, a social marketer asks, "What is it about the consumer that I do not understand enough so that I can bring the consumer to want to do what my program recommends?" (p. 49)

"Thank you," Katie said, smiling; but moments later she "forgot" the brochure about "How to Choose Child Care" on a chair in the center director's office. Outside, this well-educated mother commented to her companion, "I don't care about their checklists. I'll know the right place for my son when I see it. These places either feel right or they don't—never mind the details."

Second, use of a "much wider array of methods than survey research" (Andreasen 1995, 97) to listen to parents' unique perspectives may help us to incorporate more "parent culture" into our definitions of best practices. NAEYC recently held proceedings to reflect on a decade of accreditation. One participant commented that "we have a responsibility to understand and know what parents' perception of quality is, and include that."

Third, use of a different arsenal of behavioral change techniques than that commonly used in traditional educational campaigns may increase our likelihood of achieving our goals.

Finally, early childhood parent-education initiatives have not necessarily been evaluated on the basis of their outcomes. In a social-marketing framework, "consumer behavior is the bottom line" (Andreasen 1995, 14). It is unrealistic to expect behavioral change to occur because "messages were distributed and received . . . and people have apparently learned some facts. Learning is only important if it leads to a desired outcome" (p. 13).

As long as loving parents choose, and are satisfied with, substandard care and education, efforts to increase the supply of quality programs must be accompanied by efforts to understand parents' needs and values and to influence their choice of quality programs.

References

Andreasen, A. R. 1995. *Marketing social change: Changing behavior to promote health, social development, and the environment.* San Francisco: Jossey-Bass.

Bogat, G. A., & L. K. Gensheimer. 1986. Discrepancies between the attitudes and actions of parents choosing day care, *Child Care Quarterly* 15 (3): 159–69.

Bredekamp, S., & C. Copple, eds. 1997. *Developmentally appropriate practice in early childhood programs.* Rev. ed. Washington, DC: NAEYC.

Bryant, C. A., J. Coreil, S. L. D'Angelo, D. S. Bailey, & M. Lazarov. 1992. A strategy for promoting breast-feeding among economically disadvantaged women and adolescents. *NAACOG Clinical Issues in Perinatal and Women's Health Nursing* 3 (4): 723–30.

Far West Laboratory. 1993. *Essential connections: Ten keys to culturally sensitive child care.* Prod., J. R. Lally, creat., P. Mangione, (Videotape and video magazine.) (Available from the Bureau of Publications, Sales Unit, California Department of Education, Sacramento, CA).

Helburn, S., & M. L. Culkin. 1995. Cost, quality, and child outcomes in child care centers: Key findings and recommendations. *Young Children* 50 (4): 40–44.

Lally, J. R., A. Griffin, E. Fenichel, M. Segal, E. Szanton, & B. Weissbourd. 1995. Development in the first three years of life. In *Caring for infants and toddlers in groups: Developmentally appropriate practice.* Washington, DC: Zero to Three, National Center for Infants, Toddlers and Families.

Mitchell, A., E. Cooperstein, & M. Larner. 1992. *Child care choices, consumer education, and low-income families.* New York: Columbia University, School of Public Health.

Rubin, L. B. 1976. *Worlds of pain: Life in the working-class family.* Scranton, PA: Harper-Collins.

Zinsser, C. 1987. *Over a barrel: Working mothers talk about child care.* (Available from the Center for Public Advocacy Research, Inc., 12 West 37th Street, New York, NY 10018.)

 Article Review Form at end of book.

How can parents plan and organize for effective family communication?

Making Time for Family

Rita Newman

Recently, a friend commented to me, "Last night, Hannah was sound asleep before I realized I didn't answer her questions about an upcoming field trip. And breakfast this morning was so busy that she left for school without my listening to her. I am determined that today I will organize myself better to make sure I have time to listen to her."

Most families today find themselves with the problem of not having enough time to spend with their children. Stephen Covey, author of *The 7 Habits of Highly Effective Families* (1997), notes that no family is free from this challenge in today's fast-paced society. Covey, a father of nine and grandfather of 27 addresses this problem in his book by sharing his own stories, mistakes and achievements, as well as those of other families. Here, I review his seven basic and universal principles. Think carefully how time plays an important factor in each habit and how you could find or take the time to have a highly effective family.

Habit 1: Be proactive and responsible for making choices.

Habit 2: Have goals in order to shape your future.

Habit 3: Put first things first—have regular family times.

Habit 4: Think win-win to have understanding and cooperation, and to benefit all.

Habit 5: Try to listen and understand another family member's thoughts and feelings.

Habit 6: Respect and value individual differences and build on strengths.

Habit 7: Establish rituals or regular family traditions.

When asked, "When will I have time to do all this?" Covey responds by noting how much time adults and children spend in front of the television and how that habit prevents communication. He says you may talk "love" and "family fun," but if you never plan time together, then your lack of organization gets in the way of your goals.

Time to Plan for Time

The most important step for working parents to take is establishing priorities. Pillsbury (1994) recommends the following ways to focus on organization and communication:

- Hang a large erase-board in the kitchen or hallway near a calendar and/or telephone

- Establish a place for notes from school and check it every day

- Make individual, personal family mailboxes in which to drop notes, phone messages, reminders, invitations, etc.

- Set aside a regular time every day to ask your children about school, tell them about your day and listen in general

- Take time while driving to talk without distractions, or just listen to music together

- Make a bedtime routine that is free from the telephone or other distractions

- Schedule family game nights

- Walk the dog together—or just walk together.

Byalick and Saslow (1993) agree that finding sufficient time is the biggest challenge when juggling work, home and family. They emphasize that the most important part of the three-career couple (work, home and family) is children. They recommend establishing special rituals (secret handshakes, pet names) and creating specific routines (who picks up whom, where do we go after school) to avoid confusion and to build confidence. Plan ahead for time together each day or on the weekend; go to a museum, visit the zoo or ride bikes. Planned routines instill a teamwork attitude in the family.

Time for Awareness of Quality Time

Gilbert (1983) advises us to think about how we can set aside a period each day to concentrate on our children, no matter how overwhelmed or tired we are. Such time does not have to involve a big event. Just sharing chores can make everyone feel closer. Larger amounts of time can be spent together on vacations and days off. Spend smaller amounts of time planning events for those vacations. Quality time can also mean doing nothing except being together quietly.

Lague's (1995) practical definition of quality time is when families are enjoying the same thing at the same time, even if it is just being together at home or in the car. Quality time can be either planned or unplanned. Working parents most likely would benefit from planned time.

Lague, a working mother herself, recommends 10 ways to put quality time into the average weekday evening, including letting an answering machine pick up calls, sending out for pizza or using microwaveable foods. These time-savers enable us to set our priorities on relaxing with our families. Spend the time working on a jigsaw puzzle, playing cards or going out for ice cream. Lague says, "In quality time, be it with the individual or with a group, it is the intensity of the attention, the understanding, the quality of the conversation, and the laughter that count, not the banality of the chore or the glamour of the adventure."

Time to Have Two-Way Communication

Communication with children requires talking, listening, smiling and paying attention (Brazelton, 1984; Ginott, 1969; Goldman, 1993; Holt, 1989). To have a real conversation you must: be there; be quiet at times; listen with your voice, face and body; ask open-ended questions; and provide a role model of storytelling (Levy, 1997).

Faber and Mazlish (1983) wrote a book for those parents who want to learn about how to talk so their kids would listen, and how to listen so that their kids would talk. They provide examples, suggestions and ideas on how to:

- listen to and understand your child's concerns
- have cooperation without nagging
- deal with emotions
- find alternatives to punishment
- help your child attain a positive self image

They focus on the importance of communication and bring out new principles and skills to put into practice, as well as new patterns to learn and old patterns to unlearn.

Remember that parents do make a difference in their child's academic achievement. Taking time to listen to your child's conversation about school and to praise their achievements will positively affect their own attitudes toward school (Bernard, 1997).

Time for Family Moments

Some of the most treasured times for children might last only a few minutes. O'Neal (1995) offers 105 ways to make the most out of busy days, such as writing a message on a mirror with shaving cream and tucking a "Good luck on your test!" note into a lunchbox or bookbag. The goal is to seize moments during busy days to celebrate and enjoy being together. The Bennetts (1994) offer 365 ways to reclaim the family dinner hour as a time to spend together. They provide numerous conversational topics.

Your library or bookstore can be a wonderful place to spend time together. Browsing through the shelves together and consulting one another about a choice can lead to great discussions. There are many resources that provide great ideas for other things to do together as a family (see References and Resources).

Time to Reflect

When I retired last year, after 27 years in public education as a working mother with three sons, my youngest son (now 40) got up during the program and read the following: "Love is a special way of feeling. . . . It is the good way we feel when we talk to someone and they want to listen and don't tell us to go away and be quiet" (Anglund, 1988). He told me later that we had first read that book when he was 5 and that it said everything about the times we spent together. I hope you will take the time to realize how important the time you spend with your children is and then take the time to explore new ways to spend precious minutes or hours with them.

References and Resources

Anglund, J. W. (1988). *Love is a special way of feeling.* New York: Harcourt Brace & Co.

Bennett, S., & Bennett, R. (1994). *Table talk!* Holbrook, MA: Bob Adams, Inc.

Berg, E. (1992). *Family traditions: Celebrations for holidays and every day.* New York: Reader's Digest Association.

Bernard, M. E. (1997). *You can do it!* New York: Warner Books.

Brazelson, T. B. (1984). *To listen to a child.* New York: Addison-Wesley.

Bravo, E. (1995). *The job/family challenge.* New York: John Wiley & Sons, Inc.

Byalick, M., & Saslow, L. (1993). *The three career couple . . . her job, his job and their job together—mastering the fine art of juggling work, home and family.* Princeton, NJ: Peterson's.

Chaback, E., & Fortunato, P. (1981). *The official kids' survival kit. . . how to do things on your own.* Boston: Little, Brown & Co.

Covey, S. R. (1997). *The 7 habits of highly effective families.* New York: Golden Books.

DeFrancis, B. (1994). *The parents' resource almanac.* Holbrook, MA: Bob Adams, Inc.

Faber, A., & Mazlish, E. (1983). *How to ask so kids will listen & listen so kids will talk.* New York: Avon Books.

Gilbert, S. (1983). *By yourself.* New York: Lothrop, Lee & Shepard Books.

Ginott, H. G. (1969). *Between parent & teenager.* New York: Avon Books.

Goldman, K. W. (1993). *My mother worked and I turned out OK.* New York: Villard Books.

Holt, H. J. (1989). *Learning all the time.* New York: Addison-Wesley.

Kennedy, M. (1994). *100 things you can do to keep your family together.* Princeton, NJ: Peterson's.

Kleeberg, I. C. (1985). *Latch-key kid.* New York: Franklin Watts.

Kyte, K. S. (1983). *In charge —a complete handbook for kids with working parents.* New York: Alfred A. Knopf.

Lague, L. (1995). *The working mom's book of hints, tips, and everday wisdom.* Princeton, NJ: Peterson's.

Levy, C. W. (1997, November 1). A penny for your thoughts. *Woman's Day, 72,* 78.

Lott, L., & Intner, R. (1995). *The family that works together.* Rocklin, CA: Prima Publishing.

Matthews, S., & Nikuradse, T. (1993). *Dear dad, thank you for being mine.* New York: Bantam Books.

O'Neal, D. T. (1955). *Family fun—105 easy ways.* Nashville, TN: Dimensions for Living.

Peters, J. K. (1997). *When mothers work.* Reading, MA: Addison Wesley.

Pillsbury, L. G. (1994). *Survival tips for working moms: 297 real tips from real moms.* Los Angeles: Perspective Publishing.

Article Review Form at end of book.

What parental behaviors contribute to appropriate discipline of children?

Say What You Mean. . .

. . .and mean what you say. Discipline isn't merely a way to get your child to toe the line—it's a means of instilling good values.

David Markus

David Markus, a former editor-in-chief of Parenting, is the editorial director of the online service Thrive@Healthy Living (http://www.thriveonline.com, or the keyword "Thrive" on AOL.

There may be more important challenges for parents than how to discipline their kids, but I can't think of many. Having helped raise one child to the brink of adolescence and watching as the other now steps into that tricky world, I've always believed that discipline should be placed high atop a parent's priority list. And not just because your child could grow up to be a Visigoth if you don't, but because knowing how to conduct himself appropriately with family, with friends, and perhaps most important, with people he hardly knows is an indispensible ticket to success in a civilized world.

That said, I have a confession to make. I have never been terribly keen on discipline. Not as a kid, not as an adult, not as a parent, not even as the editor-in-chief of this magazine several years ago, when,

as now, discipline was what readers wanted to hear about most. My reticence was personal, dating from the guilt-suffused days of my occasionally wayward youth, when the D-word would boom from the mouths of teachers, priests, and football coaches. By its very definition—control obtained by enforcing compliance or obedience—the idea of discipline is unnerving and more than a little intimidating.

Control, compliance, obedience, enforcement? Those concepts are a hard sell to kids, let alone toddlers. Nevertheless, to the parents of a 14-month-old trying to stand tall in the struggle against spoon-to-wall food flinging, a little obedience on their child's part certainly has its appeal. And therein lies the problem: We don't want to rein in our children's free spirit. Neither do we want our little loved ones to run roughshod over us on their way to the cliffs of perpetual misconduct. How, then, to toe the thin gray line between capitulation and constraint? The simplest and smartest strategy, in my view, is to redefine your objectives.

Better a Teacher Than a Cop

What if, in the noble effort to teach our children how best to behave, a child's obedience becomes not the goal but the by-product? What if we approach discipline as an ongoing effort to build good values in our children rather than as a campaign of psychological containment? What if instead of acting like cops for 18 years, we become, well, evangelists to our kids? Unflappable proponents of the principles we hold dear, whose words stem from our convictions and whose disciplinary actions are the logical extensions of our words.

I know, I know. This sounds like hot air from a theorist high in his ivory tower—especially when you're deep in the trenches of chronic noncompliance à la "No, I won't give you the scissors; it's my laser sword!" But the truth is, good discipline is the result of learning good values. After all, the word *discipline*, like *disciple*, comes from the Latin *disciplus*, meaning one who learns.

"Say What You Mean . . ." by David Markus and "Smart Discipline" by Valerie Fahey from PARENTING Magazine, May 1997. Reprinted by permission of Parenting Magazine, a division of Time Publishing Ventures.

Of course, you shouldn't expect the kind of quick, decisive results that a cop gets when he foils a purse snatcher. Learning values requires repeated lessons. Few of us—adults or kids—absorb new ideas right off the bat.

The cop in us quite naturally pulls her hair out when young Genghis lofts his SpaghettiOs skyward. But the teacher is more patient. She doesn't expect the little fella to immediately grasp that noodles are meant to go in his belly, not all over Mom's hornrims. And so, when she tells her son that his favorite spoon is drawer-bound unless he stops throwing his food, and then, for a few minutes, he actually desists, she experiences a small victory.

All About Expectations

In one very important way, disciplining kids is an expectations game—managing our own, that is. If you're the hapless Officer Krupke forever endeavoring to keep the Jets and Sharks at bay, your expectations and definitions of success may set you up for failure and frustration. Dramatic results don't come quickly; whining is not eliminated in one or even a dozen swift surgical strikes. So don't be discouraged: Even when it looks like she's thumbing her nose, she's learning.

In fact, parents' unrealistic expectations are often at the root of discipline battles. If, for instance, Mom expects her three-year-old to make her own bed every day, she's going to be disappointed, her child will be frustrated, and the bed will remain a mess. If, on the other hand, Mom does the bulk of the work and merely asks her child to fluff the pillow, the results will be more satisfying for everybody: The child will begin to pick up the message that making the bed is important, and before long, she'll want to do it herself. If you hang tough and hang patient, the larger victories will come. Sooner or later, your child will stun you, appearing one school-day morning unbidden at your door, fully dressed and ready to rock. Trust me.

Consistency Is King

Hang tough, hang patient, and perhaps most crucial of all, hang consistent. At some indefinably peculiar age—it could be five or seven or nine—most children decide that it's their solemn duty to test every request a parent makes, from turning off the TV to getting to bed on time. Before you start imploring the heavens with *why me's*, it's worth asking yourself if this clash of wills is due to something other than your child's breathtaking pigheadedness. Could it be, perhaps, that you have not been as clear and consistent as you might have been?

Consistency comes down to this: saying what you mean, and meaning what you say. If you're in the park and you tell your child that it's time to head home for dinner and that he has five more minutes to play, then you really do have to leave in five minutes. Not six. Not ten. And if he fusses, it may require picking him up and carrying him to the car. By giving in to his pleas for one more trip down the slide, you'll give him the message that there are no hard-and-fast limits, that the line you've drawn in the sandbox is constantly shifting.

Picking Your Battles

But even consistency has a flip side. Standing firm on a meaningless request does nothing more than set you up for failure. When you insist that your child eat the last pea on her plate, is it really important to you that she do it, or are you just flexing your muscles? In the end, making an unnecessary request only sets you up to be inconsistent.

Avoid the Hot Zones

These tussles with your child are not epic contests between good and evil. There is no shame in occasionally refusing to take the field. You can reduce the need for discipline by anticipating (and avoiding) situations that you know will call for action. Why take your child grocery shopping, knowing you'll have to wheel her down the candy aisle just before her appointed snack time?

Make it a point to know your child's meltdown moments. They usually come like clockwork: when leaving the house in the morning, at naptime, when you come home from work, at bedtime. Likewise, certain places— Toys "R" Us, fast-food joints—are notorious hot spots. Steer clear of them whenever you can.

Watch Your Language

Another trap well worth avoiding is the desire to crank up the volume. You don't need to shout to get your message across, although sometimes you're going to want to. Fight the urge, because if you go that route, chances are your child will, too. And who needs a war of the decibels every time the two of you have a difference of opinion? Put the energy into choosing your words wisely. Try to remove any ambiguities. With younger children, especially, use short, to-the-point sentences. A preschooler is much more apt to respond to "Dinner's ready. Time

Smart Discipline: Ten Top Childrearing Experts Offer Their Best Tips

By Valerie Fahey

Adele Faber

Educator, author of *How to Talk So Kids Will Listen*, on the right way to praise

There's helpful and unhelpful praise. Unhelpful praise evaluates a child. For example, when you say, "You're so bright," the child may doubt you and say to herself, "I'm not that smart. I nearly failed my test." Children reject that type of praise because it's judgmental.

Helpful praise describes what a child has done, rather than evaluating her. You might say, "I see you put your Legos away and your dirty clothes are in the hamper. It's a pleasure to look at this room." Now the child can say to herself, "I can take a messy room and turn it into order."

When you describe what she's done, you give her a verbal snapshot of her own abilities. She will have it forever, and she can pull it out and look at it whenever she needs to. Now, that's power.

David Elkind

Psychologist, author of *Ties That Stress*, on setting limits

Setting secure limits means saying "no" and meaning it, and consistently following through. In other words, use "no" only when you mean "absolutely not." The message for the child is, "Don't bother to throw a tantrum because this is a limit and nothing you can do will shift it." You set the limits and define the consequences for breaking those rules.

Ideally, we start setting limits when our children are babies; this prepares them to set their own in adolescence. Kids have to test the limits. How else can they discover what those limits are? But if a child does it constantly, he's discovered that limits are elastic, or inconsistent, so it's worth his while to keep probing.

Penelope Leach

Child psychologist, author of *Your Baby and Child*, on consistency

Be consistent in your principles. It's very hard to teach a child to behave it you yourself don't know how to behave. You must be a good role model. If you preach tolerance but make racist remarks, for instance, your child learns to do as you do and not as you say.

This is the only kind of consistency that matters. Your child is not a circus animal, taught to respond to a specific signal with a particular trick. He is a human being, taught to respond as best he can to a vast range of signals.

Of course, he will also accept the fact that circumstances alter the situation. For example, if it has rained for a week straight, then go ahead and let him bounce on the cushions, but just for today.

Dr. T. Berry Brazelton

Pediatrician, author of *Touchpoints*, on teaching a child to respect others

Discipline means teaching, not punishment. And respect for others comes from teaching a child values and social manners. The rules of social discourse don't come naturally to a child—they must be taught or modeled. You might start by explaining the concept of borrowing and returning a toy by saying, "You need to ask whether you can play with her truck. If she say no, that's it. If she says yes, you must return it when you're finished." In this way, you're teaching a child respect for others' things, demonstrating the manners he needs for asking, and helping him delay gratification.

Another way to do this is by modeling appropriate behavior. For example, if you accidentally jostle someone in the grocery store and say, "Excuse me," your child will learn good behavior by imitating you.

Dr. Perri Klass

Parenting contributing editor, pediatrician, on power struggles

Being a parent is equal parts creative compromise and surrender. It's important to ask yourself, is this power struggle something that I need to win so that my child will understand who's the boss? Or is it a luxury item? Is it really a problem if she wears one blue sock and one green sock?

Some things are completely unnegotiable: Certainly a child has to sit in the car seat and wear a coat when it's cold outside. But there are going to be times when your child cares about the issue at hand more than you do. Then ask yourself, Is this actually that important? If it's not harmful to life or limb, then forget it.

Valerie Fahey is a *Parenting* senior research associate.

to wash your hands," than to "Look how dirty your hands are! We can't sit down to dinner until they're clean." Better still are if/then propositions. For instance, with phrasing like "If you pick up your toys, then we'll eat," You give a child a sense of cause and effect, of how his behavior fits into the big picture.

Make It a Mantra

Whatever your verbal gymnastic of choice, few techniques can top good old-fahioned repetition. Many years ago, my little boy had trouble finding the toilet bowl when he peed. He was a little late coming out of diapers, so it was with great personal pride and celebration that he finally sauntered

Dr. Benjamin Spock

Parenting contributing editor, author of *Baby and Child Care*, on taming a tantrum

Giving in to a tantrum will only succeed, finally, in frightening your child. It gives her too much power, power that she really doesn't want or know what to do with. But tantrums do need to be dealt with. They are a child's first attempts—albeit primitive ones— at expressing and gaining control over her anger.

To calm a child, it's best to put yourself in her shoes. And by being empathetic, you'll react less from your own frustrations and be more responsive to your child. Along with that, you can hold her very tightly and say reassuring things while at the same time explaining that she can't behave this way. If all else fails, try ignoring the tantrum, which often tends to diffuse it.

Dr. Marianne Nelfert

Parenting contributing editor, author of *Dr. Mom's Parenting Guide*, on spanking

It's not OK to strike your wife or punch a stranger, so it's incongruous that it's OK to hit children. And it's not very useful to teach a child how to handle difficult feelings if you can't handle your own.

If you spank a child, you run the risk of losing control and injuring him. You're also teaching him that might makes right, that it's OK for bigger, stronger people to use force or intimidation to get their way.

What's more, spanking provides no positive information about moral behavior. It's not a useful model, because children can't and shouldn't use it themselves. For example, they're not supposed to hit a playmate. There are so many other disciplinary options, that by *not* spanking, you haven't lost anything.

Peter Williamson

Psychologist, on picking your battles

Fight the battles you can win, the ones where you control the outcome. Whenever you're in a position where you can walk away from a fight, you've won. If your child refuses to eat dinner tonight, leave her be. She'll eat tomorrow.

Parents can ignore unimportant things such as bad moods and sulky faces, and save the heavy artillery for things that really matter. If you find yourself trying to bribe a child to behave, you've lost. If you have a plan, your child won't be able to hold you over a barrel. For example, to avoid giving in to a child who's screaming for Sugar Pops in the grocery story, try shopping just after she's eaten, and establish rules about what you'll buy for her before you go.

Burton White

Psychologist, author of *Raising a Happy, Unspoiled Child*, on how not to spoil your child

Raising an unspoiled child means being nurturing without overindulging. During the first months of a baby's life, parents have to respond quickly and compassionately to the frequent cries of their child, to relieve her discomfort and to help build a healthy emotional foundation. But as she grows, if she gains attention every time she wants it, she will come to believe the world revolves around her.

What most parents don't realize is that it's fairly easy to be both loving and firm. A child does have a limited right to insist on getting her way or to repeat something to make sure she was understood. But then a parent needs to say, "No, we're not reading *Curious George* again. It's bedtime." If you stand firm, you'll usually find that your child is better behaved and happier, too.

Dr. William Sears

Pediatrician, author of *The Discipline Book*, on saying "no"

The word "no" can easily become a knee-jerk response and lose its impact. Don't say it when another expression will do. For instance, a simple "Uh-oh!" or "Wait!" often makes the point with more precision.

When you do say "no," do it with conviction. Vetoing some whims and steering a child away from danger are essential for his development and safety.

A child who's learned to accept a "no" from you will soon learn to say "no" to himself— the foundation of a healthy, balanced personality.

---

up to the "grown-up potty" and rather manfully took care of business. For this and other reasons having to do mostly with bone-deep fatigue, his mother and I were a little too slow to step in when he began irrigating the general environs of the toilet bowl instead of the bowl itself. Like a lot of boys, young and old, he enjoyed experimenting with his trajectory.

Scoldings and attempts at dissuasion had no effect. He continued to carry on like a drunken fireman—until we shifted tactics and in a moment of inspiration adopted a mantra. "Pee in a line, everything's fine," we told him. "Pee on the floor, clean up more." Over and over we told him this. And over and over we insisted that he take up his "special" towel and clean up his mess. In time— weeks, to be honest—he tightened up his aim. The mantra had become both the rule and the consequence for breaking it.

The Power of Your Voice

By holding and touching your baby, and by sharing the sound of your voice with him, you build the connection, trust, and comfort that are the underpinnings for your role as evangelist and teacher. Your voice, after all, will be the future vehicle of your lessons. Your voice will set limits: "The cars in the street can hurt you. Don't go near them." It will strike bargains: "Come off the slide now and we'll have time to watch a video." And, of course, your voice will deliver the praise and inaugurate the hugs of approval that are the most effective disciplinary tools of all.

Don't Get Physical

Using your voice is important for another reason: It is the alternative to hitting. And hitting is the cheap narcotic of discipline—the quick fix that fixes nothing and opens the door to far more hurtful behavior.

I hit my son twice. It's not something I'm proud of. The first time was an openhanded swat to the behind after he ran into the street and the path of an oncoming car. The second, a spank to the hindquarters as he fled the scene of a physical altercation with his sister. No welts or bruises or even pain to speak of.

But I was livid, not in control, and the fright I instilled in him overwhelmed any sense he had of what he'd done wrong. Afterward, he remembered my anger, not his transgression. You can't teach with fear, you can only temporarily impose your will.

A Window of Opportunity

Make no mistake: Disciplining is sticky business. You will screw up. You will lose your cool. You will obsess. At times, you may want to give up, convinced that yours is the ultimate untamable child.

From where I stand now, as I face the bewildering challenge of bringing discipline to the life of an adolescent, one particular fact jumps out at me in stark relief. The task is no longer simply to pass along my values—that I've done, for better or worse. Now I need to appeal to *her* better judgment. She will make her own choices, and I can only hope that she will opt for the principles she holds dear.

Childhood passes quickly, too darn quickly for my taste. Best not to waste your time; your window of opportunity is narrower than you think. Teach early, and teach often. Stick to the high road. And don't forget the hugs— everyone needs them.

 Article Review Form at end of book.

How can a teacher help young children successfully change from one activity to another?

Creative Strategies in Ernie's Early Childhood Classroom

Karen L. Bauer and Marilyn A. Sheerer with Ernest Dettore Jr.

Karen L. Bauer, Ed.D., is a professor and the coordinator of early childhood education at Edinboro University in Edinboro, Pennsylvania. Karen has held numerous workshops for child care professionals and is an NAEYC accreditation validator for child care programs.

Marilyn A. Sheerer, Ph.D., is the chair of the Department of Elementary and Middle Grades Education at East Carolina University in Greenville, North Carolina. Marilyn has held numerous leadership positions in early childhood and elementary education. She writes in the areas of supervision and professional development and is a consulting editor for Young Children.

Ernest Dettore Jr., Ed.D., is an assistant professor of early childhood education and a model instructor in the Early Learning Lab of Miller Research Learning Center in Edinboro, Pennsylvania. Ernie has owned and operated with his wife a family care home and child care center, and he serves as a state trainer to child care professionals.

Editor's note: An observational study conducted in this laboratory preschool program chronicles a teacher's (one of the authors) interactional skills with young children over a four-month period. The analysis focuses on particular transition periods and self-selected activity times. The teacher's philosophy, respect for children's ideas, and warm sense of humor emerge as the basis of these interactions. In various ways the teacher and classroom exemplify many of the guidance techniques promoted by NAEYC for many decades and recently encouraged again as part of developmentally appropriate practice (Bredekamp & Copple 1997).

The three-to five-year-olds in the Early Learning Lab are vying for a position in line to be the crane that picks up the blocks and loads them into a box.

"Over here, Ernie. I need to get this long one!" yells Ian, being the crane, as Ernie, the teacher "operating" the crane, guides the four-year-old's legs toward a particular corner of the room.

"I'm next," calls Hillary. "I'm picking up all those little ones!"

"While these cranes are working, how can we pick up the Legos?" asks Ernie.

"I know, I know," offers Tyler excitedly. "Let's use my big scooper!"

Tyler begins using a cardboard lid to dig into the pile of Legos and return them to their container. He makes a motor noise to add legitimacy to his endeavor.

"Alex, I want you to show us how we can clean this up. . . . Oh, he's going to use his glow gun to help him. Hm . . . m . . . m, nice invention, Alex."

Ernie responds to children's needs. He believes that guiding children's behavior is situational, and he avoids preconceived approaches.

"Children have valid reasons for their behavior," Ernie believes.

"We may not agree with or approve of the behavior, but our job is to discover why a behavior occurred and help the child find an appropriate way to behave."

Cleanup Time

Adults recognize that through cleaning up, children learn classification, seriation, organizational skills, respect for their environment, and a sense of responsibility. Adults therefore incorporate clean-up as an integral part of play or activities. Ernie uses this approach in his classroom. However, he occasionally uses cleanup time to engage children in unique play episodes or to encourage an uncooperative child to comply.

"Rigidity can increase the conflicts that arise between children and teachers." says Ernie. Instead of becoming upset when cleanup time is not going well, he takes a different tack. He focuses on the issue at hand and personalizes his responses to the children and the situation. His approach incorporates flexibility and spontaneity.

Ernie believes the most important strategy for young children is to create their own solutions. They feel empowered when accomplishing a task on their own; the experience increases self-confidence and a sense of identity.

The idea of children becoming "human cranes" evolved in response to an uncooperative child during cleanup time. Ernie recounts the story:

When I reminded Kevin that he was supposed to help clean up, he responded with "I don't feel like cleaning up." Since this wasn't typical of Kevin, I decided to try to change his mood. I said, "Well, if you won't pick up the blocks, I'm going to have to turn you into the human crane." He looked puzzled. I picked him up at the waist and gently turned him upside down. Then I told him to use his hands to pick up the blocks. I

began to make engine sound effects to maintain interest. Kevin happily put the blocks away, a confrontation was avoided, and the other children wanted to try being the crane.

Ernie employs the human crane infrequently but successfully. When he's asked why he chose to use the crane with Kevin, Ernie replies, "I sensed that Kevin needed some support and guidance and that some sort of physical intervention would be necessary. I chose to approach the situation with a sense of humor. It worked like a charm. The human crane is not a technique I would want to use all the time, but, on the occasions when I do, it works."

Creating Various Cleanup Devices

Some days the children do an incomplete cleanup job. Ernie may make a game of cleaning up the room by asking the children to each find five items that need to be put away or five pieces of paper on the floor to throw away. Not a particularly unique approach, but Ernie describes how the "human comb" grew out of such a day.

I explained the phrases "comb the area" and "go over with a fine-tooth comb." Then I instructed the children to line up side-by-side and on all fours. I told them that they were human combs and had to pick up everything in their paths and put it all away. The children were very cooperative, the room looked great, and, in addition, the children expanded their language skills.

One activity center in Ernie's preschool is a "clipping and cut-

ting service." Here the children design collages, signs, books, invitations, and lists, among other things. Supplies in the center include magazines, catalogs, wallpaper samples, construction paper, glue, tape, scissors, string, and a paper punch. A favorite activity is using the paper punch, a difficult but intriguing task for three- and four-year-olds, It's also a very messy activity.

Ernie invented the "dot picker-upper" after a big day of hole punching. When it was time to clean up, the children struggle to get the paper dots off the floor. Ernie places masking tape on the ends of small unit blocks and demonstrates how to operate the new invention. Children scurry to use the dot-picker-upper. When they discover that the invention picks up more than one dot at a time, Ernie describes,

The challenge became how many dots could be picked up at once. You could hear children calling out numbers for several minutes until all the dots were gone. In fact, the children were disappointed when there were no more dots to be found. They loved the process.

The "home for lost toys" was spawned after another not-so-great cleanup effort. As children are sometimes wont to do, toys and games are mixed together or placed in wrong bins during cleanup. "This behavior is characteristic of young children and not an effort to avoid work," says Ernie.

Rather than reprimanding the children or becoming angry, Ernie decides to approach the problem in a creative way. He sorts through the toys to collect all the misplaced items and places them in a line. Next, he tells the children how he had heard all the toys crying when he came into the classroom that morning. "I really exaggerated by picking up a block and pretending it was crying," says Ernie.

"Oh, I really miss my block family," Ernie whimpers. Sympathetic children willingly sort all the items into their proper containers.

Ernie believes that it's important to take into consideration the thinking of young children. It's his philosophy that,

You can capitalize on it to find ways to make tasks enjoyable. For example, I adapted one of Aesop's Fables, "The Greedy Dog," to encourage children to keep the room tidy. Our greedy dog puppet is the epitome of bad manners. If the room is unusually messy, I bring on the puppet and say something like, "Oo-ooo, I love messy rooms. Let's leave it like this." Of course, the children want to do the opposite, and they respond by hurriedly straightening up. They enjoy telling the puppet how *they* are going to make the room look nice. It works every time.

Children in Ernie's room also have learned how to operate the "chair bulldozer," a combination wrecker and organizer. Children building with blocks can help in the demolition and cleanup. The chair bulldozer is a preschool chair turned upside down, and the operator pushes on the back legs of the chair and scoops the blocks into a pile. Another crew stacks the blocks back on the shelves. Children take turns being the bulldozer operator.

We might ask, wouldn't it be easier just to require the children to pick up the blocks? Ernie responds, "Not necessarily. Children are generally quite willing to clean up. It's on those occasional times when things aren't going smoothly that I find a different approach."

Ernie believes that the teacher needs to respond to the situation. However, how the teacher responds determines whether there will be a confrontation. He tries to avoid pitting his will against a child's as much as possible. "That's not to say that I am never directive," says Ernie. "Sometimes it's necessary to be directive."

One morning the children just didn't clean up after being asked. I called a meeting and said, "I saw people running. I saw people throwing toys. I saw people shouting." Then I gave clear, concise directions to each child. I focused on something small that could easily be accomplished. "Your job is to put the playdough away," I said, and I doled out jobs to each child and selected one child as the model. I praised how well Alex had followed through with his task and asked the other children to do the same.

Ernie's goal is to help the children successfully complete what is asked of them. Sometimes he finds it necessary simply to tell them what needs to be done, but he has faith that children will cooperate. Ernie trusts that when he deals with the situation by focusing on the children's needs, things will turn out well.

Transitions

Cleanup time is only one transition that children are expected to make. Other transitions, while kept to a minimum, also are necessary.

"As teachers, we want to encourage children to concentrate on their activities and become engrossed in their projects," says Ernie. He believes that frequent transitions detract from this concentration. Inevitably, however, we must address transitions from one activity or area to another.

How teachers organize transitions will influence the momentum in a classroom and the success of an activity. Ernie's view is that establishing a consistent routine in which adult expectations match children's ability is vital.

Transitions require time. Young children should not be hurried nor should they be made to wait for extended periods of time. In some programs where children must share facilities such as the gym or computer room, one group may need to wait for a previous group of children to exit. This potentially restless time challenges Ernie. He uses creative planning to eliminate misbehavior.

"Let's fool our computer teacher by pretending we're a still-life painting on the wall," Ernie suggests to the children. "I'll tell her you aren't here today, so I brought down this picture. But, when the teacher comes out, you'll come alive and surprise her." Silent children were the result of this tactic.

Making Connections for Transition

Teachers should feel free to employ their own creativity to enhance many routine transitions. Making a connection between a story and a transition is extremely effective. Children in Ernie's room were once "airlifted" to various areas of the classroom.

The class had just listened to the storybook *The Cow Who Became Famous*. In this story the cow is tied to the wings of a plane and transported across the country. Ernie employs this idea when the children are to choose where in the classroom they want to work. He picks up a child, has her spread her arms like airplane wings, and flies her to the selected area. As Ernie guides the child, he asks questions such as, "How are you going to keep from crashing?"

The reading of *Mouse Paint* was to be followed by activities in the art center. To facilitate the movement, Ernie whispers to the children, "Pretend to paint yourselves white like the mice in the story." Once the children finish "painting" themselves, Ernie continues, "Let's see how Ashley tiptoes past the cat. See how quiet she is. Be careful, Ashley. Don't step on the cat's tail."

As Ernie interacts with the children, he asks them silly questions. "Travis, can you get to the art center safely? Would it be a good idea for you to use the cat's tail as a paintbrush?" Such questions amuse the children but actually require their critical thinking.

"World Famous People Pancakes" was a hit with the children as well. After reading the book *Pancakes,* children are to cook their own. Ernie creates a safe and deliberate strategy. He pretends to make people into pancakes, while another adult helps children cook. Chanting the recipe, Ernie adds plastic milk, eggs, and butter. He calls one child at a time by name to get into the batter. Next, he stirs the batter with a plastic spoon and pours out the people pancake. He instructs each child to slowly roll over to the cooking center. As the activity continues, the children join in chanting the recipe and stirring the batter. Double batches are made as the children's attention dwindles.

Children should be given choices and encouraged to help during transition times. Ernie queries, "Do you want to walk on eggshells or creep like a cat? Would you like to walk on thin ice or sneak past the guard?" "Such choices provide children with an opportunity to make decisions while abiding by the classroom rules," Ernie points out.

Effective transitions can be enhanced by voice changes. Ernie uses cartoon voices or animal voices. Children may select which voice they want him to imitate. Talking softly is another way to get children to listen and lower their own voices. Ernie pretends he is losing his voice: "I can't talk very loud because I'm losing my voice. You'll have to help me by listening quietly while I whisper your names."

Since the goal during transition is to help children successfully change from one activity to another, any creative approach can be considered. A limitless number of ways makes the process fun and enjoyable for children and teachers.

Self-Control

Helping children learn to control their own behavior is an integral part of life in the Early Learning Lab. Feelings are still new to three- and four-year-olds. They need help in learning how to deal with them. The ultimate goal is for children to develop inner control.

"I try to be nonjudgmental and show plenty of patience," Ernie explains. He consistently demonstrates developmentally appropriate practices in his daily interactions with children.

When the children break the rules, Ernie asks questions but doesn't interrogate. "The questions," he says, "are my attempt in understanding what happened. I try to get the children to state the problem. I reflect what they say and help them to verbalize their feelings." Ernie frequently begins by saying "I was wondering. . ." or "I noticed. . . ." These phrases are neutral and avoid putting children on the defensive.

It is common to see Ernie with his arm around a child's shoulder. He gets down to the child's level, makes eye contact, and talks. His tone is calm. His body language communicates concern.

"It's important for the adult to remain objective instead of emotional," he explains. "Children need to know the adult is in control. I want children to respond to their own behaviors. My role is to devise ways to help children monitor their behavior."

Developing Some Control Approaches

Ernie has some unique approaches for helping children develop self-control. Noting that young children are active and often become so excited that their voices or the activity gets too high, he does not try to shout instructions over the noise, which seems only to escalate the situation. Teachers need to find more effective ways to enable children to lower their own voices and control their own bodies.

The "control meter" devised by Ernie provides a direct physical means for children to monitor their bodies. As he describes it, "When a child begins to run around inappropriately or reaches a frustration level and begins to scream, I calmly ask him to put his hand over his heart to check his control meter. I point out that a wildly beating heart is a sign of being out of control."

Ernie never humiliates children, nor does he ever tell them they are bad. His control meter serves to temporarily extinguish an undesirable behavior and helps the child regain control.

What he ultimately wants is for the child to become responsible for regaining control.

Playing on the preoperational thought processes of preschoolers, Ernie employs a "volume control button" as another way to change behavior. "I designed this strategy," he says, "to also help children gain self-control. I developed the notion of children having volume control buttons like TVs, tape recorders, and radios." At the teacher's suggestion, the volume control button helps children lower their voices. Ernie simply mentions to the child that her voice is loud and ask her to use the volume control button to lower it.

Occasionally, Ernie asks if he may lower the volume control button. Once when he attempted to lower the button for a child without asking, the child said, "You turned it the wrong way." "I had to turn the button the opposite way," Ernie recalls.

Would you be upset with that response? Some teachers would view that behavior as inappropriate. It is important to respect a child's attempt to maintain autonomy.

"This child was willing to lower his voice," Ernie points out, "but I broke the ground rules. I didn't ask if I could lower the control button. After I moved the button the opposite way, the child grinned and lowered his voice to an acceptable volume. That was what I wanted, and the child complied."

In an attempt to stop a distressed child's whining, the "whine box" emerged. Ernie asks a child if she knew she was whining and then suggests that together they put her whiny voice in the whine box and place it in the refrigerator.

"This idea is so ridiculous that the child laughs and goes along with it," Ernie relates. "When the whining returns, we go to check the box for leaks." When someone starts to whine in Ernie's classroom now, a child in the room suggests the whine box.

Adapted from *The Wizard of Oz*, the "oil can" is effective in cheering up sad or grouchy children. Ernie notes that a child looks unhappy, and he comments that her "smile elevator" lines must be stuck. The teacher or another empathetic child then pretends to click oil into the smile lines to loosen them up.

Ernie describes what happens: "Children almost always respond by smiling. Then they begin to frown-smile-frown to perpetuate the game. Usually others who aren't even grumpy ask to play. The result is lots of smiling faces."

Sometimes Ernie has to get out the "grump remover." This is an imaginary spray that gets rid of grump. Ernie may remark to a grumpy child that "it's time to remove that miserable grump." If he sees the child responding to this bait, he then sprays grump remover all over the child's body. If this doesn't totally work, but the child appears to want to be cheered up, Ernie gets out the industrial-strength grump remover and resprays the child.

Pretend Playing Without Aggression

Some of the children in Ernie's preschool go to child care programs in the afternoon. One day a little boy said solemnly, "Ernie, I'm going to tell Susan that you let us play Mutant Ninja Turtles." "Why?" Ernie asks. "Aren't you allowed to play 'Turtles'?" "No," the child replies, "because they use violent aggressive behavior." "Oh, but you weren't using violent aggressive behavior. What were your turtles doing?" The child thinks a moment, then says, "They were using tools."

Ernie does not forbid children to pretend to play Mutant Ninja Turtles or Power Rangers or other superheroes, but he also does not permit them to use aggression. "Children are intrigued with these figures and it's difficult to eliminate them," points out Ernie. He says, "I take the best out of them and extend the play; I use them to help children learn."

Recently an observer in the Early Learning Lab saw two boys lying under a table painting on paper that was taped to the underside of the table. "I'm Michelangelo," explains the one child. "He painted on ceilings a long time ago." "Yeah," replies the second child, "we saw some pictures of him painting in a book."

Ernie takes the children's interest in superheroes and redirects it in an appropriate way. He says, "It is easier to move children beyond those aggressive play behaviors by redirecting them. If you forbid the play, then it emerges when you aren't watching or children engage in the play elsewhere. I believe that at least I have extended their knowledge and given them another theme to use during play."

Conclusion

Our study in the Early Learning Lab yielded wonderfully rich examples of management strategies used by one early childhood teacher. The resultant videotapes show a classroom with high activity and movement, smiles and laughter, and a teacher interacting constantly with the children. These interactions are based on a high level of trust on both sides. Ernie trusts that children will be positive and cooperative, and the children trust that Ernie will be there with them, assisting them in making decisions and trying new things.

Overall, our naturalistic study in this early childhood setting uncovered the variety and complexity of approaches used by one very good teacher to create a context in which children feel empowered and important. Ernie's knowledge of child development emerges as the basis for making appropriate decisions and guiding children's growth. We believe a solid understanding of children's development is vital to all successful early childhood educators; it is the foundation from which developmentally appropriate practices emerge.

Reference

Bredekamp, S., & C. Copple, eds. 1997. *Developmentally appropriate practice in early childhood programs.* Rev. ed. Washington, DC: NAEYC.

 Article Review Form at end of book.

What key features did Daniel Olweus's program include to reduce bullying in schools?

Bullying in School

It doesn't have to happen

Being bullied in school is not "part of growing up" or just a "rite of passage." Some children who endure bullying never get over the fear and the humiliation, according to Mr. Barone. By working together, schools and parents can make going to school an experience that students will enjoy, not dread.

Frank J. Barone

Frank J. Barone is the principal of Amsterdam (N.Y.) High School.

Almost everybody can tell a story or two about having once been victimized in school by a bully. Many people can discuss in detail the incidents surrounding the experience and can even remember the name of the bully and the grade level at which the trauma occurred. Few of us go through all the years of schooling unscathed. And while most of us get over the fear and the humiliation, some do not.

Nathan Feris, a seventh-grader at DeKalb High School in DeKalb, Missouri, decided that enduring four years of taunting by other children, who called him "chubby" and "walking dictionary," was more than enough. On 2 March 1987 Feris brought a gun to school and fatally shot another student before turning the gun on himself in class. Classmates said that nobody really had anything against Nathan. "He was just someone to pick on." They said.[1]

A set of parents in Japan have filed a 22-million-yen damage suit against the Tokyo metropolitan government and the parents of two alleged bullies, claiming that their 13-year-old son's suicide was caused by *ijimi* (bullying). The parents also claim that the school principal and several teachers not only failed to intervene to stop the harassment, but actually assisted the bullies in their activities. The boy hanged himself in a railway rest room and left a note naming two classmates as the cause of his anguish.[2]

It seems that bullying has been a problem in schools for as long as there have been schools. Why is this so? Although not encouraged, bullying continues to be a problem for many children because it is widely tolerated. Teachers, school officials, parents, and other students too often seem to stand by as children are degraded, humiliated, beaten, and ridiculed.

Left unchecked, bullying in school can lead to tragic consequences akin to the two cases mentioned above. Even when suicide or murder is not the outcome, bullying can leave lasting emotional and psychological scars on children. Furthermore, research has shown that bullying can extend across the generations: the children of bullies often become bullies themselves.

Why, then, do school officials, teachers, and parents often appear to take so little notice? One

"Bullying in School, It Doesn't Have to Happen" by Frank J. Barone from PHI DELTA KAPPAN, September 1997. Reprinted by permission of Phi Delta Kappa International and Frank J. Barone, Educational Consultant, Latham, NY.

reason may be because many adults consider bullying to be a normal part of growing up. Confronting a bully is considered one of the "rites of passage" for a boy. Unfortunately for the victim, the age-old advice to "stand up to" the bully and fight back usually leads to more violent bullying. Rarely does the bully back down. A second reason why bullying continues unabated might be that educators have become desensitized to bullying and do not even see it. Thus they seldom report it. A third reason could be that the schools are overwhelmed by other issues and problems outside of education with which they must deal. And finally, schools may not want to identify bullying as a problem because they do not have the resources to address it.

Scope of the Problem

Students who are the victims of bullies and school officials who hold the power to stop them have very different perceptions of the problem. This difference has hindered effective prevention efforts.

I developed a survey that was administered in spring and summer of 1993 to two goups in upstate New York. The first group consisted of 847 eight-graders; the second group consisted of 110 counselors, teachers, and administrators in the same schools as the students. The survey contained the following definition of bullying: "Bullying is a situation when a student or group of students is mean to you over a long period of time (weeks or even months). Bullying can either be physical (hitting, kicking, and so on) or it can be verbal (threats, name calling, gossiping, or ignoring). " Using this definition, the school staff members were asked to esti-

mate the percentage of the "students in their schools" who had been victimized by bullying. On average, the staff members believed that 16% of the students had been victims of bullies. The students in the same schools were asked whether they had "ever been bothered by a bully or bullies while you were in middle school." And 58.8% of the students surveyed said that they had.

The size of the difference in perceptions between students and school staff members suggests that the staff members do not recognize the extent of the bullying that students face. Bullying just does not seem to be "that big a problem" to the staff.

Nature of the Problem

The same survey uncovered some interesting facts. Contrary to what many of us believe, bullying in school does not primarily involve boys. Popular portrayals, such as *The Lord of the Flies* and *The Lords of Discipline,* which depict only boys as both the bullies and the victims, do not reflect reality. As shown in this study, only 47% of the victims of bullying in middle school are boys. Thus, according to the students' own perceptions, the majority (53%) of the victims of bullies are girls.

Not surprisingly, the bullying that takes place among boys tends to be more physical (punching, kicking, pushing, and so on) than that which takes place among girls (which is usually more verbal in nature). Among the students who said that the bullying they had experienced was mostly physical, 89.3% were boys. Among those students who said that the bullying they experienced was mostly verbal, 67.1% were girls.

Among all students surveyed, 10% indicated that they had been physically injured by a bully in school. Furthermore, the nature of the injuries ranged from minor bumps and bruises to some injuries that required hospitalization. Of those students who said they had been injured by a bully, 76.5% were boys.

Effective Remedies

When asked to name the three most effective ways of solving the bullying problem in school, most staff members named "tougher discipline" (41.4%) followed by "better supervision" (33.7%). Only 17.4% of staff members listed "more counseling." Students, on the other hand, mentioned "more counseling" most often (43.2%); 25.8% mentioned "tougher discipline," while 22% mentioned "better supervision."

Tougher discipline is clearly important. Bullies must be held accountable for their behavior, or the behavior will continue. Victims will come forward if they can see that bullies are dealt with sternly, and bullies will be deterred.

Schools also need to improve their supervision efforts. This does not necessarily mean having more supervision, but rather making certain that the correct areas are supervised. Most adult survey respondents said that they believed bullying tends to occur in out-of-the-way and hard-to-supervise places, such as on playgrounds and in locker rooms. But 62.9% of the students surveyed indicated that most bullying in their school occurs in the hallways. (Only 10.6% of the staff surveyed felt that most of the bullying in their school takes place in the hallways.) Staff members need to improve the ways they supervise school hallways. Teachers can do this effectively by situating themselves in the doorways of their classrooms during passing time. Teachers also need to be taught what to look for when monitoring for bullying. What teachers may interpret as accidental pushing and shoving in a crowded hallway may in fact be deliberate and premediated bullying.

Finally, schools need to invest in inservice training for staff members and in counseling programs that counsel victims and bullies alike. Several programs exist that do so. Some involve large-group sensitivity training, while others interweave the issue of bullying into the curriculum.

Intervention Programs

The most widely known intervention for bullying has been used in Norway by Daniel Olweus.[3] The main goal of the program is to reduce the incidence of bullying in schools. It educates teachers, other school officials, and parents about bullying through a 32-page booklet that was distributed to all schools in Norway. Olweus describes the keys to the program's success: 1) creating a school environment characterized by warmth, positive interest, and involvement with adults; 2) setting firm limits on unacceptable behavior; 3) consistently applying sanctions against bullying; and 4) having adults act as authority figures.

In Olweus' program adults closely supervise recess and enforce "strict and straightforward" rules of behavior. School officials mete out consistent, nonphysical punishment to children who misbehave in aggressive ways. Rewards and praise are also part of the program. Parents are encouraged to teach their children to develop and maintain friendships. Though Olweus believes that the peer group can play an important role in discouraging bullying, he places the main responsibility for dealing with bullies on the adults in the school.

E. Roland, also of Norway, has offered his own suggestions for dealing with bullies.[4] The first involves having a class read and discuss a story about bullying. The second asks students to hand in written work that deals with a child's feeling and thoughts about being bullied. The third approach involves role-playing, often reversing the role of the bully and the victim. A fourth approach involves the use of peer sponsors, who are students who assume responsibility for looking after younger children. And finally, Roland discusses the use of class meetings in which the group assumes responsibility for the well-being of all its members.

An evaluation of Olweus' model was conducted in Bergen, Norway. After 20 months of implementation, the number of students who reported being bullied declined by 50%, and there was a general reduction in other antisocial behaviors, such as vandalism, theft, and truancy.

C. St. John-Brooks describes a school in North London where the head teacher has made a point of attempting to reduce bullying by encouraging all students to tell someone when they have been bullied. Students new to the school are told: "You have a right to come to school without being afraid. This is a 'telling school.' The rule that you must not tell was invented by bullies, and you will only get into trouble if you don't tell."[5]

D. Stead reports that some British schools have established "bully courts" to deal with bullying behaviors. Once a week the court, made up a faculty advisor and four students, convenes to read descriptions of bullying behavior and mete out such punishments as after-school detention and eating lunch in isolation.[6]

Andrew Mellor's study of bullying in Scotland outlines some proven strategies for combating bullies. First, the school must acknowledge that the problem exists and that it hurts students. Second, victims will not come forward unless bullying is unequivocally condemned throughout the school. Finally, parents, teachers, and pupils need to be involved in formulating an anti-bullying policy so that they will have a vested interest in making it succeed.[7]

Stuart Greenbaum lists and discusses 10 prevention and intervention strategies that schools can employ to deal with bullying.

- Use a questionnaire to determine the scope of the problem.

- Communicate clear standards of behavior, and consistently enforce them.

- Monitor playgrounds closely.

- Establish a recording system for incidents of bullying.

- Provide children with opportunities to discuss bullying.

- Never overlook intentionally abusive acts.

- Contact the parents of both the victims and the bullies when a problem occurs.

- Establish intervention programs.

- Encourage parent participation.

- Provide support and protection for victims.[8]

   It is important to recognize that bullying does not have to be part of a child's school experience. It is not "part of growing up," nor is it a "rite of passage." By working together, schools and parents can make going to school an experience that students will enjoy, not dread.

1. Stuart Greenbaum. "What Can We Do About Schoolyard Bullying?," *Principal*, November 1987. pp 21-24.

2. M. Kikkawa. "Teachers' Opinions and Treatments for Bully/Victim Problems Among Students in Junior and Senior High Schools: Result of a Fact-Finding Survey." *Journal of Human Development.* vol. 23, 1987.

3. Daniel Olweus. "Bully/Victim Problems Among School Children: Basic Facts and Effects of a School-Based Intervention Program." In Debra J. Pepler and Kenneth H. Rubin. eds., *The Development and Treatment of Childhood Aggression* (Hillsdale, N.J.: Erlbaum, 1991).

4. E. Roland. "Strategy Against Mobbing." Oslo, 1983.

5. C. St. John-Brooks. "The School Bullies." *New Society*, vol. 6, 1984.

6. D. Stead. "British Bullies Toppled from Pulpit." *New York Times.* 7 January 1990.

7. Andrew Mellor, *Bullying in Scottish Secondary Schools* (Edinburgh: Scottish Education Department. March 1990).

8. Stuart Greenbaum. *Set Straight on Bullies* (Malibu, Calif.: National School Safety Center, 1989).

 Article Review Form at end of book.

Why would companies redesign workplaces?

Companies in a Family Way

Some firms do much more than provide 'family friendly' programs. They've redesigned jobs with parents in mind.

Amy Saltzman

This is the paradox of the American workplace: Most companies now realize they must make concessions to a world where both parents work, and an increasing number offer flextime, child care, and other programs to help employees cope. But the same companies expect their most ambitious and devoted workers to forgo such options or to take advantage of them only in order to spend more hours at the office. They adhere to a blueprint for success drafted 40 years ago when men went to work and women stayed home. In this conception, work is firmly in the center and "personal life" is squeezed into whatever space remains.

At a handful of companies around the country, however, an experiment is underway that turns this formulation on its head. Rather than appending "family friendly" programs to a traditional conception of office life, these firms are redefining the nature of work itself, making balanced lives for employees a central tenet around which the rest of the company is designed.

Like most new philosophies, this one was born of necessity. Studies show workers want more balanced lives, and companies are wise to adapt if they want to stay competitive. Most corporations start out offering traditional job flexibility programs, but few employees take advantage of them. Child care would seem a good way to help workers handle family responsibilities, but in some cases it adds a new level of anxiety. With emergency child care available, for example, an employee can now come to work even when a child is too ill for day care, secure in the knowledge that a complete stranger is tending her toddler. "We had to ask ourselves if this is really the message we wanted to be sending employees—that work should come first no matter what," says Patricia Nazemetz, director of human resource policies and practices at Xerox.

A more radical solution seems in order, and a few companies are finding it in a growing body of work by academics, psychologists, and management gurus. That work suggests that if businesses want to help people achieve balanced lives while helping firms profit, the answer is not to add more programs but to revamp fundamental notions about how people work. "It finally dawned on us that it's the job, stupid," says Ellen Galinsky, president of the Families and Work Institute.

Things Happen

Research supports the notion that the key to balancing work and family interests is a well-designed job, one where goals are clear and where workers have control over how, when, and where they get their work done. Underlying this is a recognition that employees have personal lives that sometimes get complicated. In a study conducted at Fel-Pro, a Skokie, Ill., manufacturer of automotive products known for its family-friendly policies, researchers from the University of Chicago found that workers whose jobs allowed them autonomy and input in decisions benefited most from the company's work and family programs. These employees reported that the policies not only helped them balance work and family demands but made them more committed to their jobs: They submitted twice as many quality improvement suggestions as workers who did not use work-family benefits. If a job was designed poorly, however, offering little autonomy or control, the benefits were of little help.

Not all jobs, of course, seem to invite such reform. Factory shift workers have little choice but to report to work at specific hours. As a result, they are rarely able to take advantage of programs designed to give employees more flexibility in their lives. But if the work itself is designed in a less-structured way, with both personal and business goals in mind, even shift workers benefit.

At General Motors' Saturn Co., for example, an unusual four-day, 10-hour-a-day workweek, with rotating day and night shifts, offers workers more options while allowing the company to keep the plant operating six days a week, 20 hours a day, with minimal overtime. Workers get five consecutive days off at the end of each three-week rotation. Because they don't need to use leave time for appointments, these employees have fewer personal obligations that cut into productivity. And because teams are responsible for deciding how management's goals will be met, employees who need a day off can simply switch with another team member when personal problems do arise.

At her previous job at a GM plant, Tonya Bowden saw her son just 30 minutes a day after he got home from school: She had to report to work at 4:30. At Saturn, rotating day and evening shifts allow Bowden more time with her children, ages 16 and 7. And her days off give the single mother a chance to fix up her new house and see movies with her kids.

Few companies, of course, have the luxury of creating a new work culture from scratch, as Saturn did. But even well-established companies can learn from the innovative auto manufacturer: When such changes start at the top and are driven by business need, they are likely to succeed. Such is the story of First Tennessee Bank.

For years, internal surveys had shown that First Tennessee branches with the lowest employee turnover also reported the greatest customer satisfaction. To stay competitive, the bank had to figure out how to keep employees happy. The problem was that its workers—mostly female and paid by the hour—barely used the company's array of family-friendly programs.

Employees First

So the Memphis bank laid out a new corporate philosophy. Retaining employees was put ahead of profitability and growth in the firm's mission statement. A management training program was developed to link productivity and customer satisfaction to employee satisfaction. That meant letting workers make decisions about how to meet the needs of the customer, without management watching every move. It also meant giving employees power to decide how to balance work responsibilities with personal needs.

Over a four-month period in 1992, First Tennessee trained the bank's 1,000 managers in the art of flexibility. They played board games in which they were given a set period of time to solve an employee's work-family dilemma. They talked frankly about their own needs—many male managers admitted for the first time that they, too, yearned for time to attend their children's ballgames or care for aging parents. CEO Ralph Horn came to each training session, underscoring the message that this was a fundamental shift in how the bank conducted business.

Just how thoroughly that shift has taken hold is evident today throughout the bank. In the accounts processing department, for example, a "flex board" indicates when employees are taking flextime throughout the month. The employees worked out a schedule that requires longer shifts at the start of the month—when work is heaviest—but gives a day off to each employee later in the month. The system cut the time it takes to reconcile customer accounts from 10 days to four.

Nowhere have the results of the program been greater than in the loan operations division, which has more than doubled its loan volume with no increase in staffing or major systems improvements. Customers are happier: 98 percent now give the division a good rating, compared with 38 percent in 1992. And employees are working fewer hours, with annual overtime pay dropping from $36,000 in 1993 to $6,000 last year.

Not every manager has embraced the program. Says Horn: "Some managers just don't fit in. The sad part is that many of them were rewarded in the past for not being empowering and flexible—the very things we are now insisting they become." And while most bank managers know the lingo, few have pushed it as far as the loan operations department. Says Vice President Tina Williford, who rushes out each day at 3 p.m, beeper and cellular phone in tow, to pick up her 2-year-old son at day care: "We consider ourselves to be a role model for the company."

Such model departments may be the most realistic first step

toward sweeping cultural change. Xerox corp. was handed just such an opportunity a few years ago when the Ford Foundation sponsored several pilot projects to demonstrate the more efficient workplaces could be created if employees' desires for better work-family balance were taken into account.

Quiet Time

At one of the work sites, for example, a group of 17 engineers was working evenings and weekends to get a new printer to market and had all but given up on any reasonable family life. The question for researchers was whether the engineers were using their time as efficiently as possible. After keeping hourly logs, the engineers discovered that more than half their time was eaten up by interruptions and impromptu meetings with colleagues. The result: "Quiet times" were set aside during which interruptions were forbidden. Not surprisingly, the engineers were able to get their work done more quickly and have more time with their families. And the division had its first on-time product launch in history.

Despite its initial success, the Xerox project also provides evidence of how hard it is to make changes stick. After their successful product launch, many members of the team moved on to new projects. Quiet times gradually disappeared for all but a few diehard employees. "What we realized is that the quiet times were covering up more-basic problems," says Jeff Sisson, vice president and general manager on the project. The real issue, he says, was that employees were caught in a pattern of reacting to crises rather than finding ways to prevent them. Now the department is

Child Care: Forging Bonds between Child and Caregiver

When looking for day care, many parents concentrate on safety and cleanliness. Finding a safe, clean center is of course essential, but far more is involved in day care's likely contribution to a child's emotional development. The central goal for an infant is to form attachments to adults. Bonds with primary caregivers form the basis for the child's healthy emotional and cognitive development.

If you pay a lot of money for child care, that's no guarantee it will meet this standard. Here are qualities to look for.

• **Sensitivity.** Notice levels of attentiveness and consistency in a caregiver. Does the caregiver watch TV while the child is awake? Does he or she understand the difference between a cry of hunger and a cry of fatigue? Does he or she talk to your child?

• **Low ratio.** No matter how loving caregivers may seem, they can properly pay attention to only a few children at a time. In group settings, there should be no more than 3 infants to 1 caregiver and 4 toddlers to 1 adult. When caregivers are overworked and infants cry for attention in vain, the children "start feeling powerless," says Dr. Kyle Pruett, a child psychiatrist at the Yale Child Study Center. "Then they turn to aggression or listlessness." A child who seems depressed or angry may not be getting the attention he or she needs.

• **Low turnover.** Many parents want their children cared for by a succession of

different adults, thinking that is the best way to prevent a caregiver from replacing Mommy and Daddy. But your child needs to become attached to his or her caregiver. The younger the child, the more critical it is to have one consistent caregiver, says Alan Sroufe, an expert in attachment at the University of Minnesota. For toddlers, having a loving caregiver boosts the chances that they will view teachers in a positive light once they reach school age.

Fostering attachment, takes time. Ideally, a child should have the same caregiver for the first two or three years. That means a day-care center should have very little turnover in staff. Ideally, the same person should care for your child every day. If you choose to hire a nanny, try to ensure that she will stay with your child for at least a year—even by offering bonuses, if you can afford them. If you plan to leave your child with a relative, try to get the same kind of commitment. According to a recent study, care provided by relatives may not be better than institutional care. In some cases it can be worse, because relatives often fail to stick with a child through his first year.

• **Staff morale.** Ask caregivers how they feel about their jobs. Adults who are overworked or depressed cannot cater to the needs of their charges. Drop in at your child's day care unannounced every so often, or come home at odd times, to observe both your child and caregiver.

—*Shannon Brownlee*

crafting guidelines for making product development more systematic. But without the Ford researchers monitoring them, there is a reluctance to put this in a work-family context. "We are more conscious now of that part of it, but it is a slow process," says Sisson.

It's inevitable that change should evolve gradually at large companies like Xerox. "You can't just roll out a fundamental shift in values," says organizational expert Peter Senge, author of *The Fifth Discipline*. It is at a grass-roots

level that the push for employee-centered workplaces is taking hold. "It starts with a sales manager or branch manager opening up about his or her own personal struggles and saying we need to do something about this," says Senge. At a conference, that manager talks to another supervisor. They form a committee. Senior management starts to listen. And slowly, ever so slowly, change happens.

 Article Review Form at end of book.

How can early childhood educators avoid judging the infant sleeping routines of children from cultures different than their own?

The Cultural Context of Infant Caregiving

Navaz Peshotan Bhavnagri and Janet Gonzalez-Mena

Navaz Peshotan Bhavnagri is Professor, Early Childhood Education, Wayne State University, Detroit.

Janet Gonzalez-Mena is Professor, Napa Valley College, Napa, California.

To be prepared for the 21st century, early childhood teacher educators, educators of child care personnel, and early childhood practitioners need an expanded conceptualization of infant caregiving. Instead of preaching "universals" exclusively, cultural relativism should be an equally strong focus when preparing practitioners to work in multiple settings (e.g., early intervention programs, parent-infant centers, parent education programs, infant group care and family child care).

Significance of Culture in Caregiving

Teaching about the cultural context is critical in infant care for two reasons. First, the caregiver is a vital influence on infants' ongoing socialization and their personality development. Research indicates enormous cultural variations characterize infant caregiving in developing countries, as well as in industrial countries such as the United States (Abbott, 1992; Bhavnagri, 1986; Field, Sostek, Vietze & Leiderman, 1981; Leiderman, Tulkin & Rosenfeld, 1977). Since the 1970s, immigrants to the United States have been mostly from Asia, Latin America and the Middle East (Jackson, 1980; Kitano & Daniel, 1988). They represent greater ethnic, racial and socioeconomic diversity than immigrants from earlier areas, who were primarily European (Grant, 1995). Therefore, their caregiving practices are usually very different than the prevalent Euro-American practices (Lieberman, 1995).

Recent empirically developed models on immigrant acculturation (e.g., Garza & Gallegos, 1985; Hareven, 1982; Rueschenberg & Buriel, 1989) suggest that immigrant families do not simply shed old values for new ones, as accepted previously (e.g., Gordon, 1964; Handlin, 1951); rather, they selectively maintain some of their old values and practices, modify some, and alter others. As a result, these immigrants flexibly operate in at least two cultures. Additionally, these new models view the acculturation as a bi-directional process in which the new immigrants modify the mainstream culture, and at the same time individuals in the mainstream culture also change to effectively adjust the immigrants' ways (Patel, Power & Bhavnagri, 1996).

Given this large influx of non-European immigrants who are undergoing rapid but selective acculturation and the non-immigrants also undergoing adjustments, we need to retool early childhood training. Well-intentioned professionals armed with child development research are increasingly baffled by new immigrant parents' very different practices, belief systems, perceptions of their children's capabilities, goals for child rearing, world views and life experiences. Therefore, we need to prepare child care professionals to face these challenges.

Second, a dramatic change affecting infants in the United States further necessitates cultural awareness. Whereas in 1977 only 32 percent of the mothers of infants were employed, the figure increased to 48 percent by 1985 (NICHD Early Child Care Research Network, 1996). Currently, more than 50 percent of mothers with infants are in the workforce (Hofferth, Brayfield, Deitch & Holcomb, 1991). It is estimated that 278,000 infants and 791,000 toddlers were in child care arrangements in 1988 (U.S. Bureau of the Census, 1992). Institutional group child care is growing, of which infant care is the fastest growing segment (Gonzalez-Mena, 1997). By 1990, more than 50 percent of infants under 12 months were being cared for by adults other than their mothers (e.g., a relative, baby sitter, nanny, family child care provider, or staff in center-based care).

It would be best for these multiple caregivers to work in unison, thereby promoting families' resiliency (Lynch, Fulcher & Ayala, 1996). This coordinated approach can occur when all caregivers understand, respect and support each others' efforts, share similar goals and beliefs on infant rearing, and perceive infants' abilities in a similar manner. That is not always the situation, however, especially when multiple caregivers are from different cultures. When professionals *do* offer culturally consistent caregiving, conflicts and culturally assaultive approaches are minimized (Gonzalez-Mena, 1992, 1995). Therefore, we need to prepare professionals for culturally consistent caregiving and empower them to communicate effectively with each other (Anderson & Fenichel, 1989; Phillips, 1995).

Given the above rationale, this article asks professionals first to question the universality of all child development theory and research. Next, it asks readers to reflect on sleep-time practices from a comparative child development perspective. This example will help us re-examine our view of "appropriate," "normal" and/or "best practices." Finally, the authors will recommend strategies to facilitate a paradigm shift from a universal to a cultural view of child development and care.

Questioning the Universality of Child Development Theory and Research

Early childhood professionals should be fully cognizant that the generally understood universals (e.g., "developmental tasks," "developmental milestones," and "effective," "optimal" or "best practices") in child development are actually based on an extremely small sample of the world's population. The data from these universal determinations come mainly from the Western world, and principally from middle-class people of European extraction (Levine, 1989; Werner, 1979). Furthermore, this Western research is predominantly from the United States. Lozoff (1977) states that the children studied in the context of modern industrialized societies, such as the United States or Europe, are a select group that is not representative of most other cultures and during most of human history.

New (1994) reports that only 9.3 percent of the studies published in *Child Development* between 1986 to 1990 (i.e., the second half of the International Decade of the Child) were studies on culturally and linguistically diverse populations outside the United States. Of these limited studies, still fewer of them explicitly focused on culture in their research designs or provided ethnographic background material for examining the results. Additionally, less than 3 percent of the studies reported focused on children developing in cultures outside the United States.

Bornstein (1991) states that ". . . it is a truism of contemporary psychological study that the cultural contexts in which children are reared constitute central, yet often neglected, factors in developmental study" (p. 3). Developmental psychologists are just starting to address this gap, as evidenced by the growing research in comparative child development (e.g., Bornstein, 1991; Field, Sostek, Vietze & Leiderman, 1981; Munroe & Munroe, 1975; Rogoff, Mistry, Goncu & Mosier, 1993; Wagner & Stevenson, 1982; Whiting & Edwards, 1988).

Comparative child developmental research provides a unique opportunity to: 1) expand the range of normal behavior, 2) raise awareness of how culture contributes divergent pathways to children's development, 3) test specific social science hypotheses, 4) generate new hypotheses, 5) test the generalizability of child development theories, 6) integrate multiple research methodologies and disciplines, 7) develop effective policies for international aid and 8) force us to reflect on our beliefs and practices regarding optimal and normative child development (Bornstien, 1991; Harkness, 1980; Hopkins, 1989; Jahoda, 1986; Levine, 1989; New, 1993, 1994; Rogoff & Morelli, 1989).

Given the above arguments, how can early childhood professionals mobilize themselves to challenge their assumptions on "universal" child development principles and practices? According to Dewey (1933), individuals should be encouraged to

> We need to prepare professionals for culturally consistent caregiving and empower them to communicate effectively with each other.

give active, persistent and careful consideration to any supposed form of knowledge or beliefs in light of the grounds that support it and the conclusions that are drawn from it. He defines this process as reflective thinking, and recommends it for solving real-life problems.

Let us, therefore, reflect on one infant caregiving practice—namely, sleep-time routine. According to Ferber (1985, 1986), sleeping is an issue of great concern and a "real problem," even more than feeding and toilet training. At least half of all concerns that American parents raise with their pediatricians involve their children's sleeping habits.

Cultural Caregiving on Sleeping Routines

Caregivers need to reflect upon the following cultural issues related to sleeping routines:

1. Early childhood professionals need to realize that while mothers and infants sleeping together may be considered "abnormal" by many in the United States, it has been a common and normal practice in most other societies. Barry and Paxson (1971) analyzed data from 169 societies and found that none of them practiced putting an infant in a separate room to sleep. Whiting, Kluckhohn and Anthony (1958) reported that out of their sample of 56 world societies, only five had sleeping arrangments similar to those of U.S. Americans, where, typically, parents share a bed and the baby sleeps alone. Their study revealed that less than 10 percent of the ethnography of societies they surveyed have infants sleep in a crib or cradle. In other countries, even when the infant has a cradle or cot, it is generally placed within easy reach of the mother's

bed. Cultures that practice cosleeping include both highly technological and less technological communities (Morelli, Rogoff, Oppenheim & Goldsmith, 1992). Only in Western societies, notably in the middle class of the U.S., do infants have bedrooms of their own (Whiting & Edwards, 1988).

2. Professionals need to recognize that sleeping arrangements are strongly mandated by value-laden cultural customs, and upheld by elders or "expert" specialist such as pediatricians or psychologists. Frequently, nationally known American pediatricians who are also specialists on parenting (e.g., Brazelson, 1978, 1979, 1989; Ferber, 1985; Spock, 1968, 1984) discourage the practice of mothers and infants sleeping together. Spock and Rothenberg (1992) state, "I think it's a sensible rule not to take a child into the parents' bed for any reason" (p. 213). Brazelton (1989) recommends, "A child shouldn't fall asleep in her parent's arms; if she does, then the parents have made themselves part of the child's sleep rituals" (p. 69). Ferber (1985) advises, "Sleeping alone is an important part of [the child's] learning to be able to separate from you without anxiety and to see himself as an independent individual" (p. 39). Eighty-four percent of the pediatricians surveyed in Cleveland asserted that an infant should never sleep with his or her parents (Lozoff, Wolf & Davis, 1984). At one time, almost all U.S. hospitals separated the mother from the child at birth. Although neonates in hospitals often stay with their mothers they still do not share the same bed; instead, they have their own crib.

Trevathan and McKenna (1994) advise, "It is important for parents to know that when pediatricians give advice as to where their infants and children should

sleep, they are dispensing cultural judgments and not advice based in scientific findings" (p. 101). To foster "optimal" development some cultures put a high value on promoting individuality (e.g., the United States), while other cultures place greater value on relating to others (e.g., Japan) (Caudill & Plath, 1966; Kawasaki, Nugent, Miyashita, Miyahara & Brazelton, 1994; Levine, 1989; Rogoff, 1990). Such cultures believe that we need to attend to an infant's need for dependency by allowing a child to sleep with the mother, and thereby creating a secure base from which later independence, autonomy and exploration can grow. Gonzalez-Mena (1991) states that, "The word individual is downplayed in some cultures, and the word private is practically nonexistent" (p. 31).

3. Early childhood educators need to be informed of the consequences of parents and infants sleeping in the same bed, so that they can confidently discuss this practice with parents. The proponents of this practice state that infants are vulnerable, immature and poorly regulated. Therefore, human contact during sleep helps infants regulate their body temperature and maintain homeostasis. Research also indicates that Sudden Infant Death Syndrome (SIDS) is infrequent in cultures that accept cosleeping (Gantley, Davies & Murcett, 1993; McKenna & Mosko, 1993). Moreover, studies show that mother-infant states of sleep are synchronized when they sleep together (McKenna, Mosko, Dungy & McAninch, 1990). Keefe (1987) also reports that newborns who slept in the same room as their parents slept more quietly and cried less compared to those who slept in a separate nursery room. Additionally, sleeping together is more convenient and efficient for breastfeeding. Lastly, children are less likely to need transitional objects (e.g., "security" blankets, teddy bears) as psychological substitutes for human contact when parents cosleep and have frequent daytime contacts (Anders & Taylor, 1994).

Early childhood educators also need to be aware of opposing views on the practice. Opponents believe it interferes with the child's independence, intrudes into parental privacy, sexually arouses the oedipal child, and causes more sleep problems (Wolf, Lozoff, Latz & Paludetto, 1996). Anders and Taylor (1994) report that since most child development literature and professional advice is on how to help the baby sleep through the night, parents have those expectations, and deviations from that practice are viewed as "problems." Nighttime awakenings, however, are not viewed as a "problem" in those cultures where parents are socialized to expect it.

4. Early childhood educators who want to make "developmentally appropriate" decisions need to reflect on the infant's "development" in relation to other primates' development (i.e., comparative child development from an evolutionary perspective) to determine what is "appropriate." Trevathan and McKenna (1994) recommend that instead of expecting infants to be independent, caregivers need to accept infants as what they actually are— namely, the least neurologically mature of all mammals at birth. Consequently, human infants have to rely far more on their caregivers for their regulation and survival than infants of other mammalian species. To provide this continuous care all primate adults sleep with their infants,

with the exception of human infants, who need the most care. Over centuries, human infants have adapted to sleeping with their mothers, and only recently, in an evolutionary sense, has this adaptive mechanism been disrupted. Even monkey infants show significant detrimental effects (e.g., decrease in body temperature, release of stress hormones, cardiac arrhythmias, sleep disturbances and compromised immune systems) when separated from their mother for only three hours. Therefore, an evolutionist would consider it "developmentally inappropriate" to expect infants to sleep separately from their mothers.

5. Early childhood educators should not sanctimoniously judge sleeping apart as a totally unacceptable practice, but instead understand the historical roots of this practice in Western cultures. From the 16th to the 18th centuries, some European countries enacted laws requiring infants to sleep separately from parents, ostensibly in order to prevent suffocation. In reality, these laws were a response to infanticide trends. Parents often killed their children because of food shortages, and then would claim to have accidentally rolled over onto the infant during sleep. Around the same time, the husband-wife bond became more prominent than the parent-child bond. The notion of romantic love gained popularity, contributing to the trend for separate sleeping arrangements for parents and children. Additionally, churches supported separate sleeping, to maintain children's purity (Trevathan & McKenna, 1994).

The cultural development of mother and infant sleeping together also needs to be understood. Levine (1977) explains that

infant mortality rates were high in all cultures at one time. Therefore, the parent's overriding goal and concern was the child's survival, which was expressed by keeping the infant in close proximity. This continuous surveillance of the infant's well-being resulted in the mother and infant sleeping together. Over time, this effective survival strategy became encoded as a customary practice within a culture, and was socially transmitted from one generation to the next.

6. When faced with conflicting values, professionals need to reflect and arrive at creative solutions that are in the child's best interests. At one child care center where each infant had a crib, for example, a baby who had just arrived from Southeast Asia protested mightily at naptime. The staff discovered that he had never slept apart from his mother and had never even seen a crib. His distress was significant. Noting that he could only go to sleep in the noisy playroom, the staff went along with his inclination. A licensing worker objected to the arrangement after finding the infant asleep on a cushion in the corner, citing a law that read, "each child has the right to quiet undisturbed sleep." She interpreted this regulation to mean that babies must sleep in cribs in a special dark and quiet room, apart from the playroom. Twardosz, Cataldo and Risley's (1974) found, however, that infants can sleep as well in a bright, noisy, common play and sleep room as they can in a darkened, quiet and separate sleep area. The head teacher was able to convince the licensing worker that the only way this particular child could get quiet, undisturbed rest was in the midst of people, and thus the licensing law was not violated. The center was granted a waiver for this child! Early childhood professionals can be helped by discussing such creative resolutions.

7. *When sharing the above-mentioned cross-cultural evolutionary, historical and medical research perspectives, we need to help students reflect on their own practices.* Reflection will help students understand that what they may have considered "abnormal" and "inappropriate" may be considered "normal" and "appropriate" by others. This awareness itself often makes students feel uncomfortable and generates emotional dissonance. For example, some students reported that they "disobeyed" their doctor's advice and had their baby in bed with them for a very long time, but did not tell others because they felt guilty. They are relieved to know of great variations in infant care. Others view these multidisciplinary research perspectives as eye openers, yet are still uncomfortable in directly questioning their long-held beliefs on infant rearing.

The following are some questions to prompt students' reflection: What if a practice is culturally relevant but somewhat developmentally inappropriate? Where does one draw a line? What cultural practices are benign to infants' development and what practices are unquestionably harmful? What is the criteria and who makes this criteria? How are parents' practices adaptive to the original culture? How adaptive are they to current culture? Should they be practiced exactly as before, or should they be modified? Who should decide? How does one reconcile what one strongly believes in, based on research, with what parents believe, especially when the gap between

the two is enormous? Are we acting responsibly and sensitively by saying nothing to parents when we disagree with them, or are we abdicating our responsibilities? How can we be sensitive to differing practices and yet be professionals and share our expertise? On what issues must one take a stand, and which ones must we concede as crucial to the parent's and child's reality?

Recommendations

Overall, the authors recommend including culture as an integral component of all relevant courses (e.g., parent education, family life education, child development, infant child care, developmentally appropriate curriculum). Multicultural early childhood educational courses, which typically and almost exclusively focus on cultures that influence the curriculum during formal schooling, should also reflect how different cultures influence socialization practices in infant rearing. Finally, early childhood faculty should broaden their personal definition of multicultural education to readily incorporate this recommendation.

We recommend including in the coursework comparative developmental data generated by many disciplines, such as anthropology, sociology, medicine, social work, history and linguistics, as well as child development. Ethology and attachment theory, for example, can be used to explain Konner's work (1977) regarding significant changes in infant rearing over time; population psychology to explain Levine's work (1977) on parental goals in infant rearing; and psychocultural theory to explain the Whitings's world famous studies on child rearing in six cultures (Whiting, 1963; Whiting, 1977). Also noteworthy are Brofenbrenner's (1979) ecologi-

cal theory, Triandris's (1979) cross-cultural model and Lester and Brazelton's (1982) biosocial model (see Bhavnagri, 1986, for details on these models). Discussions on Vygotsky's (1978) cultural-historical theory (Wertsch & Tulviste, 1992) as applied by Luria (1976) and Rogoff (e.g., Rogoff, 1990; Rogoff, Malkin & Gilbride, 1984; Rogoff, Mistry, Goncu & Mosier, 1993) would explain the cultural context of infant caregiving. Readings from some of the sources cited here and from journals such as *Anthropology and Education Quarterly* and *OMEP-International Journal of Early Childhood* would help students.

The authors earlier recommended a reflective approach to deconstruct the universality of child development theories. This same reflective and dialectic approach is an effective tool for reconstructing culture's contribution to child development. Instead of prescriptively "pouring in" knowledge we should encourage the co-construction of knowledge on cultural relativism by facilitating student-teacher and student-peer dialogues. Schon (1987) believes that such "reflection-on-action" and "reflection-in-action" helps students to confront unique situations in the real world of practice, when they feel uncertain and have value conflicts. Infant-rearing issues are fettered with uncertainties, value conflicts, and moral and ethical dilemmas for students to reflect upon and question. Finally, reflection could permit students to co-construct a position that is truly accepting of divergent practices.

In addition, when teacher educators use this reflective and dialectical approach, they empower their students to use this same approach with parents of the infants in their care. When students use reflective practices with parents, they empower parents to reflect on their own cultural practices in an enlightened manner and to consider multiple options in infant rearing. Teacher educators should also offer well-guided learning experiences, in which students frequently, meaningfully and reflectively interact with parents of diverse cultures. This practice will reduce students' apprehensions, help them confront their preconceived belief systems about diverse families and offer continuity between the center and home care (Chang & Pulido, 1994; Harry, Torguson, Katkavich & Guerrero, 1993; Whaley and Swadener, 1990). In conclusion, such reflections are necessary for both professionals and parents if they are to work together as a team in the best interests of the child.

References

Abbott, S. (1992). Holding on and pushing away: Comparative perspectives on an Eastern Kentucky childrearing practice. *Ethos, 20,* 33–65.

Anders, T. F., & Taylor, T. R. (1994). Babies and their sleep environment. *Children's Environments, 11,* 123–134.

Anderson, P. P., & Fenichel, E. S. (1989). *Serving culturally diverse families of infants and toddlers with disabilities.* Washington, DC: National Center for Clinical Infant Programs.

Barry, H., & Paxson, L. (1971). Infancy and early childhood: Cross–cultural codes 2 *Ethnology, 10,* 466–508.

Bhavnzgri, N. (1986). Mother–infant interactions in various cultural settings. In L. G. Katz (Ed.), *Current topics in early childhood: Vol 6* (pp. 1–32). Norwood, NJ: Ablex.

Bronstein, M. H. (Ed.). (1991). *Cultural approaches to parenting.* Hillsdale, NJ: Lawrence Erlbaum Associates.

Brazelton, T. B. (1978, October). Why your baby won't sleep. *Redbook,* p. 82.

Brazelton, T. B. (1979, June). What parents told me about handling children's sleep problems. *Redbook,* pp. 51–54.

Brazelton, T. B. (1989, February 13). Working parents. *Newsweek,* pp. 66–77.

Bronfenbrenner, U. (1979) *The ecology of human development.* Cambridge, MA: Harvard University Press.

Caudill, W., & Plath, D. W. (1966). Who sleeps by whom? Parent-child involvement in urban Japanese families. *Psychiatry, 29,* 344–366.

Chang, H. N. L., & Pulido, D. (1994). The critical importance of cultural and linguistic continuity for infants and toddlers. *Zero to Three, 15*(2), 13–17.

Dewey, J. (1993). *How we think.* Boston: DC Heath and Company.

Ferber, R. (1985). *Solve your child's sleep problem.* New York: Simon and Schuster.

Ferber, R. (1986). Sleepless child. In C. Guilleminault (Ed.), *Sleep and its disorders in children* (pp. 41–163). New York: Raven Press.

Field, T. M., Sostek, A. M., Vietze, P., & Leiderman, P. H. (Eds.). (1981). *Culture and early interactions.* Hillsdale, NJ: Lawrence Erlbaum Associates.

Gantley, M., Davies, D. P., & Murcett, A. (1993). Sudden infant death syndrome: Links with infant care practices. *British Medical Journal, 306,* 16–20.

Garza, R. T., & Gallegos, P. I. (1985). Environmental influences and personal choice: A humanistic perspective on acculturation. *Hispanic Journal of Behavioral Sciences, 7,* 365–379.

Gonzalez–Mena, J. (1991, July / August). Do you have cultural tunnel vision? *Child Care Information Exchange,* pp. 29–31.

Gonzalez-Mena, J. (1992). Taking a culturally sensitive approach in infant-toldler programs. *Young Children, 47*(2), 4–9.

Gonzalez-Mena, J. (1995). Cultural sensitivity in routine caregiving tasks. In P. Mangione (Ed.), *Infant/toddler caregiving: A guide to culturally sensitive care* (pp. 12–19). Sacramento, CA: Far West Laboratory and California Department of Education.

Gonzalez-Mena, J. (1997). *Multicultural issues in child care* (2nd ed.). Mountainview, CA: Mayfield.

Gordon, M. (1964). *Assimilation in American life.* New York: Oxford University Press.

Grant, R. (1995). Meeting the needs of young second language learners. In E E. Garcia, B. McLaughlin, B. Spodek, & O. N. Saracho (Eds.), *Meeting the challenge of linguistic and cultural diversity in early childhood education* (pp. 1–17). New York: Teachers College Press.

Handlin, O. (1951). *The uprooted.* Boston: Little, Brown.

Hareven, T. (1982). *Family time and industrial time.* New York: Cambridge University Press.

Harkness, S. (1980). The cultural context of child development. In C. M. Super & S. Harkness (Eds.), *Anthropological perspectives on child development: Vol. 8. New direction for child development* (pp. 7–13). San Francisco: Freeman.

Harry, B., Torguson, C., Katkavick, J., & Guerrero, M. (1993). Crossing social class and cultural barriers in working with families. *Teaching Exceptional Children, 26*(1), 48–51.

Hofferth, S., Brayfield, A., Deitch, S., & Holcomb, P. (1991). *National child care survey, 1990.* Washington, DC: Urban Institute.

Hopkins, B. (1989). Culture, infancy and education. *European Journal of Psychology of Education, IV* 289–293.

Jackson, K. (1980). The old minorities and the new: Understanding a new cultural idiom in U.S. history. In M. Kritz (Ed.), *U.S. immigration and refugee policy: Global and domestic issues* (pp. 313–335). Lexington, MA: Lexington Books.

Jahoda, G. (1986). A cross–cultural perspective on developmental psychology. *International Journal of Behavioral Development, 9,* 417–437.

Kawasaki, C. Nugent, J. K., Miyashita, H., Miyahara, H., & Brazelton, T. B. (1994). The cultural organization of infants' sleep. *Children's Environments, 11,* 135–141.

Keefe, M. R. (1987). Comparison of neonatal night-time sleep-wake patterns in nursery versus rooming-in environments. *Nursing Research, 36,* 140–144.

Kitano, H. L., & Daniel, R. (1988). *Asian Americans: Emerging minorities.* Englewood Cliffs, NJ: Prentice-Hall.

Konner, M. (1977). Evolution of human behavior development. In P. Leiderman, S. Tulkin, & A. Rosenfeld (Eds.), *Culture and infancy: Variations*

Leiderman, P. H., Tulkin, S. R., & Rosenfeld, A. (Ed.). (1977). *Culture and infancy: Variations in the human experience.* New York: Academic Press.

Lester, B. M., & Brazelton, T. B. (1982). Cross cultural assessment of neonatal behavior. In D. A. Wagner & H. W. Stevenson (Eds.), *Cultural perspectives on child development* (pp. 20–53). San Francisco: W. H. Freeman.

Levine, R. A. (1977). Child rearing as cultural adaptation. In P. Leiderman, S. Tulkin, & A. Rosenfeld (Eds.), *Culture and infancy: variations in the human experience* (pp. 15–27). New York: Academic Press.

Levine, R. A. (1989). Cultural environments in child development. In W. Damon (Ed.), *Child development today and tomorrow* (pp. 52–68). San Francisco: Jossey–Bass.

Lieberman, A. F. (1995). Concerns of immigrant families. In P. Mangione (Ed.), *Infant/toddler caregiving: A guide to culturally sensitive care* (pp. 28–37). Sacramento, CA: Far West Laboratory and California Department of Education.

Lozoff, B. (1977, March). *The sensitive period: An anthropological view.* Paper presented at the Biennial Meeting of the Society for Research in Child Development, New Orleans.

Lozoff, B., Wolf, A., & Davis, N. (1984). Cosleeping in urban families with young children in the United States. *Pediatrics, 74,* 171–182.

Luria, A. R. (1976). *Cognitive development: Its cultural and social foundations* (M. Lopez-Morillas & L. Solotaroff, Trans.). Cambridge, MA: Harvard University Press.

Lynch, E. W., Fulcher, J. L., & Ayala, E. (1996). Cross-cultural competence in infant care and intervention: Recognizing resilience. *Focus on Infancy, 8*(3), 1–4.

McKenna, J. J., & Mosko, S. (1993). Evolution and infant sleep: An experimental study of infant-parent cosleeping and its implications for SIDS. *Acta Paediatrica Supplement, 389,* 31–36.

McKenna, J. J., Mosko, S., Dungy, C., & McAninch, P. (1990). Sleep and arousal patterns of co-sleeping human mothers/infant pairs: A preliminary physiological study with implications for the study of Sudden Infant Death Syndrome (SIDS). *American Journal of Physical Anthropology, 83,* 331–347.

Morelli, G. A., Rogoff, B., Oppenheim, D., & Goldsmith, D. (1992). Culture variation in infants' sleeping arrangements: Questions of independence. *Developmental Psychology, 28,* 604–613.

Munroe, R. L., & Munroe, R. H. (1975). *Cross-cultural human development.* Belmont, CA: Wadsworth.

New, R. (1993). Cultural variations on developmentally appropriate practice. In C. Edwards, L. Gandini, & G. Forman (Eds.), *The hundred languages of children: The Reggio Emilia approach to early childhood education* (pp. 215–231). Norwood, NJ: Ablex.

New, R. (1994). Culture, child development, and developmentally appropriate practices: Teachers as collaborative researchers. In B. Mallory and R. New (Eds.), *Diversity and developmentally appropriate practices* (pp. 2–9). New York: Teachers College Press.

NICHD Early Child Care Research Network, The. (1996, Spring). Child care and the family: An opportunity to study development in context. *SRCD Newsletter,* pp. 4–6.

Patel, N., Power, T., & Bhavnagri, N. P. (1996). Socialization values and practices of Indian immigrant parents: Correlates of modernity and acculturation. *Child Development, 67,* 302–313.

Phillips, C. B. (1995). Culture: a process that empowers. In P. Mangione (Ed.), *Infant/toddler caregiving: A guide to culturally sensitive care* (pp. 2–9). Sacramento, CA: Far West Laboratory and California Department of Education.

Rogoff, B. (1990). *Apprenticeship in thinking: Cognitive development in social context.* New York: Oxford University Press.

Rogoff, B., Malkin, C., & Gilbride, K. (1984). Interaction with babies as guidance in development. *New Directions for Child Development, 23,* 31–44.

Rogoff, B., Mistry, J., Goncu, A., Mosier, C. (1993). Guided participation in cultural activity by toddlers and caregivers. *Monographs of the Society for Research in Child Development, 58,* (8, Serial No. 236).

Rogoff, B., & Morelli, B. (1989). Perspectives on children's development from cultural psychology. *American Psychologist, 44,* 343–348.

Rueschenberg, E., & Buriel, R. (1989). Mexican American family functioning and acculturation: A family systems perspective. *Hispanic Journal of Behavioral Sciences, 11,* 232–244.

Schon, D. S. (1987). *Educating the reflective practitioner.* San Francisco: Jossey-Bass.

Spock, B. (1968). *Baby and child care.* New York: Meredith Press. (Originally published in 1945).

Spock, B., & Rothenberg, M. B. (1992). *Dr. Spock's baby and child care.* New York: Pocket Books.

Spock, B. J. (1984, December). Mommy, can I sleep in your bed? *Parents Magazine,* p. 129.

Trevathan, W. R., & McKenna, J. J. (1994). Evolutionary environments of human birth and infancy: Insights to apply to contemporary life. *Children's Environments, 11,* 88–104.

Triandis, H. C. (1979). Cross-cultural psychology. In M. E. Meyer (Ed.), *Foundations of contemporary psychology* (pp. 544–579). New York: Oxford Press.

Twardosz, S., Cataldo, M. F., & Risley, T. R. (1974). Open environment design for infant and toddler day care. *Journal of Applied Behavior, Anal., 7,* 529–546.

U.S. Bureau of the Census. (1992). *Who's minding the kids? Child care arrangements: Fall 1988.* (Current Population Report, 30). Washington,DC: Author.

Vygotsky, L. S. (1978). *Mind in society: The development of higher mental processes.* Cambridge, MA: Harvard University Press.

Wagner, D. A., & Stevenson, H. W. (Ed.). (1982). *Cultural perspectives on child development.* San Francisco: W. H. Freeman.

Werner, E. E. (1979). *Cross-cultural child development* Belmont, CA: Wadsworth.

Wertsch, J. V., & Tulviste, P. (1992). L. S. Vygotsky and contemporary developmental psychology. *Developmental Psychology, 28,* 548–557.

Whaley, K., & Swadener, E. (1990). Multicultural education in infant and toddler settings. *Childhood Education, 66,* 238–240.

Whiting, B. B. (Ed.). (1963). *Six cultures: Studies of child-rearing.* New York: Wiley.

Whiting, B. B., & Edwards, C. P. (1988). *Children of different worlds: The formation of social behavior.* Cambridge, MA: Harvard University Press.

Whiting, J. W. M., Kluckhohn, R., & Anthony, A. S. (1958). The function of male initiation ceremonies at puberty. In E. E. Maccoby, T. Newcomb, & E. Hartley (Eds.), *Readings in social psychology* (pp. 359–370). New York: Holt.

Whiting, J. W. M. (1977). A model of psychocultural research. In P. Leiderman, S. Tulkin, & A. Rosenfeld (Eds.), *Culture and infancy: Variations in the human experience* (pp. 29–48). New York: Academic Press.

Wolf, A. W., Lozoff, B., Latz, S., & Paludetto, R. (1996). Parental theories in the management of sleep routines in Japan, Italy and the United States. In S. Harkness & C.M. Super (Eds.), *Parents' cultural belief systems* (pp. 364–385). New York: Guilford.

Article Review Form at end of book.

WiseGuide Wrap-Up

- The needs of children and their parents should direct the care and educational experiences.

- All children deserve quality, inclusive programs that provide opportunities to

engage in developmentally appropriate activities.

R.E.A.L. Sites

This list provides a print preview of typical **coursewise** R.E.A.L. sites. There are over 100 such sites at the **courselinks**™ site. The danger in printing URLs is that web sites can change overnight. As we went to press, these sites were functional using the URLs provided. If you come across one that isn't, please let us know via email to: webmaster@coursewise.com. Use your Passport to access the most current list of R.E.A.L. sites at the **courselinks**™ site.

Site name: I Am Your Child
URL: http://www.iamyourchild.org/
Why is it R.E.A.L.? Local and national resources about early childhood development (0–3) are available for parents and child caregivers. Information about brain development and children's ages and stages is presented with visuals.
Key topics: brain development, early experiences, families
Activity: Find *Parent Questions*. What are the three most pressing questions parents ask about children from 0 to 3 years of age?

Site name: American Academy of Pediatrics
URL: http://www.aap.org/
Why is it R.E.A.L.? This site represents pediatricians' commitment to infants, children, adolescents, and young adults. The web site provides ideas about professional education, advocacy, and research related to the physical, mental, and social health of children and adolescents.
Key topics: brain development, early experiences, social and emotional development
Activity: The *Advocacy* option will lead you to *Violence Prevention Resources.* Describe the *Portrait of Promise,* how to order the video, and its cost.

Site name: Bright Futures
URL: http://www.brightfutures.org
Why is it R.E.A.L.? Bright Futures responds to the health promotion and disease prevention needs of infants, children, adolescents, families, and communities. The resource is divided into areas: infancy, early childhood, middle childhood, and adolescence.
Key topics: social and emotional development, cognition/intelligence, parenting
Activity: Select and print out two activities from the *Bright Futures Activity Book.*

section 4

Acceptance of All Young Children:
How Will We Recognize and Celebrate Each Child?

WiseGuide Intro

Human life experiences are universally similar. What makes children alike and different are the rich and varied cultural contexts that diversify their lives. The culture, historical events, regional locations, societal privileges, and individual capabilities influence each child's development. These influences create varied perceptions about other communities and their life styles. Communities with many cultures must work persistently and proactively to promote the acceptance of our many colors, social standings, and ways in which we live and behave. The authors of "Enhancing Multicultural Awareness through the Storybook Reading Experience" in this section include a quote from Alice Walker, who counsels us to "Keep in mind the present you are constructing. It should be the future you want."

The present now under construction brings children together from enormously different backgrounds. Technology enables children in North Dakota to computer-chat with students in Florida. Children in Texas study weather conditions presently occurring in New Jersey. Positive attitudes open opportunities for students to participate in school activities. Unbiased multicultural and multilingual practices look at children's strengths first, embracing each moment to strengthen self-identity.

The five readings in Section 4 confirm the benefits of inclusive and multicultural programs for children. Self-concept, valuable for every individual's development, is critical for young children acquiring awareness of their own identity. The first reading, "Ethnic Awareness and Attitudes in Young Children," discusses the value of learning experiences that enable children to build positive self images.

Continuous activities help children develop awareness of their own identity and build respectful attitudes about differences. The readings "Multicultural and Nonsexist Prop Boxes" and "Enhancing Multicultural Awareness through the Storybook Reading Experience" review specific activities that facilitate positive awareness, attitudes, and appreciation of diversity.

Strategies for responsible education of special needs children are considered in the last two readings. In "Let's All Sign! Enhancing Language Development in an Inclusive Preschool," teachers report that signing affords advantages for normal-hearing children and hearing-impaired children. Teacher educators outline a vision in the reading "Adapting Instruction for Students with Special Learning Needs, K–8." Special learning differences may be better met when appropriately modified experiences encourage reasoning abilities.

Key Points

- Positive self-concept development is closely linked with perceptions of ethnic and racial identity.

- Playing with authentic multicultural and nonsexist props enhances children's attitudes about their own identity and appreciation of others.

- Building acceptance may be attainable by simply inviting parents and children to daily read storybooks about diversity.

- Inclusive preschools enhance language development for all children.

- Children with special learning needs require opportunities to develop mathematical reasoning and problem-solving skills with appropriate instructional adaptations.

108

Questions

Reading 20. Studies show that young children of color display a significantly lower percentage of selecting friends within their own ethnicity than Anglo-American children. Why?

Reading 21. What are the contributions of prop boxes to children's growth and development in an early childhood setting?

Reading 22. How can early literacy development foster positive attitudes and awareness of diversity?

Reading 23. What are some of the benefits for hearing children in a preschool for hearing and nonhearing children?

Reading 24. How might primary school teachers create opportunities for children with special learning needs to collaboratively problem-solve?

Studies show that young children of color display a significantly lower percentage of selecting friends within their own ethnicity than Anglo-American children. Why?

Ethnic Awareness and Attitudes in Young Children

Karen Chia-Yu Liu and Susan Blila

Karen Chia-Yu Liu, an associate professor in the Department of Elementary and Early Childhood Education at Indiana State University, Terre Haute, has written numerous articles in the field of early childhood education. Susan Blila is a graduate student in the Department of Elementary and Early Childhood Education, School of Education, Indiana State University.

There has been a vast amount of research attempting to determine the age at which ethnic awareness, attitudes. and prejudice first appear in children. Some of the earliest investigations were made by Kenneth and Mamie Clark (1939), and the result of their studies indicated that Black American children growing up in a White society had difficulty accepting their Blackness and had serious social identity problems.

Clark's studies played a significant role in the United States Supreme Court 1954 decision to desegregate schools in the United States (Davey, 1983). Clark's findings were confirmed by further investigations (Stevenson and Stewart, 1958; Morland, 1966).

Over a quarter of a century ago, research confirmed that age, race, socioeconomic status, and geographic location were some of the factors which influence the development of young children's ethnic awareness. Do those factors still play a major role in influencing the development of children's racial awareness? Why is it still important to determine the age at which a child becomes aware of ethnic differences?

Piaget's theory indicates that children in the preoperational stage develop their cognitive ability to recognize the differences in size, shape, and texture of objects. They also develop the ability to distinguish color differences. It is natural for children at younger ages to develop the ability to perceive ethnic differences.

Ethnic awareness is the perception and acknowledgement of racial or ethnic distinctions in individuals and groups. Aboud (1988) indicated that racial awareness precedes the formation of racial attitudes, either positive or negative, and this awareness plays a major factor in a child's self-identification process.

Is the development of ethnic awareness related to prejudice? Aboud (1988) indicated that ethnic awareness comes before prejudice; it does not cause prejudice. However, Aboud (1988) believed that identifying with one's own ethnic group affects preference and that perceived differences between one's own ethnic group and others' affects prejudice. With this knowledge and understanding, preschool teachers will be able to create an environment that provides learning experiences to help young children form strong, positive self-concepts and to enable them to grow into mature adults who are able to respect and accept people who are different from themselves (Derman-Sparks, Gutierrez & Phillips, 1989).

A successful early childhood program should be able to meet each child's basic needs, including a positive self-concept.

Methodology

The Racial Awareness Response Form was used to determine children's self-concept, self-esteem, racial awareness, and knowledge of racial terms, racial attitude, and racial preference. The interview survey form was adopted from Stacey York's book, *Developing Roots & Wings* (1992). One hundred and fifty-six (156) children (30 Anglo-American children, 39 Hispanic children, 31 African-American children, 26 Native American children, and 30 Asian-American children) between the ages of three and 10 were interviewed by a graduate student majoring in early childhood education. Those interviewed children were from Indiana, Texas, and Illinois and were enrolled in preschool or day care programs.

Magazine pictures of Anglo-American, Hispanic, Asian-American, African-American and Native American children were used. Children three and four to years of age were presented with the Lakeshore ethnic dolls instead of or in addition to the magazine pictures.

Each child was interviewed individually. To assess a child's development of self-concept, the interviewer displayed the photos or dolls and asked the child, "Which one looks like you?" and "How are you and that child alike?" To assess the child's development of self-esteem, the interviewer asked the child to color a picture of himself or herself. The interviewer recorded the child's comments while drawing.

To assess a child's racial awareness and his/her knowledge of racial terms, the interviewer mixed up a matched set of multi-ethnic people picture cards, laid out the pictures in front of the child, and asked the child to match the people. After the child had matched the pairs, the interviewer then pointed to each matched set and asked, "What do you call these people?" To identify a child's racial attitude, the interviewer showed the child color squares, such as light brown squares, dark brown squares, yellow squares, black squares, etc. With each color, the interviewer asked the child, "What do you think of when you see the color brown (or other selected color)?", and "How does the color brown (or other selected color) make you feel?"

To assess a child's racial preference, the interviewer laid out the magazine pictures of ethnic children and/or ethnic dolls and asked the child the following questions: "Of these children, who would you like to play with?", "Who could be your friend?", "Whose house would you like to visit?", and "Is there anything else you want to tell me about these pictures?"

Result

Self-Concept

When asked to choose a picture or a doll that looked like themselves, seventy-five percent of Anglo-American children chose a picture or a doll that resembled themselves. The ability to choose correctly increased with age. Hispanic children in this sample have the least ability to identify themselves with their own ethnicity. Among the five ethnic groups, some of the Hispanic, Native American, and Asian children had difficulty distinguishing themselves from the children who have similar hair, skin, and eye colors. The majority of the African-American children who failed to identify their own ethnicity chose a Hispanic child with the same hair and eye color as their own.

Self-Esteem

Generally speaking, three- and four-year-old children were unable to draw a self-portrait with similar skin tone, hair, and eye color. Between the ages of five and seven years, the children's drawings became more consistent with reality as to skin tone and hair color. Eye color was less often accurate. The African-American children and the Native American children were the least accurate overall, drawing themselves with lighter skin and hair than they actually had. By the age of seven, the children drew pictures that were consistently realistic.

Racial Awareness

Without exception, the children from each ethnic group could easily recognize distinct ethnic differences. The children had no difficulty differentiating between the African-American picture or doll and the Anglo-American picture or doll when they were presented side by side without the other ethnic dolls in view. When all five ethnic groups of dolls or pictures were presented together, the children had more difficulty distinguishing distinct differences. Hair style appeared to influence choices.

Racial Attitude

All five ethnic groups were quite consistent in their attitude toward color. The vast majority of all the children liked all colors and had positive feelings about black and white. The color that evoked the most negative feeling was brown. Less than fifty percent of the children in each group had any specific thoughts come to mind when asked to think of the colors black, brown, or white. They all needed prompting to make color association.

Racial Preference

The majority of the Native American, Asian, Hispanic, and African-American children chose friends outside their own ethnic groups. When choosing friends, Asian, Hispanic, and Native American children frequently chose children with hair, skin, and eye coloring similar to their own. These choices could be considered in-group choices. The ethnic differences between the African-American children and their out-group choices are more distinct, suggesting that the African-American children may be rejecting their own ethnic group when choosing friends.

Discussion

The result of this survey showed that Anglo-American children gave evidence of a viable self-concept. They showed a preference for and assigned a positive value to the group with whom they shared physical characteristics. Since the Hispanic, Native American, and Asian doll or picture have similar skin tone, some children had difficulty in distinguishing the ethnicity of each group. Most of the children in the survey were highly aware of the physical differences between Anglo-American and African-American dolls or pictures.

Dermans-Sparks (1989) indicated that children of color, more often than White children, may verbalize disliking the color, texture, or shape of their skin, hair, or eyes. In this survey, only a small percentage of the children from each of the ethnic groups drew pictures that were reason-

able facsimiles of themselves as far as skin tone and hair color were concerned. Eighty-seven percent (87%) of the African-American children, 73% of Native American, and 51% of Hispanic children drew themselves with significantly lighter skin tones and lighter hair.

Ethnic awareness has often been associated with skin color recognition. Research indicated that color connotations are learned at an early age. Renninger and Williams (1966) explored the development of the evaluative meanings of black and white colors among preschool children. Their research has shown that evaluative meanings of black and white were learned during preschool years at which time children have begun to develop their ethnic attitudes. This survey showed that children younger than five years old thought of nothing when considering colors of black, brown, and white. Generally speaking, the vast majority of all the children surveyed liked black and white, but not brown.

At the present time, "Black" is still an accepted term among many African-Americans. Goodman (1964) stated that to label children "Black" when they are actually brown or light brown, is a significant mistake. Children at three or four years old can recognize color difference, and if they do not see black on their skin when they are called "Black," it is very confusing to them. It is important for preschool teachers to help children understand the proper way of categorizing different racial groups.

It is interesting to note that when choosing friends, children of color showed a significantly

lower percentage than Anglo-American children of selecting friends within their own ethnicity. Children of color need help in developing more positive own-race acceptance. It is recommended that parents and teachers of young children should make a conscious effort to reinforce positive own-race acceptance (Durrett & Davy, 1970).

Implication

Development is a continuous, interactive, and cumulative process. This developmental process can be seen in the progression of children's awareness of and attitude toward human differences (York, 1991). Early childhood educators need to understand a child's developmental process in becoming aware of ethnic differences and in the formation of racial attitudes.

A successful early childhood program should be able to meet each child's basic needs, including a positive self-concept. It is important to carefully evaluate materials used in a program for young children and to avoid or remove any that contain biased messages (Derman-Sparks, Gutierrez, and Phillips, 1989). It is equally important that materials be appropriate to the focus of young children and to their level of development.

Teachers also need to evaluate honestly their own feelings and attitudes about people from different cultural and ethnic backgrounds.

Early childhood educators should be able to create an environment in which young children feel comfortable being themselves and are encouraged to express feelings about their own ethnicity.

References

Aboud, F. (1988). *Children and Prejudice,* Basil Blackwell, Inc., New York, New York.

Clark, K. & Clark, M. (1939). The Development of Consciousness of Self in the Emergence of Racial Identification in Negro Preschool Children. *Journal of Social Psychology,* 10, 591–599.

Davey, A. (1983). *Learning to be Prejudiced,* Edward Arnold Ltd., London, U.K.

Derman-Sparks, L. (1989). *Anti-Bias Curriculum,* National Association for the Education of Young Children, Washington, D.C.

Derman-Sparks, L., Gutierrez, M. and Phillips, C. (1989). *Teaching Young Children to Resist Bias.* National Association for the Education of Young Children, Washington, D.C.

Durrett, M. & Davey, A. (1970, October). Racial Awareness in Young Mexican-American, Negro, and Anglo Children. *Young Children,* 16–24.

Goodman, M. (1964). *Race Awareness in Young Children.* New York: Collier Books.

Morland, J. (1966). A Comparison of Race Awareness in Northern and Southern Children. *American Journal of Orthopsychiatry,* 36, 22–31.

Renninger, C. & Williams, J. (1966). Black-White Color Connotations and Racial Awareness in Preschool Children. *Perceptual & Motor Skills,* 22, 771–785.

Stevenson, H. & Stevenson, N. (1960). Social Interaction in an Inter-Racial Nursery School. *Genetic Psychology Monograph,* 61, 37–75.

Stevenson, H. & Stewart, E. (1958). A Developmental Study of Racial Awareness in Young Children. *Child Development,* 29, 399–409.

York, S. (1992). *Developing Roots & Wings: A Trainer's Guide to Affirming Culture in Early Childhood Programs,* Redleaf Press.

York, S. (1991). *Roots & Wings: Affirming Culture in Early Childhood Programs,* Redleaf Press.

Article Review Form at end of book.

What are the contributions of prop boxes to children's growth and development in an early childhood setting?

Multicultural and Nonsexist Prop Boxes

Gloria S. Boutte, Irma Van Scoy, and Susan Hendley

Gloria Swindler Boutte, Ph.D., is an associate professor at the University of South Carolina at Columbia. Gloria has authored several articles on diversity issues, made numerous state and national presentations on the topic, and is preparing a book on the subject.

Irma J. Van Scoy, Ph.D., is an associate professor in early childhood education at the University of South Carolina at Columbia. Irma has worked for 10 years with early childhood teacher education students in the development and use of prop boxes.

Susan Goldstein Hendley, Ph.D., is an assistant professor of education at the University of South Carolina at Sumter. As a teacher educator, she researches diversity issues, specifically authentic multiculturalism.

There has been a resurgence of interest in prop boxes, as evidenced by articles appearing in early childhood journals (Soundy & Gallagher 1992; Myhre 1993), yet little emphasis has been placed on multicultural and nonsexist possibilities of prop boxes. Although multicultural education extends far beyond activities and materials alone (Boutte & McCormick 1992), teachers must plan for multicultural dimensions in all activities and set up the environment to represent diversity (Brewer 1995). Materials and props facilitate the process. As children play with props and interact among themselves, teachers have many opportunities to discuss diversity issues and model acceptance of differences.

When teachers fail to include a wide variety of multicultural and nonsexist props in their dramatic play areas, they unconsciously reinforce monocultural ideas about how a business or home setting is "supposed" to look. The absence or infrequent use of multicultural props often reflects teachers' attitudes toward diversity.

Rationale for Prop Boxes

Play, including prop boxes, encourage children's holistic development (social, emotional, language, cognitive, and physical) and easily lends itself to integration across the curriculum. Although prop boxes are most commonly found in preschools and kindergartens, they also provide wonderful learning opportunities for children in the primary grades. Prop boxes with multicultural themes can be developed in a complex and detailed manner to expose children to diversity issues. When multicultural concepts are integrated into regular play routines, the experiences are more authentic (Boutte & McCormick 1992) than when taught in isolated lessons or units.

From a Piagetian (constructivist) perspective, prop boxes are excellent for fostering children's construction of knowledge and providing them with an "active" education (DeVries & Kohlberg 1987). A particular strength of prop boxes is that they allow children to build on spontaneous activities. Children begin to note commonalities among genders, ethnicities, and cultures while playing with nonsexist and multicultural props. They find common elements in how people from different cultures cook, eat, dress, live in families, and carry out daily activities (Brewer 1995).

DeVries and Kohlberg (1987) suggest four methods that actively engage children's minds and appeal to children's spontaneous activities: interest, play, genuine exploration, and cooperation. Each method is briefly discussed to illustrate why the dramatic play area is an ideal and natural area to focus on diversity.

Interest

DeVries and Kohlberg (1987) emphasize that unless children are interested, they will never make the constructive effort to make sense out of their experiences. Passive approaches such as drills and lectures do not typically gain or sustain children's interest. Most children begrudgingly engage in repetitive tasks, such as completing worksheets, primarily to oblige the teacher. On the other hand, prop boxes and other active methods elicit children's interest naturally. Children gravitate toward prop boxes on their own volition, without prodding from the teacher.

Since play is inherently interesting to most children, prop boxes place learning within a relevant context. For example, children are more compelled to learn their telephone numbers when the numbers are used during play routines (written down on message pads, listed in appointment books, or filed in a Rolodex) to "call" classmates about business issues. The concept of time is emphasized when children use a clock and calendar to set "appointment" times. Children are motivated to count money if they pretend to pay a bill. They will add, subtract, multiply, divide, or use a calculator when there is a clear purpose for doing these activities. Other concepts naturally emerge as children classify items by attributes, measure objects, put things in order, and so forth. Since young children also are very interested in differences and similarities among people, teachers can use multicultural props to extend understanding of diversity issues.

Play

DeVries and Kohlberg (1987) point out that play is usually neglected by traditional schools because it appears to be devoid of functional significance. By contrast, constructivist educational methods, and the progressive education philosophy that preceded it, include a large component of play. However, teachers must be adept at observing children's play to determine how to facilitate learning (including knowledge of and attitudes about other cultures).

Experimentation

Genuine experimentation and authentic work are salient characteristics of education. Experimentation should be embedded in natural contexts. Prop boxes, less threatening than formal methods, encourage experimentation. Experimentation provides time and opportunities for children to make errors, rediscover, or reconstruct their knowledge.

Unlike approaches that focus on correct answers, prop boxes are open-ended and allow children a chance to derive *horizontal* (deeper) understandings. Since the process of knowledge construction is ongoing, each time children engage in dramatic play activities, the possibilities of deepening their understandings increase. Learning is not a series of facts that children accumulate (*vertical* learning). Rather, the emphasis is on enhancing children's reasoning processes and understandings. Multicultural and nonsexist prop boxes provide children with opportunities to experiment with different cultural artifacts.

Cooperation

Cooperation does not mean "submissive compliance or superficial good-naturedness" (DeVries & Kohlberg 1987, 30). Rather, it implies interactions (including conflict) between teachers and children. DeVries and Kohlberg note that social interaction is necessary for the development of logic. The social context offers possibilities for children to become aware of differences in perspectives. Through social interactions, children can be led out of egocentrism or subjectivity in thought to reciprocity and objectivity. For example, children learn that certain cultural habits that are familiar to and preferred by them may be foreign and distasteful to others. As children play with props, they inevitably face disagreements with and intellectual challenges by their peers and/or teachers. Such conflicts encourage accommodation (learning) and discourage ethnocentrism (believing that people like you are the best people).

When children use stereotypes, teachers can discuss misconceptions and dispel myths. Teachers may purposely select props that stimulate children's multicultural and nonsexist awareness. It is not uncommon to observe children debating different play schemas such as what foods to serve (for example, tacos or hamburgers). Culturally loaded judgments and terminology can be discouraged by encouraging children to use terms such as "different" instead. After extended periods of play and cooperation, children will undoubtedly leave dramatic play areas with increased levels of multicultural awareness. Children also learn that many foods, clothing, and so forth are shared across a number of cultures.

Multicultural and Nonsexist Prop Boxes

Authentic multicultural experiences should be thoroughly integrated in curricula and activities rather than being presented through formal units or lessons

(Boutte & McCormick 1992). Many teachers, in an effort to avoid a "tourist" approach to multiculturalism, have difficulty conceiving relevant ways of emphasizing similarities and differences among people. While they want to avoid promoting stereotypes by presenting cultural artifacts to represent cultures, teachers have to find ways of exposing children to the wide variety of cultural possibilities and beliefs.

Prop boxes should encourage all children to try out various roles. A hair salon, for example, should include men's products as well as women's. Girls and boys can be doctors, nurses, mail carriers, flight attendants, firefighters—whatever. Numerous ethnic groups and cultures should be represented through pictures, magazines, and the like.

At first glance, it may appear that the prop items are simply add-ons that contribute to the tourist approach of multiculturalism. However, closer examination will reveal that children are exposed to cultural artifacts that normally may not be included in the regular classroom or only included as part of special units. Hence, children learn very little about cultural information and artifacts that are very important to various cultures.

Teachers do not need to explicitly point out multicultural and nonsexist items. Rather, they need to observe and listen to children's comments and follow up with rich discussions. Otherwise, children will not get the full benefit of the multicultural and nonsexist props.

For example, children may ask questions about various hair products—after encountering the hair "grease" [oil] used by many Blacks, a White child may ask,

Listen to These Children Learn

Ebony (Black female): (Talking to self while styling a doll's hair.) "Hold still, girl, so I can grease your scalp."

Elizabeth (White female): (Frowning) "What's that stuff?"

Ebony: "Hair grease."

Elizabeth: "Hair what?"

Ebony: "Girl, don't you know what hair grease is? Don't your mama put it on your hair?"

Elizabeth: "No."

Ebony: "What do you use then?"

Elizabeth: "This one." (Points to an empty container of shampoo that her mother donated to the collection.)

Ebony: "Oh, I don't use that."

On the surface, hair may seem to be a trivial subject, but it is closely related to the development of children's self-esteem and how they feel about themselves. This scenario lends itself to subsequent discussion about many issues dealing with hair care. The two girls are confronted with the fact that they each use different types of hair products.

Teachers can share books like *Cornrows* (Yarborough 1979) to reopen the discussion. (Often Black products and hairstyles are not seen on advertisements, and children and adults assume that the process of taking care of hair is universal.) The teacher may find ways to discuss differences in hair textures and frequency of shampooing. Many Black females wash their hair only once every two or three weeks, as compared to daily (or every other day) shampooing by many White females. Discussions about straightening hair could be stimulated by including a straightening comb in the collection.

Informal follow-up by the teacher is important in order to curb ethnocentrism. Too often Black females are not taught to feel proud of their hair. The important message for children to learn is that we all have hair, but there are vast differences in hair care techniques. Although we have focused on Black and White females here, other ethnic groups, as well as males, also have different hair care needs and customs.

"What's this sticky stuff?" Without teacher clarification, such comments could lead Black children who use these products to feel embarrassed or White children to view hair grease as "weird" or "gross."

Children grow multiculturally when they learn that there are numerous, varied techniques and products for hair care. Teachers can extend children's knowledge by making comments that show appreciation for different hair care methods, visiting hair salons that cater to different ethnic groups, or inviting children and their parents to discuss various hair products and methods they use. The box on this page includes a dialogue that was observed while two children played with multicultural hair products.

Children also may voice objection to different types of music and artwork. Such reactions and comments may point out voids in the curriculum, unresolved questions that children have, and issues that are confusing to them. The addition of listening to a diverse collection of music and artwork on a regular basis has the potential for broadening children's multicultural horizons. By continuous

Children become more tolerant because multicultural activities are integrated daily rather than in the isolated units that are few and far between in many classrooms.

exposure to cultural variations, children learn to appreciate and accept these musical variations as the norm rather than as a deviation from "mainstream" culture. Teachers can invite discussion of multicultural issues that arise in children's play.

The following section highlights some of the multicultural possibilities of prop boxes. Content areas that naturally emerge through interaction with prop box activities are emphasized. We assume that the reader will be able to think of *typical* props to go with each theme (refer to Myhre 1993 or Soundy & Gallagher 1992); therefore, we will focus only on multicultural and nonsexist items and activities.

Generic Multicultural Possibilities

The multicultural possibilities provided in this section are not intended to be exhaustive. They are elements designed to enhance prop boxes and dramatic play and to stimulate other extensions.

We reiterate that if items are used only once or twice to accompany isolated units, they simply reinforce stereotypes. Although the items listed for specific prop boxes will be unique to some children, they are part of ordinary cultural orientation for others. As children play with a wide range of multicultural props, they become familiar with the myriad of ways that humanity manifests itself. Teachers may first need to research some of the items to determine their cultural significance and appropriate use.

Specific Multicultural Possibilities

This section provides examples of multicultural items and extensions that can be used with six

Art

Multicultural artwork can be displayed to accompany most prop boxes. Artwork should cover a variety of periods and styles (impressionist, cubist, and so on). Museums often sell calendars with reproductions of such work. Sculptures, vases, baskets, masks, pottery, mobiles, and other forms of art also provide a cultural flavor to the dramatic play area. Photos and magazine pictures can be used to decorate the prop boxes and to create posters for display in the dramatic play center. Choose pictures that portray men and women of different races, ages, and abilities engaged in a variety of roles.

A number of books with artwork can be placed in language centers—for example, *Picasso* (Venezia 1988), written on a child's level with pictures of the Spanish artist's painting; *Linnea in Monet's Garden* (Bjork 1987), a collection of the French impressionists's work; and *Father and Son* (Lauture 1992) or *Noah* (Gauch & Green 1994), both featuring illustrations by African-American artist Jonathan Green of South Carolina.

Cultural Artifacts

A wide variety of cultural artifacts can be included with any prop box (for example, kimonos, saris, kilts, grass skirts, wooden shoes, sombreros, African kufis, quilts, baskets).

Literature

Integrate literature with prop boxes whenever possible. Many books can be used to reinforce themes.

Items for Special Needs

Include objects that are used by people with special needs (for example, portable wheelchair, child-size crutches, walking cane, sign language alphabet posters, braille cards, and so on).

Music

Most businesses play background music. In the same way, music can be played softly in the background during dramatic play activities.

A wide variety of musical styles (for example, country, classical, soul, reggae, appropriate rap, Native American, Asian, Latino) should be recorded. Most public libraries have a wide assortment of music. To avoid repeated trips to the library, we have found it useful to record the music on a cassette player. Children learn to appreciate different music styles and to critique them as well. Additionally, when children hear music that is similar to the type that they hear at home, the school-home transition/link is strengthened.

Foods

Cultural dishes often should be served as snacks to help children develop a tolerance for—perhaps even an appreciation of—other foods. Parents often are willing to cook a traditional dish to share at school. Possibilities include sushi (a vegetable and rice version), red beans and rice, and the like. These should not be presented as unique and exotic snacks; rather, they should be a regular part of the menu. Children will begin to understand that some people do not eat pork or other meats. But they also will realize how much people have in common—for example, that rice is an important staple in many cultures even though it may be prepared differently.

Shoe Store

Include a selection of shoes (for example, moccasins, Chinese slippers, sandals, boots) for males and females of many different cultures. Supply knee highs that represent many different skin tones. Read books about various types of shoes—for example, *Try on a Shoe* (Moncure 1973) or *A Pair of Red Clogs* (Matsuno 1960).

Bakery

Create simulations of baked goods representing many different cultures (baklava, pitas, tortillas, challah, and the like.) Simulations may be made with homemade or commercial playdough. When possible, provide the real thing for snacks. Many parents are willing to bake goods. Children also enjoy baking in the classroom.

Cookbooks featuring baked goods from many different cultures can be created by children and their families. Scrapbook pictures can be cut out of food magazines or other magazines such as *Good Housekeeping* and *Ebony*. Books such as *Bread, Bread, Bread* (Morris 1989) can be shared.

specific prop boxes: beauty/barber shop, shoe store, bakery, restaurant, grocery store, and department store. Curriculum areas can be included in each prop box. For example, for math extensions, children can create price lists, total bills, and pay for services.

Teachers' Attitudes and Actions Are Important: Teachers Should Not Merely Be Providers of Props

We urge teachers to remember the integral role they play in reinforcing attitudinal multicultural competencies. The simple provision of materials without teacher guidance

Beauty Shop/Barber Shop (Hair Salon)

Wherever children congregate, we sometimes have problems with the spread of head lice, ringworm, and the like. If you are having this type of problem, we suggest that children style doll's hair instead of their own. Provide a multicultural collection of male and female dolls that authentically represent many cultures. If wig heads are used, they also should be multicultural.

Collect an abundance of hair care materials that focus on differences: rollers of various sizes; wigs of many textures, lengths, and colors; a collection of empty containers representing male and female hair products from many cultures (for example, curl moisturizer, oil sheen, hair "grease," perms for Black and White hair, men's hair cream); beads for braids, hair for weaves, barrettes, ribbons, and the like; male-oriented materials such as razors (remove blades, of course), hair clippers (with cord and plug cut off), and empty aftershave containers; different types and sizes of combs (feather, afro, straightening); and various headdresses such as turbans and yarmulkes. While we recommend using empty containers, we suggest that teachers ask children and/or parents to share one hair product during show-and-tell. The teacher may also bring extra products (for example, hair grease) for the children to explore and experiment with.

Provide manicure materials that appeal to both boys and girls and include cotton balls, cardboard emery boards, empty bottles of nail polish, and so on.

Children can cut out pictures of various hairstyles from magazines, make collages, and learn to attend to and appreciate diverse hair styles. Also collect hair salon books that feature hairstyles for males and females of all cultures. Teachers can help children classify hairstyles by color, texture, length, etc. Children's literature about hairstyles can be included or read, such as *Cornrows* (Yarborough 1979), *Straight hair, Curly Hair* (Goldin 1965), *Uncle Jed's Barbershop* (King-Mitchell 1993), *Afrotina and the Three Bears* (Crump 1991), or *Rapunzel* (both the classic and African-American edition [Crump 1992]).

Include a wide variety of magazines that appeal to many cultures and both genders. For example, *Sports Illustrated, Ebony Man,* or *Sport* may appeal to boys, *Ebony* or *Essence* to Blacks, or *Scoop Today* to Asians. (Screen all magazines for appropriateness. We remove suggestive pictures prior to placing any magazine in the dramatic play area.) Often parents have such magazines at home and would willingly contribute them to the classroom.

Department Store

This prop box has unlimited possibilities since department stores sell a variety of products. Be sure to include departments for both males and females. Offer clothing that represents many different cultures (kimonos, dashikis, saris, and so on). Children and teachers can create cardboard male and female mannequins that feature characteristics of various ethnic groups. In the accessory department, provide a collection of multicultural and nonsexist hats and scarves (yarmulkes, turbans, and so on). Read Ann Morris's book *Hats, Hats, Hats,* (1989).

The jewelry department could feature a variety of costume jewelry including Native American and African beads, shell necklaces, simulated pearls and gems, and silver- and gold-tone chains. The cosmetic department can include empty foundation bottles representing many skin tones, simulated lipstick and eye shadow colors in a range of colors, and a wide variety of small bottles featuring exotic perfumes and aromas (put a drop of cologne or oil in a cotton ball and stuff the ball into the bottle). A wide variety of knee highs representing many skin tones should be included in the hosiery department. The home interior department could include African sculptures, Asian vases, a variety of dishes and baskets, and so forth.

Restaurants

Several types of restaurants (soul food, Chinese, Indian, Jamaican, Mexican, etc.) with accompanying cooking utensils, dishes, and props can be set up. Try to obtain menus as well as empty food containers and boxes from ethnic restaurants.

Many children have not tasted ethnic foods and are hesitant to try new foods. Ideally, field trips to restaurants could be taken. Parents and teachers also may cook some of these dishes for snacks. In a related extension activity, children could taste herbal teas from all over the world.

Cookbooks complement this prop box. Children's literature such as *Everybody Cooks Rice* (Dooley 1992), *Latkes and Applesauce* (Manushkin 1990), *The Perfect Present* (Thomson & Thomson 1988), *Too Many Tamales* (Soto & Martinez 1993), and *Strega Nona* (dePaola 1975) also can be read.

Grocery Store

Ask parents to save containers and boxes from the grocery store. Include a variety of products that appeal to many cultures and both genders (for example, taco or rice boxes, men's aftershave containers). Create simulated bagels, burritos, and other foods with playdough and other media. Many children are unfamiliar with foods such as these. Teachers can discuss how many foods are eaten by people from different cultures. Empty spice bottles and containers can expose children to the wide variety of seasonings used in various cultures (for example, curry, anise, ginger, cayenne pepper).

Multicultural children's books and magazines can be "sold" in the magazine section of the grocery store.

does little for developing multicultural awareness. Children become more tolerant because multicultural activities are integrated daily rather than in the isolated units that are few and far between in many classrooms.

References

Boutte, G. S., & C. B. McCormick. 1992. Authentic multicultural activities (Avoiding pseudomulticulturalism). *Childhood Education* 68 (3): 140–44.

Brewer, J. 1995. *Introduction to early childhood education.* Needham Heights, MA: Allyn & Bacon.

DeVries, R., & L. Kohlberg. 1987. *Constructivist early education: Overview and comparison with other programs.* Washington, DC: NAEYC.

Myhre, S. M. 1993. Enhancing your dramatic-play area through the use of prop boxes. *Young Children* 48 (5): 1–6.

Soundy, C. S., & P. W. Gallagher. 1992. Creating prop boxes to stimulate dramatic play and literacy development. *Day Care and Early Education* 21 (2): 4–8.

 Article Review Form at end of book.

How can early literacy development foster positive attitudes and awareness of diversity?

Enhancing Multicultural Awareness through the Storybook Reading Experience

Mary Ann Wham
University of Wisconsin–Whitewater

June Barnhart
Northern Illinois University

Greg Cook
University of Wisconsin–Whitewater

The purpose of this study was to examine the effects of combining home and classroom reading experiences of multicultural storybooks on the awareness and attitudes of kindergarten, second grade, and fourth-grade students, towards individuals representing other cultures, circumstances, or lifestyles. Two classrooms of students at each of the three grade levels participated in the study with one classroom at each grade level randomly specified as the Storybook Reading Group; the other served as the Control Group. The following question guided the study: Are pupils' attitudes toward multicultural diversity enhanced by exposure to multicultural literature? At the beginning and at the end of the study, all participants responded to a survey which examined their attitudes toward aspects of diversity. Administration of the instrument at posttest time indicated that positive gains occurred in the Storybook Reading Groups at Grades 2 and 4. For kindergartners, positive gains occurred on six of the nine survey items. A different, and surprising pattern occurred in the control groups where there was overall negative change at all three grade levels. These findings suggest that without a diversity program children's appreciation of diversity may actually decrease across the schools year.

Children do not come to school as blank slates on the topic of diversity. Rather, research by Katz (1981) suggests that infants, as early as 6 months of age, notice skin color differences, and by the age of 2 years, begin to ask questions about differences among people. This awareness continues to develop as children mature; and by the age of nine, research by Aboud (1988) suggests that children's attitudes towards diversity tend to stay constant unless altered by life changing events.

Within the educational community as well as within the general population, reading aloud to children has been regarded as beneficial for a variety of reasons. Primarily, research reports have documented the correlation between being read to and certain aspects of literacy development. Studies have found, for example, that the experience of being read to figures prominently in the histories of children who come to school already reading (Durkin, 1966; Gardner, 1970; Hoffman, 1982; Plessas & Oakes, 1964; Tobin, 1982). Furthermore, numerous correlational studies have now documented the relationship between reading stories to children and their subsequent advantage on reading readiness tests and success with beginning reading (Chomsky, 1972; Durkin, 1974–75, 1988; Yaden, Smilkin, & Conlon, 1989). Teale (1984) suggests that reading to children helps foster four areas of early literacy development, including (a) awareness of the functions and uses of written language, (b) concepts about print, books, and reading, and the form and structure of written language, (c) reading strategies, and (d) attitudes toward reading.

Today, most elementary classrooms include children representing a variety of cultural backgrounds. However, regardless of the classroom composition, all children need exposure to literature that incorporates a wide variety of cultural groups (McGee & Richgels, 1996).

Several reports have described efforts to use literature in the classroom as a vehicle to increase multicultural awareness among elementary grade students (Bishop, 1987, 1992; Lichter & Johnson, 1973; Nicolai-Mays & Oulahan, 1991; Norton, 1990; Perkins & Long, 1991; Walker-Dalhouse, 1992). It is believed that incorporating multiethnic literature into the curriculum can expand appreciation and decrease negative stereotyping of individuals representing other cultures (Walker-Dalhouse, 1992). Although literature for children has been recognized as a potent factor for multicultural learning, Rasinski and Padak (1990) propose that its full potential for multicultural awareness has yet to be realized.

Because of the recent focus on the multicultural heritages within the United States, schools have been encouraged to help students learn to appreciate the members of other cultures and to promote an awareness of and appreciation for the contributions of cultures coexisting within our country. Multicultural perspectives have expanded to include studies of gender equality, an understanding of physical disabilities, and a focus on the similarities among people rather than viewing differences as deficiencies (National Counsel for Accreditation of Teacher Education, 1981).

Children cannot be expected to develop a sensitivity towards others merely because they are told to do so. Attitudes are difficult to change. Perhaps "what cannot be taught through facts may be taught through the heart" (Bieger, 1996. p. 308). Literature allows individuals to share in the lives of others; it can also provide an avenue for multicultural understanding. It allows individuals to experience other people's feelings, appreciate, and understand those whose cultural backgrounds differ from their own.

Among the general population, there is growing recognition that schools and parents must become active participants and supporters in the education of their children. The positive effects of organized parent participation have been documented through research (Henderson, 1988). Intergenerational projects (for example, Parents as Partners in Reading and the Parent Readers Program) have begun to receive attention and support throughout the country (France & Hager, 1993).

With this knowledge as a framework, we decided to implement a program that would incorporate several aspects of existing research. Essentially, we, as researchers, sought to build on the efforts of others by examining the effects of combining home and classroom reading experiences of multicultural storybooks on the awareness and attitudes of kindergarten, second grade, and fourth-grade students towards individuals representing other cultures, circumstances or lifestyles.

We began the study with the following question as our main focus: Are children's attitudes toward multicultural diversity enhanced by exposure to multicultural literature? In addition, it was of interest to see if the effectiveness of the program would generalize across grade levels.

Participants

Our participants for the study were 128 students (55 females, 73 males) who attended a public elementary school in a small Midwestern community. The composition of the student population can best be described as middle-class Caucasian and is reflective of the community as a whole where greater than 99% of the population is Caucasian.

Two classrooms of students at each of three grade levels participated in the study with one classroom at each grade level randomly specified as the Storybook Reading Group (SRG); the other served as the control group (CG). There were 35 students in the kindergarten sample (*n* = 19, SRG: *n* = 16, control), 45 students in the second-grade sample (*n* = 25, SRG; *n* = 20, control) and 48 students in the fourth-grade sample (*n* = 25, SRG; *n* = 23, control).

Data Collection Procedures

At the beginning of the study, one of the researchers met with the parents of the students designated to be in the Storybook Reading Groups to explain the project to them. The researcher discussed the benefits of reading aloud to children and elaborated on the value of the social interaction between parent and child during the storybook reading experience. The parents were encouraged to discuss the books with their children. The parents were informed that the understanding of a text is enhanced by encouraging children to ask questions and relate their own experiences to the story. The researcher asked that, after each daily read aloud session, the parent and child fill out a reading record on which they would record the number of pages read and comment on their feelings about the contents of the book. All of the parents who attended the session and almost all of those we contacted by phone were eager to participate in the project. They agreed to read to their child for at least 15 minutes per day. There were two families at the fourth-grade level who chose not to participate in the study.

Through a university grant, we were able to purchase multiple copies of tradebooks written about various aspects of diversity. There were stories about single parent families, the elderly, the unemployed, families representing different cultures and ethnic groups,

and children with physical and mental disabilities (see Appendix A for a complete bibliographic list*). The books, which were fiction as well as nonfiction, were sent home with the students in the Storybook Reading Groups on a regular basis over a 7 month period. Some children took home several books a week; others chose longer chapter books and kept them for extended periods of time. In addition, subjects in all three-grade levels who were in the Storybook Reading Group were exposed to classroom routines that included daily storybook reading episodes by their classroom teachers of one or more of the books selected for the study. Teachers of students in the control group classrooms were asked to continue with their daily routines, and if that included a read aloud session, not to include any of the books that had been selected for the study.

At the beginning of the school year in September, all of the subjects responded to a survey instrument constructed for this study. Nine of the questions on the survey dealt with some aspect of multicultural diversity, including the hearing impaired, visually impaired, elderly, impoverished, divorced, and physically disabled. Three questions dealt with general reading attitudes and were not analyzed for the current study. The entire survey instrument can be found in Appendix B.*

To determine the reliability of the instrument, a test-retest procedure was implemented. This procedure, accomplished on successive days, used a pilot set of data and did not involve participants from the present study. A Cronbach Alpha formula was computed on the two sets of test scores. The obtained alpha coeffi-

*Not included in this publication

cient (*r* = .9267) indicated that the test appears to be highly reliable.

The questions on the survey asked subjects to respond to hypothetical situations in which they would be reading about or participating with individuals representing a range of diverse backgrounds. Subjects were given answer sheets on which there were numbered rows with three faces per row. Each face within a row was the same except for the mouth. The first face showed a broad happy smile, the second, a straight line indicating a neutral response, and the third, an inverted smile, indicating displeasure. In March, the survey instrument was again administered as a posttest to all subjects.

Administration of this instrument at the pre and posttest times was carried out by one researcher reading the questions to the subjects and directing them to "Mark the face that best indicates your feeling about the situation described in the question". Implementation of the storybook reading experience occurred over a 7-month period between pre and posttests.

Data Analysis

At the conclusion of the study, all responses to the diversity questions on the surveys administered to the subjects at the pre and posttest times were converted to ordinal numbers in order to facilitate data analyses. Each response corresponding to a face with a broad smile was assigned a 3, a face with a straight line was assigned a 2, and a face with an inverted smile was assigned a 1. Comparisons between treatment and control groups were performed to analyze for changes in the frequency of responses coded as 3s (positive attitude responses) across the nine questions in the survey. Additionally comparisons across grade levels were performed to analyze for differences in responses coded as 3s.

Results

The primary question guiding the study asked whether children's attitudes toward multicultural diversity would be enhanced by exposure to multicultural literature. Tables 1a, 1b, and 1c* show the number of children at each grade level who gave the most positive rating (3) on the pretest and posttest for each of the nine diversity questions assessed. Positive gains occurred in the experimental condition (SRG) at Grades 2 and 4. For kindergartners, a positive change occurred on five of the nine questions on the survey while there was negative change on three of the items resulting in no overall gains. For second graders, there was a positive change on six items in the SRG and no negative changes. For fourth graders a positive change occurred on six of the nine items and a negative change on three items. A different pattern occurred in the control groups where there was an overall negative change at all three grade levels.

In the Storybook Reading Groups, the percentage of increase in positive responses towards diversity ranged from no overall percentage change among kindergartners to a 14% change in the second-grade group. Fourth graders recorded a 3% change in attitude after the storybook reading experience. Decreases in positive responses in the control groups ranged from 1% in the fourth-grade group to 7% in the second-grade group with kinder-

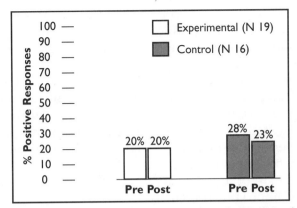

Figure 1. Change in attitude toward multicultural diversity kindergarten subjects.

gartners recording a 5% decrease (Figures 1–3**).

These findings indicate that, across the school year, attitudes toward multicultural diversity became more positive or remained steady in the Storybook Reading Groups and became more negative in the control groups.

Since the largest increase and decrease both occurred in the second grade, it appears that this is a time when multicultural attitudes might be most modifiable. Without positive intervention, second graders seem to be at greatest risk for showing decreases in positive multicultural attitudes, while with intervention, they show the greatest potential for increases in positive attitudes.

Parental Evaluation

Parents who participated in the study were asked to complete a short survey evaluating their participation in the Read To Me program. We found their comments enlightening and gratifying. One parent wrote, "We all learned from the books." Another wrote, "Our most sensitive child is beginning to realize his emotions are shared by other children." And a third who urged us to offer the program at more grade levels responded, "It was a fun time together enjoyed by

both parent and child—no pressure on my child to perform. It was also a nice alternative to TV watching."

Limitations of the Study

We, as researchers, recognized that the study had limitations. For example, we had no control over the quality of the parent-child interactions during the story time reading experiences. It is possible that some parents reinforced the positive messages in the books during their conversations with their children.

In addition, we did not attempt to control over the children's choices of books. Perhaps some of the books contained a stronger, more influential message than did others. We also recognized that the children who completed the survey became aware, during the course of the year, that certain attitudes were "politically correct" and responded to the posttest in that manner.

Conclusions

Before the study began, we had hypothesized that attitudes toward diversity would probably become more positive in both the SRG and control groups, but we hoped that the reading program would enhance the positive growth in the experimental group. We were therefore surprised that

*Not included in this publication
**Figures 2 and 3 not included in this publication.

the number of positive ratings actually declined in the control group. This finding is alarming because it suggests that, without a diversity program children's appreciation of diversity may actually decrease across the school year. If so, we believe that it is critical for intervention programs to be implemented in order to enhance appreciation of individuals representing other cultures, circumstances or lifestyles.

At the beginning of this article, a reference to Aboud (1988) was included in which she suggested that attitudes tend to stay constant unless altered by a life changing event. We believe that reading aloud to children on topics reflective of diversity provides such an event and may serve as a catalyst in forming positive attitudes towards members of diverse cultures. By providing books on diverse topics that parents and children could read together at home, and teachers could read in the classroom, we were able to reverse a negative trend and show some positive gains in attitudes toward most of the diversity topics.

It seems appropriate, therefore, to suggest that multicultural literature may be a potent factor in moving students to broader levels of awareness and understanding of diverse groups. Based on the results of this study, we are comfortable in urging educators to incorporate the reading of multicultural literature into the classroom curricula and to urge parents to support these efforts through storybook reading in the home.

A statement by Alice Walker (1989) sustains our ideas of early intervention as a way of building a world of acceptance. She states, "Keep in mind the present you are constructing. It should be the future you want" (p. 238). Clearly, this is a worthy and deserving concept—one that appears to be attainable in part through the simple sharing of storybook reading. We believe that educators who feel a sense of responsibility toward a world of unity will respond in kind and participate in this easily implemented activity.

References

Aboud, F. (1988). *Children and prejudice.* London: Basic Blackwell.

Bieger, E. M. (1996). Promoting multicultural education through a literature-based approach. *The Reading Teacher, 49,* 308–313.

Bishop, R. S. (1987). Extending multicultural understanding through children's books. In B. E. Cullinan (Ed.). *Children's literature in the reading program.* 60–67. Newark, DE: International Reading Association.

Bishop, R. S. (1992). Multicultural literature for children: Making informed choices. In V. Harris (Ed.). *Teaching multicultural literature in grades K–8.* 37–53, Norwood, MA: Christopher-Gordon.

Chomsky, C. (1972). Stages in language development and reading exposure. *Harvard Educational Review, 42,* 1–34.

Durkin, D. (1966). *Children who read early.* New York: Teachers College Press.

Durkin, D. (1974–75). A six year study of children who learned to read in school at the age of four. *Reading Research Quarterly, 10,* 9–61.

Durkin, D. (1988). *Teaching them to read* (5th ed.). Boston: Allyn & Bacon.

France, M., & Hager, J. (1993). Recruit, respect, respond: A model for working with low income families and their preschoolers. *Reading Teacher, 46,* 468–472.

Gardner, J. (1970). Early reading skills. In *Reading skills: Theory and practice.* London: Ward Lock Educational Books.

Henderson, A. T. (1988). Parents are a school's best friend. *Phi Delta Kappan.* 149–153.

Hoffman, S. J. (1982, March). *Preschool reading related behaviors: A parent diary:* Paper presented at the third Ethnography in Education Forum, Philadelphia.

Katz, P. (1981). Development of children's racial awareness and intergroup attitudes. In Lilliian Katz (Ed.). *Current Topics in Early Childhood Education, 4,* 19–54.

Lichter, J. H., & Johnson, D. (1973). Changes in attitudes toward Negroes by White elementary students after the use of multiethnic readers. *Journal of Educational Research, 65,* 295–299.

McGee. L., & Richgels, D. (1996). *Literacy beginnings: Supporting young readers and writers.* Needham Heights, MA: Allyn & Bacon.

National Council for Accreditation of Teacher Education, (1981). *Standards for the accreditation of teacher education* (rev. ed.). Washington D.C.

Nicolai-Mays, S., & Oulahan, A. (1991). Making a difference. Multicultural literature for young children. Illinois *Reading Council Journal, 19*(1), 21–27.

Norton, D. E. (1990). Teaching multicultural literature in the reading curriculum. *The Reading Teacher, 44,* 28–40.

Perkins, F. D., & Long. R. (1991). Author studies: Profiles in black. *Teaching Pre K–8, 21,* 51–53.

Plessas, G. P., & Oakes, C. R. (1964). Prereading experiences of selected early readers. *The Reading Teacher, 44,* 28–40.

Rasinski. T. V., & Padak, N. D. (1990). Multicultural learning through children's literature. *Language Arts, 67,* 576–580.

Teale, W. (1984). Reading to young children: Its significance for literacy development. In H. Goelman, A. A. Oberg, & F. Smith (Eds.). *Awakening to literacy,* 110–122. Exeter: Heinemann.

Tobin, A. W. (1982, March). *Social and psychological correlates of precocious reading achievement.* Paper presented at the annual meeting of the American Educational Research Association, New York.

Walker, A. (1989). *The temple of my familiar.* New York: Pocket Books.

Walker-Dalhouse, D. (1992). Using African-American literature to increase ethnic understanding. *The Reading Teacher, 45,* 416–422.

Yaden, D. B., Smikin, L. B., & Conlon, A. (1989). Preschoolers' questions about pictures, print conventions, and story texts during reading aloud at home. *Reading Research Quarterly, 24,* 188–213.

 Article Review Form at end of book.

What are some of the benefits for hearing children in a preschool for hearing and nonhearing children?

Let's All Sign!

Enhancing language development in an inclusive preschool

Irma Heller
Diane Manning
Debbie Pavur
Karen Wagner

*Irma Heller (deceased), Head Teacher, Newcomb College Nursery School, New Orleans, Louisiana. **Diane Manning,** Coordinator, Early Childhood Program, Department of Education, Tulane University, New Orleans. **Debbie Pavur,** Coordinator, Newcomb College Nursery School, New Orleans, Louisiana. **Karen Wagner,** Early Childhood/Special Education Coordinate Major, Newcomb College, New Orleans, Louisiana.*

When co-teachers Irma Heller and Debbie Pavur learned that two children with hearing impairments would be included in their afternoon class for 3-year-olds, they decided almost immediately that they would teach the entire class sign language. Neither teacher knew anything about signing, but what they knew about young children convinced them that this was the best course for everyone. Not only would the two children who were hearing impaired be provided with the least restrictive social environment, but the children with nor- mal hearing might also gain unex- pected benefits. Their classroom would be bilingual, where signing would be employed simultane- ously with spoken English.

Newcomb College Nursery School (NCNS), a preschool on the campus of Tulane University, has a 70-year history of develop- mentally appropriate curriculum and is accredited by the National Association for the Education of Young Children (NAEYC). Whereas several children with ex- ceptionalities such as Down syn- drome had been included previously, these two youngsters were the first children with hear- ing impairments at NCNS. In the mornings, the children would at- tend Bright School, a school for children with hearing impair- ments, where they would be in- structed in sign language. These children learned English Sign Language (ESL), one of the two major sign languages for English- speaking countries; the other is American Sign Language (ASL). The children's afternoons would be spent at NCNS where they would be fully included in all activities.

Understanding Signing as a Language

The two teachers began taking classes in ESL over the summer to be ready by fall. As they became more proficient, their appreciation for the language deepened. Heller recalled:

Previously I had considered signing as the use of hands to represent words, which deaf people never heard. It looked pictorial or, better yet, like "picture writing in the air." Very soon it became apparent that signs were not pictures; they were complex, abstract symbols with complex inner structures.

As the teachers' proficiency grew, so did their appreciation of the fact that signing is an actual language. They understood that their class would be truly bilin- gual. They began to think about what effects this would have on the children who were not hearing impaired. They asked themselves questions other preschool teachers have wondered about bilingual in- struction and signing. Would the second language interfere with the learning of the first? Since young children are kinesthetic learners, wouldn't signing augment the other senses in the child's quest to mastering spoken and written English?

The teachers decided to do a little investigation into what other teachers had learned. They located a number of recent articles that advocated the use of signing for children whose hearing is normal (Good, Feekes, & Shawd, 1993–1994; Zeece & Wolda, 1995). A few had discovered some benefits of signing for young children with normal hearing (Brown, 1990; DeViveriros & McLaughlin, 1982; Ellison, Baker, & Baker, 1982; Wilson & Hoyer, 1985), but their reports tended to be limited to particular skills or based on very small numbers of children. An exception was Daniels (1994), who found that African-American children in pre–K classes in Chapter I schools had superior receptive language scores on the Peabody Picture Vocabulary Test (PPVT) after 1 year of instruction in signing compared to children not taught signing.

Although the NCNS teachers could not find answers to all their questions, they knew from experience that the 3-year-olds in their class would be slowly moving from the concrete to the world of the abstract (Vygotsky, 1987). Heller and Pavur concluded that the concrete, physical expression of signing should enhance and hasten the children's movement from simple to complex, from concrete to abstract (Solit, Taylor, & Bednarczyk, 1992).

Integrating Sign Language into the Whole Curriculum

Consistent with their philosophy of full integration, the teachers de-cided early that signing would be a part of the whole curriculum. Their approach was to use signing concurrently with spoken language in all communications with all children as needs arose naturally. Otherwise, the usual curriculum was not modified. All children participated in the activities of the NCNS curriculum to the best of their ability. Except for the addition of signing, the class was no different from other classes of 3-year-olds.

Signing as an Accompaniment

From the first day, the teachers introduced the children to signing as an accompaniment to speech. Teachers greeted the children and parents at the door verbally and by sign. Signs were introduced naturally as they were needed to accomplish the daily activities of classroom life. Children caught on rapidly and began to imitate the teachers' fingers. Before long, the teachers came to realize signing had additional personal benefits, as they signed to each other from one side of the play yard to the other or from far across the room without using their voices.

Working with Parents

Parents were brought into the process early. The teachers and administrators were eager for all the parents to be prepared for the addition of the two new children with hearing impairments. They wanted to allay any concerns par-ents might have that accommodating the needs of the integrated youngsters would have negative effects on the language development of the other children.

Parents were invited to a meeting about signing and the reasons for it during orientation week. All parents agreed to their children participating in signing. Regular classroom newsletters kept parents informed about the progress of the class, and further opportunities for discussion occurred during routine parent conferences. Parents themselves became interested in signing and often reported anecdotes to teachers about how it carried over into the world outside of school. Frequently, parents would report that the children were teaching them signing at home.

A 2-Year Pilot Study

At the end of the first year, the teachers' efforts to achieve full inclusion through signing seemed successful in many ways. Both parents and teachers were pleased, and it seemed increasingly likely that other children with hearing impairments would be enrolled at NCNS in future years. While the teachers initially had not thought of their program as a vehicle for studying the effects of signing in a mainstream setting, they began to recognize that a more formal assessment of the program's impact was needed.

> **Did you know signing or "talking with your fingers" is a language? I arrived at this wonderful realization during my work with children. It all started when I was informed there would be two deaf children in my nursery school class for 3-year-olds in September, and it was recommended that I study sign language to communicate with them effectively.**
>
> **—Irma Heller**

Research Begins

A university researcher was brought onto the team to help design a 2-year pilot study. Obviously, the design would be limited by the nursery school's rather unique history and setting and the predominantly middle-class background of the students and teachers.

The question the teachers hoped to answer was, "What is the effect of using signing on the receptive English vocabulary of middle-class preschoolers who have normal hearing and language development?"

Research on Signing

In sign language, people learn signs for the ideas and actions they want to express. Signing is a visual language capable of expressing every emotion and discussing any topic, concrete or abstract, as effectively as speech. In usage, it ranks fourth in the United States after English, Spanish, and Italian (Wilbur, 1979).

Neurological support for the claim that signing is an actual language comes from Neville (1989), who demonstrated that signing uses the left hemisphere of the brain predominantly, the side biologically specialized for the function of language. This confirmed that signing is treated by the brain as language even though it is visual, not auditory, and spatial, not sequential.

Based on their informal observations, they hypothesized that after 1 academic year, the receptive English vocabulary of these children would be equal to that of 3-year-olds in other NCNS classes who had not used signing. They chose the PPVT as their measure of receptive vocabulary. The PPVT is a reliable, nationally standardized instrument for persons 2.6 through adulthood.

Participants, Curriculum, and Teachers

The participants in the study were 54 students in four classes for 3-year-olds at NCNS. The signing group included 29 children with normal hearing who used signing as part of the regular curriculum, as described earlier. The nonsigning group included 25 children who were not taught signing and who had no classmates who were hearing impaired. All students came from middle-and upper-middle class backgrounds, and 99 % were Euro-American. Children ranged in age from 2.11 at pretest to 4.2 at posttest.

At pretest time, the children's receptive language development was above the national average in all classes. This "bias" would make it harder to show a gain at posttest time, since there would be less room for the children to grow. There were no initial differences among the four classes.

The curriculum and the teachers were the same in all classes in both years. The average teacher:pupil ratio was 1:7. The adult:child ratio often was even lower because of Newcomb College student workers. At least one teacher in each classroom

> Since the first day of school, children's hands and enthusiasm never stopped "flying." How could it be otherwise when everyone in the class agreed their favorite sign is "I love you!"
>
> —Irma Heller

changed between the first and second year of the pilot study, lessening the possibility that results could be due to the influence of a particular teacher.

Results

At the end of the school year, children who had been taught signing had significantly higher receptive vocabulary scores on the PPVT than did children who had not been taught signing. Mean scores for the signing classes were 111.62 at pretest and 117.31 at posttest. Mean scores for the nonsigning classes were 107.48 at pretest and 112.48 at posttest. A two-way analysis of variance indicated that the main effect of signing was highly significant (F (1,53) = 719.04, p < .01). That is, children who used signing were clearly superior in language development to those who had not. There was only one chance in a hundred that the results were due to random chance (see Table 1).

What Did the Pilot Study Show?

The results of the pilot study demonstrated that the benefits of

| Table 1 | One-Way ANOVA of Signing Vs. Non-Signing Children on PPVT |

Source of Variance	Degrees of Freedom	Sums of Squares	Sums of Means	F-Ratio
Between groups	1	7118.52	7118.52	F (1,53)=719.04
Within groups	53	524.81	9.90	
Total	54	7643.33		

Note: ANOVA = analysis of variance; PPVT = Peabody Picture Vocabulary Test. p < .01.

full inclusion programs can extend beyond social and emotional domains to the cognitive realm. When sign language instruction was integrated in a naturalistic way into the general preschool curriculum, both hearing and nonhearing children benefitted. After 1 year in an inclusive, signing classroom, children without hearing impairments had language development superior to that of their peers. All children profited cognitively when they used signing in a natural setting to communicate with each other.

> As the teachers' proficiency grew, so did their appreciation of the fact that signing is an actual language.

We hope this pilot study will encourage other teachers to do their own investigations of the potential benefits of signing in inclusive classrooms. There is still much to learn. Would the results have been the same for children who learned signing in a noninclusive classroom? How important was the "real" need to sign to classmates who had hearing impairments?

These and other questions remain to be answered by teaching colleagues in other schools. For now, it is encouraging to discover that fully including children with hearing impairments by teaching the whole class to sign turns out to be the best choice for everyone.

References

Brown, V. (1990). *Integrating drama and sign language: A multisensory approach to language acquisition and its effects on disadvantaged preschool children.* Unpublished doctoral dissertation, New York University.

Daniels, M. (1994). The effect of sign language on hearing children's language development. *Communication Education, 43(4),* 291–298.

DeViveriros, E. C., & McLaughlin, T. F. (1982). Effects of manual sign use on the expressive language of four hearing kindergarten children. *Sign Language Studies, 35,* 169–177.

Ellison, G., Baker, S., & Baker, P. (1982). Hand to hand: The joy of signing among hearing children. *Young Children, 37(4),* 53–58.

Good, L. A., Feekes, J., & Shawd, B. (1993–94). Let your fingers do the talking: Hands-on language learning through signing. *Childhood Education, 70(2),* 81–83.

Neville, H. J. (1989). Cerebral organization for spatial attention. In J. Stiles-Davis, M. Kritchesvky, & U. Bellugi (Eds.). *Spatial cognition: Brain bases and development:* Hillsdale, NJ: Lawrence Erlbaum.

Solit, G., Taylor, M. & Bednarczyk, A. (1992), *Assess for all: Integrating deaf, hard of hearing, and hearing preschoolers.* Washington, DC: Gallaudef University.

Vygotsky, L. S., (1987). *Thinking and speech.* New York: Plenum.

Wilbur, R. B. (1979). *American sign language and sign systems.* Baltimore: University Press.

Wilson, R. M., & Hoyer, J. P. (1985). The use of signing as a reinforcement of sight vocabulary in the primary grades. In L. B. Gambrell (Ed.). *New directions in reading research and practice* (pp. 43–51). Silver Spring: University of Maryland. (ERIC Document Reproduction Service No. ED 255 885)

Zeece, P. D., & Wolda, M. K. (1995). Let me see what you say: Let me see what you feel! *TEACHING Exceptional Children, 27(2),* 4–9.

 Article Review Form at end of book.

How might primary school teachers create opportunities for children with special learning needs to collaboratively problem-solve?

Adapting Instruction for Students with Special Learning Needs, K–8

Carol A. Thornton

Professor of Mathematics, Illinois State University

Graham A. Jones

Professor of Mathematics, Illinois State University

If you don't let your grasp extend your reach, then you'll never extend your reach.

—Woody Allen, 1992

Traditionally mathematics for students in special education has focused on basic skills, primarily low-level computation, and has been largely perceived as a hierarchy of skills. This perspective of mathematics instruction denies students with special learning needs access to some of the more creative aspects of mathematics, and essentially prepares them for the "yesterdays" but not the "tomorrows."

In this paper we present a vision of what could be. In particular, in an environment that accommodates special learning differences, we focus on the teaching of "big ideas" in mathematics and emphasize

problem-solving experiences that encourage reasoning. These themes embrace the philosophy that rich, challenging problems focusing on mathematical thinking and complemented by appropriate instructional modifications and adaptations can help mathematics teachers meet the challenges inherent in a diverse student population. Moreover, programs consistent with these themes embody multiple approaches that enable students' learning differences to be capitalized upon. As a result students with special learning needs can respond within their specific limitations and succeed at levels previously considered to be beyond their reach.

There is a critical need to redefine "good mathematics" for students with special learning needs. We need to look beyond what is and envision realistically what could be. Without that vision, we prepare students with special learning needs for the *yesterdays* but not the *tomorrows*.

Traditionally mathematics for students in special education has

focused on basic skills, primarily low-level computation, and has been perceived as a hierarchy of skills that are learned in a particular sequence. Suggestions for helping low-achieving students in special education improve their performance in mathematics have centered on "more active instruction and feedback, more redundancy, and small steps with higher success rates." In the classroom this translates to "more review, drill and practice, and thus more lower level questions" (Brophy & Good, 1986, p. 365).

This perspective of mathematics instruction denies students with special learning needs access to some of the more distinctive and creative aspects of mathematics. In particular, this perspective precludes these students' involvement with on-going problem-solving experiences in mathematics and limits opportunities for them to engage in discussions about their own mathematical thinking (Haberman, 1991).

A vision of *what could be* requires that we thoughtfully rethink mathematics instruction for students with special learning needs. Three themes that have emerged from recent studies (Behrend, 1994; Borasi, Packman, & Woodward, 1991; Jones et al., in press; and Langrall, Thornton, Malone, & Jones in press), illustrate successful engagement of students with special learning needs in problem solving and higher-level thinking. These three themes suggest ways of adapting instruction for students with special learning needs: (1) focus on "big ideas" in the curriculum and in the selection of mathematics learning goals and curriculum materials; (2) engage students more routinely in problem tasks that require them to *think* rather than rely on memorized procedures; (3) be sensitive to the unique ways in which different students "learn best." The following sections elaborate on these themes.

Teaching for "Big Ideas"

At the present time identifying and focusing on "big ideas" is a major thrust in mathematics instruction (Greenes, 1995; NCTM, 1989, 1991). Consistent with this thrust is the need to base Individualized Education Plans (IEPs) for students in special education on only the most important mathematical ideas, as these students typically require more time to learn. Focusing on less but carefully selecting content allows important topics to be covered in greater depth, increases the potential for higher-level engagement by students and, in the long run, promotes greater learning. In this sense, *less is more* for students with special learning needs.

"Big" instructional ideas promoted by the National Council of Teachers of Mathematics in their Standards documents (1989, 1991) and in their *Windows of Opportunity: Mathematics for Students with Special Needs* (Thornton & Bley, 1994) emphasize several important thrusts. These instructional ideas, listed below, are intended for all students—including those students serviced by special education:

- Collaborative problem solving and reasoning.

- Multiple ways of communicating and justifying thinking to accommodate diversity in thinking and learning.

- Connections among what is said, done, and written while carrying out mathematical tasks; and natural connections between mathematics and relevant in- and out-of-school situations.

- "Number sense" and the redefining of computation to emphasize estimation, mental math, and appropriate use of technology.

- A *broader, more balanced* curriculum addressing appropriate skills but emphasizing the on-going development of concepts and relationships in problem contexts.

- A *broader, more balanced* curriculum including significant noncomputational work: for example, experiences requiring geometric and spatial reasoning, interpretation of data and chance situations, and exploration of numeric and spatial patterns.

The following classroom snapshot illustrates several "big ideas."

Classroom Snapshot: "Big Ideas"

In broadly planning how to approach her third grade mathematics class, Mrs. Algonqua decided to start with a noncomputational unit as a major focus, but also to involve the students in addition-subtraction problem solving for a short time each day to review basic facts and whole number computation.

At first, in the daily review sessions, Ms. Algonqua used smaller numbers in the problems she posed. When she discovered that a significant group of her students had forgotten the "harder" number facts over the summer, she set aside time to use 10-frames and counters during one session to explore "adding through 10" (e.g., 8 + 5 is "a 10-frame and 3": 13), and during another to explore "subtracting through 10" (e.g., 14–9 leave *one* counter in the 10-frame and 4 others: 5).

Then, based on her belief that basic facts would be further reinforced through repeated problem-solving experiences, she continued during subsequent sessions to present problems with larger numbers: For example,

Farah's sticker book held 250 stickers. She got 125 from Dad, 56 from Mom, and 28 from her brother on her birthday. Did she have enough to fill her book? Explain.

Frequently Ms. Algonqua encouraged her students to "think, pair, share" (McTighe & Lyman, 1988). That is, she first asked the students to try to think of one or more different ways of solving a problem, and to share their thinking with a partner. As time allowed, Ms. Algonqua then called on different students to share the approach(es) they used and their solution(s). Alternately, she allowed time for pairs of students to exchange their approaches with each other after they had written out their own solutions. "Why did you add?" or "Why did you subtract?" were frequent questions. "Who did it a different way?" and "Convince me your answer 'makes sense'" were frequent challenges. This instructional environment emphasized reasoning about concepts and relationships, and invited estimation. There was a premium on *thinking*, and an open attitude toward different approaches that accommodated a variety of learning levels and styles.

For the sticker problem, for example, Gina (a child serviced by special education) reported that "Me and Joey think the book wasn't full, because 125 and 28 stickers are about 150, and another 56 makes about 200. More, really." Erica solved the problem a different way. She said she thought about the 100s Chart and counted on to find the "real" number of stickers: "125 and 28: that's 125, 135, 145, 155 and back 2 makes 153; then 56 more: that's 200 and 9 more, 209."

The preceding snapshot illustrates how Mrs. Algonqua captured the spirit of "big ideas" in her teaching. In a problem context she involved students in collaborative settings, encouraged diverse thinking and approaches, established ways of building connections, and nurtured number sense and number relationships in a variety of ways.

If you had visited Mrs. Algonqua's class later the same day you would have seen her students working on a probability unit. The task for the day was to engage in a race game which required determining "which sum is most likely when two dice are rolled." For this game, Mrs. Algonqua had labeled each die

with the numbers 4 through 9. As part of the wrap-up, the teacher had pooled the data from all groups, and the students had noticed that the sum of 13 came up most frequently.

After students had discussed with a partner "why" this had happened, Terry, a bright student affected by cerebral palsy, spoke excitedly: "There's more ways of getting 13." Picking up on Terry's idea, the class was able to list all six ways, and agreed that a sum of 13 could be formed in more ways than any other sum. Terry couldn't help but comment, "In this case, 13 is the lucky number, not the unlucky number."

By having the students engage in probability experiments, Mrs. Algongua was clearly providing a *more balanced* curriculum for her students. In the task described above, she also designed the experience to integrate the study of probability with her ongoing review of number facts.

Teaching with Problems That Invite Reasoning

Problem solving has traditionally been a difficult area for students with special learning needs. This difficulty has been exacerbated by the fact that students supported by special education have not typically and regularly been engaged in problem solving, and hence have not had opportunities to develop their own mathematical reasoning. In essence, large numbers of students in special education have not had the "opportunity to learn" to problem-solve.

However, recent research (e.g., Behrend, 1994: Bulgren & Montague, 1989) has revealed that students serviced by special education can succeed beyond current expectations if they are exposed to

developmentally appropriate and meaningful problem tasks that are complemented by appropriate instructional modifications. Moreover, research also indicates that students experiencing difficulty with computation or basic facts should not be excluded from engaging in regular problem-solving experiences, as these skills can actually be developed and reinforced through problem solving (e.g., Carpenter & Moser, 1984; Cawley & Miller, 1989; Ginsburg, in press).

Classroom Snapshot: Using Problems That Invite Reasoning

The following snapshot focusing on Jeremy, Amanda, and Ellamae illustrates the different ways three first grade students, supported by special education, used mathematical reasoning to solve a developmentally appropriate, meaningful problem.

The Toy Factory Problem   The toy factory makes caterpillar pull toys. Each caterpillar has 10 wheels for feet—5 on each side. If 95 caterpillar wheels are in a box, how many caterpillars can be made? Would all the wheels be used? Explain.

Ellamae, Jeremy, and Amanda were assigned to different working groups. After one student in Jeremy's group put out 95 cubes, 9 tens and 5 singles, Jeremy suggested that they build models of the caterpillars. To demonstrate this, he broke a 10-train in half, and put five wheels on each side. The group worked together to make all the bugs they could, then Jeremy counted them: nine caterpillars and five extra wheels.

In her group, Amanda simply put up ten fingers to represent one caterpillar. She opened her hands repeatedly and counted by 10s—10, 20, 30 . . . , 90. Another student in her group kept track of the number of times Amanda counted to determine that there were nine caterpillars. Ellamae's group used a more sophisticated version of Amanda's strategy, orally counting by 10s and using their fingers only to keep track of the number of caterpillars. Ellamae imitated and joined in on the count, as did others in the group.

In solving this problem Jeremy, Amanda, and Ellamae each approached the task in their own way—one that "made sense" to them. Consequently, all three modeled the problem, but in different ways and at different levels of sophistication. This situation illustrates what can happen when students are allowed sufficient time to understand and more fully address a problem. Repeated exposure to rich problem tasks like this one increases the likelihood that students with special learning needs will use their diverse strengths to generate appropriate solution strategies and will begin to think independently at higher levels (Scheid, 1990).

Teaching to Accommodate Special Learning Differences

Different students have different learning strengths. Students with **auditory** strengths may only internalize and retain important mathematical ideas if given adequate opportunity to verbalize their thinking, or to reverbalize ideas in their own language. For **visual** learners, seeing is believing. While these students may "listen poorly," they are more likely to remember what they have seen or read. **Kinesthetic**

learners, on the other hand, find comfort in movement and "hands on" involvement. These students benefit from "acting out" ideas and demonstrating relationships. They have a greater need for time to *feel* an idea, and may want a teacher to talk more slowly and allow more wait time.

In the case of students supported by special education, their strengths can be used to compensate for any identified deficits. Perhaps the most effective teachers are those who become informed about the way a learning disability or special learning characteristic affects individual children in their classes. Teachers become informed by interacting with special education staff and parents, and by grasping every opportunity to observe their students working independently and in small groups. Given this informed perspective, teachers can select from a variety of instructional styles and approaches to reach students with diverse learning needs and disabilities (see Bley & Thornton, 1994). Always, the goal is to assist students to understand and compensate for any learning deficits and to become as successfully independent as possible.

Classroom Snapshot: Accommodating Learning Differences

This snapshot depicts an inclusion classroom solving an open-ended problem, although a similar scene might have occurred in a self-contained or pull-out setting among special education students. The sixth grade teacher Mr. Richards set the scene for the day's basketball problem (next column) by having Carlos, a kinesthetic learner, use a Nerf ball and hoop in the classroom to demonstrate the difference

between a free throw, a 2- and a 3-point shot. Mr. Richards then posed the problem and provided time for students to work in groups of three or four to solve it.

The Basketball Problem   The annual lunchtime basketball tournament was going on at Columbia Middle School. Michael scored 30 points yesterday, including 4 points at the free throw line. How many 2-point shots and 3-point shots could Michael have made? Explain.

As soon as he had finished his Nerf ball demonstration, Carlos joined his group and began tearing bits of paper. He got others to help him label them with a 2 or a 3—for the 2-pointer and the 3-pointer shots. Next they made groups of 2s and groups of 3s and checked to see if the sum was 26. Mr. Richards was amused but not surprised by the "hands on" approach Carlos initiated.

In a nearby group Tiffany sat quietly, watching the others in her group construct a table for 2-point shots, and 3-point shots. Under each of these headers, the students tried various pairs of numbers, multiplied, and checked each sum. When Mr. Richards came to the group and noticed that Tiffany was not as involved as the others, he asked her to explain the group's strategy for solving the problem.

Without hesitation Tiffany relayed what she had seen: "This [pointing to the first column] is the multiply by 2 column, and this [pointing to the second column] is the multiply by 3 column, and the total has to be 26. We just keep trying till the numbers work." Mr. Richards nodded and remarked, "Good, Tiffany! You really could 'see' the strategy and explain it."

Kenisha's group started by trying pairs of numbers randomly.

Fortuitously, one student found a workable pair almost right away—"4 two-pointers will work with 6 three-pointers, because 8 and 18 make 26—and the 4 free throws make 30." Hearing their conversation, Mr. Richards probed: "Is that the only way it could have happened?"

The students shrugged, but went back to work. One student said, "I'd like to try 10. It often works." Another countered, "But I'm already starting with 8." Listening to the conversation, Kenisha protested: "4 worked for the 2-pointers. Shouldn't we check 5 and then 6, and then get to other numbers up to 10 in order?" When asked "why" by others in her group, Kenisha smiled as if discovering the reason for herself and said: "So we don't miss any!" Perhaps unknowingly, others in the group played right to Kenisha's auditory strength by forcing her to clarify and articulate her thinking aloud. *I internalize when I verbalize; I learn when I hear myself speak!*

Even though Carlos, Tiffany, and Kenisha were students with special conditions that had an impact on the way in which they learned, each of them was able to respond to the open-ended problem situation by using their learning strength. By so doing each made a worthwhile contribution to their group's collaborative problem-solving effort. Without modifying the curriculum, Mr. Richards was able to capitalize on these students' different learning strengths

- by frequently using rich problem tasks,
- by orchestrating group work and other supportive mediums for student interactions, and
- by giving appropriate prompts and probes to heighten

individual involvement and stimulate mathematical thinking.

In some mathematics classrooms, teachers work together to design a *balance* of rich problem activities for each major topic presented, so that it is possible to select those which are appropriate for different learners. Usually a slight modification of the task itself, careful assignment of individual roles within a collaborative group, or the support of a buddy or others in a learning group enables a student from special education to "keep up" with most aspects of the regular lesson.

At times, however, specific curriculum modifications may be necessary to meet individual needs. A major modification may be to *pare down* the scope of what is addressed, as was emphasized earlier in the section on teaching for "big ideas." While it may be important, for example, to take a close look at basic skills, a great deal of skill learning can be introduced, developed, and reinforced in a problem-solving context.

Modifications may include resequencing texts, omitting some parts and supplementing or replacing other parts. If replacement units or investigations are used, teachers must insure that "activity" doesn't preempt the learning of important mathematics, and that student explanations and debriefings are augmented by the teacher to highlight the big mathematical focus of each unit or investigation.

Sometimes, for specific individuals, it may be necessary to design a parallel task, one which focuses on the topic other students are learning but is pitched at a simpler level. For example, if other students are making a drawing to scale, a student with serious mental limitations might

be delegated the task of *measuring* the scaled figures and describing (in writing, orally to a partner, or orally into a tape recorder) any relationships between the original and the scaled drawing.

Concluding Comments

This article has presented three major themes: focusing on "big ideas" in mathematics, using problems that invite reasoning, and accommodating special learning differences. These themes embrace the philosophy that rich, challenging programs focusing on mathematical thinking, complemented by appropriate instructional modifications and adaptations, can help mathematics teachers meet the challenges inherent in a diverse student population. Moreover, programs consistent with these themes embody different approaches, thus allowing students to capitalize on their learning differences. As a result such students can respond within their specific limitations, find their niche, and succeed at levels previously considered to be beyond their reach.

References

Behrend, J. L. (1994). *Mathematical problem-solving processes of primary-grade students identified as learning disabled.* Unpublished doctoral dissertation. University of Wisconsin, Madison.

Bley, N. S., & Thornton, C. A. (1994). Accommodating special needs. In C. A. Thornton & N. S. Bley (Eds.). *Windows of opportunity: Mathematics for students with special needs* (pp. 137–163). Reston, VA: National Council of Teachers of Mathematics.

Borasi, R., Packman, D., & Woodward, A. (1991). *Supporting middle school learning disabled students in the mainstream mathematics classroom.* National Science Foundation.

Brophy, J. E., & Good, T. L. (1986). Teacher behavior and student achievement. In M. C. Wittrock (Ed.)

Handbook of research on teaching (pp. 328–375). New York: Macmillan.

Bulgren, J., & Montague, M. (1989, June). *Report from working group four.* Paper presented at the Information Center for Special Education Media and Materials Instructional Methods Forum. Washington, DC.

Carpenter, T. P., & Moser, J. M. (1984). The acquisition of addition and subtraction concepts in grades one through three. *Journal for Research in Mathematics Education, 15,* 179–202.

Cawley, J., & Miller, J. (1989). Cross-sectional comparisons of the mathematical performance of children with learning disabilities: Are we on the right track toward comprehensive programming? *Journal of Learning Disabilities, 22,* 250–254.

Ginsburg, H. P. (in press). Mathematics learning disabilities: A developmental perspective. *Journal of Learning Disabilities.*

Greenes, C. (1995) Mathematics learning and knowing: A cognitive process. *Journal of Education, 177,* 1, pp. XX.

Haberman, M. (1991, December). The pedagogy of poverty versus good teaching. *Phi Delta Kappan,* 290–294.

Jones, G. A., Thornton, C. A., Putt, I. J., Hill, K. M., Mogill, A. T., Rich, B. S., & Van Zoest, L. R. (in press). Multidigit number sense: A framework for instruction and assessment. *Journal for Research in Mathematics Education.*

Langrall, C. W., Thornton, C. A., Malone, J., & Jones, G. A. (in press). *Journal of Teacher Education.*

McTighe, J., & Lyman, F. T., Jr. (1988). Cuing thinking in the classroom: The promise of theory-embedded tools. *Educational Leadership, 45* (7), 18–24.

National Council of Teachers of Mathematics. (1989). *Curriculum and evaluation standards for school mathematics.* Reston, VA: The Council.

National Council of Teachers of Mathematics. (1991). *Professional standards for teaching mathematics.* Reston, VA: The Council.

Scheid, K. (1990). *Cognitive-based methods for teaching mathematics to students with learning problems.* Columbus, OH: Information Center for Special Education Media and Materials.

Thornton, C. A., & Bley, N. S. (Eds.). (1994). *Windows of opportunity: Mathematics for students with special needs.* Reston, VA: National Council of Teachers of Mathematics.

 Article Review Form at end of book.

WiseGuide Wrap-Up

- A society that encourages positive self-concept and self-identity allows each child to achieve a sense of belonging.

- Building acceptance calls for inclusive settings that provide appropriate educational opportunities for all children.

R.E.A.L. Sites

This list provides a print preview of typical **coursewise** R.E.A.L. sites. There are over 100 such sites at the **courselinks**™ site. The danger in printing URLs is that web sites can change overnight. As we went to press, these sites were functional using the URLs provided. If you come across one that isn't, please let us know via email to: webmaster@coursewise.com. Use your Passport to access the most current list of R.E.A.L. sites at the **courselinks**™ site.

Site name: Stand for Children
URL: http://www.stand.org/
Why is it R.E.A.L.? Supporters of children will find updates about child care, community diversity, and advocacy efforts. *Stand for Children Day* is held in June.
Key topics: child care, community, cultural sensitivity/diversity
Activity: Find the picture labeled Milagros. Click on the picture and describe the featured piece.

Site name: The Council for Exceptional Children (CEC)
URL: http://www.cec.sped.org/
Why is it R.E.A.L.? An extensive menu will connect you to training and events, professional standards, a job bank, publications, and the ERIC Clearinghouse on Disabilities and Gifted Education.
Key topics: inclusion, language/literacy, special needs
Activity: Write a brief paragraph describing why you think that special education teaching conditions need to improve. Transmit your statement to *Tell CEC What You Think.*

Site name: Native Child
URL: http://www.nativechild.com/core.html
Why is it R.E.A.L.? Culturally appropriate and sensitive curriculum activities and materials are available at this site. The colorful drawings provide links to curriculum units and Head Start/Preschool Programs using the Native Child materials.
Key topics: cultural sensitivity/diversity, identity, multicultural
Activity: Click on *curriculum,* then *curriculum material,* then *colors.* Describe the available materials and colors.

Site name: The National Information Center for Children and Youth with Disabilities (NICHCY)
URL: http://www.nichcy.org/
Why is it R.E.A.L.? The focus of this national information and referral center is on children and youth with disabilities. Publications, organizations, and links to related topics are available.
Key topics: inclusion, special needs, technology
Activity: On the first page of the NICHCY site, click on *Mini Posters.* Summarize your reaction to the message in the Zebra poster.

section 5

Family-Centered Communities Benefit Young Children: What Policies Enhance the Developing Child?

The way communities value children may very well determine their sense of belonging. Feelings of belonging profoundly enhance a child's development. The spirit of contemporary society must grasp the meaningfulness of emotions, family relations, and school experiences in order to create supportive communities that benefit the growth of each child.

Community and school leaders can begin the process of building family-centered communities by first acknowledging that societal challenges and stresses affect families and their children. Family-friendly communities, including service agencies and businesses, enable significant adults to nurture and model. Schools that consider all dimensions of the child's development welcome and facilitate parent involvement. Families, neighbors, community members, and educators together create a web of support that contributes to the healthy and meaningful growth of children.

As educators formulate goals for parent involvement, they should consider the contexts in which children live and learn. The first reading, "Challenges to Family Involvement" by Mick Coleman and Susan Churchill, provides themes for guiding family-school interaction. Parental attitudes and expectations about the educational setting will affect the degree of parental involvement in a child's school.

Dr. James Comer answers questions about his School Development Program in the second reading, "Building Schools as Communities: A Conversation with James Comer." His emphasis is on "close-knit community interaction" and caring adults, communities, and schools. The reading "Keep Community 'Real' for Urban School Success" reviews Dr. Comer's program and techniques that guide authentic school communities.

The third reading, "Family Involvement with Assistive Technology," defines family interactions for those children who require assistive technology. Family members participate in all levels of assessment and implementation of plans. The reading "Migrant Head Start: What Does It Mean to Involve Parents in Program Services?" validates many of the similar concepts related to parent involvement. Parent involvement is a process that depends on collaboration and careful attention to local conditions and circumstances of the particular community.

The Network Preschools in Alexandria demonstrate how a community can proactively increase children's and their families' chances for success. In "A Safe and Caring Place," Carolyn R. Pool details this community's establishment of quality preschools that include high levels of parental involvement.

The definitions of work and business will acquire new meaning as more parents elect to work at home. In "Caring for Your Child While Caring for Your Business," Tina Egge reports that home and work needs change as the children and the business grow. Responding to changes at home, at work, and in the community with family-centered policies will allow every child's optimal development.

Questions

Reading 25. List one theme and the related goals detailed in the guide for family involvement.

Reading 26. What features for child-friendly schools does Dr. Comer suggest?

Reading 27. What are three applications of videotaping for assessment of special needs children?

Reading 28. What should the teaching staff consider when parental involvement is expected in Migrant Head Start?

Reading 29. How are parents involved in school improvement?

Reading 30. Why do parents trust the Network Preschools?

Reading 31. Finding the right kind of child care depends on what three factors?

List one theme and the related goals detailed in the guide for family involvement.

Challenges to Family Involvement

Mick Coleman and Susan Churchill

Mick Coleman is Associate Professor and Susan Churchill is a doctoral student in the Department of Child and Family Development, University of Georgia, Athens.

The percentage of 3- and 4-year-olds enrolled in early childhood education programs has risen more than three-fold since the mid-1960s (U.S. General Accounting Office, 1990). Public schools increasingly provide child care, preschool education and before- and after-school care for young children. Such school-based early childhood programs reflect a growing interest in early educational enrichment experiences for children in general, as well as an expansion of compensatory education programs for children who are judged to be at risk for school failure because of poverty, lack of proper health care, inadequate home-learning environments and a lack of adult protection (Swick & Graves, 1993, pp. 26, 93).

Recognizing the mutuality of families' and schools' concerns about children's growth and development, educators are seeking new ways to involve families in their children's education (Boyer, 1991; Silvern, 1988; U.S. Department of Education, 1991). While family involvement is a concept that has wide appeal, only limited institutional support exists (Epstein & Dauber, 1991; Greenberg, 1989; Swick & McKnight, 1989).

Challenges to Family Involvement

No conclusive evidence exists that family involvement programs are uniformly effective (White, Taylor & Moss, 1992), despite the many positive ways families can affect their children's academic efforts (see, for review, Henderson, 1988; Hess & Holloway, 1984; Peters, 1988; Rutter, 1985; White et al., 1992), and the many positive ways quality early childhood programs can affect families (see Pence, 1988; Powell, 1989; Schorr & Schorr, 1988). Family involvement efforts face two challenges aside from the difficulties associated with the diverse methodologies used in family involvement studies (White et al., 1992).

• *Ambiguous definitions of family involvement.* It is hard to find consensus on the meaning of family involvement (Haseloff, 1990; White et al., 1992). Family involvement may include the following elements, among others: providing parents with facts about their child's development, teaching parents to become effective change agents for their child, providing parents with emotional support, training parents to guide and teach their child, exchanging information about a child between parents and teachers, hosting joint parent/teacher activities like childhood assessments or program planning, and helping parents get access to community services (McConachie, 1986; Peterson & Cooper, 1989).

Ambiguous definitions of family involvement can result in programs that are merely a series of disconnected activities with little relevance to family or classroom environments. To be effective, family involvement planners must address the ambiguous boundaries that exist between home and school (Johnston, 1990), and the resulting sense of intrusion and power imbalance that can occur when parents and teachers attempt to coordinate their interactions with children (Haseloff, 1990).

In practice, family involvement planning must include the formulation of a family involvement philosophy and supportive goals. In the course of conducting inservice workshops on family involvement, the authors have discovered that sufficient attention is not always paid to this conceptual process. Subsequent discussions about the meaning and purpose of family involvement, however, often uncover a common set of philosophical themes (see Table 1). Teachers can use the themes in Table 1 as an aid to beginning the reflective process. Teachers should delete from, or add to, the list so that it meets their schools' particular concerns and interests.

The list of themes is used as a planning device so that teachers can prioritize their family involvement goals while thinking about past family involvement experiences. In most cases, teachers can select one theme that best reflects their family involvement goal for the upcoming year. They can then develop specific family involvement objectives that reflect their school's diverse family-school environments.

• *Diversity of family-school environments.* The call for greater collaboration between families and schools is admirable in that it recognizes the different contexts in which children learn. Nevertheless, the discontinuities between a young child's home and school lives can pose numerous challenges (Hess & Holloway, 1984; Peters, 1988; Silvern, 1988). A school's customs, schedules, spaces, resources, expectations, experiences, languages and values, for example, may not be reflected in the same way or to the same degree at home. This may be especially true for children from racial and cultural minority families, as well as those from lower socioeconomic families.

In particular, school environments may fit better with the family environments of children from middle-class families because public schools are often staffed with middle-class administrators and teachers. Middle-class families subsequently may be more responsive to school policies and family involvement programs than lower socioeconomic families.

Parent education and family socioeconomic status are two factors that may create discontinuity between schools and families. Although it is true that parents with higher levels of education and from higher socioeconomic backgrounds show greater family involvement, this trend does not necessarily indicate differential *interest* in family involvement (Epstein & Dauber, 1991; Stevenson & Baker, 1987). In fact, parents from low-income families are as supportive of the family involvement concept as parents with higher incomes (Chavkin & Williams, 1989).

One way parents from lower and higher income families may differ is where they are willing or able to be involved in their children's education. Researchers have found a positive relationship between socioeconomic status and school-based family involvement activities such as parent conferences and volunteering, as well as teacher perceptions of parent support; socioeconomic status, however, has not been associated with home-based activities like tutoring (Hoover-Dempsey, Bassler & Brissie, 1987). This finding may reflect the difficulty or hesitancy parents from lower socioeconomic backgrounds may experience when directly interacting with schools. Some parents may have conflicting work and family demands. Others may limit their involvement with schools because of their own negative school experiences and feelings of academic inadequacy.

Parents with higher levels of education tend to be more involved in school activities, and their children are more likely to be

Table 1 Themes for Guiding Family Involvement Philosophies*

Theme	Goal
Empowerment	To provide families with the information and support they need to actively participate in school-related discussions regarding their children's education
Parenting	To support parents in nurturing and guiding their children
Family strengths	To assist families in identifying and developing strengths and coping mechanisms as a means of managing family life stressors
Child-siblings	To prepare school-age children and their younger siblings for schooling
Community resources	To provide parents with the information, support and skills necessary to identify and manage community services
Educational modeling	To involve parents in identifying education objectives and providing supportive in-home learning opportunities for their children
Family-teacher relations	To improve the quality of interpersonal relations between teachers and children's families

*The purpose of the themes is to help structure ideas about family involvement and their implications for planning practical family involvement strategies. Some overlap is expected.

doing well in school (Stevenson & Baker, 1987). These findings may reflect parental attitudes, work schedules and lifestyle priorities that are congruent with those found in schools. Parents with more education may have more positive attitudes toward school, resulting in more frequent and positive interactions with teachers and more reinforcement of classroom activities in the home. Parents with higher levels of education also may have more flexible work schedules, allowing them to assist with homework projects and attend school functions. Also, these families' adult-child interactions and childhood behavioral expectations may resemble more closely those found in the school.

To develop strategies that link the early learning experiences in home and school settings, planners must address the discontinuities between those environments. The authors have summarized in Table 2 some of the themes that they have found useful in helping family-school coordinators and teachers link family and school environments.

Teachers can use Table 2's themes to further expand their family involvement philosophies. Using the guides, for example, can facilitate the planning and implementation of enrollment interviews, home visits, parent-teacher meetings and classroom activities. Some teachers use the themes to formulate questions and possible explanations about family-school disagreements (e.g., home-school differences in behavior management and self-help expectations). Or, the themes can be used to structure classroom activities that build upon children's home experiences (e.g., childhood interests, home routines, family relation-

Table 2 Themes for Guiding Family-School Interactions

Theme	Example
Home routines	Child's typical daily schedule and activities
Child's interests	Child's favorite toys, television programs, foods, games, books, etc.
Behavior management	Types of encouragement, reinforcements, limits and consequences used by parents to guide child's behavior
Communication	Verbal and nonverbal strategies used by parents to instruct, deliver explanations and make requests of child
Child's fears	Objects, events and situations feared by a child
Community involvement	Community events, activities and institutions that families attend (e.g., church, library, recreational, cultural)
Relationship	Child's most important interpersonal relationships within and outside the home setting
Self-help expectations	Self-help skills relating to personal hygiene and home chores that parents expect child to perform
Instructional strategies	Strategies used by parents to teach a child (e.g., instruction, demonstrations, play)

ships). The themes in Table 2, like those in Table 1, are only a beginning point. Teachers can add themes that reflect their school's individual concerns.

Working with Family Professionals

Stamp and Groves (1994) suggested that family involvement be viewed as a "third institution" whose primary purpose is to strengthen family-school linkages. As we already have noted, the diversity of family structures and lifestyles can present barriers to creating such a "third institution."

On the other hand, a conclusion that families and schools cannot be linked would be based on too narrow an interpretation of family and school goals regarding early childhood education. The traditionally stated goals of child care (protection, nurturing and socialization) and school (education and socialization) always have been interdependent (Caldwell, 1990). Today, more than ever, aca-

demic education (learning to read and write) and life-skills education (learning self-help and social responsibilities) are mutually supportive endeavors that occur across family and school settings. Likewise, parents and teachers, although sometimes depicted as adversarial, have similar educational goals (Epstein, 1991) and philosophies (Stipek, Milburn, Clements & Daniels, 1992).

Thus, creating a "third institution" of family involvement is not impossible, although greater attention must be given to devising practical strategies for linking families and schools (Sexton, Aldridge & Snyder, 1994). The authors will now examine some ways in which three types of family professionals can work with schools to develop practical strategies for strengthening family involvement.

■ *Teacher training: Family life educators.* Teachers whose training in family relations is limited have only their own family experiences to guide them when developing a family involvement program. Family life educators can help address teachers' questions about potential barriers to family involvement. During inservice training, teachers should brainstorm questions. Some common questions regarding family involvement follow:

- What are the challenges that confront families from different socioeconomic backgrounds, and how do they influence families' involvement with schools and other social institutions?

- What concerns do families from different ethnic, religious, racial and sexual orientation backgrounds have regarding how their families are depicted in school?

- What are the potential stressors associated with divorce, death and remarriage in relation to child-teacher and parent-teacher relations?

- What strategies can be used to acknowledge the roles of foster parents, grandparents and other extended family guardians?

Barriers to family involvement go beyond school-based issues. Family life educators can help coordinate and facilitate the following professional learning experiences:

- Selected teachers might receive release time for social service internships in order to better understand the diversity of family life within a community context.

- Teachers might be asked to develop a family involvement program that is tied to a youth program, or that is based at a work site, community center or church.

- Inservice training can be provided to highlight the different roles that parents can play in supporting their children's development and education within and outside school and home settings.

One of the most popular topics in education today is diversity (Jacob & Jordan, 1993; McCracken, 1993; Neugebauer, 1992). Teachers need opportunities to explore their own respective cultures, as well as those of others, in relation to curriculum issues. They should be careful, however, not to overgeneralize or stereotype, since all families are unique regarding their rates of cultural assimilation or their racial, ethnic, religious, socioeconomic and sexual orientation backgrounds. Family life educators can facilitate the following activities:

- Keep personal journals related to positive and negative family-school interactions to encourage reflective thought on teaching practices involving children from different family backgrounds.

- Discuss the meaning of "family diversity" and its implications for classroom practices to facilitate group creativity and problem-solving. The authors have found it useful to ask teachers to reflect upon their own meaning of "family" as a beginning reference point.

- Ask teachers to develop parent workshops on topics of their choosing that take into account the different family backgrounds represented in their respective classrooms.

■ *Community education: Family life advocates.* Early childhood advocates warn that educators must not promise more than early childhood programs can deliver,

since legislators tend to view early childhood programs as a means by which to achieve sweeping education and social reforms (Morado, 1986). Family life advocates can work with teachers to ensure that family involvement expectations are kept realistic.

- Form task forces to identify barriers and recommend strategies for strengthening family-school-community linkages. School-community linkages may be needed, for example, to ensure the efficient delivery of social services to families who are recent immigrants and/or who have limited means of transportation or income.

- Encourage school administrators to make family life education an integral part of the curriculum. The concept of "families" rather than "family" should be stressed in order to reflect the diversity of family structures and lifestyles in contemporary society.

- Provide training to expand parents' child advocacy efforts. Such training might include establishing parent advisory boards, arranging co-teaching experiences and informing parents of child advocacy efforts in the community.

■ *Family involvement research: Family researchers.* Although the effectiveness of family involvement programs has not been adequately documented, parents and teachers continue to search for meaningful ways to support each other. Teachers can work with family and education researchers to clarify the importance of family involvement through examination of the following questions:

- Are parents better able to understand and implement information regarding child guidance and education when it is presented in parent-led support groups as opposed to teacher-led educational groups? A study about strategies for coordinating family-school expectations and practices regarding children's guidance and education would be useful.

- Do children from certain family backgrounds (e.g., well-established versus recently immigrated; different socioeconomic levels) perform better in the classroom when classroom activities include materials found in their homes, rather than standard classroom materials? Teachers could benefit from learning how to use home materials to support and expand the classroom curriculum.

- Are community-based programs that link families with human services agencies more effective than similar school-based programs? This question could be answered by comparing the joint efforts of teachers and family service workers with those of schools and human service agencies.

- In what ways does family involvement serve as a mediating variable in children's short- and long-term academic and social adjustment? Educators could benefit from studies about family involvement programs' timing, structure and content.

- What are the secondary effects of family involvement programs? Research is needed, for example, on how family involvement programs may benefit younger siblings still at home and the ability of parents to advocate for their children across community settings.

Conclusion

Understanding family lives is central to building a meaningful family involvement program. Family professionals can work with school administrators and teachers to meet the challenges associated with family involvement by helping to develop a family involvement plan that is both practical and relevant to community needs.

References

Boyer, E. L. (1991). *Ready to learn: A mandate for the nation.* Lawrenceville, NJ: Princeton University Press.

Caldwell, B. M. (1990). Educate: A new professional identity. *Dimensions, 18,* 3–6.

Chavkin, N. F., & Williams, D. L. (1989). Low-income parents' attitudes toward parent involvement in education. *Journal of Sociology and Social Welfare, 16,* 17–28.

Epstein, J. L. (1991). Paths to partnership: What we can learn from federal, state, district, and school initiatives. *Phi Delta Kappan, 72,* 344–349.

Epstein, J. L., & Dauber, S. L. (1991). School programs and teacher practices of parent involvement in inner-city elementary and middle schools. *The Elementary School Journal, 91,* 289–305.

Greenberg, P. (1989). Parents as partners in young children's development and education: A new American fad? Why does it matter? *Young Children, 44,* 61–75.

Haseloff, W. (1990). The efficacy of the parent-teacher partnership of the 1990s. *Early Child Development and Care, 58,* 51–55.

Henderson, A. T. (1988). Parents are a school's best friends. *Phi Delta Kappan, 70,* 148–153.

Hess, R. D., & Holloway, S. D. (1984). Family and school as educational institutions. In R. D. Parke, R. N. Emde, H. P. McAdoo, & G. P. Sackett (Eds.). *Review of child development research: The family* (Vol. 7) (pp. 179–222). Chicago: University of Chicago Press.

Hoover-Dempsey, K. V., Bassler, O. C., & Brissie, J. S. (1987). Parent involvement: Contributions of teacher efficacy, school socioeconomic status, and other school characteristics. *American Educational Research Journal, 24,* 417–435.

Jacob, E., & Jordan, C. (1993). *Minority education: Anthropological perspectives.* Norwood, NJ: Ablex.

Johnston, J. H. (1990). *The new American family and the school.* Columbus, OH: National Middle School Association.

McConachie, H. (1986). *Parents and young mentally handicapped children: A review of research issues.* Cambridge, MA: Brookline Books.

McCracken, J. B. (1993). *Valuing diversity: The primary years.* Washington, DC: National Association for the Education of Young Children.

Morado, C. (1986) Prekindergarten programs for 4-year-olds. Some key issues. *Young Children, 41,* 61–63.

Neugebauer, B. (1992). *Alike and different: Exploring our humanity with young children.* Washington, DC: National Association for the Education of Young Children.

Pence, A. (1988) *Ecological research with children and families.* New York: Teachers College Press.

Peters, D. L. (1988). Head Start's influence on parental and child competence. In S. K. Steinmetz (Ed.), *Family and support systems across the life span* (pp. 73–97). New York: Plenum.

Peterson, N. L., & Cooper, C. S. (1989). Parent education and involvement in early intervention programs for handicapped children. In M. J. Fine (Ed.), *The second handbook on parent education: Contemporary perspectives* (pp. 197–233). New York: Academic.

Powell, D. (1989). *Families and early childhood programs.* Washington, DC: National Association for the Education of Young Children.

Rutter, M. (1985). Family and school influences on cognitive development. *Journal of Child Psychology and Psychiatry, 26,* 683–704.

Schorr, D., & Schorr, L. (1988). *Within our reach: Breaking the cycle of disadvantage.* New York: Doubleday.

Sexton, D., Aldridge, J., & Snyder, P. (1994). Family-driven early intervention. *Dimensions, 22,* 14–18.

Silvern, S. (1988). Continuity/discontinuity between home and early childhood education environments. *The Elementary School Journal, 89*, 147–159.

Stamp, L. N., & Groves, M. M. (1994). Strengthening the ethic of care: Planning and supporting family involvement. *Dimensions of Early Childhood, 22*, 5–9.

Stevenson, D. L., & Baker, D. P. (1987). The family-school relation and the child's school performance. *Child Development, 58*, 1348–1357.

Stipek, D., Milburn, S., Clements, D., & Daniels, D. H. (1992). Parents' beliefs about appropriate education for young children. *Journal of Applied Developmental Psychology, 13*, 293–310.

Swick, K., & Graves, S. B. (1993). *Empowering at-risk families during the early childhood years*. Washington, DC: National Education Association.

Swick, K., & McKnight, S. (1989). Characteristics of kindergarten teachers who promote parent involvement. *Early Childhood Research Quarterly, 4*, 19–29.

U.S. Department of Education. (1991). *Preparing young children for success: Guideposts for achieving our first national educational goal*. Washington, DC: Author.

U.S. General Accounting Office. (1990). *Early childhood education: What are the costs of high-quality programs?* (GAO/HRD–90–43BR). Washington, DC: Author.

White, K. R., Taylor, M. J., & Moss, V. D. (1992). Does research support claims about the benefits of involving parents in early intervention programs? *Review of Educational Research, 62*, 91–125.

 Article Review Form at end of book.

What features for child-friendly schools does Dr. Comer suggest?

Building Schools as Communities

A conversation with James Comer

What children need as much as computers or books, says James Comer, is relationships with caring adults. After a quarter-century, the School Development Program is continuing to model how educators can work with families to create caring communities in schools.

John O'Neil

James Comer is Maurice Falk Professor of Child Psychiatry at the Yale University Child Study Center, Associate Dean of the Yale University School of Medicine, and Director of the School Development Program, 230 S. Frontage Rd., New Haven, CT 06520–7900. John O'Neil is Contributing Editor of Educational Leadership.

John O'Neil: Recently there's been a surge of interest in the social and emotional aspects of learning. That's been the focus of your lifelong work, of course. How did your interest develop?

James Comer: My interest developed from the fact that the friends I grew up with—poor African-American youngsters who were just as bright as I—went on a downhill course in life. When I looked back at this, I realized that the only difference was that I received support for my emotional and social development that my friends did not receive. My mother and father taught me respect and gave me the social skills to solve problems and promote well-being.

For example, like most kids I enjoyed "exploring" my environment. While doing so when I was 11, I visited a house where known "problem behavior" took place. Before I even got home, my father knew about it, because one of the "sisters" from our church had called him. Fortunately, he didn't scold or spank me. He simply pointed out that if I wanted to be respected by people in the neighborhood and in my church, there were things I could and could *not* do. So I learned not to do troublesome things. This close-knit community interaction taught me to seek respect, as well as to respect others.

My mother also arranged for me and my brothers and sisters to play with children of people she felt would be good role models—my doctor's son, in particular. To prepare us, she taught us social skills. One lesson I remember was her advice: "Now, talk enough to be interesting, but don't tell all your business." Because we had good social skills, friends of the family took us many places that my parents could not afford: Chicago Cubs games, amusement parks, and so on.

The importance of these lessons was reinforced when I began training in child psychiatry. It became very clear to me that it is a child's overall development—not simply cognitive or intellectual development—that makes academic learning possible.

Yet the public wants schools to get back to basics; many people seem to think curriculum designed to address social or emotional issues detracts from academic work.

Well, that's because many people misunderstand what intelligence is. Intelligence is really the capacity to gain and use knowledge to solve problems and promote well-being. It has several components: the cognitive, the affective or emotional, and the expressive. People use different terms, but there is now clear recognition that the cognitive is only one dimension of intelligence. To be successful, one needs a threshold level of cognitive ability. But many other things are just as important: creativity, personal discipline, the ability to relate to other people. I call this "effective intelligence"—all the things that come into play in problem solving.

We all see examples of people who have outstanding cognitive skills but who founder because they lack self-insight or have trouble working with others.

Right. And if you talk to employers, they'll tell you they want employees who are able to think, take initiative, get along well with other people, solve problems, be disciplined and responsible. But schools are being influenced by another factor: the demand to produce high test scores. The accountability structures we've created are driving academic activity, driving the way schools are organized. We have overemphasized the cognitive—we think we can measure it, although I'm not sure we even do that very well!

Take us back to the late 1960s, when you began the School Development Program in New Haven. How did you go about providing for students' social and emotional development?

First, we immersed ourselves in the schools and tried to understand what was wrong. We realized that the children were bright and able but that the climate wasn't right. We also realized that the teachers wanted to succeed, but they were stuck with a mechanical model of teaching and did not understand what else was necessary. They weren't prepared to respond to students lack of social and emotional skills, which led to students' acting out or withdrawing from classroom activities. The teachers' response was to try to control the behavior, to "get the badness out of the children." That led to difficulty with the parents, who themselves very often had not done well in school. Parents ended up withdrawing from the school or attacking it. So children, parents, and teachers all wanted to succeed, but all behaved in ways that kept them from being successful.

Next, we build a structure that enabled parents, educators, and other specialists to develop a comprehensive school plan together. The plan had both a social-emotional and an academic component. As we created a good social climate in the school, we then were able to integrate academic learning and social emotional development.

Even at the early states, did parents really have an authentic voice in making decisions? This was way before the heyday of school-based management.

Our School Development Program contained the essential elements of school-based management. Parents served on the governance and management team, and they had their own parent team. The parents helped design a program to support the academic and social program that the school planning and management team came up with. The parents and the teachers worked together on those activities.

Can you give some examples?

We started out with things like Welcome Back to School pot luck suppers and so on. We didn't do them just because they were nice to do, however. We wanted to establish relationships among the adults, to create authority figures for the children to identify with and become attached to. Our idea was to bring all the adults together to support children's growth along the developmental pathways—the social interactive (how to interact well with other people), the psychoemotional (how to control your emotions or handle your impulsivity), the moral-ethical, the linguistic, the intellectual-cognitive, and the physical. It is growth along *all* those pathways that facilitates intellectual academic growth.

Originally, one of your primary teams was called the Mental Health Team. That wasn't designed to "treat" students with emotional problems, though, was it?

To avoid confusion, we now call it the School Support Team. The initial idea was that a Mental Health Team would help children with specific problems. But we found that those problems often grew out of conditions in the school that weren't child-friendly. We learned what we had to do to change the school. The Mental Health Team often took the leadership. For example, we found that children who transferred into the

> What children need more than anything is the chance to attach to adults who are meaningful and important to them.

school were often dumped there without adequate support. What happened? Often, they would act up. One boy kicked the teacher and ran out of the classroom. When the Mental Health Team discussed that with the staff, we all learned together about what support children need during difficult transition periods when they are removed from a supportive environment and put into a new one that is threatening. Then we designed ways to support transfer students when they come into the school.

Although we would help children with a particular problem, we made sure to look more closely at what the school was doing. In the traditional way, the child who kicked the teacher might be sent to the principal's office, be punished, and return to the classroom. When he got there, the other kids would laugh, a fight would start, and this would go round and round until the child was labeled "disturbed." In our program, we learned from these experiences how we could change the school and prevent that kind of outcome.

Can you talk a bit about the curriculum in those early schools, and then in today's schools? How did you develop it and how is it distinctive?

We eventually developed the Social Skills Curriculum for Inner-City Children, which we are now revising. It's a curriculum for *all* kids; it just happens that we were working primarily in the cities when we created it.

We involved parents in developing the curriculum by asking them what they wanted for their children as adults. We found that they wanted the same things that middle-class parents wanted

—good jobs, families, responsible citizenship. We then ask them what kinds of activities would help their children develop the capacity to achieve those things. As we talked about it, our discussion converged on the areas of politics and government, business and economics, health and nutrition, and spiritual and leisure-time skills. So we developed units in those areas that integrated the teaching of basic academics with social interaction skills and appreciation of the arts.

> We found that the problems children had often grew out of conditions in the school that weren't child-friendly. So we learned from children's problems what we had to do to change the school.

In the process of carrying out these activities, staff members learned how they could help the children with their impulsivity and with any other behavioral problems. I believe that living with and helping children to successfully carry out activities is a much more effective approach than lecturing to them in the abstract about what is right or wrong, good or bad.

Some of today's social/emotional programs focus a lot on teaching kids explicitly to manage their emotions, control their impulsivity, and so on. Is that a bad approach?

I don't disagree with it, but I argue that it's easy to get caught up in a specific curriculum that teaches various social or emotional skills but doesn't address the quality of life in the school. The key question is: Are the adults interacting in a way that creates a climate where children feel comfortable, safe, and protected, where they can identify with and attach to adults? It is difficult to internalize a sense of well-being, high self-esteem, and a

passion for achievement in an environment that is chaotic, abusive, or characterized by low expectations for students.

Is it possible for a school to have a traditional curriculum but still be faithful to your model?

I think so. Some people who want great change believe that test scores are unimportant and that we need to teach for deep understanding. I believe that you can do both. If the school climate is supportive enough, you can teach in a way that will enable the young people to pass whatever exam is out there and still help them become deep thinkers and problem solvers.

Your network of Comer schools has received an enormous amount of attention. How big is it now?

We now include more than 650 schools. About 120 are middle or high schools, and the rest are elementary schools. We're now in districts that have as many as 50 different ethnic groups. We are in some majority white middle-class and poor districts, some predominantly Hispanic districts, some predominantly black districts. Some are in rural areas.

That kind of diversity is encouraging. Do affluent districts think they need programs to foster students' social and emotional literacy?

They're beginning to understand. If you look at the trends in social problems, the greatest growth is in the white middle class. Teenage pregnancy was once three times as great among blacks as whites.

It's now one and a half times higher. Thirty years ago, Daniel Patrick Moynihan made us aware of the disturbing fact that 25 percent of black homes were headed by single parents. That's now true of the white community. So we're dealing with a systemic problem; it just happened to show up in the most vulnerable group first.

When you look back to the schools that you began to work with in the late 1960s and 1970s, have they been able to sustain their improvements and build on the structures that had been established?

Some have sustained the reforms, some have not. I'd estimate that about one-third of schools made significant changes, one-third made modest changes, and one-third made no changes. Now hitting .333 is pretty good in baseball. But in school change, we need to hit .900. This will require immense changes in the condition of teaching.

What are some of the lessons you've learned about what it takes to bring about and sustain change?

First, to sustain reform, you really have to change the way we train, select, and support school staff. We need to train a large body of people, as well as retool existing staff members, so that they're capable of creating good organizations in every school. Every school must become a place that supports the development of children. Until we do that, school cannot sustain any program that deals with emotional and social growth. And they limit academic learning, too, because social and emotional growth are so important to academic learning. The im-

portance of preparing and training teachers is a major focus of my new book, *Waiting for a Miracle: Schools Can't Solve Our Problems—But We Can*, which will be published this fall.

What else have you learned?

That continuity and stability are absolutely vital for kids. What children need more than anything is the chance to attach with and bond to adults who are meaningful and important to them. But look at all the examples of discontinuity and instability we have in our education system: superintendent turnover, principal turnover, the movement of teachers from school to school. Many children move frequently and experience no continuity. We have 45-minute classes, even though we know we can't teach for deep understanding in that time. Schools are becoming more and more fragmented.

We are trying to make this commitment to continuity much more central in our relationships with the schools we work with now. District offices need to understand that you don't bring three new teachers into a building without major efforts to prepare them. And you have to look very hard at the effects of teacher turnover within and between schools. It takes so much to change a school, but you can wipe it all out with one or two careless assignments.

As persuasive as your arguments are, a segment of the public is very opposed to having schools play a more active role in students' social and emotional devel-

opment. *There's a feeling that schools are taking over a role that belongs to parents. Is that something you've had to fight?*

For the most part we haven't, because you can't argue with success. Where children are doing better, because families and teachers are all working together, you don't get many arguments. Also, we're very clear that we're not taking over the family's prerogative; we're involving the family in the work of the school. We probably led the call for deeper family involvement in the work of the school. That's the opposite of what's being charged.

The reason we need to strengthen the ties between families and schools is that the nature of our society has changed. We've experienced massive economic changes, technological changes, and the high mobility that technology has made possible. Neighborhoods are not natural communities anymore. And with the growth of mass communications and computers, children are being bombarded with more information than ever before. For the first time in the history of the world, information goes directly to children rather than through important adults who can filter it. What we've got to do is reestablish or create a tighter fabric of support for children's development. To even have a chance to counter the negative aspects of these new developments, you have to connect home and school.

You mentioned that in growing up, you had adults in your community

> To be successful, one needs a threshold level of cognitive ability. But many other things are just as important: creativity, personal discipline, the ability to relate to other people. I call this "effective intelligence."

who took collective responsibility for children. What's happened to our sense of community?

Without question, we've had a breakdown in the sense of community. In the past, we tended to overlook how important community is. It provided social and emotional support for children, but we didn't see how that related to academic learning. This is still not widely understood. Now we're experiencing a breakdown in our communities, and we still need to help students attain high levels of academic achievement. The solution is to restore a sense of community. And that is what our program has always been about: restoring community, and doing it within the school.

Editor's note: For more information, contact Cynthia Savo, School Development Program, 53 College St., New Haven, CT 06510; (203) 737-1020 (e-mail: cynthia.savo@yale.edu). The SDP Web site is http://pandora.med.yale.edu/comer/welcome.html.

Article Review Form at end of book.

What are three applications of videotaping for assessment of special needs children?

Family Involvement with Assistive Technology

Roger Kroth and Mary-Dale Bolson

Roger Kroth is a professor emeritus, University of New Mexico, where Mary-Dale Bolson is a doctoral student.

Regarding adaptive technology, are there differences between the expectations for family involvement and the subsequent behaviors of family members and professionals as opposed to typical parent involvement with children with special needs? YES, there seems to be!

The differences appear to be subtle. It is the purpose of this article to address some of these differences. A basic philosophical difference is in how significant others (family members and professionals) view the person who has special needs. This philosophy drives some assessment and treatment procedures.

Traditionally, the design of special education evaluation and treatment is a deficit model. How can the child be made eligible for special needs services? And are there behaviors and traits that need to be remediated? Therefore, referring a child for special education services becomes almost a self-fulfilling prophecy. Conversely, sometimes families are disappointed after assessment, if the recommendation is not to use any assistive technology (AT) devices. Subconsciously, the hope is that whatever AT solution is recommended, the device will have magical properties to "normalize" the child. Whatever the decision or process, family involvement is critical. And it's precisely this area of involvement that may be avoided by busy professionals. Working with families initially adds a time requirement to an already overloaded system. It is our premise, though, that "a stitch in time saves nine." Or for an assistive technologist "A switch in time saves time!"

At the Research Institute for Assistive and Training Technologies (RIATT) in Albuquerque, NM, family members participate in the process from beginning to end. Who knows the individual's strengths better than those who are around the person? Who knows how much time and effort the student can expend better than those who live with him/her? And who knows how much time and energy the family can expend to learn to implement the procedures laid out? In a family systems approach, the family structure and resources are carefully attended to in order to provide a usable and useful treatment program.

Assessment Procedures

Early in the training program for assistive technologists at the University of New Mexico, research and experience proved the benefits of home visits, especially when visits with the individual who needs services were videotaped. While this sounds time consuming, it succinctly addresses the goal to provide services or devices to a person with special needs, appropriately tailored and cost efficiently delivered.

Videotaping the family in their home environment provides the assistive technology team with data to review before bringing the child and family to the clinic for a more formalized assessment. During the home visit, family members verbally and nonverbally demonstrate lifestyle needs of the child.

"Family Involvement with Assistive Technology" by Roger Kroth and Mary-Dale Bolson from CONTEMPORARY EDUCATION, Fall 1996, Vol. 68, No. 1, pp. 17–19. Reprinted by permission.

Once when a team was making a home visit, they were questioning the parents about things the child could do. One of the siblings was playing at the side but, as is often the case, he was listening to what was going on with his brother. After a while, he seemed unable to contain himself any longer. "He can do that. I'll show you," and he proceeded to do just that.

At this stage, the role of the assistive technologist and the team members is to provide families with an opportunity to demonstrate the skills and abilities of the person with special adaptive needs. The family members show how they have compensated with their own solutions, which then leads to a meaningful discussion about next steps. In other words, family involvement demonstrates a strength model rather than the more common deficit approach.

Listening and Observing

When working with the family, professionals learn to attend not only to the words but also the message behind them. It is particularly important to observe eye communication. Dr. Adamson, Director of RIATT, refers to his eye test when observing a child for the first time. Did the eyes "say" to the examiner, "There is something in here you need to tap?" While it is important to review standardized tests for information, often the condition and special needs of the person invalidate test results. Hatred and love show in the eyes; therefore, this "eye test" is not as subjective as you might think. Intelligence may very well be in the eyes of the beholder. Family involvement is important at this stage to verify whether the goals of the professionals and the family are really the same.

A number of years ago at a family learning vacation at a school for the deaf and hard-of-hearing, professionals were intent on finding some assistive device for a child who was severely and profoundly physically impaired. *Their* goal was to develop some sort of communication system. Later, the mother shared with one of the camp counselors that they, the parents, would be pleased if the child could just hold his head up for feeding!

Good listening and interviewing techniques could have saved much time and frustration. Parents often think professionals know what is best, and professionals often try to anticipate what they think the parents want (Kroth, 1985, Perl, 1995).

Probability and Possibility

One of the most interesting phenomena in working with families is the different ways professionals and parents perceive a given situation. Professionals predicted that the child would die before his sixth birthday. Family members accepted the prognosis. It affected the family lifestyle. Trips were out of the question. Baby-sitters were not often used. The family was afraid to leave their son in respite care, although some very good respite care opportunities were available. But he didn't die. After a while, they called him Lazurus, because he kept coming back from the dead. He actually lived until he was 21.

A parent once said, "You professionals want to talk about probabilities, and we want to talk about possibilities." Norman Cousins (1989) said, "Accept the verdict, but do not accept the consequences." Writers such as Bill Moyer, Bernie Siegel, and Norman

Cousins, emphasize the importance of not taking the *hope* away. Normally accepted predictive assessment tools such as standardized tests and professional past experiences may do just that.

Empowerment

Good family involvement programs seek to empower the parents and put professionals in the role of consultants. An additional goal in assistive technology programs is to empower the individual with special needs (Dunst & Trivettee, 1987). Wraparound service providers should collaborate with that in mind. One problem that occurs when diverse support professionals meet is lack of common language. Frequently, team members use words and phrases common to their disciplines but not common for family members or other professionals. Reference booklets simply written are sometimes useful.

Jeanelle Livingston-Pasternack, being sensitive to this issue, developed a handbook for parents. She realized that parents of children in her camp program were not familiar with the role of at least some support professionals. She used a question and answer format— "questions to ask an occupational therapist," or "questions to ask an audiologist," and so on. She tried to facilitate and familiarize language and roles of involved professionals for families. For instance, parents might wonder why their child is seeing an *occupational* therapist—particularly if the child is young. Occupation normally means job or a way to earn a living. The question format and strategy allowed professionals to define themselves by their answers.

Specific issues must be addressed with written handbooks or handouts for families. One is the average reading ability of the intended audience. Another is the primary language used by the family. A third is family culture.

Training

Training family members and support professionals in the intended use of assistive technology devices recommended for a particular person in need is an often overlooked step. Special education teacher Joanne Keane and a few of her co-workers at Inez Elementary School in Albuquerque develop videotapes to be sent home to families. Since survey research of families report that most homes have a television and VCR, this is an effective communication and training tool. It provides an up-to-date visual and auditory evaluation of the child. It demonstrates normal classroom activities and involvement by the child. Mary Hartley, a speech and language therapist, created videotapes for parents on sign language. An added value of the videotape method is that families can play it over and over, and then, the tape can be recycled.

Certainly, one key to any successful use of an assistive device is training provided for family members and school personnel. Assistive devices often look forbidding to those who are not used to the world of technology. If they seem to be too much trouble, the devices sit unused, and this happens at schools as well as in homes. Expecting families to be excited about the possibility of having a device is unrealistic. Or if they are excited, their enthusiasm may wane when they find out they have to help with the implementation of the program.

As we tried to set up a training session, a mother once said, "I have eight children, my husband has shot at me twice, I am on welfare, and I can hardly keep clean clothes on the children and food on the table. I don't have time to come to another meeting." She was right.

Compendium

Family involvement is required by law, but what is even more important, it is necessary for successful assessment and implementation of plans for individuals with assistive technology needs. Hope and love are not ingredients easily measurable, but remember the mom who said, "Don't talk to me about the probabilities, tell me the possibilities." Taking time to understand the family structure and considering the number of professionals involved and how one impinges on the other will assure a program and interaction that does more good than harm (Doernberg, 1978). Assistive technologists who develop skills in observation and communication tempered with compassion have a sound opportunity to provide successful fulfillment of assessment, training, and treatment plans for those with assistive technology needs.

Comparison of Differences of Family Involvement of Assistive Technology and Special Education

Category	Assistive Technology	Special Education
Philosophy	Strengths model (What can the person *do*?)	Deficit model (Is the person eligible?)
Assessment	Direct Observation (parents very much involved)	Normative testing (structured testing)
Goals	Specific	More general
Predictability	Possibilities	Probabilities
Empowerment focus	Client	Parents
Communication	Frequent initiation by either party	Seldom and initiated by agency
Special devices	*Always* and often provided by agency	Usually traditional

References

Castro, G. & Mastropieri. M.A. (1986) The Efficacy of Early Intervention Programs: A Meta-Analysis. *Exceptional Children, 52*(5) 417–424.

Cousins, N. (1989), *Head First: The Biology of Hope*. New York, New York: E.P. Dutton.

Doernberg, N. (1978) Some Negative Effects on Family Integration of Health and Educational Services for Young Handicapped Children. *Rehabilitation Literature, 39*(4) 107–110.

Dunst, C.J. and Trivettee, C.M. (1987) Enabling and Empowering Families: Conceptual and Intervention Issues. *School Psychology Review, 16*(4), 443–456.

Kroth, R. (1985). *Communicating with Parents of Exceptional Children: Improving Parent-Teacher Relationships* (second edition) third edition with Edge, D. (in press). Denver, Colorado: Love Publishing Co.

Moyers, B. (1989) *Bill Moyers: a World of Ideas. Conversations with Thoughtful Men and Women about American Life Today and the Ideas Shaping Our Future*. New York, Doubleday.

Perl, J. (1995, Fall) Improving Relationship Skills for Parent Conferences. *Teaching Exceptional Children,* 29–31.

Siegel, B. (1988) *Love, Medicine & Miracles: Lessons learned about Self-Healing From A Surgeon's Experience with Exceptional Patients*. New York: Perennial Library. Harper & Row, Publishers.

 Article Review Form at end of book.

What should the teaching staff consider when parental involvement is expected in Migrant Head Start?

Migrant Head Start

What does it mean to involve parents in program services?

Frank Fuentes, Virginia D. Cantu, and Robert Stechuk

Frank Fuentes is Deputy Associate Commissioner, Child Care Bureau, Administration for Children and Families, U.S. Department of Health and Human Services.

Virginia D. Cantu is a Social Services Specialist with the Academy for Educational Development, Migrant Head Start Technical Assistance Support Center in Washington D.C. Ms. Cantu has more than 20 years experience in early childhood education and child care administration. She has served as Social Services/ Parent Involvement Coordinator and Program Assessment Specialist with Head Start and Migrant Head Start Grantees, and has worked with the Texas Department of Human Services.

Robert Stechuk is an Education Specialist with the Academy for Educational Development Migrant Head Start Technical Assistance Support Center in Washington D.C. Mr. Stechuk also served in Head Start for 10 years as an Education/ Disabilities Coordinator and as a Home-Base Program Director.

Since its inception, Head Start has worked to foster child development through services that are both comprehensive and interdisciplinary. That is, Head Start programs provide an extensive variety of services to address all areas relevant to development. Furthermore, programs provide services through collaborative efforts, not only among program staff but also in conjunction with the parents of enrolled children. The philosophy of Head Start is not only that "parents are a child's first and most important teachers," but also that parents should be involved in the full range of program operations, from direct services through decision making and evaluation. Although the inclusion of parents in service provision is not typical of most other organizations or agencies, this aspect of the Head Start program is one of its most striking.

Parent Involvement in Migrant Head Start

Within the Head Start community, the Migrant Programs Branch funds 26 grantees which operate programs in 38 states. During FY 93/94, approximately 34,000 children were enrolled in Migrant Head Start (MHS) programs.

Like all Head Start programs, those serving migrant families must operate in compliance with the Performance Standards (45-CFR 1304) and Transmittal Notice 70.2, which mandate extensive parent involvement in all areas of program operation. The extent of parent involvement includes not only parents' direct service participation (e.g. as classroom volunteers, assisting with field trips), but also parents' active roles in policy and program decision-making (approval of curriculum, staff hiring), and within the evaluation of program services (SAVI/OSPRI).

MHS programs may operate for as few as six weeks per calendar year, or for as long as nine to 10 months. Individual MHS Centers may run from 8–12 hours per day for 5–7 days per week. In addition, children enrolled in MHS may range from six weeks to five years in age.

"Migrant Head Start: What Does It Mean to Involve Parents in Program Services?" by Frank Fuentes, Virginia D. Cantu and Robert Stechuk from CHILDREN TODAY, Vol. 24, No. 1, pp. 16–18. Reprinted by permission of the authors.

Migrant Workers, Head Start Parents

Agriculture is a labor-intensive operation; so too is agricultural employment an intensive undertaking for those who perform the labor. Typically, both parents work together in the fields or orchards while their children attend the MHS program. Their working days often begin well before sunrise and end after sunset, and the work week is often longer than five days. Not surprisingly, the long hours, exposure to the elements and the physically demanding nature of job tasks leave parents exhausted at the end of the day. Once a particular season or harvest is completed, families often move hundreds of miles to obtain other employment. The question for MHS programs thus becomes: How can MHS respond to the challenges posed by the nature of agricultural work, so that programs can support optimal parent involvement in program operations?

MHS: Service Options for Family Needs

In order to address the needs of migrant families, MHS programs must begin with an understanding of the families they serve. The challenge is twofold: first, how to *obtain* the trust, respect and confidence of parents; and second, how to *build upon* and develop these qualities so that parents involve *themselves* in the program. To establish this, parent involvement must be conceived of and implemented as a process, in which lines of communication between parent and program are first opened and then expanded.

One step in this process is to initiate and develop methods of communication which inform parents that they have the right to involvement in their children's program. In many cases, MHS parents possess a deep and profound respect for education and educators. One way of demonstrating this respect is not to question or attempt to influence what programs do or how programs operate. In order to achieve parent involvement, therefore, programs must first communicate that involvement is not only possible but desired by program staff.

Second, programs must consider multiple options for establishing communication. For some families, a written invitation to attend a program function may not be understood or may simply be too impersonal. Some families may respond to a personal invitation from staff who make site-visits to the camps, or from the bus drivers and/or aides who transport the children to and from the MHS program. In any case, using many forms of communication helps demonstrate that programs desire the involvement of their parents.

A third step is for programs to develop an understanding of what motivates parents. Not surprisingly, this usually turns out to be an interest in the growth and development of the child or children enrolled in the program. By providing services for children which are safe, appropriate and comprehensive, parents become oriented to the comprehensive nature of the Head Start approach. Later, through involvement in activities that are meaningful to them, parents come to see the variety of ways in which they can support the development of their children, their child's program, and themselves.

Over time, MHS parents begin to involve other parents in program activities and operations. For example, Margarita Arevalo, who migrates between Texas and Minnesota with her family, has been a Head Start parent for 16 years. At first, Margarita became involved "because I wanted to know and understand what was happening at my child's center. I wanted to better my program." Now, building upon her experiences, "I teach other parents what I've learned. I motivate them, give them rides to meetings." This level of personal involvement, in which parents take over the tasks of defining and creating ways to participate in program functioning, embodies "involvement" in its optimal form. Here, parents with Head Start experience serve as role models, trainers and advocates for those families who are more recently enrolled.

Parent Involvement: A Process

Yet achieving this high level of participation takes time. MHS programs have come to learn that by maintaining high quality programs for children, they will attract the attention of the children's parents. Further, when parents are asked to assist in defining program operations—such as setting hours of operation, the length of the program year, and the times, locations and content of training opportunities—they can begin to see themselves as equal partners in the process. MHS programs must plan to inform parents regarding the full range of choices open to parents and accommodate different levels of time and energy.

For example, families with newborns may only be able to participate occasionally, while other families may choose more frequent participation. In order to offer services that meet the needs of migrant families, program staff must collaborate to learn from families (concerns, areas of interest, services desired etc.), and then incorporate parents' expressions into program services. Many programs choose to accomplish this communication process by:

- making communication convenient for families, including translating written materials into the native language of the family, or making site visits to camps, when appropriate;

- polling parents about their concerns and preferences;

- conducting home visits to both give and receive information with families;

- contacting employers (growers, contractors, crew leaders) to understand their specific labor requirements and ways in which they might collaborate with the MHS program;

- incorporate all program staff into the process: Teachers, Center Directors, Parent Involvement Coordinators and bus drivers may not all play the same role, but all have a role to play;

- informing parents that they may ride to and from their child's center on the bus (in the event that weather conditions or mechanical break-downs provide them with time off from work);

- holding meetings in the evenings or on weekends;

- revising schedules to accommodate "spontaneous" parent volunteers who are available when rain interrupts work schedules;

- providing child care (including infant child care) and nutritious meals during parent meetings and training opportunities;

- planning and conducting parent meetings at the labor camps;

- providing transportation when meetings are conducted at the Head Start center.

Parent-Program Collaboration

The *specific* methods of communication that programs select depend upon local conditions and circumstances. While an individual option may appear straightforward or simple, it will only be successful after hours are invested in planning and implementation. For example, providing child care and nutritious meals may be crucial to obtaining parent attendance at meetings. By offering these elements as part of the meeting, programs provide service offerings that are *consistent with family routines*. Expecting families to attend a Head Start meeting after a full day of labor and then go home to prepare dinner will probably yield lower levels of participation. Conducting meetings at labor camps may minimize travel time and expenses for families and will demonstrate that programs really do want parents to be involved. By raising and exploring these and other issues with their parents, MHS programs develop working relationships that are mutually beneficial to parents and program staff.

Parent Involvement: Going Beyond

How might Head Start parents benefit from programs that offer flexible and creative options for their involvement in program activities? Julieta Lopez, who has participated in Head Start experiences for eight years, provides this answer: "[I've learned to] value myself as a person, to better myself so that my children can better themselves. I'm their role model. I've been able to use what I learned in the Migrant Head Start program in my job."

Ultimately, then, "parent involvement" can exist on as many levels as there are parents to be involved. Parents who are offered communication that is accessible to them and options that are meaningful to them thereby become capable of empowering themselves in conjunction with their local MHS program. Through MHS offerings which get and then *keep* parents involved, parents can support both the development of their children and the development of themselves, as parents and as employees. By translating the Head Start philosophy into practical activities at the local level, MHS can benefit families long after they and their children leave the program.

MHS staff therefore combine both creativity and flexibility in their work. In order to achieve success in involving parents, staff must be willing to review and evaluate their efforts to accomplish parent involvement. In doing so, staff proceed from national standards, which mandate extensive parent involvement program activities, to local responses, which combine creative thinking, flexibility, and plain hard work.

 Article Review Form at end of book.

How are parents involved in school improvement?

Keep Community "Real" for Urban School Success

Darren W. Woodruff

From Theory Into Practice.

Darren W. Woodruff is a research associate at the School Development Program, Yale University, New Haven, Connecticut, where inquires on the School Development Program may be directed. Condensed from Theory Into Practice, 35 (Autumn 1996), 278–82.

In past times, urban-school parents could almost count on running into their child's teacher at the market, shopping center, or church for up-to-the-minute reports on behavior and academic standing. Their children were consistently exposed to positive teacher-parent interactions and received a sense of their parents, teachers, and others within the community talking, thinking, and contributing as a unified whole to their development. These relations between the school and the wider community allowed the school and its teachers to function as a central component in the child's development.

In present times, schools and teachers have released their status as centerpieces within the community. Many working in urban schools travel long commutes and leave quickly to beat rush-hour traffic. Such teachers cannot develop the tools to properly understand, teach, and improve their students.

A mostly untapped bridge between urban teachers and more desirable levels of student knowledge is the local community itself. Schools and curricula are most effective when rooted in children's needs and experiences. What goes on in a school, therefore, should be as much about a child's overall life as it is about academics. To this end, life in the home/community and life at school should interact in relation to one another. Classrooms should be organized to make children feel significant and cared for.

We must bridge gaps between urban schools, parents, and students.

One way to do this is by creating schools that reflect and value the child's community, belief systems, and culture. When school staff are unable to reflect the life and needs of a child, the school loses its relevance as a valid source of knowledge. When teachers fail to connect with their students by tapping into their learning and cultural styles, barriers grow between the school's goals and the children's innate abilities.

Parents can be powerful allies in bringing schools, students, and the community into sync. Unfortunately, in many urban schools, parent-teacher interactions do not exist. In fact, one of the most difficult and unresolved issues for urban schools has been the problem of involving minority and low-income parents in the education of their children. Misunderstandings between two cultures—school and community—have been cited as a key roadblock to desirable home-school relationships and academic focus among students.

When there is agreement—or consonance—between the prevailing school culture and that of the local community, an interpersonal and interactional sync is achieved. Harmony between the school and the wider community can then extend into a linking of concerns, behavioral styles, and modes of communication. Such coordination is critical for stimulating parental involvement and teacher effectiveness with students.

Currently, however, the interpersonal style in the urban community is often at odds with the school's, creating problems rooted in cultural dissonance.

James Comer defines this dissonance as "an extremely high degree of distrust, anger, and alienation between home and school—the two most important institutions in the developmental life of a child—that were only vaguely apparent and routinely misunderstood." He says school staff saw parents' poor participation as lack of concern, while parents often felt staff to be distant, rejecting, sometimes even hostile.

Gaps between urban schools, parents, and students need to be actively bridged: Schools, teachers, and parents must move toward a goal of "keeping it real." This involves installation and development of authentic, contextually sensitive school communities that welcome students and parents as equal participants into the broader goals of learning and school success. Teachers should acquire the knowledge and skills for working with diverse student groups and for helping them develop positive attitudes about themselves.

Community-sensitive teaching —particularly in the use of relevant language, communication styles, and curriculum materials— is rich in its connections to cognitive development. Cognitive demands of problem-solving tasks are lessened when the tasks are framed in ways that are familiar and connect to the student's existing knowledge background.

In this way, culturally relevant pedagogy helps to unclog the pipeline of knowledge acquisition from teacher to student. Linking pedagogy with contextual relevance enables teachers to "personalize" their schools and

classrooms in the direction of student needs and perspectives on the world.

The School Development Program (SDP), a school empowerment model developed at Yale University by James Comer, works to close the gulf between students, parents, and schools. It actively recruits and involves parents and others from the community in the everyday functioning of schools on all levels. Management and policy decisions, teacher pedagogy, and child development theory, as well as the social life of the school, are areas incorporating full parent involvement under the SDP model.

This systemic reorganization of the school into a functioning community provides multiple levels and opportunities for heightened parent-staff interactions, affective bonding experiences, and greater cultural understanding. SDP teachers report that "We can get involved with the curriculum much more quickly because we spend less time on disciplinary issues. . . . With the model in place everyone at the school has really begun to enjoy being here so much more—there's much more teamwork going on."

The result of this school climate change is a natural push among parents and teachers toward a greater focus and motivation for positive student development and an opportunity for teachers to participate in critical developmental pathways. In short, says Comer: "Children are able to meet the (social/behavioral) expectations of the school, and [then] elicit a positive response from school people. As a result, a positive attachment and bond [can] occur between children and school people similar to the attachment and bond that occurs between parents and their

children. This enables school people to relate the school program to the children . . . including an appreciation of academic learning."

The original SDP schools mirrored the frustrations cited by urban school principals—poor achievement, attendance, and morale. Most of the children were perceived as "bad," undermotivated, and lacking in academic potential. In examining the culture within these schools, Comer noted a pervasive lack of trust between parents, teachers, and administrators. He recognized the need for structural mechanisms that could lead to positive change.

To meet this need, Comer and his colleagues developed these components for school improvement:

- A school planning and management team (SPMT) involving teachers, parents, and staff working together at decision making.

- A mental health support team (MHT) using child development theory in the organization of the school and for prevention of negative behavioral issues.

- A parents program to systematically include parents at every level within the school.

- A comprehensive school plan for academic goal setting and social programming throughout the school year.

- Staff development to create programs and workshops to enable the staff to move toward the goals of the comprehensive school plan.

- Collaboration and consensus decision-making between all school stakeholders with the principal as recognized leader.

This process for positive school change has been implemented and developed over the years and has resulted in significant achievement and climate gains in schools across the country. SDP has produced significant math and reading improvements in many of its schools. There are now over 600 SDP schools across the country.

The success of this model, with its emphasis on active construction of positive, equitable relations between teachers, students, parents, and the wider community, distinguishes it from reforms that focus solely on teaching technique or perceived student limitations. SDP is unique in its efforts to change the nature and quality of human interactions—i.e., the cultural system—at work in schools. The focus on people and relationships in SDP schools helps develop a school-wide climate that is both progressive and oriented toward effective management, teaching, and learning.

Because of this focus on climate change—restoration of schools as a foundation within the community—SDP is an important model for school policymakers. It can help provide instructors with the cultural and community foundation for engaging in relevant and sensitive pedagogy, an approach crucial for improving educational outcomes for students in urban schools.

Without continuity between the home, school, and wider community, successful development of children is impossible. Under current conditions at many schools, urban students and others outside the cultural mainstream are most at risk for being failed by schools. SDP is specifically designed to bridge the gap between ineffectual schooling and more effective, relevant approaches.

When teachers—most often representatives of mainstream, middle-class culture—come into contact with students not of their culture or group (i.e., urban/

minority children), assumptions are often made regarding their capacity for achievement. These assumptions are rooted in systemic ignorance of the contexts, views, and strengths that these children bring with them into the classroom. Without broader recognition and understanding of the diverse group characteristics and strengths found in urban settings, teaching practices in these schools will continue to increase the probability of student failure.

All school stakeholders should reflect and respond to the diversity found in urban schools. Students in these settings need exposure to powerful educators who are able to "keep it real"—by bringing a sense of community and positive interaction into the practices of the school and in the classroom.

 Article Review Form at end of book.

Why do parents trust the Network Preschools?

A Safe and Caring Place

The mission of the Alexandria Community Network Preschools is to remove the barriers that children in poverty face when they enter public school.

Carolyn R. Pool

*Carolyn R. Pool is Senior Editor of Educational Leadership. **Barbara Mason**, the Executive Director of the Alexandria Community Network Preschools, can be reached at 2210 Mt. Vernon Ave., Alexandria, VA 22301.*

Meet Susanne and Brittany, a mother-daughter team enrolled in the Alexandria Community Network Preschools, a private, nonprofit preschool system that serves more than 125 children and their families from low-income neighborhoods in Alexandria, Virginia.

Brittany, a bright 5-year-old, enjoys writing and art and is always thinking of new things to do in the classroom. Her older brother and sister have also attended the preschool, and her mother, Susanne, became a paid parent assistant several years ago. Susanne's experiences at the preschool led her to apply for another training program to become a licensed home day-care provider. After several months, she received her license and now cares for several children in her home.

According to Barbara Mason, the Executive Director of the Network Preschools, this family and many others now have a chance to break the welfare cycle that dominates the lives of many people in their neighborhood. The story of Susanne and Brittany is one of many Network success stories.

The Network Preschools follow the principles for a high-quality early childhood curriculum formulated by the High/Scope Educational Research Foundation (Schweinhart et al. 1993), and they are accredited by the National Association for the Education for Young Children (1997). The curriculum is based on a child's natural development—particularly in language skills, social and emotional growth, and physical motor development—and encourages children to be independent learners. Speaking, listening, singing, looking at pictures, running, skipping, hopping, hugging, drawing, coloring, playing with blocks—all these are in the curriculum, as well as cleaning up, sharing, and saying thank-you.

Parents are important partners in this curriculum. For example, parents volunteer in the classroom, take basic education classes offered at the school, obtain training and employment as paid parent aides and child-care providers, and work with teachers who visit their families at home.

Preschool Beginnings— and Struggles

The Network Preschools began with five children in 1984. A group of mothers living in a public housing project started a school when they found out that all of their children had failed kindergarten. Local churches helped them set up their new school, offered with no charge to the parents. Results of that first year? All the children who attended the preschool passed kindergarten. The program has grown to four schools and nine classes—and tuition is still free.

Because preschool is not part of Alexandria's public school system (except for special education preschools), there is usually a long waiting list (30–50 children) for the Network schools, which are separate from the local Head Start schools. Even those schools have a waiting list of 160 children —more than the Network preschools could accommodate. It is difficult to estimate the total number of unserved preschoolers in the city, because many of them come from families who are undocumented immigrants. But if you simply add the waiting lists, you get at least 200 known children—and families—who still need a high-quality preschool program.

Where do the funds come from for such programs? That's a problem the Network Preschools struggle with daily. The program receives no state or federal funding (apart from the school lunch program). One-third of the Network's funds come from the city of Alexandria; one-third, from private foundations; the remainder, from private donors, including the United Way. And a new Target Department Store in Alexandria just announced a gift of $1,000 to the preschools. Mason says she spends most of her time writing grants—when she would rather be focusing on school programs and the needs of children in the community. Mason also recently attended the White House Conference on Child Care, where Hillary Rodham Clinton called the state of U.S. child care an "invisible crisis."

Preschool Where the Action Is

All Alexandria Network Preschools are located in the communities they serve. Two are in recreation centers in public housing projects, and two are in apartment buildings in low-income areas. In one building, the preschool is across from the laundry room. At one recreation center, the preschool is at the hub of activity, located next to the new citizen project, down the hall from meetings of a support group for young

black males, and near the gym where neighborhood adolescents play basketball. Because the schools are part of the community, young mothers and fathers regard them as "a trusted friend," says Mason.

One mother and her 4-year-old daughter, Juanita, recently found how true a friend the school could be. One day Juanita just stopped coming to school, and the staff sent note after note home, finally preparing to drop her from enrollment. After three weeks, the mother came to school in tears and told the horrifying story of how her child had been raped and hospitalized, and that now all Juanita wanted was to come back to school. Mason said the hospital provided this non-English-speaking mother with no counseling—just a business card printed in English. So the staff welcomed mother and daughter back into school and found crisis-counseling services in Spanish.

The school provides similar services to all enrolled children and their families (including siblings). Regardless of the level of trust, and staff knows that many cases of rape and abuse go unreported. Mason often tells Juanita's story to teachers, saying, "Don't you ever think that what you're doing is not meaningful."

What Is High-Quality Early Childhood Education?

The four Network Preschools make a concerted effort to provide comprehensive, neighborhood-based services to young children at risk and their families. Here are some of the principles that preschool staff follow:

The curriculum is based on a child's natural development and encourages children to be independent learners.

What Do the Children Say?

On a recent Monday morning, during circle time, a child began telling the class about an instance of domestic violence that had occurred in her home. Concerned, the teacher looked to the child's mother, who happened to be working as an aide that day. The mother signaled to let her daughter continue.

Once the child had finished her story and the mother assured the teacher that the police knew about it, the teacher turned her attention to the class and decided to teach the children some new strategies she had just learned in a workshop on this topic.

She first reminded them of what to do first in such a situation—remove themselves from immediate physical danger. Then she asked them to close their eyes and envision themselves in a safe place—something they could do at home, too.

After a few minutes, she told the children to open their eyes and asked for volunteers to share the safe place they had chosen. The teacher was overcome by emotion: Out of 11 children in the circle, 7 had chosen the classroom as their safe place. Of all the places and people they could have envisioned, these children felt most protected right where they were—in school with their teacher.

• *Use developmentally appropriate practices with young children.* Children learn through play. That is the essence of a high-quality preschool program. Mason says.

We set up an environment that is conducive to learning so that every toy or item available to a child can be used in a mode of learning. But the child makes the choice; the child charts his or her course, and the teacher asks the right questions to guide the child.

Children have many choices in the classroom, from playing in the house corner, to playing at the sand or water tables, to painting at the art table, to listening to tapes, to playing with blocks.

They visit the library often for special story times, and students from metropolitan elementary schools come to the preschool to read to them.

Many of the parents take a class called "Answers," which engages them in hands-on activities that show how young children learn—and why the preschool doesn't focus on the ABC's of reading and writing. According to Mason,

Some parents get upset when their children come home and say they played all day. But we show parents that when children play in the house corner, they're creating a story—their own story. And when they are building with blocks, they're doing math.

• *Enable and encourage parent and community involvement.* Many parents serve as both paid and unpaid assistants in the classroom; others participate in literacy programs or child-care training programs. Area churches, businesses, and city agencies participate in Community Service Days; workshops on parenting, immigration issues, health and safety, and fire and home safety; and the family literacy project (recording children's books on tape; see box, p. 76*).

• *Provide for the health and nutrition needs of children and their families.* Children receive healthy lunches and snacks at school, and parents who are home-care providers receive meals for their families. Regular vision and hearing screenings and referrals keep children—and parents—healthy. The school was bequeathed an annual gift of $5,000 to help pay medical expenses of families that are not paid by Medicaid or another source, Mason says.

*Not included in this publication.

If a child needs eyeglasses, we take the child and the parent to the optometrist and pay for the exam and the glasses. If needed, we pay for the child's required physical exam, and we pay for neurological and other exams that are not covered.

• *Provide connections and easy referrals to social services.* Preschool staff include social service interns and therapists who provide direct services to children and help parents find food stamps, transportation, and other assistance.

• *Employ specially trained staff and parent aides, with a low student-teacher ratio.* All Network teachers have degrees in early childhood education, and some have master's degrees. In most classrooms, the ratio is four adults for 15 children: a teacher, two assistants, and a parent aide. Recent monthly workshops for staff and parent aides have included "Using the C.O.R. Assessment Tool" (a way to record observations of children), "Adult-Child Interaction," and "Movement and Music."

• *Provide safe and secure settings.* In inner-city neighborhoods, many children are either victims or witnesses to domestic violence. In an era of drive-by shootings and a rising poverty rate, schools like the Network Preschool provide a safe haven for children and a way for parents to learn nonviolent childrearing practices (see box, p. 159).

• *Include children of poverty, children from limited-English-speaking families, and children from all ability groups, including children with disabilities.* Families served by the preschools are

Because the schools are part of the community, young mothers and fathers regard them as a trusted friend.

mostly black and Hispanic, and all live in low-income neighborhoods. One school serves Spanish-speaking immigrants new to the area. Children with mild disabilities receive all needed services at the preschools, and children with more severe disabilities attend a special education program for half the day at a city school. About one-third of the children receive special services of some sort, and 97 percent qualify for free lunches (provided through the U.S. Department of Agriculture school lunch program).

• *Provide child-care for families who need them.* Extended day-care services are available at one preschool. In addition, a new program provides interested parents—like Susanne—with training in becoming licensed day-care providers in their own homes. The preschool employs these providers, equips them, and supervises them, and even provides evening and weekend child care to those who need it.

• *Consider the needs of the community.* A new, rapidly expanding Parent Literacy program attempts to meet the needs of community members for basic education and instruction in English. In learning to read, parents also learn good parenting behavior and improve their chances at employment. Parents attend English classes while their children are in school—down the hall—and they practice reading to their children in the classroom and at home, during home visits by staff. None of these programs is required, but many parents participate in the classes and workshops that the school offers. Mason says, "Our parent education program is developmentally appropriate, too; just as we take the children where they are, we take the parents where *they* are."

Positive Results

Walter exemplifies the success of the Network Preschools. As his teacher watched this busy 4-year-old work a puzzle, she reflected on what Walter was like just nine months earlier: "He couldn't sit still and pay attention. He couldn't play with the other children. He didn't speak a word of English, and you couldn't understand what he said in Spanish."

When he was 3, Walter's parents looked for a preschool for him, but couldn't afford any. They were afraid that their son would enter kindergarten hopelessly behind, like many children with limited proficiency in English. They found the Network Preschool, and by January of his first school year, Walter was playing with other children and speaking English sentences. Walter's father sings the school's praises:

I have seen how much it has helped Walter, how it has been good for his well-being. Everyone has been working together—the teacher, his friends, and the whole system.

Mason adds, "Walter's a fully functional child in 1st grade now, doing high-level work—he's fine."

But to the preschool staff, it's not enough to cite the success of children like Walter, Brittany, or Juanita or to say that none of the preschool graduates have failed kindergarten in the past five years. What is important is that the program changes the lives of families. Mason says:

What makes us special is how much growth we see in both the children and the mothers. While the child learns in the classroom, the mother is talking English classes and also works in the child's classroom. She also may take child-care provider training. And specially trained home visitors follow "nurturing curriculum" lesson plans to help parents incorporate what they have learned into the home environment. It usually starts with the mother—then the father, who has been watching all along, begins to join in, and then the other kids learn, too. Our program really has a big impact. It's a holistic approach that brings the family together.

For information about the Parent Nurturing Program, contact SCAN (Stop Child Abuse Now), 2210 Mt. Vernon Ave., Alexandria, VA 22301.

References

National Association for the Education of Young Children. (1997). "NAEYC Position Statement." World Wide Web: (http://www.america-tomorrow.com/naeyc/position/dap3.htm).

Schweinhart, L.J., H.V. Barnes, and D.P. Weikart. (1993). *Significant Benefits: The High/Scope Perry Preschool Study Through Age 27*. Monograph No. 10. Ypsilanti, Mich.: High/Scope Educational Research Foundation.

Article Review Form at end of book.

Children learn through play: That is the essence of a high-quality preschool program.

Finding the right kind of child care depends on what three factors?

Caring for Your Child While Caring for Your Business

Tina Egge

For the homebased working parent, the idea of child care may seem like a contradiction in your lifestyle choice. The reason you left full-time employment was to balance work and family commitments and tip the scale towards family.

Yet, here you are successfully growing a business at home and child care with its associated perplexities are facing you once again. Besides the guilt associated with sending your kids to daycare, there is the ever-present stress associated with the expense of using a child care provider. For some of you, your business is growing, but your bank account may be shrinking. This factor can be additionally strained by the fact that your household budget is tighter because you've moved from a dual income to only one steady income, plus the added expenses of starting your business are heaped on top.

It's important to remember that child care is a necessity and is used by all mothers, including stay-at-home moms, to ease bur-dens. If your business is growing, you can't ignore you'll need concentrated, uninterrupted time to be successful. In their book "Mompreneurs", Ellen Parlapiano and Patricia Cobe cite a survey of work at home mothers that shows 89% used some form of child care, with over half spending between $0 and $5,000 annually. Remember, although you are utilizing child care as you did when employed full time, you are now in control of your time as a homebased worker.

Evaluate Your Needs

Choosing the right kind of child care will depend on three main factors: the nature of your business, the age of your children and your financial position. These requirements will change as the three factors change, so be prepared to make adjustments along the way to accommodate your progressive business and child care needs.

Before deciding on the kind of child care to use, you should evaluate the nature of your business and its required time commitments. For instance, if your home business primarily entails work on a computer, such as word processing or medical billing, then your use of child care may only involve a mother's helper or teenage babysitter for short periods of time. However, if your business requires you to leave your home office for extended periods, then you may need to use a more formalized approach such as center-based child care or a nanny.

Peggy Elliott, an independent marketing consultant for retirement communities and mother of three, has found that adapting to changing business demands also means adapting child care options. The nature of her business requires that she conduct presentations to groups of senior citizens promoting the retirement facility she represents. Sometimes she schedules several presentations a week, while other times she may go for several weeks without any presentations. This erratic schedule makes it ineffective for Elliot to use regular child care. So, she uses a family daycare center that her children became familiar with when she was a full-time employee. Since the center's head count changes daily due to sick kids and different schedules, they can always accommodate her changing schedule and drop in needs.

"I can't justify a regular schedule of child care, due to the fact that my work is so sporadic," says Elliott. "But, I was concerned that my children have a familiar setting to connect with. So this arrangement has worked out great." To get more consistency, Elliott takes her younger son Keelan, 3, there on occasion so he stays comfortable with the center. Peggy occasionally helps out at the center on days when she has the time. On those occasions, she can take Keelan to play while she works. In exchange, she receives free child care hours from the center.

But, again, adaptability is the name of the game. With six-month-old daughter Erin added to the family, Peggy's husband, Kevin (a recent addition to the work at home force) has to pitch in. On days Peggy gives seminars, Keelan goes to family daycare, while 6-year-old Shauna goes to school. Kevin puts Erin in the backpack and walks around the house making calls. So far, the new arrangement has worked without much conflict. But as soon as Erin becomes mobile, the Elliotts will have to look for different child care arrangements.

Besides evaluating your home business time commitments when choosing daycare, you must also consider the age of your children. If you have an infant, you will probably need and want someone to come into your home to help out. This arrangement will allow you to be close by at all times and your infant to remain in familiar surroundings. Additionally, if you are still nursing, you will be able to take the necessary breaks to feed your baby.

If your children are of preschool age, then a nursery school or daycare center may be a viable option. Of course this option is mutually beneficial to you and your child. You get the time needed to concentrate on work, and your child gets to interact socially with other children his or her age. Plus, it may be easier to separate yourself from your child and family responsibilities, which is especially beneficial if you find it difficult to work at home when your children are present.

Different Solutions

Jennifer Coborn is a new mother and she's taken a different approach to child care for her infant. She takes her daughter with her to meetings. It's an unusual approach, and not always a recommended tactic, but Jennifer's clients seem to accept her approach to balancing family and work. "I started taking my daughter to client meetings when she was 10-weeks-old," says Coburn. "I always ask if it is a problem before I bring her along."

Most of her clients respond enthusiastically, with one even holding her daughter as they finished the meeting. But, not all clients have warmed to the idea of daughter-in-tow. So, Jennifer keeps tuned to clues for acceptance. "I told one client I had a 6-month-old and would like to bring her along," says Coburn. "The client said that it was OK, but asked whether I would be able to focus." Jennifer quickly picked up on the concern and said, "let me take her to a neighbor for the hour that we are going to meet."

As a public relations writer for non-profit companies, much of Jennifer's work is done at home. But when she needs to meet with her clients, her unique form of self-child care seems to work. However, Jennifer realizes that her needs will change as her daughter becomes mobile and more demanding.

Gina Correll has adapted to her children's changing needs over the past two years. Correll is an independent representative with Jewelway International, a network marketing company. She left full-time employment when her first son Tyler was two-months-old. She started with Jewelway shortly before Tyler was born, and the homebased business quickly showed the potential of generating enough income to leave full-time work.

To take advantage of the opportunity, Correll decided she needed 20 hours of help a week so she could devote the time to growing her business. Since Tyler was still an infant, Correll decided to use a nanny. She contacted an agency and found one that would place a part time person for $100. As with many nanny horror stories, three of Correll's nannies did not work out. One was caught stealing, another was found letting Correll's infant cry because she thought it was best for him and the other was caught asleep while her 9-month-old was about to tumble down stairs. She finally found a young college aged girl who loved working with babies. Although Correll's nanny worked out for the best, there were areas of concern, one of which was the nanny's lack of interest in creating an educational environment for her son, Tyler. So when the nanny returned to college, Correll entered Tyler in a preschool

Child Care Choices

Nursery Schools

Generally, when children are between the ages of 2 1/2 and 5 and are potty-trained they can enter into nursery school programs. Most schools have several different options as to the days and hours your child can attend. Nursery schools are a wonderful option since they not only offer a social environment for your child, but also are curriculum-based, so your children are learning and not just being watched.

Most kids love to go to nursery school and play with others their age. Since the time spent there is minimal, usually two to three hour periods, the child does not feel abandoned and you won't feel the guilt traditionally associated with daycare. Nursery schools usually charge between $4 and $7 per hour depending on the area in which you live and how many hours your child attends.

Some Nursery schools offer a more academic approach than others. What you choose will depend on your child's needs, your budget and your desire for what you want your child to get from the program.

Family Daycare

Family daycare is often an attractive option for work-at-home parents since it offers a home environment typically with a small ratio of children to caretaker(s). In traditional center-based care many states allow up to a 12:1 ratio. Most family daycare centers take only a few children and are often run by other stay-at-home mothers. The smaller family environment allows for more attention to be given to your child. The costs are generally the same as center-based care, although they can be higher due to the loss of economies of scale associated with running large centers.

Another advantage of family daycare is that many will allow you to drop off your child on non-scheduled days, allowing for some flexibility in your need to respond to customers or tight deadlines. Since many family daycare centers do not advertise, you should check with other parents, schools and churches to find references for these centers.

Center-Based Child Care

Center-based child care is a fragmented industry, usually run as mom-and-pop type operations. Although there are some national franchises such as Kindercare and Children's Discovery Centers, they only account for 10% of the child care centers. Thus, you still have to do your research to determine the quality of each center. Daycare centers are usually filled with children whose parents work full-time outside the home. Still, they do provide different scheduling options for the part time user.

A newer type of center is the "drop in" child care center; a convenient option for the occasional user, or when your regular provider is closed. These centers charge a slightly higher hourly rate, but can accommodate you on a last minute basis. The downfall of relying on this set-up is that there will be little consistency for your child, which could present problems especially for the under 5 age group. Center-based child care costs anywhere from $75-$150 a week on a full-time basis, or $3-$5 per hour on a part time basis, with discounts for multiple children. There is usually a registration fee required, so be sure to choose one you think you can stick with for a while.

Nanny

Nannies are individuals who come into your home during the day, or can be program where he could get social and educational interaction. Now that Correll has a 9-month-old daughter, Raegan, she's hired a 60-year-old, former family daycare owner to help watch her daughter. Correll has also branched out from Jewelway and is now promoting postpartum exercise videos. When Raegan gets older, Correll says she will probably enroll her in preschool and eliminate her need for a nanny.

Laina Schechtman, owner of Gotta-Go-Travel Accessories, has changed her child care arrangement as her business and children have grown. Initially, her travel accessory company was run from home during nap times. But, as the business grew, she soon had to find help, as well as, move the assembly and shipping portion of the business out of her home. Although she still works from home and the car and the playground, she does go into her office a few hours each day. During those times she utilizes both a grandmotherly babysitter and a college student to watch her children. Although one would think nap time is a good time for Laina to do work, she feels better having someone help during this time. Laina says, "you can always delegate your work but not your children."

Finally, your financial situation will have the greatest impact on your selection of child care. The most expensive option is to hire a nanny. Generally, good nannies require substantial wages, based on their experience. Depending on the area in which you live, nannies can cost anywhere from minimum wage to $300 a week for full-time care, plus sick pay and vacation pay for full-time employees. Of course, tax laws require you to withhold and pay employee taxes including FICA. So, your actual outlay is more than just the nanny's wage. However, if you have several children, this option may be more live-ins who help you with child care and other household duties. Although the most expensive type of care, nannies are also the most convenient since they come to your home and you don't have to take your child elsewhere. You can use an agency to help you find a nanny, but be prepared to pay for it. Charge can range from $300 for a part-time placement upwards to $3,000 for placing a nanny full-time. Although they do all the background checks and screenings, you can perform these functions yourself. Many of the nannies who go through agencies also respond to advertisements for help.

Nannies are typically younger women, but as the older population grows, there are many empty-nesters and grandmothers looking for this type of work. If you hire a nanny and pay them more than $1,000 per quarter, you will be considered their employer and obligated to follow federal employment laws including withholding of taxes.

Nanny's charges range anywhere from minimum wage to $10 per hour, depending on your geographic location and the number of children being watched. If you do go this route, be sure to include other household duties your nanny can perform to relieve some of those responsibilities. Finally, in looking for a good match, make sure the nanny is comfortable with you working at home.

Mother's Helper

A mother's helper can be anyone—a grandmother, a college student or a teenager. Typically, a mother's helper comes into your home a few hours a day to help entertain or babysit your kids. Using a neighborhood teenager is often a good choice since they are cheaper and you are still there to oversee the caretaking. With a growing senior population, you may find an experienced grandmother to help. Some parents opt to pay for a babysitting class, including CPR, for the mother's helper for extra assurance. Since you will probably be using a mother's helper infrequently, you probably won't reach the $1,000 per quarter mark required for making this person an employee and paying the required taxes.

Babysitting Co-ops

Babysitting co-ops have been used in an informal sense for many years by stay-at-home mothers as an inexpensive (i.e., free) way of gaining child care help. The informal set-ups usually consist of two or three parents exchanging babysitting duties while the others get a break to get work done. You may wish to look for other work-at-home parents whose goals are the same as yours. Or you may want to swap with another stay-at-home parent.

In looking for a match, you probably want to find someone who has children in a similar age bracket and shares your basic child rearing philosophies. If you want to be more formal and include many more parents in the co-op, you could set up a simple agreement with terms and conditions and swapping cards which assures that no one parent takes on more than they receive in benefits.

The basic benefit of this set up is that it only costs you time, which you would have been devoting to your child anyway. With a growing number of people joining the homebased ranks, this type of co-op should expand. So, where do you find other interested parents? Try your neighborhood, schools, church and local homebased business associations.

cost effective since most daycare centers charge per child.

The least expensive form of outside help is a free form of child care called *babysitting* co-ops or *exchanges*. In these instances, parents may look for other home business owners, or stay-at-home mothers who have children of similar ages and who need help. Some babysitting co-ops are very formalized with rules and limits on the number of participants. Most, though, are informal arrangements where parents agree to swap babysitting duties to get work done.

As a stay-at-home working mother, my use of child care has evolved as has my business. When my daughter was a year old, I left full-time employment to work at home. I stayed on as an employee with my company for 6-months, telecommuting from home four to six hours a day. I would work early in the morning, during my child's naps and in the evenings when my husband was home. This routine worked well, especially because my daughter took long naps.

When the term ended with my company and I started my homebased business, I found my time requirements for work changed as did my daughter's requirement for sleep. I quickly realized that I would need some concentrated time to work without worrying about interruptions. So I enrolled my daughter in two half days of preschool and used that time to complete my most concentrated work and return phone calls. Paying for preschool was a hard decision to make since my business was not generating an income. But, if I didn't get help I would not have been able to grow my business. I also took advantage of sharing a babysitter one day a week for three hours with a neighbor.

This set-up worked nicely since we could split the babysitting fee and our two daughters could play together. Later, I increased my daughter's preschool schedule to three days a week, and decided not to use the part-time sitter. I also worked out an arrangement with another work-at-home mother to swap babysitting duties. This no cost option is a great bonus because it has allowed me to devote more time to my business without the added cost of daycare. Now, with a newborn, I'm going to have to juggle child care options again, probably utilizing someone in the home.

Whatever your choice for child care, be assured that your concerns for its quality are shared by all parents. Child care has become an emotionally charged issue with the intense public debate. With Hillary Clinton and other prominent figures highlighting the inadequacies of our current child care system, improvements in the system will be a national focus. Improving the access and quality of child care will benefit all working parents.

Tax Considerations

When evaluating the financial aspects of daycare, you should also consider the tax benefits of different kids of care. Randall Peterson is a CPA in Encinitas, Calif. He recommends his clients who run a home business take a look at the qualifications for child and dependent care expense deductions (IRS Publication 2441) before selecting the type of daycare.

Currently, the Dependent Care Tax Credit allows for a tax credit for children under the age of 13 of 20% up to $2,400 for one child or up to $4,800 for two or more children. For the home business owner filing jointly, this credit can be used as long as your business is making a profit. Although any tax credit is welcomed, a $480 credit for a $5,000 outlay may seem minuscule. If you've hired a nanny to come into your home as an employee, then you may have better tax deduction options. If your business is set up as a C-Corporation or S-Corp, where you hire employees and provide child care expenses for those employees, then that child care cost can be deducted. But you must offer the benefit to all employees. If you are the only employee and you hire child care help, then that expense would be deductible. It is recommended that you contact your tax consultant regarding these credits and deductions.

Your choices for child care are varied. The key is evaluating your own needs and matching them to the options. Find one that allows you to care for your child *and* your business.

 Article Review Form at end of book.

WiseGuide Wrap-Up

- Family involvement in strong, caring schools will positively affect the social and emotional development of children.

- Communities are family-centered when agencies, businesses, and schools collaborate with parents to nurture the changing needs of children.

R.E.A.L. Sites

This list provides a print preview of typical **coursewise** R.E.A.L. sites. There are over 100 such sites at the **courselinks**™ site. The danger in printing URLs is that web sites can change overnight. As we went to press, these sites were functional using the URLs provided. If you come across one that isn't, please let us know via email to: webmaster@coursewise.com. Use your Passport to access the most current list of R.E.A.L. sites at the **courselinks**™ site

Site name: Families and Work Institute

URL: http://www.familiesandworkinst.org/

Why is it R.E.A.L.? The Family and Work Institute is dedicated to research about families and the work force. The institute is a national nonprofit organization that sponsors the "I Am Your Child" campaign. *Rethinking the Brain: New Insights into Early Development* can be ordered from this foundation- and corporation-sponsored organization.

Key topics: child care, families, working parents

Activity: Locate the *Strategies to Support Young Children and Their Families*. What corporations and agencies are involved in successful community collaborations?

Site name: Head Start Training and Technical Assistance Regional Network

URL: http://www.acf.dhhs.gov/programs/hsb/regions.htm

Why is it R.E.A.L.? The Administration for Children, Youth, and Families offers numerous resources about Head Start, including specialized references for American Indian and Migrant Programs. Head Start is divided into regions with training and assistance provided in the specific areas.

Key topics: Head Start, migrant families, family involvement

Activity: Locate the Migrant Head Start icon. Record the first principal objective for Migrant Head Start Quality Improvement Center and sign their guestbook.

Site name: For Mentors (The National Mentoring Partnership)

URL: http://www.mentoring.org/formentors.html

Why is it R.E.A.L.? For Mentors offers a complete online resource for mentors, including *A Year's Worth of Mentoring* and ways to organize communities. The National Mentoring Partnership affiliates are also listed.

Key topics: community, guidance, social and emotional development

Activity: The mentor role is described. Write a response to the listed roles (*What a Mentor Is*), indicating how you personally will meet each responsibility.

section

6

Key Points

- Child care and caregivers are concepts that become necessary and popular 150 years ago in North America.

- Howard Gardner adds naturalist intelligence to the list of multiple intelligences, expanding the importance of each child's individual differences.

- Preschoolers' cognitive development may be enhanced with computer-assisted instruction that features levels of scaffolding.

- Computers increase accessibility to knowledge and open new pathways for learning.

- Information age schools will feature accessible technologies in exploratory environments.

Societal Changes That Impact Early Childhood Education:
How Will Children, Families, and Professionals Adapt?

WiseGuide Intro

Changing family patterns, urbanization of society, and technological advances affect children. Urbanization and technology are altering the way children's routine needs are met including approaches for care and learning. Can we foresee a world where children and families adapt to this consistent whirl of changes? Will we be able to promise understanding adults, relevant education, and caring communities? Can we harness the benefits of technology and urbanization while we maintain valuable patterns that enhance families and the development of their young children?

Academic disciplines review the past to better understand today and tomorrow. This retrospective process shows that intrinsic needs of children are constant. Section 6 begins with the reading "Quality of Care in Historical Perspective," which looks at the historical view of child care. The discussion reveals interesting similarities regarding health and safety of children and the pervasive needs of poor working mothers.

Transition into the next century calls for identification of the abilities and skills that will guide children's success and achievement. Howard Gardner adds another intelligence to his list of seven. Discussion in the reading "The First Seven . . . and the Eighth: A Conversation with Howard Gardner" points out that children will need to use their minds to probe, understand, and problem solve. Similarly, in the selection "Technology and Change of Mind: An Interview with Robert Ornstein," Joy Starry Turner, editor of *Montessori Life*, documents that the culture will require more visual and oral skills.

Changes have created the information age that calls upon educators to create developmentally appropriate information-age schools with computer-assisted instruction. The research reviewed in the reading "Computer Assisted Instruction and Cognitive Development in Preschoolers" demonstrates that microcomputers may be valuable for the promotion of preschoolers' cognitive development, but this technology is not magical. In the reading "Creating the Information Age School," Vicki Hancock features the idea of self-initiated and self-paced learning in multiage groups. Teachers at all levels will need to shift from dispensing facts to becoming coaches who arouse curiosity, ask questions, and stimulate discussion.

Society will continue to change and influence the care and learning of young children. Early Childhood Education is the profession positioned to model a perspective that articulates a commitment to young children in the twenty-first century.

Questions

Reading 32. Whose needs were met by the NYN and TN?

Reading 33. How is learning style different from multiple intelligences?

Reading 34. What is CAI?

Reading 35. Will computers make teachers and schools obsolete?

Reading 36. How will the teacher's role change in information-age schools?

Whose needs were met by the NYN and TN?

Quality of Care in Historical Perspective

Larry Prochner

Concordia University

The study of quality of care in two mid-nineteenth-century day nurseries in North America indicates that quality was associated with saving children's lives within a context of charity-based social welfare. The concern for the health and safety of children led to the entrenchment of a custodial mode of child care. Child care staff developed "coping strategies" that served to modify the quality of care in the institutions. The resilience of the custodial mode in day nurseries throughout the nineteenth and early twentieth centuries is discussed.

Quality of care emerged as a central issue in child day care research in the mid-1980s. Since then, studies have examined the relationship of such variables as staffing, staff training, child/caregiver interaction, health and safety, and quality of care (Davis & Thornburg, 1994; Scarr & Eisenberg, 1994). Quality is usually measured by assessing the impact of the variables on their own and in combination on aspects of child's development. However, some researchers believe definitions of quality rely too heavily on child development research (Farquhar, 1990; Katz, 1994; McKim, 1993; Singer, 1993). They claim that quality has multiple meanings and requires the consideration of multiple perspectives, for example, those of staff, parents, children, cultural communities, and the larger society. This article presents a further source of ideas about quality care through the historical case study of two infant nurseries founded in the 1850s: the Nursery for the Children of Poor Women in New York (NYN) and the Public Nursery in Toronto (TN).[1]

Ideas about children, child development, and early education are socially constructed and historically situated (Aries, 1962; Singer, 1992; Kagan, 1992; White, 1979). However, historians often present a decontextualized interpretation of child care quality, using the current standard as a yardstick to judge care offered in the pioneer day nurseries. In this

[1]The Nursery for the Children of Poor Women changed its name to the Nursery and Child's Hospital in 1856. The Toronto Public Nursery changed its name to the Girls' Home and Public Nursery in 1860. To avoid confusion, the nurseries will be referred to as the New York nursery (NYN) and the Toronto nursery (TN) throughout the article.

way, the field of early care and education is portrayed as having made significant advances, at least in its conception of what contributes to quality care. However, history written as a story of progress reveals little about the meaning of quality in the early day nurseries. The study presented here sheds light on the nature of care in earlier times and suggests reasons for the mode of care provided in the pioneer day nurseries.

The day nursery idea (Steinfels, 1973, p. 35) has taken a variety of forms during the past 150 years. The essence of the idea is that children are cared for by adults other than their parents, while their parents are temporarily occupied elsewhere. The various components of this basic idea have been qualified differently at different times. For example, where should caregiving take place (parents' home, small-scale or large-scale institution, in school)? Who are the children (age, gender, social class)? Who are the caregivers (mothers, wet nurses, professionals)? How long is temporary (2 weeks, 10 out of 24 h)? How are parents occupied (employed, shopping, as students)?

Correspondence and requests for reprints should be sent to Larry Prochner, Concordia University, Education Department, 1445 de Maisonneuve Blvd. W., Montreal, Quebec 113G 1M8 Canada.

Who are those whose interests child care serves (parents, children, employers, the state)? The answers to these questions in turn influence definitions and measures of quality care. Is care intended to be safe, educative, or loving? Is quality measured by decreased mortality, family support, or enhanced development? In short, the day nursery idea—just as the idea of early education—is a complex historiographical problem. However, it is not treated as such in most renditions of the history of child care. Historians have typically favored the period beginning with the Golden Age (Steinfels, 1973, p. 34) of day nurseries in the 1880s and 1890s and glossed over earlier developments. However, the NYN and the TN are an important part of the story of child care in North America. They provide a rare opportunity to study the Victorian vision of quality issues in group child care beyond those employed in the more popular foundling hospital and orphan asylum. The principal sources of data for the study were the organizational records of the two nurseries, including annual reports, the Minutes of the Board of Managers of the Nursery and Child's Hospital in New York, and a daily register of children from the Girls' Home and Public Nursery in Toronto.[2] This article briefly outlines the founding and management of the nurseries before discussing quality issues in relation to the managers, mothers, and children.

Founding the Nurseries

The NYN and TN were established at a time of tremendous change in urban North America resulting from a wave of immigration in the 1840s and the first half of the 1850s. Many of the new-comers were Irish escaping from the years of famine. The effect of the immigration was profound; in Toronto, the population doubled from 21,050 in 1847 to 41,760 in 1856. New York was the principal port of entry for immigrants to the United States at midcentury. In 1854 approximately 70% of the 460,474 immigrants to the United States came through New York (Stott, 1990, p. 287). Despite considerable out-migration, in the period 1850 to 1860, the population of New York increased from 515,500 to 814,000. There were a variety of charities in New York and Toronto dedicated to aiding the poor, sick, and aged. However, there were few services for the very young, and none specifically for children under the age of 2 years (Breton, 1991; Quiroga, 1986). Although poorhouses and orphanages offered day nursery services for infants in North America from the late eighteenth century (Michael, in press; Rooke & Schnell, 1983), the NYN and the TN were the first child care settings to be loosely modeled after the French creche (first established in Paris in 1844). The period during which they functioned on a *daily* basis as nurseries was quite brief, and neither offered daily care after its first few years of operation. For this reason the NYN is better known as the beginning of one of the first children's hospitals in the United States, and the TN as the forerunner of an orphan home.

The NYN was founded in 1854 by a committee of wealthy charitable women led by Mary DuBois. The idea grew out of DuBois's concern over the private

[2] The minutes of the Board of Managers, Nursery and Child's Hospital will be abbreviated as NCHMBM. The Register of the Girls' Home and Public Nursery will be abbreviated as GHPNR.

child care arrangements made by wet nurses (Quiroga, 1986, p. 197). Mothers working as wet nurses faced the dilemma of what to do with their own infants. Typically, they left their infants with siblings, neighbors, or relatives, or on their own. Because most non-maternal caregivers were unable to breastfeed their young charges, wet nurses' own children often died from gastrointestinal bacteria caused by bottle-feeding (known as hand-feeding). The TN (established in 1857) was one of several nurseries developed on the model of the NYN in the late 1850s (Dubois, 1886; NCHMBM). As in New York, it stemmed from the contact of wealthy women with poor families and the plight of the babies of wet nurses. In the Toronto story, members of the founding committee visited the local poorhouse and witnessed the problems of housing very young children and adults in the same facility (Breton, 1991). Young children in mixed-age institutions risked being exposed to disease. It was also feared that they would learn to depend on charity for their livelihood, rather than on their own labor. These concerns stimulated a reform movement that pressed for the creation of orphan asylums and children's homes. Thus, the NYN and TN were part of a trend in North America to create separate institutions for children and adults (Rooke & Schnell, 1981).

This changed in the second half of the nineteenth century, when large-scale institutions of all kinds were recognized as creating their own set of problems. Thus, day nurseries of the 1880s and 1890s grew out of a spirit of anti-institutionalism. During this period the NYN and TN (then a hospital and an orphanage, respectively) came under increasing pressure to change to a boarding-home system. An indirect stimulus for the NYN and TN was industrialization. Braun and Edwards (1972, pp. 41–42) argued that industrialization stimulated a boom in institutional forms of early education in Europe and North America in the first half of the nineteenth century. However, infant care facilities such as the NYN and the TN, like the crèche in France, had their roots in the infant welfare movement and not in early education. Although the increase in the numbers of mothers and older children employed outside the home changed the ability of the family to provide full-time care for very young children, most mothers of children in the NYN and TN were not industrial workers or even day laborers. Instead, they worked for wealthy New York and Toronto families as servants and wet nurses.

The Administration of the Nurseries

The organization of the nurseries followed the usual pattern of women's charity work in the nineteenth century. The socially prominent women who founded the nurseries sought out other women interested in the idea and formed a club. Finances for rent, heat, food, and salaries were secured through membership fees and door-to-door fundraising. Club members elected an executive committee (hereafter referred to as the managers) to set policy, direct public relations, and manage the day-to-day operation of the nursery. A male advisory board comprised of doctors, lawyers, and businessmen lent credibility to the venture and ensured the connection of the nurseries with the medical, legal, and financial communities.

Nursery policy was a mixture of crèche regulations (Marbeau, 1845) and the organizational principles that guided North American foundling and orphan homes. The aim was to offer services to as many clients as possible for the least possible cost. The regulations of the TN are almost identical to those of the NYN (Nursery for the Children of Poor Women, 1854; Toronto Public Nursery, 1857b). From the regulations we know that the nurseries were open for daily boarders from 6:00 A.M. to 7:30 P.M.[3] The nurseries admitted children from birth to 6 years of age and charged a fee for daily or long-term boarding. Children unclaimed for more than 1 week were taken to the local poorhouse.[4] The managers at the TN arranged the adoption of long-term boarders if their fees were unpaid for more than 3 months. The supervisors, who were called matrons, kept a registry of wet nurses seeking employment, and mothers could work at the nursery until they found work with a private family. Most of the rules and regulations provided a guide for the efficient and economical management of a charitable institution. Rules relating to children's well-being focused on health and hygiene and were based on contemporary medical knowledge. The origin of the regulation governing staffing (1 caregiver to 12 infants) is more obscure, but its roots may have been in the standard set in one of the first infant nurseries, founded in Paris in 1801 (Maire, 1888, p. 2223). However, although the published rules and regulations describe management policy and the conception of a minimum standard of quality care, they give only a partial picture of life in the institu-

[3]The NYN opened at 5:30 A.M.

[4]Children were sent to the almshouse after 2 days at the NYN.

tions. The remainder of this article incorporates other organizational records—minutes of meetings and registers of children —in order to compare the official standard with the actual practice of day nursery care in the 1850s.

The Clients of Nurseries

Although some historians have classed the progressive-era day nursery as adult oriented (O'Connor, 1995; Varga, 1993), this distinction was not clear in the cases of the NYN and the TN. In the face of high rates of infant mortality, the essential needs of infants were health and safety. Rapid urban growth, high unemployment, low wages, congested housing, and the absence of public health measures, led to large numbers of infant deaths in the poorest wards of New York and Toronto. The month before the NYN opened, 35% of all recorded deaths in New York City were of infants under 1 year of age ("City Mortality," 1854)—a figure roughly consistent with that of Toronto (Nicolson, 1985). Cities deserved their reputation as infant abattoirs (Meckel, 1990). Therefore, the original missions of the NYN and TN stressed the importance of infant welfare through the "maintenance and care of the children of wet-nurses" and "daily care of infants whose mothers labor away from home" (Nursery and Child's Hospital, 1857, p. 6; Toronto Public Nursery, 1857a, p. 6). Although the nurseries doubled as recruitment centers for servants and wet nurses, they were not oriented solely to adult needs. Rather, they had two sets of clients, mothers and children, with intersecting needs. The nurseries assisted mothers to earn a meager living to support their families and provided infants with an increased chance of survival. The nurseries also met the needs of the managers. As female members of the elite of society it was their moral and social duty to give practical assistance to the less fortunate. Moreover, as employers of servants and wet nurses at a time when there was an acute shortage of domestics, they benefited from the nursery in a practical and self-serving way.

Four different categories of mothers used the services of the nurseries. The largest group was mothers who worked as wet nurses or servants in private homes while the nurseries boarded their children. The second and smallest group were parents who brought their children to the nurseries on a daily basis, akin to current day care practices. Only four children attended the TN as "daily boarders" in a 7-year period (GHPNR).[5] There is no evidence that the daily service was more popular at the NYN. Although the NYN annual reports did not list daily boarders separately, the large number of wet nurses on staff indicates that most children were long-term boarders (Nursery and Child's Hospital, 1859). The registers and annual reports of the nurseries reveal that two categories of women used the nurseries in addition to those targeted by the original mission. The first was the staff themselves. The distinction between client and staff was often unclear. Mothers lived at the nurseries with their children, using their employment in the nursery as servants and nurses—the generic term for child caregivers—as short-term relief in hard times.[6] Following several weeks or months of employment in the nursery, some mothers continued to board their children

while working elsewhere. In the initial years, the matrons in charge were also mothers with young children. Most staff were women in very difficult circumstances; all were poor and many were widows or single mothers.

A second category not predicted by the mission were destitute parents who used the nurseries as orphanages. In some cases fathers were absent or deceased, or mothers were in prison or a lunatic asylum. In its first months of operation, 8% of mothers of children at the NYN were in an institution of some type. (NCHMBM). By 1863 the NYN acknowledged its new function as a long-term home for children whose mothers were not wet nurses by noting the establishment of a "Hospital for Foundlings" in its annual report (NCH, 1863).

The novelty of the NYN and TN in the 1850s is that they implemented the day nursery idea in an institution not associated with an orphanage or poorhouse. At the same time, they adopted many of the practices of these charities, meaning that children were treated to a minimum standard of what we now call custodial care. Most wage-earning mothers, whether wet nurses or daily laborers, used the child care services of family members or neighbors (Auerbach & Woodhill, 1992). Long-term or permanent care options (foundling hospitals and orphanages) were available for children of destitute, deceased, or otherwise absent parents (for example, those in jail, hospital, or lunatic asylum). In better times, after periods of months or even years, parents or relatives would

sometimes retrieve their children from orphanages. Many orphanages also offered care to a small number of children on a daily basis. As foundling and orphan home systems of institutional child care were familiar to mothers, managers, and staff, it was natural that the nurseries took on some of their characteristics in relation to such activities as feeding, housekeeping, and recreation.

The Provision of Care

The utility of the nurseries rested in their ability to help poor families survive. Thus, they offered a range of flexible services to meet the immediate needs of mothers for employment and of young children for food and shelter. The primary health risk for infants in any group child care setting was malnutrition or gastrointestinal-related illness, so that feeding was a dominant focus of care. Unlike the French crèche, which at least intended mothers to feed their own infants, North American nurseries employed wet nurses or permitted hand-feeding. Although the preferred option was the use of a wet nurse, these were difficult to recruit. Wet nurses in institutions were responsible for feeding several infants in addition to their own. Wet nurses preferred to work for private families, and managers and other club members competed for their services in what would now be called a conflict of interest. DuBois (1886) also noted the reluctance of wet nurses to accept sick infants, particularly those infected with syphilis, for fear of infecting themselves and their own child.

In addition to feeding, the general labor of child care centered on housekeeping activities. Work included washing diapers and other linen, ironing, sewing,

[5]Although the Register is labeled 1859–1870, the last entry is in 1866.

[6]The term "nurse" was used in the nineteenth century to refer to women who worked as child-caregivers. Although a distinction was sometimes made between wet nurses and dry nurses, in time all caregivers of very young children bore the title of nurse.

cleaning feeding devices, and preparing food for older children and staff. All the staff, as well as the older children, shared in the labor. It was common practice for residents of most institutions—including orphanages—to contribute labor to the upkeep of the facility. In the nurseries, older children also served as caregivers and were an important complement to paid staff. The presence of long-term boarders at the nurseries meant that they housed children with a wide range of ages, for example, up to 10 years of age at the NYN (NCH, 1863). Many children lived in the NYN for years, despite the official age limit of 6 years. The TN accepted older girls, particularly if they came with younger siblings. Older children were a mixed blessing for the managers. The managers of the NYN blamed them for taking spaces from the infants of wet nurses (NCH, 1873). Older children also required more stimulating activities, which prompted the managers of the NYN to start a school in 1863. However, the children's labor more than compensated managers for the cost of a part-time teacher. The NYN and TN actually increased the numbers of older children by opening servants' schools for girls in 1859. The curriculum consisted of hands-on experience in kitchen work, laundry, sewing, and, of course, child care.

Although nursery rules stipulated time for play, the duties of the staff did not include engaging children in play-oriented activities. The routines of feeding, washing, and sleeping provided the structure of the children's day. Infants rarely left their cribs, and older children created their own amusements during their free time. The guideline for staffing, 1 nurse for 12 infants, would have

precluded closer attention. The high ratio of children to staff indicates that staff-child interaction was not considered an important aspect of quality care. There was no staff allocated to the older children except for the part-time teacher in the case of the NYN. In general, the nurseries were chronically understaffed (i.e., beyond the 1:12 ratio) because of the conception of nursery employment as short-term relief, as well as the oppressive working conditions. The first matron at the NYN left after several months because the "sickness and death . . . affected her nerves" (NCHMBM, 1854, July 13). Significantly, managers did not view increased staffing as a priority.

The lax staffing practices and demands of institutional life worked against the nurseries achieving even the minimum standards of quality for the safe, hygienic, and kindly care described in their policies. Understaffing and overcrowding were normal conditions, and staff developed strategies in order to cope. Occasionally, these strategies severely compromised the quality of care and were challenged by mothers and other staff. For instance, staff reported the head nurse of the NYN to the managers for giving narcotics to the babies to keep them quiet and being "unkind to an infant, in using cold water to check it crying" (NCHMBM, 1854, October 26). The infant subsequently died, which the child's grandmother attributed to the actions of the nurse. Although the managers fired her, they concluded that "it is not in the power of the matron or Manager to prevent a head Nurse from doing secretly whatever she wills" (NCHMBM, 1854, October 26). Drugging children was an accepted practice in infant

care institutions and infant care in general. Apparently, this particular nurse overstepped the bounds of what was permissible. Another coping strategy was child packing, meaning crowding children together into "small, contained, and easily supervised spaces" (Miller, 1989, p. 161). Children spent most of their time indoors in a single room. As a result, highly contagious diseases such as measles and conjunctivitis, spread easily throughout the entire nursery. Although the managers recognized the benefits of space, fresh air, and outdoor play for older children, staff shortages and the intensive labor of caregiving did not permit it. Nevertheless, managers of the NYN required staff to take older children outdoors twice each day (NCHMBM). This led to confrontations between the staff and matron. One nurse "on 2 or 3 occasions, had the coats and hats put on the little ones to take them out as ordered, and then when the Matron's back was turned, taken [sic] them off again" (NCHMBM, 1854, November 28). The managers interpreted this as insubordination, rather than an indication that they should hire more staff or accept fewer children.

The NYN managers attributed declining attendance in the early years to a growing reputation for poor quality care. Staff beat some children, lost others (older children ran away or "eloped" in the terminology of the time), and generally neglected housekeeping duties. Managers visiting the nursery found crib mattresses—and the slats beneath them—soaked with urine (NCHMBM). They observed that "there seems to be a growing feeling among the poor that our babies do not receive the care they ought" (NCHMBM, 1855, October

25). Concerns about the turnover of staff prompted the managers to adopt the principle of "retaining as far as circumstances would allow, the same nurse for each child" (NCH, 1857, p. 2). In their defense, the managers of the NYN claimed that it was being unfairly represented as an inferior institution. The annual report (NCH, 1857) listed 1 nurse with 11 months of service, and 7 with at least 4 months. Thus, under pressure from parents and embarrassment from negative reports in the press, the managers modified their idea of quality care to include consistency of staff. In this and other examples, mothers and the staff themselves played a role in regulating the quality of care in the nurseries. If not for the complaints of staff and the grandmother of the abused child in the example just described, the nurse's actions would likely have escaped detection. The managers' action also indicates that they were sensitive to particular challenges to the nursery's standard of care. Staff turnover, rather than numbers of staff, was a critical issue for the managers, along with the general upkeep of the institution. Managers considered the efficient management of staff and housekeeping to be within their sphere of influence. However, they had a different view of mortality in the nursery. Managers were resigned to child deaths as being beyond their power to control, even if they occasionally resulted from staff mistreatment.

In fact, despite the criticism they engendered at the time, the nurseries did have some success in their mission to save the lives of wet nurses' own children. What is not clear, however, is whether this was the result of any specific activity on the part of the nurseries. In its first 7 months of oper-

ation, the mortality rate at the NYN was 10% (NCHMBM) in comparison with 35% in a single city ward in March of the same year. At other times, the record was far worse. In August 1856 more than half of the 24 children admitted died (NCHMBM), likely from gastrointestinal problems, although the cause of death was not disclosed. The pattern of mortality was similar at the TN. During the period 1859–1866, 9% of children in the nursery died. The mortality rate of children under the age of 2 years—who were more likely to be wet nurses' own children—was much higher (46%). However, mortality rates in the nurseries compared favorably with the records of other institutions that housed very young children. In the Montreal Foundling Hospital, which took in over 600 infants each year throughout the 1860s, mortality was consistently as high as 90% (Carpenter, 1869, p. 28). A survey of organizations caring for foundlings in Massachusetts during the same period revealed that "in some well-managed hospitals" the rate was from 40% to 60%, in "good asylums" from 30% to 50%, and in "good single families" (private boarding homes) from 20% to 35% (Carpenter, 1869). An overall mortality rate of 9% or 10%, as in the NYN and the TN, would therefore be exceptionally low for the period. Even the mortality of infants (wet nurses' own children) was not unusually high for a "good asylum." However, nursery managers did not view these grim statistics as a measure of success. Deaths of child-clients were routinely underreported in annual reports and generally blamed on the deceased child's fragile condition on admission rather than the inadequacies of the nursery.

Over time the functions of both the NYN and the TN expanded to include servant's schools and long-term care of older children. Another branch of work—hospital care for sick infants—was unique to the NYN. The managers recognized the new orientation by changing the name to the Nursery and Child's Hospital in 1856. From the beginning the NYN had a liberal policy of admitting sick infants (which had the effect of increasing the numbers of deaths in the nursery). In the first summer the managers used the bedroom of the laundress as a makeshift infirmary to isolate a sick child and hired a girl specifically for her care (NCHMBM). Although the NYN continued to offer boarding for children of wage-earning women, it took on a stronger identity as a hospital. Whereas mothers needing child care had choices, however limited, those with sick babies had no alternatives to the NYN. By 1859 the daily nursery at the NYN appears to have ceased to function. The attending physician in that year listed the NYN functions as a home for neglected infants, a dispensary, and a hospital (NCH, 1959). Mothers, nursery managers, and doctors transformed the nursery according to their own particular needs. Mothers needed care for their sick infants; the managers needed an opportunity to do charitable work in a meaningful way; and the physicians needed a site to demonstrate their expertise and dominance in pediatric medicine (Quiroga, 1986, p. 203). The situation was different in Toronto where the TN evolved into an orphan home for girls. As in New York, the managers blamed the public for failing to comprehend the meaning of a temporary child care service. It was just as likely that the distinction between temporary and permanent care, care for sick children or healthy children, was unclear to the managers themselves.

Discussion

From our current perspective the care provided in the nurseries appears woefully inadequate. The contradiction between the intentions of the managers and the day-to-day reality of the institutions they created was considerable. Although this was a characteristic of Victorian charity in general, the critical point is whether the contradiction was visible and worrisome to the nineteenth-century women who used, staffed, and managed the nurseries. The evidence presented in this article indicates that staff turnover, kind treatment of children, and the general cleanliness of the institutions were aspects of quality care that were agreed on by staff, mothers, and managers. The child-oriented indicators of quality included promoting infant health through the provision of clean milk, wet nurses, and medical services. These services went hand in hand with the conception of the nursery as a service to mothers, through the provision of employment bureaus and the availability of the nursery as a short-term refuge. This was problematic in relation to overall quality, because the managers did not seem to be able to reconcile the different needs of mothers and children. The number of mothers and children served became a basic indicator of quality. Under the direction of the nursery managers, matrons were unwilling to turn any mother away, even if it placed the mother's child at risk. This point is emphasized by the routine admission of unweaned infants in the summer months, in the face of criticism from nursery physicians.

Because staff shortages and overcrowding were permanent conditions, the quality of care in the nurseries was further compromised by the development of an alternate set of caregiving practices (in relation to those outlined in the rules and regulations). These are referred to in the literature on the sociology of the classroom as coping strategies (Hargreaves, 1978). Certain teachers behaviors stem from the mainly unavoidable aspects of schooling, for example, managing large groups of children in classrooms that are physically isolated from one another. In the case of day nurseries, caregiver behaviors developed out of similar constraints, although their child-clients were more compliant. However, not all coping strategies decreased the quality of care. Older children and students from the servants' school acted as auxiliary caregivers (just as older children functioned as monitors in schools) to help offset the effects of staff shortages.

Quality of care was understood as consisting of identifiable factors, yet it was also routinely compromised. These contradictions in the provision of care were less visible to the managers than they are to us, because quality of care was defined within a charity-based social welfare paradigm in which mother's needs were not separated from those of children. The managers were distrustful of the ability of other authorities, for example, physicians, to make decisions in the best interests of poor families. The struggle between lay and professional authorities to have the final word on quality of care continued at the Nursery and Child's Hospital until the early twentieth century (Quiroga, 1986). Custodial care was conceived as a temporary guardianship of children in the absence of their parents. The managers did the best they could for the children within their understanding of benevolent social welfare. If medical opinion conflicted with their understanding of their social duty, medical opinion was placed aside. For the managers, quality of care was imbued with a moral dimension (the belief that the poor would find redemption through their own labor) that ultimately had greater significance for the well-being of children and families than lapses in standards related to staffing, health, and hygiene.

By the time the NYN and the TN changed from their original orientations as nurseries, the day nursery idea had taken on a new form within the context of a new crisis, the American Civil War. The Day Nursery of Philadelphia, established in 1863, provided child care for mothers employed in war-related industries and widows of soldiers, rather than the babies of wet nurses. After the war it continued as a daily and short-term child care service for wage-earning mothers. By the late nineteenth century day nurseries were a popular and prolific charity, and group child care had entered what Steinfels called its "golden age." Small-scale day nurseries, modeled on the home rather than an orphanage, suited the anti-institutional mood of the day. The development of public nursing, pure-milk campaigns, and compulsory vaccination lessened some of the health risks for very young children in cities. Yet, the historical record indicates that a custodial mode of care—characterized by a predominant focus on health and safety in combination with moral elements[7]—persisted in day nurseries well into the twentieth century.

A number of questions are raised by the study of quality care in the past. How closely do current conceptions of quality reflect the increasingly diverse needs of children and parents? Are coping strategies that compromise or enhance quality built into the construction of caregiving in institutions? The resilience of the custodial mode warrants further investigation, as does the resilience of key ideas in early care and education in general.

[7]Expressed, for example, in compulsory parent education courses.

References

Aries, P. (1962). *Centuries of childhood: A social history of family life.* New York: Knopf.

Auerbach, J. D., & Woodill, G. A. (1992). Historical perspectives on familial and extrafamilial child care: Toward a history of family daycare. In D. L. Peters & A. R. Pence (Eds.), *Family daycare: Current research for informed public policy* (pp. 9–27). New York: Teachers College Press.

Braun, S., & Edwards, E. (1972). *History and theory of early childhood education.* Belmont, CA: Wadsworth.

Breton, C. (1991). Nineteenth century child rescue and the development of Toronto Girls' Home, 1860–1900. In *Social welfare in Toronto: Two historical papers* (pp. 2–27). Toronto: Faculty of Social Work, University of Toronto.

Carpenter, P. (1986). *On some of the causes of the excessive mortality of young children in the City of Montreal.* (Reprinted from the *Canadian Naturalist* for June, 1869) Ottawa: Canadian Institute for Historical Microreproduction

City Mortality. (1854, March 7). *New York Daily Times.*

David, N.S., & Thornburg, K. R. (1994). Child care: A synthesis of research. *Early Child Development and Care, 98,* 39–45.

DuBois, M. A. (1886). 30 years experience in hospital work. *32nd Annual report of the Nursery and Child's Hospital.* New York: Nursery and Child's Hospital.

Farquhar, S. (1990). Quality in early education and care: What do we mean? *Early Child Development and Care, 64,* 71–83.

Girls' Home & Public Nursery, Girls' Home Register. (1859–1870). (Available from Protestant Children's Home Papers, L30, B, Baldwin Room, Toronto Reference Library [BRTRL]).

Hargreaves, A. (1978). The significance of classroom coping strategies. In L. Barton & R. Meighan (Eds.), *Sociological interpretations of schooling and classrooms* (pp. 73–100). Driffield, United Kingdom: Nafferton Books.

Kagan, J. (1992). Yesterday's premises, tomorrow's promises. *Developmental Psychology, 28,* 990–998.

Katz, L. (1994). Perspectives on the quality of early childhood programs. *Phi Delta Kappan, 76,* 200–205.

Maier, S. (1888). Pastoret. In F. Buisson (Ed.), *Dictionnaire de pedagogie et d'instruction primaire.* Paris: Hachette.

Marbeau, J.B.F. (1845). *Des crèches: Ou, Moyen de diminuer la misere en augmentant la population* [The crèche or a way to reduce poverty by increasing the population] (2nd ed.). Paris: Comptoir des Imprimeurs-Unis.

McKim, M.K. (1993). Quality child care: What does it mean for individual infants, parents and caregivers? *Early Child Development and Care, 88,* 23–30.

Meckel, R.A. (1990). *Save the babies: American public health reform and the prevention of infant mortality, 1850–1929.* Baltimore: Johns Hopkins University Press.

Michel, S. (in press.) *Children's interests/mothers' rights: A history of child care in America.* New Haven: Yale University Press.

Miller, A. (1989). *The day care dilemma: Critical concerns for American families.* New York: Insight Books.

Nicolson, M.W. (1985). Peasants in an urban society: The Irish Catholics in Victorian Toronto. In R.R. Harney (Ed.), *Gathering place: Peoples and neighborhoods in Toronto, 1834–1945* (pp. 47–74). Toronto: Multicultural History Society of Ontario.

Nursery and Child's Hospital, Board of Management Minutes, 1854–1860. (Available from Medical Archives, New York Hospital-Cornell Medical Center [MANYH]).

Nursery and Child's Hospital, Annual Reports, 1856, 1857, 1859, 1861, 1863, 1873, 1874. MANYH.

Nursery for the Children of Poor Women. (1854). *Constitution, by-laws, and regulations of the Nursery for the Children of Poor Women in the City of New York.* MANYH.

O'Connor, S.M. (1995). Mothering in public: The division of organized child care in the kindergarten and day nursery, St. Louis, 1886–1920. *Early Childhood Research Quarterly, 10,* 63–80.

Quiroga, V.A. (1986). Female lay managers and scientific pediatrics at Nursery and Child's Hospital, 1854–1910. *Bulletin of the History of Medicine, 60,* 194–208.

Rooke, P., & Schnell, R. (1981). Child welfare in English Canada, 1920–1948. *Social Service Review, 55,* 484–506.

Rooke, P., & Schnell, R. (1983). *Discarding the asylum: From child rescue to the welfare state in English-Canada (1800–1950).* Lanham, MD: University Press of America.

Scarr, S., & Eisenberg, M. (1994). Measurement of quality in child care centers. *Early Childhood Research Quarterly, 9,* 1131–1151.

Singer, E. (1992). *Child care and the psychology of development.* New York: Routledge.

Singer, E. (1993). Shared care for children. *Theory and Psychology, 3,* 429–449.

Steinfels, M. (1973). *Who's minding the children?: The history and politics of day care in the United States.* New York: Simon and Schuster.

Stott, R.B. (1990). *Workers in the metropolis: Class, ethnicity, and youth in antebellum New York City.* Ithaca: Cornell University Press.

Toronto Public Nursery, Annual Reports, 1857a, 1858. BRTRL.

Toronto Public Nursery. (1857b). *Constitution, bylaws and regulations of The Public Nursery in the City of Toronto.* BRTRL.

White, S.H. (1979). Children in perspective. *American Psychologist, 34,* 812–814.

Varga, D. (1993). From a service for mothers to the developmental management of children: Day nursery care in Canada, 1890–1960. In *Advances in Early Education and Care,* Vol. 5 (pp. 115–143). Greenwich, CT: JAI Press.

 Article Review Form at end of book.

How is learning style different from multiple intelligences?

The First Seven . . . and the Eighth

A conversation with Howard Gardner

Human intelligence continues to intrigue psychologists, neurologists, and educators. What is it? Can we measure it? How do we nurture it?

Kathy Checkley

Howard Gardner is Professor of Education at Harvard Graduate School of Education and author of, among other books, The Unschooled Mind: How Children Think and How Schools Should Teach *(1991). He can be reached at Roy B. Larsen Hall, 2nd Floor, Appian Way, Harvard Graduate School of Education, Cambridge, MA 02138.* **Kathy Checkley** *is a staff writer for* Update *and has assisted in the development of ASCD's new CD-ROM,* Exploring Our Multiple Intelligences, *and pilot online project on multiple intelligences.*

Howard Gardner's theory of multiple intelligences, described in Frames of Mind *(1985), sparked a revolution of sorts in classrooms around the world, a mutiny against the notion that human beings have a single, fixed intelligence. The fervor with which educators embraced his premise that we have multiple intelligences surprised Gardner himself. "It obviously spoke*

to some sense that people had that kids weren't all the same and that the tests we had only skimmed the surface about the differences among kids," Gardner said.

Here Gardner brings us up-to-date on his current thinking on intelligence, how children learn, and how they should be taught.

How do you define intelligence?

Intelligence refers to the human ability to solve problems or to make something that is valued in one or more cultures. As long as we can find a culture that values an ability to solve a problem or create a product in a particular way, then I would strongly consider whether that ability should be considered an intelligence.

First, though, that ability must meet other criteria: Is there a particular representation in the brain for the ability? Are there

populations that are especially good or especially impaired in an intelligence? And, can an evolutionary history of the intelligence be seen in animals other than human beings?

I defined seven intelligences (see box, p. 181) in the early 1980s because those intelligences all fit the criteria. A decade later when I revisited the task, I found at least one more ability that clearly deserved to be called an intelligence.

That would be the naturalist intelligence. What led you to consider adding this to our collection of intelligencies?

Somebody asked me to explain the achievements of the great biologists, the ones who had a real mastery of taxonomy, who understood about different species, who could recognize patterns in nature and classify objects. I realized that to explain that kind of ability, I would have to manipulate the other intelligences in ways that weren't appropriate.

So I began to think about whether the capacity to classify nature might be a separate intelligence. The naturalist ability passed with flying colors. Here are a couple of reasons: First, it's an ability we need to survive as human beings. We need, for example, to know which animals to hunt and which to run away from. Second, this ability isn't restricted to human beings. Other animals need to have a naturalist intelligence to survive. Finally, the big selling point is that brain evidence supports the existence of the naturalist intelligence. There are certain parts of the brain particularly dedicated to the recognition and the naming of what are called "natural" things.

How do you describe the naturalist intelligence to those of us who aren't psychologists?

The naturalist intelligence refers to the ability to recognize and classify plants, minerals, and animals, including rocks and grass and all variety of flora and fauna. The ability to recognize cultural artifacts like cars or sneakers may also depend on the naturalist intelligence.

Now, everybody can do this to a certain extent—we can all recognize dogs, cats, trees. But, some people from an early age are extremely good at recognizing and classifying artifacts. For example, we all know kids who, at age 3 or 4, are better at recognizing dinosaurs than most adults.

Darwin is probably the most famous example of a naturalist because he saw so deeply into the nature of living things.

Are there any other abilities you're considering calling intelligences?

Well, there may be an existential intelligence that refers to the human inclination to ask very basic questions about existence. Who are we? Where do we come from? What's it all about? Why do we die? We might say that existential intelligence allows us to know the invisible, outside world. The only reason I haven't given a seal of approval to the existential intelligence is that I don't think we have good brain evidence yet on its existence in the nervous system—one of the criteria for an intelligence.

You have said that the theory of multiple intelligences may be best understood when we know what it critiques. What do you mean?

The standard view of intelligence is that intelligence is something you are born with; you have only a certain amount of it; you cannot do much about how much of that intelligence you have; and tests exist that can tell you how smart you are. The theory of multiple intelligences challenges that view. It asks, instead, "Given what we know about the brain, evolution, and the differences in cultures, what are the sets of human abilities we all share?

My analysis suggested that rather than one or two intelligences, all human beings have several (eight) intelligences. What makes life interesting, however, is that we don't have the same strength in each intelligence area, and we don't have the same amalgam of intelligences. Just as we look different from one another and have different kinds of personalities, we also have different kinds of minds.

This premise has very serious educational implications. If we treat everybody as if they are the same, we're catering to one profile of intelligence, the language-logic profile. It's great if you have that profile, but it's not great for the vast majority of human beings who do not have that particular profile of intelligence.

Can you explain more fully how the theory of multiple intelligences challenges what has become known as IQ?

The theory challenges the entire notion of IQ. The IQ test was developed about a century ago as a way to determine who would have trouble in school. The test measures linguistic ability, logical-mathematical ability, and, occasionally, spatial ability.

What the intelligence test does not do is inform us about our other intelligences; it also doesn't look at other virtues like creativity or civic mindedness, or whether a person is moral or ethical.

We don't do much IQ testing anymore, but the shadow of IQ tests is still with us because the SAT—arguably the most potent examination in the world—is basically the same kind of disembodied language-logic instrument.

The truth is, I don't believe there is such a general thing as scholastic aptitude. Even so, I don't think that the SAT will fade until colleges indicate that they'd rather have students who know how to use their minds well—students who may or may not be good test takers, but who are serious, inquisitive, and know how to probe and problem-solve. That is really what college professors want, I believe.

Can we strengthen our intelligences? If so, how?

We can all get better at each of the intelligences, although some people will improve in an intelligence area more readily than others, either because biology gave them a better brain for that intelligence or because their culture gave them a better teacher.

Teachers have to help students use their combination of intelligences to be successful in school, to help them learn whatever it is they want to learn, as well as what the teachers and society believe they have to learn.

Now, I'm not arguing that kids shouldn't learn the literacies. Of course they should learn the literacies. Nor am I arguing that kids shouldn't learn the disciplines. I'm a tremendous champion of the disciplines. What I argue against is the notion that there's only one way to learn how to read, only one way to learn how to compute, only one way to learn about biology. I think that such contentions are nonsense.

It's equally nonsensical to say that everything should be taught seven or eight ways. That's not the point of the MI theory. The point is to realize that any topic of importance, from any discipline, can be taught in more than one way. There are things people need to know, and educators have to be extraordinarily imaginative and persistent in helping students understand things better.

A popular activity among those who are first exploring multiple intelligences is to construct their own intellectual profile. It's thought that when teachers go through the process of creating such a profile, they're more likely to recognize and appreciate the intellectual strengths of their students. What is your view on this kind of activity?

My own studies have shown that people love to do this. Kids like to do it, adults like to do it. And, as an activity, I think it's perfectly harmless.

I get concerned, though, when people think that determining your intellectual profile—or that of someone else—is an end in itself.

You have to use the profile to understand the ways in which you seem to learn easily. And, from there, determine how to use those strengths to help you become more successful in other endeavors. Then, the profile becomes a way for you to understand yourself better, and you can use that understanding to catapult yourself to a better level of understanding or to a higher level of skill.

How has your understanding of the multiple intelligences influenced how you teach?

My own teaching has changed slowly as a result of multiple intelligences because I'm teaching graduate students psychological theory and there are only so many ways I can do that. I am more open to group work and to student projects of various sorts, but even if I wanted to be an "MI professor" of graduate students, I still have a certain moral obligation to prepare them for a world in which they will have to write scholarly articles and prepare theses.

Where I've changed much more, I believe, is at the workplace. I direct research projects and work with all kinds of people. Probably 10 to 15 years ago, I would have tried to find people who were just like me to work with me on these projects.

I've really changed my attitude a lot on that score. Now I think much more in terms of what people are good at and in putting together teams of people whose varying strengths complement one another.

How should thoughtful educators implement the theory of multiple intelligences?

Although there is no single MI route, it's very important that a teacher take individual differences among kids very seriously. You cannot be a good MI teacher if you don't want to know each child and try to gear how you teach and how you evaluate to that particular child. The bottom line is a deep interest in children and how their minds are different from one another, and in helping them use their minds well.

Now, kids can be great informants for teachers. For example, a teacher might say, "Look, Benjamin, this obviously isn't working. Should we try using a picture?" If Benjamin gets excited about that approach, that's a pretty good clue to the teacher about what could work.

The theory of multiple intelligences, in and of itself, is not going to solve anything in our society, but linking the multiple intelligences with a curriculum focused on understanding is an extremely powerful intellectual undertaking.

When I talk about understanding, I mean that students can take ideas they learn in school, or anywhere for that matter, and apply those appropriately in new situations. We know people truly

School matters, but only insofar as it yields something that can be used once students leave school.

understand something when they can represent the knowledge in more than one way. We have to put understanding up front in school. Once we have that goal, multiple intelligences can be a terrific handmaiden because understandings involve a mix of mental representations, entailing different intelligences.

People often say that what they remember most about school are those learning experiences that were linked to real life. How does the theory of multiple intelligences help connect learning to the world outside the classroom?

The theory of multiple intelligences wasn't based on school work or on tests. Instead, what I did was look at the world and ask, What are the things that people do in the world? What does it mean to be a surgeon? What does it mean to be a politician? What does it mean to be an artist or a sculptor? What abilities do you need to do those things? My theory, then, came from the things that are valued in the world.

So when a school values multiple intelligences, the relationship to what's valued in the world is patent. If you cannot easily relate this activity to some-

thing that's valued in the world, the school has probably lost the core idea of multiple intelligences, which is that these intelligences evolved to help people do things that matter in the real world.

School matters, but only insofar as it yields something that can be used once students leave school.

How can teachers be guided by multiple intelligences when creating assessment tools?

We need to develop assessments that are much more representative of what human beings are going to have to do to survive in this

The Intelligences, in Gardner's Words

- Linguistic intelligence is the capacity to use language, your native language, and perhaps other languages, to express what's on your mind and to understand other people. Poets really specialize in linguistic intelligence, but any kind of writer, orator, speaker, lawyer, or a person for whom language is an important stock in trade highlights linguistic intelligence.

- People with a highly developed logical-mathematical intelligence understand the underlying principles of some kind of a causal system, the way a scientist or a logician does; or can manipulate numbers, quantities, and operations, the way a mathematician does.

- Spatial intelligence refers to the ability to represent the spatial world internally in your mind—the way a sailor or airplane pilot navigates the large spatial world, or the way a chess player or sculptor represents a more circumscribed spatial world. Spatial intelligence can be used in the arts or in the sciences. If you are spatially intelligent and oriented toward the arts, you are more likely to become a painter or a sculptor or an architect than, say, a musician or a writer. Similarly, certain sciences like anatomy or topology, emphasize spatial intelligence.

- Bodily kinesthetic intelligence is the capacity to use your whole body or parts of your body—your hand, your fingers, your arms—to solve a problem, make something, or put on some kind of a production. The most evident examples are people in athletics or the performing arts, particularly dance or acting.

- Musical intelligence is the capacity to think in music, to be able to hear patterns, recognize them, remember them, and perhaps manipulate them. People who have a strong musical intelligence don't just remember music easily—they can't get it out of their minds, it's so omnipresent. Now, some people will say, "Yes, music is important, but it's a talent, not an intelligence." And I say, "Fine, let's call it a talent." But, then we have to leave the word *intelligent* out of *all* discussions of human abilities. You know, Mozart was damned smart!

- Interpersonal intelligence is understanding other people. It's an ability we all need, but is at a premium if you are a teacher, clinician, salesperson, or politician. Anybody who deals with other people has to be skilled in the interpersonal sphere.

- Intrapersonal intelligence refers to having an understanding of yourself, of knowing who you are, what you can do, what you want to do, how you react to things, which things to avoid, and which things to gravitate toward. We are drawn to people who have a good understanding of themselves because those people tend not to screw up. They tend to know what they can do. They tend to know what they can't do. And they tend to know where to go if they need help.

- Naturalist intelligence designates the human ability to discriminate among living things (plants, animals) as well as sensitivity to other features of the natural world (clouds, rock configurations). This ability was clearly of value in our evolutionary past as hunters, gatherers, and farmers; it continues to be central in such roles as botanist or chef. I also speculate that much of our consumer society exploits the naturalist intelligences, which can be mobilized in the discrimination among cars, sneakers, kinds of makeup, and the like. The kind of pattern recognition valued in certain of the sciences may also draw upon naturalist intelligence.

society. For example, I value literacy, but my measure of literacy should not be whether you can answer a multiple-choice question that asks you to select the best meaning of a paragraph. Instead, I'd rather have you read the paragraph and list four questions you have about the paragraph and figure out how you would answer those questions. Or, if I want to know how you can write, let me give you a stem and see whether you can write about that topic, or let me ask you to write an editorial in response to something you read in the newspaper or observed on the street.

The current emphasis on performance assessment is well supported by the theory of multiple intelligences. Indeed, you could not really be an advocate of multiple intelligences if you didn't have some dissatisfaction with the current testing because it's so focused on short-answer, linguistic, or logical kinds of items.

MI theory is very congenial to an approach that says: one, let's not look at things through the filter of a short-answer test. Let's look directly at the performance that we value, whether it's a linguistic, logical, aesthetic, or social performance; and, two, let's never pin our assessment of understanding on just one particular measure, but let's always allow students to show their understanding in a variety of ways.

You have identified several myths about the theory of multiple intelligences. Can you describe some of those myths?

One myth that I personally find irritating is that an intelligence is the same as a learning style. Learning styles are claims about ways in which individuals purportedly approach everything

they do. If you are planful, you are supposed to be planful about everything. If you are logical-sequential, you are supposed to be logical-sequential about everything. My own research and observations suggest that that's a dubious assumption. But whether or not that's true, learning styles are very different from multiple intelligences.

Multiple intelligences claims that we respond, individually, in different ways to different kinds of content, such as language or music or other people. This is very different from the notion of learning style.

You can say that a child is a visual learner, but that's not a multiple intelligences way of talking about things. What I would say is, "Here is a child who very easily represents things spatially, and we can draw upon that strength if need be when we want to teach the child something new."

Another widely believed myth is that, because we have seven or eight intelligences, we should create seven or eight tests to measure students' strengths in each of those areas. That is a perversion of the theory. It's recreating the sin of the single intelligence quotient and just multiplying it by a larger number. I'm personally against assessment of intelligences unless such a measurement is used for a very specific learning purpose—we want to help a child understand her history or his mathematics better and, therefore, want to see what might be good entry points for that particular child.

What experiences led you to the study of human intelligence?

It's hard for me to pick out a single moment, but I can see a couple of snapshots. When I was in high school, my uncle gave me a textbook in psychology. I'd never actually heard of psychology before. This textbook helped me understand color blindness. I'm color blind, and I became fascinated by the existence of plates that illustrated what color blindness was. I could actually explain why I couldn't see colors.

Another time when I was studying the Reformation, I read a book by Erik Erikson called *Young Man Luther* (1958)[1] I was fascinated by the psychological motivation of Luther to attack the Catholic Church. That fascination influenced my decision to go into psychology.

The most important influence was actually learning about brain damage and what could happen to people when they had strokes. When a person has a stroke, a certain part of the brain gets injured, and that injury can tell you what that part of the brain does. Individuals who lose their musical abilities can still talk. People who lose their linguistic ability still might be able to sing. The understanding not only brought me into the whole world of brain study, but it was really the seed that led ultimately to the theory of multiple intelligences. As long as you can lose one ability while others are spared, you cannot just have a single intelligence. You have to have several intelligences.

As long as you can lose one ability while others are spared, you cannot just have a single intelligence.

[1] See Erik Erikson, *Young Man Luther* (New York: W.W. Norton, 1958).

 Article Review Form at end of book.

What is CAI?

Computer Assisted Instruction and Cognitive Development in Preschoolers

**Rosalyn Shute and
John Miksad**

The Flinders University of South Australia

In this study, we examined the use of microcomputers with preschoolers, comparing computers and traditional resources. Fifty-one children were randomly assigned to three groups, distinguished by the level of computer-provided scaffolding: substantial, minimal, or none (control group, with minimal teacher-provided scaffolding). A pretest-posttest design was used to compare cognitive changes over an 8-week period. In terms of specific skills, Computer Assisted Instruction (CAI) software was successful in increasing verbal and language skills, but not basic math skills, and only as a function of substantial scaffolding. Results also revealed that software with substantial scaffolding features increased general cognitive abilities significantly more than minimally scaffolded instruction.

During the 1980s, thousands of microcomputers were placed in early childhood classrooms on a rising tide of popular enthusiasm (Hyson & Eyman, 1986). They are not widely used in preschools and there is a great deal of available software aimed at this age group (e.g., Perra, 1992; Pine, 1991). Young children may derive benefits such as computer familiarization and keyboard skills, but it is difficult to justify the value of computers to preschool programs on this basis alone (Tan, 1985; Zajonc, 1984). Arguments for incorporating microcomputers into preschool classrooms would be strengthened by demonstrations that they contribute to children's cognitive development. Furthermore, early childhood educators need to know the types of software that will promote optimal levels of cognitive development and under which situations (Haugland & Shade, 1988).

Although computers have been lauded as powerful learning devices that facilitate the cognitive development of preschoolers (Buckleitner & Hohmann, 1987; Grover, 1986; Lawler, 1985), such claims are offset by methodological problems common in educational computing research. In the present study, we compared the impact of computer assisted instruction (CAI) and conventional teaching resources on preschool children's cognitive development, improving on previous work by taking the nature of the software into account, by using a suitable theoretical framework and by improving the experimental design.

Positive outcomes of computer use have been claimed for a number of areas of preschoolers' learning, including alphabet recognition (Williams, 1984), numeral recognition (Hungate, 1982; McCollister, Burts, Wright, & Hildreth, 1986), counting skills

(Hungate, 1982), concept learning (Grover, 1986), and premathematics knowledge (Howard, Watson, Brinkley, & Ingels–Young, 1994). Hughes and Macleod (1986) discovered significant pretest to posttest gains on specific subscales of the British Ability Scales after 8 months of computer use with 5- and 6-year-olds. There have also been suggestions that computers are superior to traditional teaching resources owing to features such as visual/action superiority (Pezdek & Stevens, 1984), graphic animation (Hayes, Chemelski, & Birnbaum, 1981), extended attention span (Clements, 1984), instant feedback (Grover, 1986), and control over a "microworld" (Shade & Watson, 1990).

On the whole, such research does not account for different instructional methods and content material, and fails to separate treatment and novelty effects (Clark, 1985). True experiments in the field are scarce, with many descriptive and quasi-experimental studies (Goodwin, Goodwin, & Garel, 1986). Problems include small sample sizes (Clements & Gullo, 1984; Hungate, 1982; Williams, 1984), inappropriate treatments (Goodwin, Goodwin, Nansel, & Helm, 1986; Williams, 1984), non–representative samples (Buckleitner & Hohmann, 1987; Hungate, 1982), and a lack of control groups (Anselmo & Zinck, 1987; Hughes & Macleod, 1986).

Experimental evidence for general cognitive benefits from computer use is scarce. Comparisons between computer treatment and traditional resource groups have yielded no significant differences on measures of cognitive development (Clements & Gullo, 1984; Howell, Scott, & Diamond,

1987; Lehrer, Harckham, Archer, & Pruzek, 1986), although questions about the construct validity of the measures remain. Clements and Gullo (1984) used only four subscales of the McCarthy Screening Test, whereas Howell, Scott, and Diamond (1987) used only three Piagetian tasks. Only Lehrer, Harckham, Archer, and Pruzek (1986) could claim reasonable construct validity using the McCarthy Short Form (Kaufman, 1978) and the Kaufman Assessment Battery for Children. Although this study failed to find significant effects of computer use on general cognitive development, computer use improved specific cognitive skills as a direct function of the type of software used. Other limited evidence for enhancement of specific cognitive skills include the use of computer-presented graphics to encourage the language development of speech-delayed preschoolers (O'Connor & Schery, 1986; Shriberg, Kwiatkowski, & Snyder, 1986), and the teaching of specific reading skills (Gore, Morrison, Maas, & Anderson, 1989). However, Goodwin, Goodwin, Nansel, and Helm (1986) found that computer use did not significantly affect preschoolers' knowledge or prereading concepts.

Overall, there is little solid empirical work on the effects of computer use on preschool children's cognitive development. Furthermore, few studies had a sound theoretical basis (Lepper & Gurtner, 1989; Shade & Watson, 1990), providing no clear direction for future research. In the present study, the concept *scaffolding* provides a framework to compare learning support provided by software and by teachers using traditional resources.

CAI is the main type of software in use for preschoolers, (Donohue, Borgh, & Dickson, 1987), otherwise referred to as "drill and practice" software. The future of CAI research is to progress towards more adaptive and helpful software for children (Light & Blaye, 1990), identifying features which may act as a scaffold for cognitive development (Cohen & Geva, 1989).

Scaffolded instruction is a teaching strategy aimed at the zone of proximal development of the child (Paris, Wixson, & Palincsar, 1986; Wood, 1980) and derives from the interactional theory of cognitive devellopment of Vygotsky (1978). It may be defined as ". . . instructional assistance that enables someone to solve a problem, carry out a task, or achieve a goal that the person could not accomplish alone" (Paris, Wixson, & Palincsar, 1986, p. 109). The level of assistance is tailored to the learner's degree of competence.

Wood (1980) presented five levels of scaffolded instruction, derived from research investigating how mothers teach their young children tasks (Wood, Bruner, & Ross, 1976; Wood & Middleton, 1975). Level 5, full demonstration, represents the highest level of scaffolding, when the teacher performs the entire task: This is appropriate when the task is very new or difficult for the child. The other four levels are used progressively as the child learns the task and represent a gradually lower level of task involvement by the teacher and increasing task involvement by the learner. These levels are: intervention in selection and arrangement, whereby the child only has to perform the final part of task and frustration is therefore controlled;

intervention by indication, such as pointing, with the child performing the operation; establishment of parameters, which involves verbally guiding the child's activities; and, verbal encouragement to prompt the activity and gain the child's interest (Wood, 1980). The utility of these levels, which were adopted in the present study, has been amply demonstrated with large sample sizes and a variety of tasks (NcNaughton & Leyland, 1990; Pratt, Kerig, Cowan, & Cowan, 1988; Wood, 1980; Wood, Bruner, & Ross, 1976; Vandell & Wilson, 1987).

Preschool teachers, by providing suitable levels of scaffolding, play a vital role in facilitating children's learning (NAEYC, 1986). Documentation that computer software can similarly serve to scaffold cognitive development is scarce, but it is apparent that much software has been designed with this in mind (Clements, 1987; Grover, 1986; McLanahan, 1984). The criteria for scaffolding employed in the present study have been identified in a number of programs for preschool children. With the advent of voice-feedback (Lehrer, Levin, DeHart, & Comeaux, 1987), computer software is able to provide verbal encouragement and parameter-setting. Other levels, such as intervention by indication, as well as selection and arrangement, are integral features of many programs, as is full demonstration and modeling. In the present study, the 5–level scaffolding scheme provided a way of equating the type of instruction given by the teacher using conventional methods (control group) and an experimental group using CAI which incorporated similar (minimal) levels of scaffolding. The role of scaffolding in promoting preschoolers'

cognitive development through computer use was also investigated by comparing the use of minimal-scaffolding CAI with substantial-scaffolding CAI.

In the present study, therefore, we attempted to improve upon previous research by adopting an explicit theoretical framework, by including a control group, and by controlling the type of instruction given in the various groups. Other improvements included: random assignment to groups; larger sample size; specified treatments; standardization of content material across groups, with software and related non-computer activities matched as closely as possible; and efforts to match novelty and reinforcement effects across groups.

In the present study, we investigated the cognitive-developmental implications of computers and different types of software for preschool programs to answer the following research questions:

1. Given the special features claimed for computers, is the computer per se superior to traditional teaching resources when level of scaffolding is controlled?

2. Is CAI software successful in increasing specific cognitive skills? The specific skills examined were counting/sorting and word knowledge, with the hypothesis that CAI software would increase these specific skills significantly more than other cognitive skills.

3. It was hypothesized that CAI software with substantial levels of inherent scaffolding would advance cognitive development significantly more than minimal scaffolding.

Method

Participants

There were 57 preschool children, ranging in age at pretesting from 2 years, 10 months to 5 years, 0 months (M = 3 years, 11 months). At the time of posttesting, three children had moved away and three were excluded from the study for reasons to be detailed, leaving a total of 51 (25 boys and 26 girls).

The children attended one of three preschool day-care centers located in suburban Adelaide, South Australia, offering part- and full-time care to children from families in the general community. The parents of 81% of the children in the appropriate age range returned consent forms agreeing to their child's participation. All children in the sample were fluent in English as a first language and represented a cross-section of socioeconomic status.

For some of the children, this study provided a first encounter with computers (none of the centers included computers in their preschool curriculum). However, the vast majority had gained exposure to computers in some fashion, as determined by a parent-completed questionnaire. Nineteen children (37%) had access to a computer at home, spending anywhere between 5 and 120 minutes per week on it (M = 45 min.). In general, the children were considered to be at least computer-aware.

Design

A pretest-posttest experimental design was used, with three treatment groups. The independent variable was level of scaffolded computer use, namely substantial, minimal, or none (control, with minimal teacher scaffolding). The children were stratified by pretest scores on the McCarthy Short Form into below average, average, or above average ability groups, then randomly allocated to one of the three treatment conditions. The control group received instruction using traditional resources, such as balloons, animal toys, and cards with words, numbers, and pictures. Two groups received instruction via the computer one using minimal and the other substantial assistance software.

The levels of assistance in software were rated according to levels of scaffolded instruction[1] (Wood, Bruner, & Ross, 1976). For example, *Easy Counting Game: 123-TALK*, has substantial levels of scaffolding, including all 5 levels. The task of counting the balloons is fully demonstrated; there is indication by intervention, selection and arrangement, with the program counting the balloons and the child simply pressing the key to select the appropriate number; parameters are verbally established ("How many balloons are there?"); there is verbal encouragement (e.g., "Count the balloons with me", "Very good", "Ooops"). Furthermore, verbal assistance is gradually relaxed as the child progresses successfully through the program, and higher levels of difficulty are available so that teaching can be maintained within the child's zone of proximal development.

The three groups were matched as closely as possible on other relevant variables, such as teacher assistance/intervention, content material, and reinforcement/novelty effects. The teacher maintained assistance in all groups at levels 1 and 2 (verbal encouragement and establishment

of parameters), with level 3 (intervention by indication) allowed in an emergency (Wood, 1980). The content material was aimed at the same specific skills in all three groups, that is, word knowledge and counting and sorting, and the control group was provided with reinforcement/novelty effects by way of interesting activities and consistent reinforcement from the teacher.

Unavoidably, one of the experimenters was responsible for both testing and teaching. Partial blindness was obtained by this experimenter remaining ignorant of the pretest scores, which were calculated by the second experimenter, who was then responsible for the stratification process.

Materials

Hardware. An IBM-compatible personal computer was used, with an 80286 processor, 640K RAM, 15 meg. Hard drive, an EGA monitor, and an XT–configuration keyboard (The children appeared to use the keyboard satisfactorily, even though a mouse or modified keyboard has been recommended for use with preschoolers; King & Alloway, 1992).

Software. The software was selected from the Shareware catalog, for reasons of affordability and accessibility to most computer users. Programs used for the minimal group were: Brandon's Lunchbox (Countem – Game D), ABC – FUN keys (Word Pictures), and Amy's First Primer 2.2 (Bunny Letters, and Beary Fun Counting). Programs used for the substantial group were: 123–TALK (Easy Counting), Animated Math (Count the Objects), and Wunderbook (Spell the Object, and Match Word to Picture). Each child allotted to a computer group, therefore, accessed four

computer activities, two aimed at counting and two at word knowledge. The control group was provided with related activities which were directly matched to the software but using traditional resources. For instance, if the computer task involved counting balloons, then the control group counted real balloons; if the computer task involved matching words and images, the control group task involved matching pictures and words on cards.

Cognitive (Dependent) Measures

The McCarthy Short Form (Kaufman, 1977) was used, providing an overall cognitive score, as well as six subscale scores. Prior studies with preschoolers and computers have used the McCarthy subscales in one form or another (Clements & Gullo, 1984; Lehrer, Levin, DeHart, & Comeaux, 1987). The original McCarthy Scales of Children's Abilities (McCarthy, 1972) were designed for 2½-to 8½-years olds, with 18 subscales in total. Of these 18, 15 are combined to create the General Cognitive Index (GCI), which provides a score similar to traditional IQ tests, with a mean of 100 and standard deviation of 16. Although McCarthy avoids the term, the GCI is essentially an IQ measure, correlating highly with the WPPSI, WISC-R and Stanford–Binet (Davis, 1975; Davis & Walker, 1977). Kaufman (1977) proposed a short (6 subscales) form of the McCarthy as a rapid (20 minute) screening measure ideal for research purposes. The 6 subscales are Puzzle-Solving, Word Knowledge, Numerical Memory, Verbal Fluency, Counting and Sorting, and Conceptual Grouping. The scores convert to an estimate of the full scale GCI (correlation of $r = 0.92$ with the full GCI, and split-half reliability of $r = 0.88$; Kaufman, 1977). The validity and reliability of the separate subscales are more questionable. (Sattler, 1988) and should be interpreted with caution. However, this disadvantage was outweighed by matches possible between the subscales and the software to be used, by the convenience of the short form and the excellent psychometric properties of the estimated GCI.

The Boehm Test of Basic Concepts—Preschool Version (Boehm, 1986), was also used as a screening instrument. The Boehm examines 26 abstract concepts that occur frequently in the directions of teachers and curriculum materials, such as highest, lowest, all, under, around, middle, and soon; it yields an age-graded percentile score. It was included for two reasons. Firstly, basic concepts are inherent in the instructions of all major IQ tests, including the McCarthy (Kaufman, 1978). Secondly, Clements (1987) cautioned that young children should not be exposed to computers without an understanding of basic concepts inherent in most software. For this reason, three children were not included in the study, because their knowledge of basic concepts was judged to be inadequate, with a Boehm score below 20.

Procedure

Prior to pretesting, the computer was left at each center for one full day as a free-play activity with neutral games software, in an attempt to counter some of the novelty effects (Clark, 1985) although, as noted earlier, many of the chil-

dren already had access to a computer at home. During this time, parents were given a standard consent form and questionnaire. The children whose parents gave consent were then pretested with the McCarthy Short Form and the Boehm Test of Basic Concepts. All but the three children mentioned previously were stratified according to their McCarthy GCI score, classified as below the 33rd percentile (less than 108), between the 33rd and 66th percentile (108–122), and above the 66th percentile (greater than 122). Random allocation into treatment levels from the different strata ensured that intellectual ability was spread evenly over the groups.

In each group, children received one individual 20 minute session per week, for 8 weeks, with catch-up sessions provided for absentees. In the end, each child completed the full number of sessions, except for the three children who moved away during the study, who were not included in subsequent analyses. Counting and word knowledge were targeted in alternate weeks, and each child worked his/her way through the four allotted tasks over the first 4 weeks and then again over the second 4 weeks.

The availability of two experimenters, one male and one female, allowed for the control group to be run simultaneously with one of the computer groups, in two separate rooms away from the distractions of the main classroom. In effect, the control group children were not aware that they were missing out on computer time. Over the 8 weeks, the two experimenters were counterbalanced over the three groups, to control for any experimenter effects. They were also careful not

to go beyond minimal assistance, as outline previously.

Posttesting on the McCarthy Short Form occurred one week after the end of the treatment.

Results

To test the specific research questions, a series of ANCOVAs was used, along with planned comparisons between groups. The data were first examined to see whether they met the underlying assumptions of ANCOVA. The dependent measures displayed homogeneity of variance between groups. The second assumption of ANCOVA, homogenetity of regression slopes between the dependent variables and their respective covariates, was also met by all measures.

The ANCOVAs were initially performed using posttest scores as dependent measures, and respective pretest scores as covariates. These analyses produced group means of posttest measures adjusted for the effects of pretest scores (Table 1[*]), as well as Mean square error terms essential for the subsequent planned comparisons. The resultant ANCOVA using GCI scores yielded an $F (2,47) = 8.49$, $p =.001$, (Table 2[*]) and planned comparisons were carried out as described subsequently.

The first planned comparison centered on the superiority of computers as a medium of learning over traditional resources, comparing the Control group versus The Minimal Computer group. Adjusted posttest GCI scores yielded $t (47)$ obt $= 1.02$, less than $t (47)$ crit $= 2.02$, $p >.10$. Thus, there was no evidence that general cognitive development was promoted more by computer use than by traditional teaching

[*]Not included in this publication.

resources matched for level of scaffolding.

The question of whether CAI software is successful at increasing specific skills of cognitive development required the use of a series of ANCOVAs on each of the posttest GCI subscale scores, arranged in a step-down fashion according to the hypothesized skills increased (Word Knowledge and Counting and Sorting were entered first, followed by Verbal Fluency, Numerical Memory, Puzzle-solving, and Conceptual Grouping). The subscale scores were entered separately with their respective pretest GCI covariates, with each step including the addition of the previous posttest GCI subscale score as a new covariate. For instance, posttest Word Knowledge used pretest Word Knowledge as a covariate, then posttest Counting and Sorting used pretest Counting and Sorting and posttest Word Knowledge as covariates, and so on. The adjusted group means and Mean square error term were then used in planned comparisons. The resultant ANCOVAs, in order of entry, yielded $F(2,47) = 8.39$, $p< .01$ (Word Knowledge); $F(2,46) = .26$, $p>.10$ (Counting and Sorting); $F(2,45) = 4.79$, $p<.05$ (Verbal Fluency); $F(2,44) = .13$, $p>.10$ (Numerical Memory); $F(2,43) = .14$, $p>.10$ (Puzzle Solving); and $F(2,42) = .71$, $p>.10$ (Conceptual Grouping); that is, significant effects were found for Word Knowledge and Verbal Fluency only. Planned comparisons were, therefore, carried out on these two variables.

The first comparison centered on the superiority of computers as a medium of learning, comparing Control versus Minimal groups. Word Knowledge yielded $t(47)$ obt $= .21$, $p>.10$, and Verbal Fluency yielded $t(47)$ obt $= -.64$,

$p> .10$. The second comparison centered on the Scaffolding effects of CAI software, comparing the Substantial group versus Minimal/Control groups combined. Word Knowledge yielded $t(47)$ obt $= 4.09$, $p<.01$, and Verbal Fluency yielded $t(47)$ obt $= 3.21$, $p<.05$. The hypothesized increase in Word Knowledge, as a function of substantially scaffolded CAI, was therefore found, but the hypothesized increase in Counting and Sorting was not. Verbal Fluency also increased as a result of substantially scaffolded CAI, which had not been predicted.

The final set of comparisons examined the scaffolding effects of CAI software, using the adjusted means for posttest GCI, this time comparing the Substantial group versus Minimal/Control groups combined. Posttest GCI scores yielded $t(47)$ obt $= 4.01$, greater than $t(47)$ crit $= 2.97$, $p<.01$. These results generally support the hypothesis that CAI software can provide substantial levels of scaffolding for general cognitive development.

Finally, using chi-square analyses and ANOVA, a check on random allocation to groups was made. No significant differences between groups were found on sex, age, kindergarten, and GCI pretest scores (these were in any case used as covariates), presence of and access to a home computer and the kinds of software used on a home computer. In general, then, the groups, appeared to be homogeneous, increasing confidence in the causality of the treatment effects observed.

Discussion

The first research question concerned whether computers are superior to traditional teaching resources. In the past, most com-

parisons between computers and traditional resources favored computers for promoting the cognitive development of primary-aged children (Niemiec & Walberg, 1987). However, the present results demonstrate that the general cognitive development of preschoolers and specific cognitive skills are not promoted more by computers than by traditional resources when level of scaffolding is controlled. The implication of this finding is to dispel the myth of computers as magical toys, as many parents and early childhood educators may believe. The study was not designed to examine in detail the contribution of the various features of computers purported to be special, but comments may be made about two features which may be of particular salience, namely, attentional effects and instant feedback.

Informally, it was observed that the children working on the computer, even in the minimal scaffolding group, had high levels of attention. An extreme example was a child with a normally poor attention span, who had been assessed as having Attention Deficit Hyperactivity Disorder. The computer maintained his attention for the full 20 minute session, and he repeatedly requested extra sessions. Given that improved attention is expected to promote learning (Lepper, 1985), the high attention levels noted may seem at odds with the finding that the minimal scaffolding group did not develop cognitively any more than the group taught traditionally.

A possible explanation is that the attention-grabbing features distracted the children from the content-material, thus detracting from the learning process (Huguenin, 1987). For instance, the presentation of Disney characters may increase attention span, but does not necessarily enhance the educational value of the software (Dowling, 1992). Therefore, rather than overloading the limited attentional capacities of preschoolers, software should be designed to reach optimal levels of attention maintenance.

As for instant feedback, this is also regarded as a motivational feature of computers (Chaffin, Maxwell, & Thompson, 1982). The design of the present study required that the control group should also receive individual attention, and therefore instant feedback was available for both computer and control groups. Under real-life classroom conditions, the computer may indeed be beneficial by providing feedback more readily than a busy teacher.

The second research question examined the suitability of CAI for increasing specific congnitive skills. Most software in use by preschoolers is of the CAI-type (Donohue, Borgh, & Dickson, 1987), enhancing specific skills normally developed in regular preschool through drill and practice (Gore, Morrison, Maas, & Anderson, 1989). The skills include reading, writing, alphabet/-numeral/shape recognition, and counting and math skills (Clements, 1987; Goodwin, Goodwin, & Garel, 1986). The software in the present study was aimed at two specific subscales of the McCarthy Short Form (Kaufman, 1977), namely Word Knowledge and Counting and Sorting. The results demonstrate that CAI software significantly increases Word Knowledge as hypothesized, but fails to significantly increase Counting and Sorting. Unexpectedly, Verbal Fluency also increase significantly. This may have occurred due to

some overlap between the two constructs, bearing in mind the limits of the construct validity of the subscales, or possibly due to transfer of learning.

Previous research provides only limited evidence that CAI can increase preschoolers' specific cognitive skills (Hughes & Macleod, 1986; Lehrer, Harckham, Archer, & Pruzek, 1986). The present study provides strong evidence that specific language skills can be increased (Word Knowledge and Verbal Fluency). This supports findings using CAI with speech-delayed preschoolers (Shriberg, Kwiatkowski, & Snyder, 1986). However, there is no evidence in the present results to suggest that basic math skills, such as Counting and Sorting or Numerical Memory, can be increased with CAI software significantly more than traditional resources, although it may be that the Counting and Sorting subscale was not sensitive enough to demonstrate significant changes, producing a ceiling effect for the majority of children.

In summary, the results demonstrate that CAI increase language-related cognitive skills in preschoolers when substantial levels of scaffolding are present.

With regard to the final research question, the results demonstrate that CAI software with identified levels of substantial scaffolding is successful in promoting cognitive development.

The present study supports the growing realization of the importance of scaffolding features in software for preschoolers (Clements, 1987; Cohen & Geva, 1989; Lehrer, Levin, DeHart, & Comeaux, 1987). In general, there is progress towards more adaptive and helpful software for children (Light & Blaye, 1990). The present study used public domain

software rated post hoc for levels of scaffolding, but the design of software specifically incorporating scaffolding features would represent the state of the art in intelligent tutoring.

References

Anselmo, S., & Zinck, R.A. (1987). Computers for young children? Perhaps. *Young Children, 42*(3), 22–27.

Arinoldo, C.G. (1982). Concurrent validity of McCarthy's scales. *Perceptual and Motor Skills, 54*, 1343–1346.

Boehm, A. E. (1986). *Boehm Test of Basic Concepts manual: Preschool version.* New York: Psychological Corporation.

Buckleitner, W. W., & Hohmann, C. F. (1987). Technological priorities in the education of young children. *Childhood Education, 63*, 337–340.

Chaffin, J. D., Maxwell. B., & Thompson, B. (1982). The application of video game formats to educational software. *Exceptional Children, 49* (2), 173–178.

Clark, R. E. (1985). Confounding in educational computing research. *Journal of Educational Computing Research, 1*, 137–148.

Clements, D. H. (1984). Implications of media research for the instructional application of computers with young children. *Educational Technology, 24* (11) 7–16.

Clements, D. H. (1986). Effects of LOGO and CAI environments on cognition and creativity. *Journal of Educational Psychology, 78*, 309–318.

Clements, D. H. (1987). Computers and young children: A review of research. *Young Children, 43* (1), 34–44.

Clements, D. H., & Gullo, D. F. (1984). Effects of computer programming on young children's cognition. *Journal of Educational Psychology, 76*, 1051–1058.

Cohen, R., & Geva, E. (1989). Designing LOGO-like environments for young children: The interaction between theory and practice. *Journal of Educational Computing Research, 5*, 349–377.

Davis, E. E. (1975). Concurrent validity of the McCarthy Scales of Children's Abilities. *Measurement and Evaluation in Guidance, 8*, 101–104.

Davis, E. E., & Walker, C. (1977). McCarthy scales and WISC–R. *Perceptual and Motor Skills, 44*, 966.

Donohue, W. A., Borgh, K., & Dickson, W. P. (1987). Computers in early childhood education. *Journal of Research on Childhood Education, 2* (1), 6–16.

Dowling, B. (1992). *Computers in early childhood curriculum project.* Adelaide: Children's Services Office.

Goodwin, L. D., Goodwin, W. L., & Garel, M. B. (1986). Use of microcomputers with preschoolers: A review of the literature. *Early Childhood Research Quarterly, 1,* 269–286.

Goodwin, L. D., Goodwin, W. L., Nansel, A., & Helm, C. P. (1986). Cognitive and affective effects of various types of microcomputer use by preschoolers. *American Educational Research Journal, 23,* 348–356.

Gore, D. A., Morrison, G. N., Maas, M. L., & Anderson, E. A. (1989). A study of teaching reading skills to the young child using microcomputer assisted instruction. *Journal of Educational Computing Research, 5,* 179–185.

Grover, S. C. (1986). A field of the use of cognitive-developmental principles in microcomputer design for young children. *Journal of Educational Research, 79,* 325–332.

Haugland, S., & Shade, D. (1988). Developmentally appropriate software for young children. *Young Children, 43* (4), 37–42.

Hayes, D. S., Chemelski, B. E., & Birnbaum, D. W. (1981). Young children's incidental and intentional retention of televised events. *Developmental Psychology, 17,* 230–232.

Howard, J. R., Watson, J. A. Brinkley, V. M., & Ingels-Young, G. (1994). Comprehension monitoring, stylistic differences, pre-math knowledge, and transfer: A comprehensive pre-math/spatial development computer-assisted instruction (CAI) and Logo curriculum designed to test their effects. *Journal of Educational Computing Research, 11* (2), 91–105.

Howell, R. D., Scott, P. B., & Diamond, J. (1987). The effects of "instant" LOGO computing language on the cognitive development of very young children. *Journal of Educational Computing Research, 3,* 249–260.

Hughes, M., & Macleod, H. (1986). Using LOGO with very young children. In R. W. Lawler (Ed.), *Cognition and computers: Studies in learning.* Chichester, NY: Ellis Horwood.

Huguenin, N. H. (1987). Assessment of attention to complex cues in young children: Manipulating prior reinforcement histories of stimulus components. *Journal of Experimental Child Psychology, 44,* 283–303.

Hungate, H. (1982). Computers in the kindergarten. *The Computing Teacher.* 9 (5), 15–18.

Hyson, M. C., & Eyman, A. (1986). Approaches to computer literacy in early childhood teacher education. *Young Children, 41* (6), 54–59.

Kaufman, A. S. (1977). A McCarthy short form for rapid screening preschool, kindergarten, and first-grade children. *Contemporary Educational Psychology, 2,* 149–157.

Kaufman, A. S. (1978). The importance of basic concepts in the individual assessment of preschool children. *Journal of School Psychology, 16,* 207–211.

King, J., & Alloway, N. (1992). Preschoolers use of microcomputers and input devices. *Journal of Educational Computing Research, 8,* 451–468.

Lawler, R. W. (1985). *Computer experience and cognitive development: A child's learning in a computer culture.* Chichester, NY: Ellis Horwood.

Lehrer, R., Harckham, L. D., Archer, P., & Pruzek, R. M. (1986). Microcomputer-based instruction in special education. *Journal of Educational Computing Research, 2,* 237–355.

Lehrer, R., Levin, B. B., Dehart, P., & Comeaux, M. (1987). Voice-feedback as a scaffold for writing: A comparative study. *Journal of Educational Computing Research, 3,* 335–353.

Lepper, M. (1985). Microcomputers in education: Motivational and social issues. *American Psychologist, 40,* 1–18.

Lepper, M. R., & Gurtner, J. (1989). Children and computers: Approaching the Twenty-first Century. *American Psychologist, 44,* 170–178.

Light, P., & Blaye, A. (1990). Computer-based learning: The social dimensions. In H. C. Foot, M. J. Morgan, & R. H. Shute (Eds.), *Children helping children.* New York: Wiley.

McCarthy, D. A. (1972). *Manual for the McCarthy Scales of Children's Abilities.* San Antonio: Psychological Corp.

McCollister, T. S., Burts, D. C., Wright, V. L., & Hildreth, G. J. (1986). Effects of computer-assisted instruction and teacher-assisted instruction on arithmetic task achievement scores of kindergarten children. *Journal of Educational Research, 80,* 121–125.

McLanahan, J. R. (1984). Software for young children. *Day Care and Early Education, Winter.* pp. 26–29.

McNaughton, S., & Leyland, J. (1990). The shifting of maternal tutoring across different difficulty levels on a problem solving task. *British Journal of Developmental Psychology, 8,* 147–155.

National Association for the Education of Young Children. (1986). Position statement on developmentally appropriate practice in programs for 4- and 5-year-olds. *Young Children, 41* (6), 20–29.

Niemiec, R., & Walberg, H. J. (1987). Comparative effects of computer-assisted instruction: A synthesis of reviews. *Journal of Educational Computing Research, 3,* 19–37.

O'Connor, L., & Schery, T. K. (1986). A comparison of microcomputer–aided and traditional language therapy for developing communication skills in nonoral toddlers. *Journal of Speech and Hearing Disorders, 51,* 356–361.

Paris, G. S. Wixson, K. K. & Palincsar, A. S. (1986). Instructional approaches to reading comprehension. *Review of Research in Education, 13,* 91–128.

Perra, L. L. (1992). *The status of computing in public schools in the West Kootenay region of British Columbia.* Unpublished doctoral dissertation. Nova University, B. C., Canada.

Pezdek, K., & Stevens, E. (1984). Children's memory for auditory and visual information on television. *Developmental Psychology, 20,* 212–218.

Pine, S. (1991). A basic collection of software for children. *School Library Journal, 37,* (10), 39–43.

Pratt, M. W., Kerig, P., Cowan, P. A., & Cowan, C. P. (1988). Mothers and fathers teaching 3-year-olds: Authoritative parenting and adult scaffolding of young children's learning. *Developmental Psychology, 24,* 832–839.

Sattler, J. M. (1988). *Assessment of children.* San Diego, CA: Jerome M. Sattler, Publisher.

Shade, D. D., & Watson, J. A. (1990). Computers in early education: Issues put to rest, theoretical links to sound practice, and the potential contribution of microworlds. *Journal of Educational Computing Research, 6,* 375–392.

Shriberg, L. D., Kwiatkowski, J., & Snyder, T. (1986). Articulation testing by microcomputer. *Journal of Speech and Hearing Disorders, 51,* 309–324.

Tan, L. E. (1985). Computers in pre-school education. *Early Child Development and Care, 19,* 319–336.

Vandell, D. L., & Wilson, K. S. (1987). Infants interactions with mother, sibling, and peer: Contracts and relations between interaction system. *Child Development, 58,* 176–186.

Vygotsky, L. S. (1978). *Mind in society.* Cambridge, MA: Harvard University Press.

Williams, R. A. (1984). Preschoolers and the computer. *Arithmetic Teacher, 31* (8), 39–42.

Wood, D. J. (1980). Teaching the young child: Some relationships between social interaction, language and thought. In D. R. Olson (Ed.), *The social foundations of language and thought* (pp. 280–296). New York: Norton.

Wood, D., Bruner, J. S., & Ross, G. (1976). The role of tutoring in problem solving. *Journal of Child Psychology and Psychiatry and Allied Disciplines, 17,* 89–100.

Wood, D., & Middleton, D. (1975). A study of assisted problem-solving. *British Journal of Psychology, 66,* 181–191.

Zajonc, A. G. (1984). Computer pedagogy? Questions concerning the new educational technology. *Teachers College Record, 85,* 569–577.

[1]Full details are available from the authors on request.

Thanks are due to Leanne Miksad for experimental assistance and to the directors, staff and participating children and parents of Conyngham St., Tilbrook and Parkside Childcare Centres, South Australia.

Correspondence should be addressed to:
   Rosalyn Shute
   School of Psychology
   GPO Box 2100
   Adelaide 5001
   South Australia

 Article Review Form at end of book.

Will computers make teachers and schools obsolete?

Technology and Change of Mind

An interview with Robert Ornstein

Joy Turner

Robert Ornstein, Ph.D., has the same dark beard, twinkly eyes, and wry sense of humor I remember from our first encounter almost 20 years ago, at a seminar he had organized called *Educating Both Halves of the Brain* (4 years *before* Sperry and Hubel's 1981 Nobel for their work on brain organization and functioning.) A neurobiologist, Dr. Ornstein was involved at that time in both experimental studies of the brain and their implications for health care, an interest that led him to organize other symposia: *The Healing Brain* (1980) and *Understanding the Brain* (1985).

The seminars were one of Ornstein's strategies for closing the gap between scientific knowledge of the brain and the application of that knowledge in the culture, especially in terms of how it deals with science and education. Another strategy was to write books about it, and Ornstein has turned out more than 20, including *New World New Mind* (1989, with Paul Ehrlich) and the best-selling *The Psychology of Consciousness* (1975).

In his keynote address to the AMS Fall Regional Seminar in Santa Monica, CA, Ornstein shared ideas from his most recent book, *The Axemaker's Gift: A Double-Edged history of Human Culture* (1995), coauthored with award-winning television host James Burke (*Connections*, on PBS). One of the reviewers says on the cover, "This fascinating new book tells a gripping story about how we humans have used our minds throughout history in a way that has led to both our biggest successes and our biggest problems." The book also offers a sophisticated and original way to recapture hope for the future.

Currently head of the Institute for the Study of Human Knowledge, Ornstein works and lives, with his wife, Sally, in Los Altos, CA.

Joy Turner: Dr. Ornstein, your work poses a number of questions about the relationship between human nature and the problems of the world we have created: What is it about us that makes us act the way we do? Why have we built this world the way we have, a world that's turned out to be overpopulated, polluted, violent, and difficult—and what can we do about it?

Robert Ornstein: *The Axemaker's Gift* is about how the tool-making left hemisphere took over the world. The axemakers are, in this view, the people who learn to operate in sequence, in order to make tools. To cut up the world and rearrange it, that's what we do that nobody else does. We make computers out of sand, we make telephone lines out of plastic. We're able to change the world like nobody else, but it has also given us a very limited way of looking at the world, so that the people who are very good at this kind of analytic thinking are the people who've taken over the world; they're the people who make up the IQ tests, the people who do well in business, the people who do a lot of things.

We have to remember that all of us are exactly the same *biologically* as the nomads who lived 30,000 years ago. But when we first started to cut stones into tools and used those tools to cut up the world, we changed the world forever. Until then, and still now, every other animal lives in a cycling world where nothing really changes in their lifetime or in their history. The life of your cat is probably awfully similar to the life of a similar cat in Egypt. There's Purina Cat Chow, of course, but it's not as different from the lamb and rice an Egyptian cat got to eat as, say, space travel and computers are from the pyramids. We're the only species who have had the capacity to cut into the world and change it. You might call that development sequential thinking: make this cut, make that cut, make this cut, make that cut, in this tool, then use it to cut this tree, this way, cut it up this way, put these things in this order and you have a house, you have settlements, you have a very different world.

JT: When you say that technology has "changed our minds," what does that mean? What effect has technology had upon humans?

RO: It's an awfully big question that would take much more than a single book to answer. We're so changed by the nature of the world that there is clearly no way we could ever go back to nature. For instance, our world has a lot more right angles, squares and corners, than the natural world has; seeing those as you grow up changes your visual cortex, so that you tend to look at things in terms of angles and borders. People who don't grow up in the "built" world don't see the world that way. So we already grow up in a world that's carpentered; it's built. We see it very differently and our brains get organized very differently. I think the main thing we should be concerned about is that our technology, especially in the way we've learned to express ourselves and communicate, has in fact changed not only the nature of education, but the nature of our mental system. Being able to represent ideas in speech and

language in a certain sort of way has promoted one of the main human talents way beyond its completely rightful place in the whole team of talents that we have, so that the ability to speak and express ourselves in language has sort of become the sine qua non of what human beings do. And all history from Greece to our current civilization has shown that people are more and more able to represent the world in a particular way, that is, reduce it to numbers, reduce it to letters, and so forth.

JT: What are *the talents you think we have neglected—or promoted out of balance?*

RO: Everybody comes into the world with hundreds of different abililites—the ability to match colors, to dance in a particularly graceful way, to play music, to understand what other people are needing, or the ability to construct an environment that people are happy in or to move a sofa out of the room in the right way or the ability to know where we are and where we need to go. There are lots of talents besides our abilities to calculate, represent, and express verbally.

JT: Do we lose those other abiities—or have we just devalued them?

RO: For both a society and an individual, if you don't develop them early enough, you lose them, at least to a great extent, just as you and I have lost our ability to learn Japanese, for instance. Obviously if we'd been born in Tokyo, we would be speaking as fluently as we speak English; but if you try to learn it now, in adulthood, it seems totally impossible, though any 3-year-old can do it. It's not *quite* that strong with other abilities, but what happens in the

The people who gave us the world in exchange for our minds. . . . They are the axemakers, whose discoveries and innovations, over thousands of years, have gifted power in innumerable ways. To emperors they gave the power of death, to surgeons the power of life. Each time the axemakers offered a new way to make us rich or safe or invincible or knowledgeable, we accepted the gift and used it to change the world. And when we changed the world, we changed our minds, for each gift redefined the way we thought, the values by which we lived, and the truths for which we died. And we always came back for more, unmindful of the cost. . . . The Earth was so rich and so vast that for a long time the damage caused by the indiscriminate axe was not worth consideration. . . . Today, that disregard expresses itself in distressing terms. While some now celebrate a few improvements to the environment, millions starve, and the developed nations have used their immense technological and scientific capabilities to pave almost half their cultivable land. . . one–third of Earth's forests have disappeared, the population is exploding, the oceans are getting depleted. . . and the atmosphere remains severely polluted. Axemaker knowledge and the destruction of the environment are inextricably linked.

Prologue, *The Axemaker's Gift*
Burke and Ornstein (1995)

development of an individual is that certain talents get emphasized by the early educational system and others don't. That's the general education, of course; it's not something your kind of teaching does.

JT: Yes, the Montessori approach seems to include a lot of right-brain activity, as well. And at least a few people consider it to be very negative that we don't develop these abilities, or overdevelop the other capacities, perhaps at their expense.

RO: Right, It's certainly limiting to a lot of individuals. On the other hand, high development of that ability to sequence has brought us a civilization that's been unparalleled in human history, so it's certainly not all negative. In the industrialized nations, people are healthier, wealthier, better fed, more informed, and more mobile than anybody ever. But the problem is twofold: one is, a lot of people are trying to fit a mold that fits only a few—those who really need to be symbolically literate. That's the first thing. And the second, which I think is even more important, is that the modern technologies like computers and multimedia and other systems have begun to make it possible for people to return to their more natural abilities and deal with the world more as it really is.

JT: Are you referring to the amount of information the technology makes available? Or do you mean that things like CD ROM can make experiences more multisensory?

RO: Both, really. First of all, it means there will be lots of different ways to access world knowledge again, rather than just the kind of limited, drip-by-drip, word-by-word channel, so that people whose talents are not particularly verbal and analytic might be empowered to learn in a different way, their own way, and to follow their own curiosity as opposed to the kind of formal lesson plans everybody has to deal with in school at the moment. For at least 2500 years, since the time of Greece, our society has more and more emphasized abstract representation of the world. If you wanted to learn about Beethoven, for example, what you'd generally do is read about him. It would be reduced to a set of letters. But with modern technology, you can listen to the way Beethoven composed, on the instruments he

composed it for; you can get a view of Vienna, hear what other composers were doing, change Beethoven's music around to see how he worked with it. That's a very different kind of learning experience; you don't really need to read about something if you can listen to it and look at it. So modern technology is now beginning to bring education back to what we start with in the world, listening and looking. People have more direct access to what they're trying to learn about. And with this kind of access, they will need to know a lot less about reading and writing.

JT: Although that is wonderful and marvelous, people of my age may feel a little depressed to consider that it may represent the end of civilization as we know it. In many ways that's not at all a bad thing, if it happens peacefully; yet it also threatens that it's too late for me personally to cope with the new technology and learn to look at the world in a completely new way. It feels a bit like being passed by. Is this revolution going to make teachers and schools obsolete?

RO: Not obsolete, but it will make it possible for people to follow their own paths much more easily, simply because the information available to them is going to be multiplied by hundreds of thousands. There are knowledge bases today and many under construction that will provide information options on an enormous scale—like going to a video store today and being able to choose from 10,000 movies one that you can rent for two bucks. The same thing is going to happen with the world of information. Right now, with the Library of Congress digitizing all the stuff, it will fit for any school into something the size of a little CD chamber. Any student would be able to get access

to anything within days or maybe even minutes. Every school, for several thousand dollars, could have the equivalent of a million-dollar library. That's going to be a big difference, let alone the other stuff that creative people will do. It won't make teachers obsolete, but it will make people much more able to learn what *they* want to learn rather than what the system needs them to learn.

The second thing, as we're already beginning to see now, is that lots of people who are in their 20s and highly intelligent just don't read as much. They move through information space, they look at things in a very, very different way, so that the culture is going to move toward being much more visual and oral, rather than literate. Why do you need arithmetic so thoroughly when you have a calculator to do all your work for you? It's decried a lot by people of our age, you know, that the younger generation doesn't value books and all this other stuff; but in fact, why do they need it?

JT: Certainly they will still need to know how to read!

RO: They will. And they will learn how to read. But they won't need to do it as exclusively as they do now, and people who read well won't always be at the top of the tree.

JT: What about broader implications, for example how people will earn a living?

RO: A lot of people earn their living in these industries, plus a lot of people's work now doesn't necessarily involve reading, but instead responding to visual and other kinds of information.

JT: And yet that's still abstract experience because it's secondhand.

RO: Well, of course it is. But it's still closer to the way we're normally built to deal with the world than is highly abstracted information. When we have somebody there that we're supposed to educate, we've got to know about their mental system. Yet most of the time people don't really understand how the mind works, or why the world changes so fast sometimes, and why some things are very *hard* to change.

So I want to give you four points about how the mind works. The first principle is *What have you done for me lately?* What that means, really, is that whatever happens in the last 10 minutes is really the most important thing, or whatever happens in the news over the last period becomes very important. You see it in the O.J. Simpson business—all of a sudden spousal abuse is made to be a big deal, even though the instance that was so heavily reported was just one more instance. If an airplane goes down in a crash in Japan, people get terribly worried about whether they should fly; if the wife of the U.S. President gets breast cancer, the next morning millions of women who should have gone in for checkups now do it. Why are we like this? Well, we're like this because we're short-term animals, we're animals who are really designed to respond to what's going on at the moment. We're *not* animals who are organized very much for our times. It's one of the contributors to our difficulties.

Principle Two is *Don't call me unless something new and exciting happens* The mind is specialized for the perception of the news; it's headline news that the mind wants to know. You never pick up the newspaper and see "Last night 226 million of the 250 million people in America had a

pleasant dinner. Then they went to sleep, got up and went to work, 9 million had meat loaf, 30 million had sex, "etc. What goes on over and over again is just not interesting to us. Again, that's because we're not organized to see the world as it is; we're only organized to see a *few* things that are very important.

The third principle was enunciated by the famous psychologist and comedian Henny Youngman when he was asked, "How do you like your wife?" and he said, *"Compared to what?"* Comparison is one of the ways we actually look at the world. We don't really look at the world as what it is. Everything is relative, and it's often relative to our *expectations*. For example, if you expect a bonus in your job of $5,000 at the end of the year and your boss hands you $2,000, it's a very different experience than if you weren't expecting a bonus at all. The actual event is you got $2,000; on one hand you're thinking, "I'm $3,000 down"—and on the other you're thinking, "I'm $2,000 up." So we judge almost everything we look at by what our expectation is. Changing expectations is very important, and keeping them under control is very important.

And the fourth and final principle is *Get to the point,* which you might be thinking yourself. Last summer, you probably saw a billion leaves or a million automobiles. And you probably don't remember any of them. Or maybe there was one leaf you kept or one car you bought. But most of our experience is simply thrown away; what we remember of what goes on is a millionth of what happens to us. And we pick a few things. A police siren is very important; although it's got no meaning in itself, it's important because it means *danger.* A tragic

event in your life means a lot, because your life is going to get changed. But most of the time we go about the world in a very simplified way, which means that what goes on in our *little* world makes a big difference.

The truth is that people are just not very reasonable or balanced, none of us are. We all respond to what's going on just at the moment and we act in a very simplified way because of this simplified mental system. The key is to find the things that actually move you along, and educational experiences that are more involving than print may do that better, for most people. When the newest technologies get fully into the educational system, it will change enormously, and that will also mean secondarily that a different sort of people will be able to come to the fore.

JT: You spoke of the axemakers being only a few people. What is your estimate of the percentage?

RO: Well, it depends. From the beginning of time, the movement is toward more and more people becoming empowered, with access to information. At first, the shamans had the exclusive control of information. When we get to Greece, all of a sudden literacy jumped to about 10%, and the modern world really began. People began to discuss ideas, compare ideas, write different versions of ideas, et cetera. With the Gutenberg revolution, the information available increased dramatically again. When more and more people are educated, they are able through that technology to participate in what's going on in the culture. Today if you want to send a message to the White House, you can do it on your computer without any trouble. Now it's true that not everybody has a computer; but that is changing and it's going to change more and more, the way 97% of families in the U.S. now have a television. There will always be the have-nots, but the ability of everybody who has one will increase radically.

JT: *And the axemakers of the future: who are they?*

RO: A lot of them are going to be the people who deal with the large-scale information systems—which brings up one of the things you *would* want to deal with, in terms of the problems of the future: who is going to control them. But what's happening is that the more information that gets out, the harder it is to control. It's one of the reasons the Soviet Union finally collapsed; you just could not have a Commissar in every TV set or deal with what people got to reproduce with photocopiers. And that, multiplied a millionfold, is what's going to happen tomorrow.

JT: *When will "tomorrow" come? Or is it here already?*

RO: Well, certainly in the first decade of the next century. By that point many, many schools will have access, within days or hours, to what you might call the accumulated world knowledge base. It means, really, that everybody *can* have everything. *Finding* it is going to be another matter, but I think teachers are going to become much more like guides.

JT: *Well, it certainly sounds as if computers have to be a part of the education of the teacher.*

RO: They will be, they will be.

JT: *Want to guess how many teacher education schools do it now? I'll bet it's a very small number.*

RO: Oh, I'm sure. But it will have to change. And as people get com- puters in their homes, their kids will teach them. What teacher education schools need now is a whole bunch of 8- to10-year-olds! One of my colleagues, who is very computer literate, is constantly overwhelmed by what his 9-year-old does. And again, a lot of it *will* have passed us. It will be like learning a language and, you might say, a way to navigate the world. But what it argues for is a very diverse basic education, which I think is very similar to the kinds of things Montessori people are interested in. We do face lots of difficulties and we can't ignore a lot of the havoc we've wreaked on the world, all over the world. It has happened, there are people in central Europe who are told not to open their windows because the air is so bad. Life expectancy is decreasing in a lot of countries because of the pollution. So it's not as if there aren't serious problems, and if they were left unchecked, we could be in serious trouble. We *are* in serious trouble.

JT: *So we need axemakers who will work on it.*

RO: Well, the point is, we *have* to. We have to know how to move this giant juggernaut so that it works for the rest of us. One point *The Axemaker's Gift* tries to make is that this particular way of doing things is a relatively short period in human history, say 2500 years out of 30,000. Maybe the axemaker mentality is not necessarily

> A holist view of life … examines all social decisions for their effect on the community and the environment ….The web (and all the support processes it could provide) might make small communities viable once more, functioning in a way that ought to become commonplace all over the planet, where the maxim would be: "Think globally, act locally." And it would take only the kind of currently available renewable energy systems such as solar or geothermal or wind power to make such communities energy-independent and ensure the survival of many cultures that will otherwise face the axe in the next few decades …. For such communities, the most valuable skills would be generalist rather than specialist. They would be generalist rather than specialist. They would prize the ability to connect, to think imaginatively, to understand how data are related, to see patterns in machine-generated innovation, and to assess its social effect before releasing it on society ….We can use our technology as it has been used time and again through history. We can use it to change minds, but this time for our own reasons in our own terms and at our own pace, if we use the coming technologies for what they could be: instruments of freedom ….The culture we live in … has given us the wonders of the modern world on a plate. But it has also fostered beliefs that have tied us to centralized institutions and powerful individuals for centuries, which we must shuck off if we are to adapt to the world we've made: that unabated extraction of planetary resources is possible, that the most valuable members of society are specialists, that people cannot survive without leaders, that the body is mechanistic and can only be healed with knives and drugs, that there is only one superior truth, that the only important human abilities lie in the sequential and analytic mode of thought, and that the mind works like an axemaker's gift. We have also been persuaded to think that it is unacceptable to be different or even to acknowledge that differences in abilities exist between us. But our survival may depend on the realization and expression of humanity's immense diversityu. Only if we use what may be the ultimate of the many axemaker's gifts—the coming information systems—to nurture this individual and cultural diversity, only if we celebrate our differences rather than suppressing them, will we stand a change of harnessing the wealth of human talent that has been ignored for millennia and that is now eager, all around the world, for release. (Burke & Ornstein, 1995, pp. 308–311)

the way things are, but really more a *detour* in human history. In fact, I think the last tool of the axemakers, the computer, is going to be the end of that domination. Once you can look at and play with multimedia material, you don't have to be as literate as you used to be. Maybe that period that started in classical Greece is going to end with the computer, because the modern media are going to change the way people look at the world and the way they think. In some ways, it's going to be a change *back* to the way people were before the axe started.

References

Burke, J., & Ornstein, R. (1995). *The axemaker's gift: A double–edged history of human culture.* New York: G. P. Putnam's Sons.

Ornstein, R. (1975). *The psychology of consciousness.* New York: Viking.

Ornstein, R., & Ehrlich, P. (1989). *New world new mind: Moving toward conscious evolution.* New York: Simon & Schuster.

 Article Review Form at end of book.

How will the teacher's role change in the Information Age Schools?

Creating the Information Age School

Six schools that demonstrate the characteristics of an Information Age school provide insights into what educators must do to give students the skills they need to succeed in the workplace and the community.

Vicki Hancock

Vicki Hancock is Director of New Ventures at ASCD (e–mail: vhancock @ascd.org).

Most school-age children in the United States interact every day with a variety of information media—television, video games, multimedia computer systems, audio- and videotape, compact discs, and print. At the same time, workplaces are retooling with advanced technologies and acquiring access to complex, comprehensive information systems to streamline operations. Our youth have so much exposure to technological gadgets and information resources that one would think the transition from school to workplace would be second nature. Not so. According to recent projections, only about 22 percent of people currently entering the labor market possess the technology skills that will be required for 60 percent of new jobs in the year 2000 (Zuckerman 1994).

To eliminate this mismatch between schools and workplace, we need "Information Age" schools. But what does an Information Age school look like, and how do you begin to create such a school?

What It Looks Like

Researchers (Breivik and Senn 1994, Glennan and Melmed 1996, Cuban 1997) point to at least six attributes that characterize an Information Age school. The following descriptions of these attributes include examples of exemplary schools, along with contact information. I have "found" each of the schools by making site visits in my former role as an ASCD regional director and by serving as a judge in a variety of technology competitions.

Interactivity

In schools demonstrating interactivity, students communicate with other students through formal

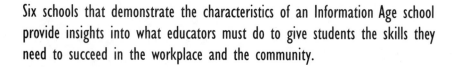
The most probing questions come from the learners, who are curious about a variety of issues and intent on communicating what they discover.

presentations, cooperative learning activities, and informal dialogue. Students and teachers talk to one another about their learning tasks in large groups, small groups, and one-to-one. Students have constant access to and know how to use print and electronic information resources to inform their learning activities. They recognize the value of the information in their own communities and interact with various community members, including businesspeople, social service staff, arts professionals, athletes, older adults, and volunteer workers, enhancing their curriculum studies with authentic information from primary sources.

At the Sun Valley Elementary School in Winnipeg, Manitoba, 4th grade students regularly participate in "keypals" activities to exchange cultural information with schools around the world. Students in grades 5 and 6 use resources from their school and community to develop "talking books" that provide graphic, textual, and auditory lessons on animals, foods, weather, and other classroom topics for the 1st grade class. The librarymedia specialist helps students develop interactive multimedia projects for their classes and the community. One such project takes citizens on an adventure tour of Winnipeg.

Contact: Sun Valley Elementary School, 125 Sun Valley Dr., Winnipeg, Manitoba R2G 2W4, Canada; (204) 663–7664.

Self-Initiated Learning

When students initiate their own learning, they participate in productive questioning, probing for information they can use rather than waiting for the next question on a test or from a teacher. Information resources are central, not peripheral, in day-to-day learning activities. Students gather their own data to learn about topics, using a variety of sources and practicing effective research techniques. They are able to examine the large quantity of information they have gathered, synthesize it, and reduce it to usable quantities for their purposes. They can analyze and interpret information in the context of the problems or questions they have identified, and they can evaluate not only the quality of the information they've gathered but also the processes they've used to gather it.

The most important role for information technology at Taylorsville Elementary School in Taylorsville, Indiana, is to support a commitment to self-paced, individualized learning. Students participate in a program that emphasizes high expectations in core subjects and allows them to

work at their own pace. Teachers use instructional strategies like multiage, multiyear groupings and team–based project work. Teachers facilitate, rather than direct, student learning, and they are comfortable using a variety of information technologies. Two days each school year are devoted to ongoing technology training, and a technology coordinator and three part-time aides assist teachers with their technology-related problem solving.

Contact: Taylorsville Elementary School, 9711 Walnut St., Taylorsville, IN 47280; (812) 526–5448.

A Changing Role for Teachers

To develop self-initiated learners in the Information Age school, the teacher's role must evolve away from dispenser of prefabricated facts to coach and guide. In this continuously changing role, teachers leave fact-finding to the computer, spending their time doing what they were meant to do as content experts: arousing curiosity, asking the right questions at the right time, and stimulating debate and serious discussion around engaging topics. In fact, every adult in the school community communicates the power of knowledge by modeling a love of learning. Preservice and inservice programs require the use of information resources and technologies as an integrated part of teachers' certification and recertification. Teachers create a community among themselves in which they are willing to plan together, share successes, resolve challenges, and model strategies for one another.

Professional development in information technologies is available daily at Adlai Stevenson

High School in Lincolnshire, Illinois, in a specialized lab for teachers staffed by a full-time trainer. Proficiency with technology resources is a hiring requirement for teachers. All teaching staff have a three-year period to demonstrate proficiency with voice, data, and video technologies. The rigor of staff training reflects the school's commitment to providing students with an environment that promotes lifelong learning, provides opportunities to access global information and create knowledge, encourages participation from the community, and develops the skills of collaborative problem solving. Teacher and students use information technologies constantly for instruction, assessment, exploration, management, and the school's day-to-day operation.

Contact: Adlai Stevenson High School, One Stevenson Dr., Lincolnshire, IL 60069; (847) 634–4000; Internet: http://www.district125.k12.il.us

Media and Technology Specialists as Central Participants

Media and technology specialists are critical in the Information Age school, and their role is twofold. Working with students, they are project facilitators. They can ask the initial questions that help students develop a focus for inquiry. They are thoroughly familiar with the school's and district's information resources and can direct students to multidisciplinary materials suitable for their investigations. With their technology skills, they can expose students to resources in a variety of media as well. They can assist students in their efforts to develop technology-enhanced products and presentations.

Working with teachers, they are instructional designers—partners in curriculum development and unit planning. Their expertise with information resources can inform teachers' exploration of curriculum topics and assist them in locating the materials they need. And, because ongoing professional development is an integral part of the work in an Information Age school, media and technology specialists contribute their expertise to the design and delivery of technology-enhanced inservice programs.

Traditionally, students learned information skills in isolation as part of elementary- and middle-level "library skills" development. Technology "literacy" programs took place in computer labs during pull-out programs or in separately scheduled classes. In the Information Age school, such skills are taught on an as-needed basis, and they are integrated throughout the curriculum.

As a result of a districtwide effort to reform curriculum and instruction, the school day at Christopher Columbus Middle School in Union City, New Jersey, is organized into blocks of 90 minutes to two hours. Longer class periods have allowed teachers to create a project-focused, research-based curriculum that integrates the traditional subject areas with access to local and remote information resources through a variety of technologies. In addition to a central computer lab for whole-class instruction and walk-in use, each of the school's 12 classrooms has five computers, a printer, and a video presentation station. Students also have access to multimedia production equipment, computer video editing capabilities, and Internet connectivity from all PCs. Teachers receive three days of paid technology training each year, and a full–time technology coordinator conducts student computer classes, consults with teachers, and handles troubleshooting.

Contact: Christopher Columbus Middle School, 1500 New York Ave., Union City, NJ 07087; (201) 271–2085.

Continuous Evaluation

Everyone in the Information Age school recognizes the need for continuous evaluation not limited to scheduled standardized assessments. They engage in a high level of introspection, asking questions about the appropriateness of information resources, the efficiency of information searches, and the quality of information selection and evaluation. They also examine the quality of the products and presentations they use to share the results of their inquires, as well as the communication process itself.

The Maryland Virtual High School of Science and Mathematics is a collaboration of 15 schools. They use information technologies to focus on computational science studies, accessing the Internet for mentoring, sharing projects, and assessing science resources. Students and teachers search and communicate online through local area networks (LANs) attached to each school's Internet hub. They use various software applications to create computational models of processes such as climate phenomena, animal population changes, and planetary motion. Teachers from the participating school attend several three-day professional development sessions each year, as well as a five-day workshop at the end of each school year. Project staff are available for schoolwide training and outreach efforts in the various school communities.

Contact: Maryland Virtual High School of Science and Mathematics, 31 Wayne Ave., Silver Spring, MD 20901; (301) 650–6600; Internet: http://www.mbhs.edu

A Changed Environment

An Information Age school has a different look and feel than a traditional school. Classroom methods link information retrieval, analysis, and application with strategies such as cooperative learning, guided inquiry, and thematic teaching. Information technologies are easily accessible, not locked away in media closets or labs. Student projects and products proliferate—not just as display items but as resources for other students and information for future investigations. Classrooms and hallways are frequently the scene of discussions and debates about substantive issues—topics important to both the curriculum and to the students investigating them. Most important, the most probing questions come from the learners, who are curious about a variety of issues and intent on communicating what they discover: How do you know that? What evidence do you have for that? Who says? How can we find out?

The curriculum at Patton Junior High School in Fort Leavenworth, Kansas, is "driven by students' needs to be productive members of an ever-advancing Information Age" (U.S.D. 207 Technology Initiatives

> In the Information Age school, information skills are taught on an as-needed basis, and they are integrated throughout the curriculum.

brochure 1996). Instruction reflects the district's efforts to maintain high standards of achievement while encouraging learners to investigate a variety of topics in an exploratory environment. Students use technology tools and develop life skills in a 26-module program that includes topics such as robotics, audio broadcasting, maintaining a healthy heart, and becoming a confident consumer. The media center and classroom computers all provide Internet access. Teachers can use a centralized media management system to remotely schedule videotape, laserdisc, and interactive CD presentations without the need to check out and transport bulky equipment.

Contact: Patton Junior High School, 5 Grant Ave., Fort Leavenworth, KS 66027; (913) 651–7373; Internet: http://www.ftlvn.kl2.ks.us

How to Begin

To transform your school into an Information Age school, begin by using information technologies to encourage experimentation with the school's program. Focus on improving the connections between curriculum content and school process. Lengthen class periods. Consider multiage grouping. Experiment with interdisciplinary, problem-based, or thematic approaches to instruction. Develop individualized instructional plans for every student. Implement ongoing assessment measures that reflect students' continuous learning (portfolios projects, performances). Encourage community members to regularly contribute their time and expertise throughout the school. Include them as part of decision-making groups for curriculum and technology planning. Provide incentives to teachers and administrators who demonstrate their willingness to try new methods and share what they've learned with their peers. Hire technology support staff with teaching experience to consult with teachers as well as troubleshoot equipment. Pay teachers to participate in professional development activities.

Rather than sitting back (like passive television viewers) marveling at the ever-increasing quantity of information and the rapidity of change, educators must lead students through a careful, cumulative acquisition of information literacy and technology skills. Teams of school professionals can plan integrated activities focusing on important content while encouraging students to practice these skills. Learners should engage from their earliest years in rich, complex, authentic experiences that provide a tension between cre-

ativity and utility. These experiences should also offer frequent opportunities for feedback and an environment of trust and open communication. This "orchestrated immersion" (Palmisano et al. 1993) can help ensure that students will leave their school years better prepared to participate actively and flexibly in their communities and the workplace.

References

Breivik, P., and J. Senn. (1994). *Information Literacy: Educating Children for the 21st Century.* New York, N.Y.: Scholastic.

Cuban, L. (May 21, 1997). "High-Tech Schools and Low-Tech Teaching," *Education Week on the Web* (http://www.edweek.org/ew/current/34cuban.h16)

Glennan, T., and A. Melmed. (1996). *Fostering the Use of Educational Technology: Elements of a National Strategy.* Santa Monica, Calif.: RAND.

Palmisano, M., M. Barron, and L. Torp. (1993). *Integrative Learning System: Rationale, Overview, and Reflections.* Aurora, Ill.: Illinois Mathematics and Science Academy.

Unified School District 207. (1996). "Patton Junior High School Technology Initiatives." (Pamphlet). Ft. Leavenworth, Kan.: Author.

Zuckerman, P. (July 18, 1994). "America's Silent Revolution." *U.S. News and World Report* 117, 3:90.

 Article Review Form at end of book.

WiseGuide Wrap-Up

- Societal changes will continue to impact children and families while their basic needs remain the same.

- Families, schools, and communities will best guide children in the information age by accepting that there are different ways to learn and access knowledge.

R.E.A.L. Sites

This list provides a print preview of typical **coursewise** R.E.A.L. sites. There are over 100 such sites at the **courselinks**™ site. The danger in printing URLs is that web sites can change overnight. As we went to press, these sites were functional using the URLs provided. If you come across one that isn't, please let us know via email to: webmaster@coursewise.com. Use your Passport to access the most current list of R.E.A.L. sites at the **courselinks**™ site.

Site name: The Future of Children

URL: http://www.futureofchildfren.org/

Why is it R.E.A.L.? *The Future of Children* is a free publication produced by the Center for the Future of Children, sponsored by The David and Lucile Packard Foundation. Subjects related to the well-being of children are prepared with objective analysis and evaluation for a mutidisciplinary audience in order to effect policy about children and families.

Key topics: caregiving, families, twenty-first century

Activity: Identify the authors of *The Future of Children* study entitled "Environmental Policy and Children's Health."

Site name: Children Now

URL: http://www.childrennow.org/

Why is it R.E.A.L.? Children Now is an independent, nonprofit group committed to improving children's life circumstances, especially those of children who are at risk and who live in poverty. Issues such as media, gender, and new legislation are addressed.

Key topics: child-centered, early experiences, intervention

Activity: Access *Talking with Kids*. Read the section "How to use this booklet." Explain why you either agree or disagree with the suggestions.

Site name: The Children's Partnership

URL: http://www.childrenspartnership.org/

Why is it R.E.A.L.? Timely information and resources are available for the benefit of children. There are links to other resources and special features about the needs of the nation's children.

Key topics: computers, parenting/parents, technology

Activity: Find and click on *The Next Generation Report*. Locate *Information Tools for Community Leaders*. What are the three main issues reported in the online *Special Report* summary?

Site name: Parents Guide to the Internet

URL: http://www.ed.gov/pubs/parents/internet/

Why is it R.E.A.L.? The U.S. Department of Education, Office of Educational Research and Improvement, Office of Educational Technology establishes this page specifically to provide resources about technology for parents. Tips, benefits, and a valuable glossary help parents navigate the superhighways.

Activity: Start with *Supporting School Use of Technology*. Record the web site for NetDay.

Index

Note: Entries in boldface type indicate the authors and the page numbers of readings.

G

Galinsky, E., 16, 19
Gallagher, P.W., 119
Gallegos, P.I., 100
Gallimore, R., 37, 40
Gandini, L., 69
Gantley, M., 102
Gardner, Howard, 8
    interview with, 178–182
Gardner, J., 121
Garza, R.T., 100
General Cognitive Index, 186
Gensheimer, L.K., 75, 76, 77
Geva, E., 184
Gilbert, S., 80
Gilbride, K., 104
Ginott, H.G., 80
Ginsburg, H.P., 131
Glickman, C.D., 25
Glowacki, S., 17
Goldman, K.W., 80
Goldsmith, D., 102
Goleman, Daniel, 8–10
Gomby, D.S., 16
Goncu, A., 37, 39, 101, 104
Gonzalez–Mena, J., 100–105
Good, L.A., 126
Good, T.L., 129
Goodwin, L.D., 184
Goodwin, W.L., 184
Gore, D.A., 184
Gormley, W.T., 21
Governance, levels of, 22–23
Greenbaum, Stuart, 95
Greenberg, P., 142
Greenes, C., 130
Greenfield, P.M., 37
Griffin, A., 76
Grover, S.C., 183, 184, 185
Groves, M.M., 140
Guided participation, 37
Guided reinvention, 40
Gullo, D.F., 184
Gurtner, J., 184
Gutierrez, M., 113

H

Haberman, M., 129
Hager, J., 121
Hancock, Vicki, 198-200
Hardman, M., 44
Hareven, T., 100
Hargreaves, A., 176
Harkness, S., 101
Hartman, J.A., 17
Hart, R., 58
Haseloff, W., 138
Haugland, S., 183
Hawley, Theresa, 3–7
Head Start, Migrant Head Start, 152–154
Hearing impaired, signing in inclusive
    classroom, 125–128
Helburn, S., 75
Heller, Irma, 125–128

Henderson, A.T., 18, 121, 138
Hendley, Susan, 114–119
Hess, R.D., 138, 139
Hildreth, G.J., 183
Hill, K.M., 130
Hinchman, H., 58
History, of child care, 170–177
Hofferth, S.L., 17–18, 100
Hoffman, S.J., 121
Hohepa, M., 39
Hohmann, C.F., 183
Holcomb, P., 100
Holloway, S.D., 138, 139
Home–business, child care choices for
    mothers, 162–166
Hoover-Dempsey, K.V., 139
Hopkins, B., 101
Howard, J.R., 184
Howell, R.D., 184
Howes, C., 17, 21
Hoyer, J.P., 126
Hughes, M., 184
Huguenin, N.H., 188
Hungate, H., 183, 184
Hyson, M.C., 183

I

Imagination, sensorial stimulation
    activities, 27–29
Immigrant families
    history of child care for, 171–176
    infant caregiving, 100–105
Impulsivity, negative aspects of, 9
Inclusive early childhood programs, 42–47
    and developmentally appropriate
        practice, 43–44
    elements of, 42–43
    facilitation of, 45
    sign language in, 125–128
Individualized education plans (IEPs), 130
Individuals with Disabilities Education
    Act, 42
Infants
    caregiving and culture, 100–105
    care and home-based working mothers,
        163–164
Information age schools, 198–201
    continuous evaluation in, 200
    main participants in, 199–200
    and multimedia projects, 198–199
    physical environment for, 200–201
    self-initiated learning, 199
    teacher's role, 199
Ingels-Young, G., 184
Inhelder, B., 29
Integration, 42
Intelligence
    definition of, 178
    emotional intelligence, 8–10
    multiple intelligences theory, 178–182
Intelligence tests (IQ), 179
Interpersonal intelligence, 8, 181
Intersubjectivity, by teachers, 38–39
Intervention
    for bullying, 95–96

child abuse prevention, 6
    and functional goals, 44
    monitoring of, 44
    for parenting, 5–6
Intrapersonal intelligence, 8, 181
Invisible children, 38

J

Jackson, K., 100
Jacob, E., 141
Jahoda, G., 101
Jakob, Susan, 51
Johnson, D., 121
Johnson, J.E., 60
Johnston, J.H., 138
Jones, Graham A., 129–133, 130
Jordan, C., 141

K

Kagan, J., 170
Kagan, Sharon L., 16–23, 18
Kaplan, R., 58
Kaplan, S., 58
Katz, L., 67, 170
Katz, L.G., 17
Katz, P., 121
Kaufman, A.S., 186, 187
Kaufman Assessment Battery for Children,
    184, 186–187
Kawasaki, C., 102
Kerig, P., 185
Kilmer, S., 60
KinderCare, 51, 164
King Little, Nancy, 75–78
Kirkby, M.A., 61
Klass, Perri, 84
Knauerhase, V., 60
Knowledge, of nature, 56–59
Kohlberg, L., 114
Konner, M., 104
Kroth, Roger, 149–151, 150

L

Lague, L., 80
Lally, J.R., 76
Langrall, C.W., 130
Language acquisition, 53–54
Larner, M., 75
Latz, S., 103
Lawler, R.W., 183
Lazarov, M., 77
Leach, Penelope, 84
Learning
    relationship to development, 37–38
    relationship to teaching, 64
    and teacher attention, 38–39
Learning differences
    auditory learners, 132
    mathematics instruction, 129-131
    visual learners, 132
Lehrer, R., 184
Leiderman, P.H., 100, 101

Special education
    assistive devices, 149–151
    learning differences, types of, 132
    mathematics instruction adaptations,
        129–133
    See also Inclusive early childhood
        programs
Spivak, G., 26
Spock, Benjamin, 85, 102
Staines, G.L., 19
Stamp, L.N., 140
State boards, 22–23
Stechuk, Robert, 152–154
Steinfels, M., 170, 171
Stern, W., 29
Stevens, E., 184
Stevenson, D.L., 139
Stevenson, H., 110
Stevenson, H.W., 101
Stewart, E., 110
Stipek, D., 140
Storybooks, multicultural awareness
    through, 120–124
Stress, and brain development, 5
Sweeting, T., 26
Swick, K., 138
Szanton, E., 76

T

Tan, L.E., 183
Tanner, T., 58
Taxation, child care tax credit, 166
Taylor, M., 126
Taylor, M.J., 143
Taylor, T.R., 103
Teachers
    adult/student ratios, 46, 50, 99
    family life educators, 140–141
    in information age school, 199
    licensing, 19–20
    and multiculturalism, 118
    salaries, 50
    teacher attention and learning, 38–39
    training of, 20–21
Teaching, relationship to learning, 63–64
Teaching Research Early Childhood
    Program, 42, 46
Teale, W., 121
Technology
    computer-assisted instruction, 183–189
    effect on mind, 193, 194–196
    information age schools, 198–201

Templeman, Torry Piazza, 42–47
Tharp, R.G., 37, 40
Thompson, B., 184
Thornton, Carol A., 129–133, 130, 132
Tivnan, T., 18
Tobin, A.W., 121
Training, staff development, 20–21
Transition planning, early childhood
    special education, 45, 47
Transitions, 88–92
    cleanup time, 88–89
    connections for, 89–90
    and self-control, 90
Trauma, and brain development, 5
Trevathan, W.R., 102, 103
Triandis, H.C., 104
Trimble, S., 59
Trivette, C.M., 150
Tulkin, S.R., 100
Tulviste, P., 104
Turner, Joy, 192–196
Twardosz, S., 103

U

Udell, Tom, 42-47

V

Vallet, 26, 27
Van Scoy, Irma, 114–119
Van Zoest, L.R., 130
Varga, D., 177
Vietze, P., 100, 101
Visual learners, 132
Vygotsky, L.S., 36, 39, 104, 184
Vygotsky's theory, zone of proximal
    development (ZPD), 37–40

W

Wagner, D.A., 101
Wagner, Karen, 125–128
Walker, C., 186
Walker-Dalhouse, D., 124
Waterhouse, S., 38
Watson, J.A., 184
Weikart, D.P., 16, 158
Weissbourd, B., 18, 78
Wertsch, J.V., 39, 104
Wham, Mary Ann, 120–124
Whitebook, M., 17, 21

White, Burton, 85
White, K.R., 143
White, S.H., 170
Whiting, J.W.M., 102
Whitmore, K.F., 36, 37
Wilbers, J.S., 44
Willer, B., 21
Williams, D.L., 139
Williamson, Peter, 85
Williams, R.A., 183
Wilson, R.M., 126
Wilson, Ruth A., 56–60, 58, 60
Wixson, K.K., 184
Wolda, M.K., 126
Wolery, M., 44
Wolf, A.W., 103
Wonder, 57
Wood, D.J., 184, 185
Woodill, G.A., 173
Woodruff, Darren W., 155–157
Woodward, A., 130
Workplace, family friendly workplace,
    97–99
World Wide Web. *See* R.E.A.L. sites
Wright, V.L., 183

Y

Yaden, D.B., 121
Yawkey, T.D., 60
York, S., 110
Yoshikawa, H., 16
Yygotsky, L.S., 126

Z

Zajonc, A.G., 183
Zeece, P.D., 126
Zinck, R.A., 184
Zinsser, C., 76
Zinzeleta, Ellen, 75–78
Zone of proximal development (ZPD),
    37–40
    and play, 39–40
    role of child in, 40
    scaffolding, 37, 184
Zuckerman, P., 198

Putting it in *Perspectives*
-Review Form-

Your name _____   Date _____

Reading title _____

Summarize: Provide a one-sentence summary of this reading. _____
_____
_____
_____

Follow the Thinking: How does the author back the main premise of the reading? Are the facts/opinions appropriately supported by research or available data? Is the author's thinking logical?

_____
_____
_____
_____
_____

Develop a Context (answer one or both questions): How does this reading contrast or compliment your professor's lecture treatment of the subject matter? How does this reading compare to your textbook's coverage?

_____
_____
_____
_____
_____
_____

Question Authority: Explain why you agree/disagree with the author's main premise.

_____
_____
_____
_____
_____
_____